THE BRITISH LIBRARY
STEFAN ZWEIG COLLECTION

CATALOGUE OF THE LITERARY AND HISTORICAL MANUSCRIPTS

THE BRITISH LIBRARY
STEFAN ZWEIG COLLECTION

CATALOGUE OF THE LITERARY AND HISTORICAL MANUSCRIPTS

BRITISH LIBRARY

First published 2017 by
The British Library
96 Euston Road
London NW1 2DB

British Library Cataloguing in Publication Data
A catalogue record is available from the British Library

ISBN 978 0 7123 5666 4

Typeset by Geoff Green Book Design, Cambridge

Printed in Malta by Gutenberg Press

Frontispiece: Stefan Zweig in 1912

CONTENTS

PREFACE

From its origins to the present day the collections of the British Library have been significantly enriched by remarkable acts of generosity. All who use its outstanding cultural and intellectual resources, whether for research, inspiration or enjoyment, are greatly indebted to those who choose to entrust their prized possessions to the British Library's care. Without their donations and bequests researchers and the general public would not have access to such a globally unique window on the world's cultural heritage.

It is a pleasure therefore to recognise once again, and celebrate, the extraordinary gift made in 1986 of the Stefan Zweig Collection of Literary, Historical and Musical Manuscripts. Undoubtedly one of the most significant donations ever made to the British Library, the Zweig Collection comprises over two hundred remarkable items assembled by the Austrian writer Stefan Zweig (1881-1942) and his heirs. Richly varied in form and content it offers deep insights into European culture and history over several centuries, as well as into Zweig's own modes of engagement with that heritage. As such the collection forms a worthy part of the British Library's internationally preeminent holdings.

The present catalogue provides new descriptions of the 87 literary and historical works in the British Library's Zweig Collection. In format it is modelled on the *Catalogue of the Music Manuscripts* published by the Library in 1999. In content it is the work of many hands. I am particularly grateful to two former colleagues, Pamela Porter and Rachel Stockdale, who worked on this catalogue for many years and contributed the core of what is now published. I also wish to thank the team of current curators led by Scot McKendrick, Head of Western Heritage Collections, who have brought the work to completion: Pardaad Chamsaz, AHRC Collaborative Doctoral Research Student, Richard Chesser, Head of Music Collections, Susan Reed, Lead Curator, Germanic Collections, and Sandra Tuppen, Lead Curator, Modern Archives and Manuscripts, 1601–1850. For Pardaad Chamsaz's contribution we are indebted to the Arts and Humanities Research Council and the University of Bristol. For funding to support the present publication I acknowledge with gratitude a generous grant from the Friends of the British Library.

Roly Keating
Chief Executive

ACKNOWLEDGEMENTS

A catalogue of such varied content is dependent on specialists in different languages and in different periods of literature and history. The British Library would like to thank Arthur Searle, the compiler of *The British Library Stefan Zweig Collection: Catalogue of the Music Manuscripts*, on whose work we heavily relied. The Library would also like to thank those who have kindly offered their expertise and enhanced the scholarship of this catalogue. From the British Library, we would particularly like to acknowledge, in addition to those already mentioned in the preface: Alexandra Ault, Stewart Gillies, John Goldfinch, Hilton Kelliher, Irina Lester, Chris Michaelides, Katya Rogatchevskaia and Geoff West. Out of those at other institutions who have supported our work, we would like to offer our special thanks to Oliver Matuschek, who has openly shared his research with us for many years, and whose comprehensive catalogue is cited in every entry. We also wish to thank the following for their guidance: Katharine Chandler, Free Library of Philadelphia; Catherine Faivre d'Arcier, Elisa Ghennam, Georges Gottlieb and Bernard Krespine, Bibliothèque nationale de France; Claire Lesage, Bibliothèque de l'Arsenal, Paris; David McClay, National Library of Scotland; Ed Potten, Cambridge University Library; Bruno Svindberg, Royal Library, Copenhagen; Gabriel Swift, Princeton University Library; Ian Thompson, University of Glasgow.

INTRODUCTION

Stefan Zweig: 'A Prince among Collectors of Autograph Manuscripts'[1]

In his autobiography *The World of Yesterday*, Stefan Zweig (1881–1942) sets aside his characteristic modesty to write:

> I think I am justified in saying – as I would never venture to say of my achievements in literature or any other sphere of life – that in my thirty or forty years of collecting I had become the leading authority in the field of autograph manuscripts ...[2]

This undoubted expertise created a collection of musical, literary and historical manuscripts that was welcomed in 1986 as 'at once the most important and the most generous gift that the British Library has received since its foundation.'[3] Zweig's 'world of autographs'[4] reveals some of the most sublime and creative moments in the history of European culture, in which he sought inspiration for his own life and work.[5] Pivotal artistic figures such as Goethe, Hölderlin, Kleist, Balzac, Stendhal, Dostoevsky, Tolstoy, Nietzsche, Hofmannsthal and Rilke form a bridge between the collection and Zweig's own writing. In the midst of the current Zweig revival centred on his prolific output of novellas, biographies and essays, we should not forget the writer's lifelong passion for collecting, an activity that he considered to be at least as creative as his writing, if not more so. If we understand the motivations of Zweig in all his activities as fundamentally

1 Dedication to Stefan Zweig in *English Poetical Autographs: A Collection of Facsimiles and Autograph Poems from Sir Thomas Wyatt to Rupert Brooke*, ed. Desmond Flower and A. N. L. Munby (London: Cassell, 1938).

2 Stefan Zweig, *The World of Yesterday*, trans. by Anthea Bell (London: Pushkin Press, 2009), p. 374. From here on referred to as *WoY.*

3 Foreword in *Stefan Zweig Series of Concerts, Lectures and Exhibitions 1987* (London: British Library, 1987).

4 Stefan Zweig, 'Die Welt der Autographen', originally published in *Neue Freie Presse* (7 November 1923), reprinted in Oliver Matuschek, *Ich kenne den Zauber der Schrift: Katalog und Geschichte der Autographensammlung Stefan Zweig; mit kommentiertem Abdruck von Stefan Zweigs Aufsätzen über das Sammeln von Handschriften* (Vienna: InLibris, 2005), pp. 103–7. From here on referred to as *Ich kenne.*

5 For the most comprehensive account of the history of the Zweig Collection see *Ich kenne*; see also Arthue Searle, *The British Library Stefan Zweig Collection: Catalogue of the Music Manuscripts* (London: British Library, 1999). For a more general biography of Stefan Zweig, see Matuschek, *Three Lives: A Biography of Stefan Zweig*, trans. by Allan Blunden (London: Pushkin Press, 2011) and Donald A. Prater, *European of Yesterday: A Biography of Stefan Zweig* (Oxford: Clarendon Press, 1972).

mediatory[6] – spreading cultural awareness as a counterbalance to politics and war[7] – collecting and writing become closely interconnected in their focus on and celebration of human artistic achievement. In the introduction to a collection of his essays in 1937, for example, Zweig described himself simply as a 'mediator of values and experiences, which have elevated the meaning of existence for our whole generation', serving ultimately the ideal of an 'understanding between people, attitudes, cultures and nations'.[8] Three years later Zweig wrote to fellow Austrian author Felix Braun to emphasise the very idea of serving those greater and more significant than himself:

> What makes me more sure of myself in contrast to you, is that I have not only written creatively as you have, rather I have also served – served other works, greater and more important ones – Verhaeren, Rolland, Hölderlin and how many others through interpretation, translation, mediation ...[9]

Collecting was always part of this project and it deserves to be integrated into the author's whole enterprise. In the content of some of his most prized items, it is possible to see the value Zweig placed on praising culture in a context he deemed increasingly hostile to the artistic and aesthetic aspects of life. Gabriele D'Annunzio's 'La Laude di Dante' (Zweig MS 140) is a paean to the great Italian poet; Shelley's poem for Byron (Zweig MS 188) begins, 'If I esteemed you less, Envy would kill / Pleasure', before praising Byron's genius; Romain Rolland's two-volume manuscript for *Jean-Christophe* (Zweig MSS 184–5) has as its central theme precisely the ability of art to overcome cultural differences; and in Schubert's 'An die Musik' (Zweig MS 81) are the lines that Zweig echoed in his autobiography, words that might represent his whole outlook: 'Thou lovely art, how often in dark hours, when life's wild tumult wraps me round, have you kindled my heart to loving warmth, and transported me to a better world'.[10]

Zweig shaped such an alternative world through his collection of autograph manuscripts, a world to which he often escaped in harder times. Yet, despite the extent to which he refined his collection after the sale of most of his items in 1936–7, the transcendent sublimity of some items in the collection is balanced by the presence of contemporary figures – friend and foe – that remind us of the collection's historical underpinnings. The Zweig Collection of musical, literary and historical manuscripts is therefore both an abstraction from and an insight into the first half of the twentieth century, marked by the collector's encounters, his exile, and his creative tendencies.

6 See Harry Zohn, 'Stefan Zweig, Literary Mediator', in *Books Abroad*, 26/2 (1952), pp. 137–40.

7 See Stefan Zweig, 'Geschichtsschreibung von Morgen', in id., *Zeit und Welt. Gesammelte Aufsätze und Vorträge 1904–1940*, ed. Richard Friedenthal (Stockholm: Bermann-Fischer, 1946), pp. 275–98.

8 Stefan Zweig, 'Einleitung', in *Begegnungen mit Menschen, Büchern, Städten* (Vienna: Herbert Reichner, 1937), pp. 5–6.

9 Zweig to Felix Braun (1 January 1940), *Briefe 1932–1942*, ed. Knut Beck and Jeffrey B. Berlin (Frankfurt am Main: S. Fischer, 2005), p. 267.

10 John Reed, *The Schubert Song Companion* (translations by Norma Deane and Celia Larner) (Manchester: Manchester University Press, 1986), p. 36.

Beginnings: Rarities and Relics

In the *fin-de-siècle* Vienna of Zweig's youth, the arts dominated consciousness: 'You were not truly Viennese without a love for culture, a bent for both enjoying and assessing the prodigality of life as something sacred'.[11] It was in this atmosphere that Zweig learned to revere creative artists and began to collect autographs outside theatres and cafés. Once he even received a friendly tap on the shoulder from Johannes Brahms that sent him into 'a state of total confusion'.[12] Surrounded by exceptional cultural figures, Zweig began a collection of autograph manuscripts that initially took as its principle that fame and rarity he saw in his environment – which he soon came to consider dilettantish as he developed more discerning criteria. Yet, collecting 'famous names' – and the rarest of their works – was always to be part of Zweig's acquisitive impulse. He would always insist on the rarity of his items: in the notes on his record cards, for example, his manuscripts are repeatedly described as 'Seltenheit', 'Kostbarkeit allerersten Ranges', 'Rarissimum', if not 'Unicum'.[13] His understanding of Madame Roland de la Platière's *Rêveries philosophiques ou folles* (Zweig MS 183) as the only remaining manuscript from her hand appears now to be in error; as is his view – in line with conventional wisdom at the time – that his first edition of Rimbaud's *Une Saison en Enfer* (Zweig MS 202) was one of maybe seven copies that escaped burning.[14] Zweig also considered the fragment of Goethe's *Faust* (Zweig MS 152) incomparable and more beautiful than all other fragments in private hands. While all these items are unquestionably rare, Zweig's insistence on their uniqueness shows that an element of the principle of 'famous names' and the aura of exceptionality was always close at hand for him and is the explanation for the wide variety of material in the collection that encompasses heavily corrected manuscripts, fair copies, printed books, objects, drawings, letters and musical scores. Matuschek writes of this aspect of Zweig's collecting: 'For Zweig, the collection of autographs comprised not only pieces of creative activity, but also mementos, the character of which could rise to the level of the relic'.[15] In the present collection, clippings of Goethe's hair (Zweig MS 155) represent this tendency at its extreme. Yet the reliquary aspect of the collection would reach its height in 1929 with Zweig's acquisition of what his great friend Romain Rolland called the 'Beethoven-Museum', including the composer's desk, a compass, a whisk and a lock of hair, among other items, now all housed at the Beethoven-Haus in Bonn. Rolland, a Beethoven expert, dismissed this particular acquisition, explaining how for him, 'Beethoven's notebook was worth more than a piece of his furniture', before adding, 'although I am Catholic, I do not know that cult for material objects or bodily remains. In an autograph I look above all for the hidden traces of cultural spirit [*Geist*]'.[16] According to Zweig's many essays on the subject, this was also the core motivation behind his collection. Yet a penchant for relic and aura was never far away.

11 *WoY*, p. 41.
12 Ibid., p. 63.
13 The record cards are found in British Library Add MSS 73167–9.
14 See Chris Michaelides, 'Stefan Zweig's copy of Rimbaud, *Une Saison en Enfer* (1873)', *The British Library Journal*, 14/2 (1988), pp. 199–203.
15 *Ich kenne*, p. 15.
16 Romain Rolland to Zweig (25 July 1929), quoted in *Ich kenne*, p. 50.

Thanks to his privileged upbringing Zweig was able to explore his early interest in rare autographs and relics. An inheritance from his grandparents had allowed him to purchase his first noted acquisition at auction, a manuscript from the poet Friedrich Hebbel (no longer in the collection), at the age of around sixteen. Information about his teenage years of collecting is sparse, but Zweig was also able to start developing a collection outside the competitive areas of auctions and antiquaries by engaging in correspondence with dealers and writers he admired, offering exchanges or asking for gifts. In 1898, still aged sixteen, Zweig wrote to the Austrian novelist, editor and collector Karl Emil Franzos, in order to offer some letters in his possession in return for a small manuscript of Franzos's own. Even at this stage, Zweig was beginning to narrow his interest and focus on drafts and works in progress. As he explained to Franzos, letters held 'little value' for a collector of 'manuscripts and original poems'.[17] At the end of this same letter, Zweig cites manuscripts already in his collection, naming artists such as Wieland, Goethe, Anzengruber and Beethoven – not an insignificant grouping for the young initiate.

Encounters: the World of Autograph Manuscripts

Zweig's reading had always been broad and European. During his school years he had sought out the latest trends in European poetry before they were available in German, and read Nietzsche and Strindberg under the table, while his schoolmaster lectured on Schiller.[18] These interests led him to undertake a doctorate on the French philosopher Hippolyte Taine, completed in 1904, and publish his first volume of poetry, *Silberne Saiten* (1901), as well as some essays and translations of predominantly French and Belgian poets and novelists. In 1902 Zweig had written to the Belgian visionary poet, Émile Verhaeren, to ask for permission to render his poetry into German, and thereby established the beginning of a longstanding collaboration. In this friendship, Zweig honed his mediatory role in European letters by not only translating the poet's work, but by writing a monograph[19] and organising a tour to publicise Verhaeren's poetry, then virtually unknown to German-speaking readers. Zweig's own growing renown among the reading public as well as among his fellow writers facilitated the flow of donations to his manuscript collection. Indeed, now that he was able to offer his prospective donors published works of his own in return, responses were increasingly positive.

The earliest acquisition preserved in the present collection, Hugo von Hofmannsthal's manuscript for the poem 'Vor Tag' (Zweig MS 159), was presented by the poet to Zweig in 1908, and welcomed by Zweig in a letter of thanks as 'doubly valuable: as a poem and as a sign of friendly sentiments'.[20] Even before that, Zweig had received gifts from Hermann Hesse (a manuscript for the short story *Heumond* in 1905) and Rainer Maria Rilke (two poems, probably

17 Zweig to Karl Emil Franzos (18 February 1898), *Briefe 1897–1914*, ed. Knut Beck, Jeffrey B. Berlin and Natascha Weschenbach-Feggeler (Frankfurt am Main: S. Fischer, 1995), p. 14.

18 *WoY*, p. 61.

19 Stefan Zweig, *Émile Verhaeren* (Leipzig: Insel Verlag, 1910).

20 Zweig to Hugo von Hofmannsthal (16 February 1908), in Stefan Zweig, *Briefe an Freunde* (Frankfurt am Main: S. Fischer, 1978), p. 17.

'Papageien-Park' and 'Archaischer Torso Apollos', in 1907).[21] In Zweig's approach to Rilke, nearly ten years after his letter to Franzos, he adopted a similarly reverent tone to the author and self-effacing modesty in relation to his collection. He writes, 'I am no collector of autograph manuscripts, now and again I buy myself the manuscript of a poem I like', before continuing, in a slightly contrary tack, 'I have a few nice items', listing Goethe's 'Maylied', works by Lenau, Storm, Verhaeren (Zweig MS 193) and Hesse, as if to reassure Rilke as to the company his manuscript would keep. He concludes, 'I know I demand a lot, since I understand the magic of writing, I know, in gifting a manuscript, one also gives away a secret. Admittedly, a secret that only love can reveal.'[22] This letter hints at themes Zweig continued to explore in his essays on the collection, namely love[23] and the 'secret' of creation. It also opened a close friendship with Rilke that flourished during Zweig's increasingly frequent trips to Paris over the following years.

Paris – 'the city of eternal youth'[24] – was where Zweig made many of his formative relationships. Yet, his connection with French culture extended beyond his direct experiences.

> For the Paris of 1904 was not the only one I wanted to know; my senses and my heart were also in search of the Paris of Henri IV and Louis XIV, of Napoleon and the Revolution, of Rétif de la Bretonne and Balzac, Zola and Charles-Louis Philippe, Paris with all its streets, it characters, its incidents ... In fact before I saw it with my own eyes, I had become intellectually familiar in advance with everything in Paris through the art of the poets, novelists, and political and social historians who described it. It merely came to life when I arrived there.[25]

Most of those named figures featured in his collection at some stage.[26] Zweig's intellectual familiarity with France is also evident in manuscripts that relate to a preceding generation of French authors, namely Baudelaire (Zweig MS 136), Rimbaud (Zweig MSS 181, 202), Mallarmé (Zweig MS 170), Sully Prudhomme (Zweig MS 190) and Verlaine (Zweig MSS 195–6). Furthermore, his deep interest in the French Revolution and Napoleonic periods is reflected in many other items in the collection by Joseph Fouché (Zweig MS 147), Jean Henri Latude (Zweig MS 166), Louis XVI (Zweig MS 169), Marie Antoinette (Zweig MS 171), Joachim Murat (Zweig MS 173), Robespierre (Zweig MS 182), Madame Roland de la Platière (Zweig MS 183) and Saint-Just (Zweig MS 187).

A Francophile, then, before even beginning to make Paris a second home in the pre-war decade, Zweig made friends with a community of like-minded writers with the help of Verhaeren.

21 The manuscript for *Heumond* was donated to the Österreichisches Theatermuseum in 1937. Rilke's poems are now at the Bodmer Foundation, Geneva, but Matuschek suggests it is not completely certain that these were the poems Rilke sent Zweig in 1907. See *Ich kenne*, p. 13.

22 Zweig to Rainer Maria Rilke (11 March 1907), *Briefe 1897–1914*, p. 142.

23 For example, 'Sinn und Schönheit der Autographen' (1934), originally published as a standalone essay and simultaneously in the journal *Philobiblon* 8. Jahrgang, Heft 4 (1935), reprinted in *Ich kenne*, p. 136. Zweig writes, 'In order to understand manuscripts, in order to admire them, in order to be inspired and moved by them, we have to have learned to love the person, whose life is immortalized in them'.

24 *WoY*, pp. 149–81.

25 Ibid., p. 156.

26 See *Ich kenne*, p. 304, for more on the Rétif de la Bretonne item once in the collection, and p. 350 for more on the Émile Zola manuscript.

The dedications on the manuscripts gifted by writers in his Parisian circle offer a glimpse into Zweig's personal life at this point. Although not personally dedicated, Verhaeren's *La Multiple Splendeur* (Zweig MS 193) was sent by the poet and shortly followed by a letter in which he notes, 'I am delighted that you, whom I love so much, possess, out of all my books, the manuscript of the one I love above all'.[27] The second Verhaeren manuscript, for the poem 'Le Meunier' (Zweig MS 194), includes a short description by Zweig in his provenance notes, 'Von Emile Verhaeren, Caillou qui bique, Sommer 1908',[28] colouring his acquisition with the memory of a place where he spent many fine summers. André Gide's 'De l'importance du public' (Zweig MS 151) is accompanied by the author's note explaining his difficulty in selecting the manuscript best suited to Zweig's collection, before settling on the draft for a presentation given at Schloss Belvedere in Weimar, which, he says, acts as a 'petit souvenir historique'. While Georges Duhamel's donation (Zweig MS 144) does not feature a particularly personal dedication in the vein of Gide's, adding only 'pour Stefan Z. Souvenir de Duhamel Octobre 36', it might carry within it a gesture of apology following a brief 'cooling' in the friendship. Charles Vildrac's fragment of a first draft of the play *Le Paquebot Tenacity* (Zweig MS 198) is signed by the writer, 'Souvenir offert à Stefan Zweig avec la solide poignie de main d'amitié de Charles Vildrac'. Through these items we are brought closer to the atmosphere of fraternal dialogue in this fertile period in Zweig's life – a period perhaps best encapsulated in his diary. Reflecting on a gathering at his flat with Rolland, Rilke and Verhaeren, he writes, 'It was a genuine delight to have these three people with me, who have goodness and genius in common, unforgettable hours that touched on all of life'.[29]

This French selection of dedications gives personality and context to Zweig's collecting practice – more so than in the case of the musical manuscripts, most of which were the work of composers distant in time and space from Zweig. The interactive element of the collection is not only evident between the collector and his collection, but Zweig saw connections between the autographs themselves, placing them 'im brüderlichen Schrank'.[30] Other items show his sustained attraction to artistic interrelation. Take, for example, the Shelley manuscript, written in honour of Byron (Zweig MS 188); the layers of interaction in Nietzsche's fair copy of *Die Geburt des tragischen Gedankens* (Zweig MS 175), originally copied for Cosima Wagner; or Baudelaire's two poems dedicated to Victor Hugo (Zweig MS 136). The collection of literary manuscripts therefore brings to life artistic encounters, both personal to Zweig in the pre-war Parisian period, and distant from Zweig in the form of much earlier, more legendary friendships.

Process: in the Artist's Workshop

This early highpoint of literary interaction in Paris in 1913 brought with it some of Zweig's major acquisitions for his collection. Three Stendhal manuscripts – including the will (Zweig MS 189)

27 Émile Verhaeren to Zweig (19 June 1909), *Émile et Marthe Verhaeren – Stefan Zweig: Correspondence générale (1900–1926)*, ed. Fabrice van der Kerckhove (Brussels: Labor, 1996), p. 221.

28 Add MS 73170, f. 10.

29 Stefan Zweig (17 March 1912), *Tagebücher* (Frankfurt am Main: S. Fischer, 1984), pp. 51–2.

30 Id., 'Handschriften als schöpferische Dokumente', originally published in *Berliner Tageblatt* (7 November 1926), reprinted in *Ich kenne*, p. 117.

in the present collection – as well as autograph drafts of Verlaine's *Fêtes Galantes* (Zweig MS 195) were acquired from Noël Charavay within a matter of days in March 1913. Rilke, with whom Zweig had spent much of his time during this same period, supplemented his earlier donations with the gift of a manuscript of – originally titled – *Die Weise von Liebe und Tod des Cornets Otto Rilke* (Zweig MS 179), which Zweig noted in his diary as a 'nice surprise', describing it as 'pure regularity, which distinguished everything he [Rilke] did'.[31] For Zweig, Rilke

> applied his fundamental sense of beauty to the most insignificant details. Not only did he write his manuscripts carefully on the finest paper in his rounded calligraphic hand, so that the line matched line as if drawn with a ruler, he chose good paper for even the most unimportant letter, and that calligraphic handwriting, pure and round, covered it regularly right up to the margin. He never, even in the most hastily written note, allowed himself to cross out a word. Once he felt that some sentence or expression was not quite right, he would rewrite the whole letter with the utmost patience. Rilke never let anything that was less than perfect leave his hands.[32]

Both the 'Cornet' manuscript and Rilke's letter to Alfred Wolfenstein (Zweig MS 180) show the care and finesse in handwriting and writing material that Zweig admired in Rilke, from the selection of squared paper for his manuscript (which contains only two corrections) to the detail of the letter's striking signature. Zweig's own manuscripts and letters – remarkably clear and predominantly in purple ink – likewise display his eye for fine materials and presentation. In later life Zweig also took care to have some of his more significant manuscripts exquisitely rebound.

Even in his earliest correspondence, Zweig had delineated his collection's focus on manuscripts showing works in progress. Writing to Ernst Hardt, he asked for a manuscript that 'is in a state that is still warm from creation'.[33] For the first time, in this same year, Zweig articulated his thoughts in an essay titled 'Vom Autographensammeln',[34] that were expanded a year later in the essay 'Die Autographensammlung als Kunstwerk'.[35] The few months of collecting that lay between the two versions of the essay appear to have significantly changed the title's emphasis from the general activity of collecting to the implicit suggestion that his collection could one day be considered an 'artwork'. What may have unconsciously inspired this confidence was the acquisition in 1914 of the most comprehensive example of the creative process in the collection, namely Balzac's corrected proofs of the novel *Une Ténébreuse Affaire* (Zweig MS 133). A diary entry describes the acquisition with the same haste and frenzy that Zweig associated with the writing of the proof itself:

> Then I go – alas, it rains, rains endlessly still – to the bookseller Blaisot, to whom Messein had directed me because of the auction, and buy – lightning-fast, rashly, greedily, despite the

31 *Tagebücher*, 29 March 1913, p. 58.
32 *WoY*, p. 165.
33 Zweig to Ernst Hardt (Summer 1913), in Zweig, *Briefe an Freunde* (Frankfurt am Main: S. Fischer, 1978), p. 24.
34 First published in *Vossische Zeitung* (14 September 1913).
35 First published in *Deutscher Bibliophilen-Kalender: Jahrbuch für Bücherfreunde und Büchersammler* (1914), reproduced as facsimile in *Ich kenne*.

> feeling of maybe overpaying – Balzac's novel "Une ténébreuse affaire". Then I'm excited, crazed, unable to think clearly, stirred up, and it all cools down when I go to a meeting.[36]

Zweig had already devoted a long essay to Balzac and contemplated a full-length biography, which was eventually taken up in 1939 and never completed.[37] The coup – it was one of the rare items to have slipped away from the great Balzac collector Charles de Spoelberch de Lovenjoul – compounded Zweig's commitment to the prolific novelist. On the catalogue card, Zweig is particularly effusive:

> This precious manuscript of incomparable value demands a special description and perhaps a whole book, so much one recognises Balzac's complete working process in them like no other manuscript. The perhaps 1000 pag. corrected proofs, which bound together not only the first corrected proofs, but often the second and third, are strewn with emendations, or were rather more the foundations on which Balzac built the final form of his novels.[38]

Balzac is the only author whose manuscripts and creative process became the subject of a separate essay. In 'Die unterirdischen Bücher Balzacs' (1917),[39] preceded by an epigraph from Goethe,[40] Zweig portrayed 'perhaps the greatest hero of artistic work [*Arbeit*]', whose process was like a 'volcanic eruption', the 'plunge of a gigantic waterfall', and whose manuscripts became 'an infernal labyrinth of corrections, revisions'. With over 600 folios, the manuscript in the collection is a veritable mess of print completely overwritten with annotations and includes over 200 pages of manuscript insertions, all presented on a variety of papers of different shapes and sizes.

Zweig's attraction to the 'workshop' of creativity is a consistent theme in his frequent writings on the subject. In the earliest essay, he wrote of a 'retreat of a being back to its becoming, of a creation back to its emergence'.[41] Process became significant enough for Zweig to suggest in 'Meine Autographensammlung' that he would rather call his collection a 'Werkschriftensammlung' (collection of drafts), since he only collected 'writings that showed the creative spirit in its creative state'.[42] There are many examples of heavily corrected manuscripts in the collection today. Consider, in particular, other Balzac fragments from his essay 'La Monographie de la presse parisienne' (Zweig MSS 135, 216); Duhamel's manuscript of *Le dernier voyage de Candide* (Zweig MS 144); Anatole France's annotations on a letter he received in response to an article (Zweig MS 148); André Gide's presentation 'De l'importance du public' (Zweig MS 151); the

36 *Tagebücher*, 25 March 1914, p. 76.

37 Stefan Zweig, 'Balzac', in *Drei Meister* (Leipzig: Insel Verlag, 1920), and *Balzac* (Stockholm: Bermann-Fischer, 1946).

38 Add MS 73168.

39 Stefan Zweig, 'Die unterirdischen Bücher Balzacs', originally published in *Jahrbuch deutscher Bibliophilen,* 5. Jahrgang (1917), reprinted in *Ich kenne*, pp. 96–9.

40 'Die Natur- und Kunstwerke lernt man nicht kennen, wenn sie fertig sind. Man muß sie im Entstehen aufhaschen, um sie einigermaßen zu begreifen', ('One cannot come to know works of art and nature when they are complete. One must catch them in their emergence, in order to understand them at all.'), Goethe to Carl Friedrich Zelter (4 August 1803).

41 'Die Autographensammlung als Kunstwerk'.

42 In *Philobiblon*, 3. Jahrgang, Heft 7 (Vienna, September 1930), reprinted in *Ich kenne*, p. 128.

poems by Heine (Zweig MS 156), Keats (Zweig MS 163), Leopardi (Zweig MS 167), and Novalis (Zweig MS 176); or the manuscripts from Verhaeren, Vildrac and Rolland, perhaps most evidently the latter's essays 'La jeunesse Suisse' and the famous manifesto 'Déclaration de l'Indépendence de l'Esprit' (together as Zweig MS 186).

For Zweig, who ultimately sought glimpses of 'the secret of creation'[43] in his manuscripts, the experience of the creative process was not just a matter of abstract textual engagement, but an encounter with the personality, the psychology behind the text:

> more than anything else, I was interested in the biographical and psychological aspects of the creation of a work of art. Where else can we locate that mysterious moment of transition when the vision and intuition of a genius brings a verse or a melody out of invisibility into the earthly realm, giving it graphic form, where can we observe it if not in the first drafts of creative artists, whether achieved with great effort or set down as if in a trance?[44]

In the visible and almost tangible marks and pen strokes in these corrected manuscripts, Zweig gets closer to the creator figure himself, reminding us in his essays that art is a *human* achievement one should celebrate. For Goethe – a constant reference point and the 'father of manuscript collecting' for Zweig – 'exceptional people were magically present through their manuscripts', making a manuscript a 'desirable supplement and surrogate' for an artist's portrait.[45] And what Carlo Ginzburg calls the 'shock' of the autograph is precisely the fact that 'behind the immateriality of the content ... there exists (or existed) the real bodies of men and women'.[46] That physical proximity to a creator allowed Zweig to deduce a 'moral lesson' from his collecting, that artworks were not merely 'gifts of genius to the artists, but the fruit of painstaking, rigorous, sacrificial work [*Arbeit*]', which should incite our reverence for the 'man in the artist' in two ways: as both exceptional and human.[47]

Interconnections: Writing and Collecting

In many ways, Zweig's understanding of the 'moral' sacrifices artists make when struggling for high art and ideals was paralleled by a moral imperative he threaded through his collection and his own mature writing, which included many biographies, essays on creative personalities, and eulogies, depicting the figures and works he thought deserved renewed emphasis through his words. It was the First World War that intensified Zweig's pursuit of a humanistic agenda. In a letter of 15 November 1918 to his fellow collector and publisher at the Insel Verlag, Anton Kippenberg, Zweig signalled a new direction for his activity: 'It is time for a new idealism'.[48]

43 'Sinn und Schönheit der Autographen', p. 136.
44 *WoY*, p. 185.
45 'Die Welt der Autographen', p. 104.
46 Carlo Ginzburg, Preface in Pedro Corrêa do Lago, *True to the Letter: 800 Years of Remarkable Correspondence, Documents and Autographs* (London: Thames & Hudson, 2004).
47 'Sinn und Schönheit der Autographen', p. 139.
48 Zweig to Anton Kippenberg, 15 November 1918, *Briefe 1914–1918*, p. 242.

Drawing new lines and comparisons through history and literature in his 'Baumeister der Welt' series and his historical biographies, Zweig was often inspired by subjects represented in his collection. Or, conversely, subjects of biographies later found a place in it. As he said with reference to Balzac, only those who know Balzac's manuscripts understand the real Balzac. Thus, with respect to most texts, Zweig devoted himself to primary research into his subject's original drafts and letters.

The collection and Zweig's writing overlapped, therefore, in many places. Zweig wrote laudatory monographs and essays on the same close friends who donated to the collection: Verhaeren, Rolland, Rilke. Furthermore, one of Zweig's earliest extended essays (1904) took Paul Verlaine as its subject, opening with, '[t]he works of great artists are silent books of eternal truths'.[49] Written a decade before the acquisition of *Fêtes Galantes* and even longer before the fragment of *Voyage en France par un français* (Zweig MS 196) came into the collection, this remark on the 'silence' of such works may seem less defensible in the face of the heavy corrections particularly evident in the latter item. The figures of the 'Baumeister der Welt' series of biographical triptychs,[50] namely Balzac, Dickens,[51] Dostoevsky (Zweig MS 143), Hölderlin (Zweig MSS 160–1), Kleist (Zweig MS 164), Nietzsche, Casanova,[52] Stendhal and Tolstoy (Zweig MS 191), all held a place in the manuscript collection and interacted in some way with their published portraits by Zweig. Of Dostoevsky, Zweig wrote, 'Dostoevsky writes in fever, just as he thinks in fever and lives in fever. Beyond the hand, which lets the words stream in small flowing pearls (he had the rushed writing of all feverish people) over the paper, his pulse beats twice as fast'.[53] When assessed by reference to the collection's draft of the Russian novelist's *The Insulted and Injured* (Zweig MS 143), this description appears to have been exaggerated to fit the overall portrait of a writer in feverish struggle. This particular manuscript with its minute handwriting might justify the idea of Dostoevsky's 'flowing pearls'. However, it also shows a precision somewhat contrary to fever. Indeed, fever might be better applied to the collection's manuscript of Tolstoy's *Kreutzer Sonata* (Zweig MS 191). Zweig frequently depicted prolific, biographically chaotic and tragic 'heroes' as similarly chaotic in their writing in order to lend some harmony to his portraits. The description of Hölderlin's verses as 'manic poems' with 'chaotically jumbled lines'[54] also seems less apt for the manuscripts of the poems in the present collection than for perhaps other variants or related manuscripts, of which Zweig had knowledge.

Further connections are to be found between the collection and Zweig's biographical interest in the French Revolution and Napoleonic periods. Zweig's biography of French statesman Joseph Fouché (1929) – a surprising success at the time – was followed three years later by a study of

49 Stefan Zweig, *Paul Verlaine*, trans. O. F. Theis (Dublin; London: Luce and Company, 1913), p. 1.

50 *Drei Meister*, op. cit.; *Der Kampf mit dem Dämon* (Leipzig: Insel Verlag, 1925); *Drei Dichter ihres Lebens* (Leipzig: Insel Verlag 1928).

51 The two pages from the manuscript of Dickens's *David Copperfield* are no longer in the collection. See *Ich kenne*, p. 193.

52 All three items Zweig once owned by Casanova are now at the Bodmer Foundation, Geneva, although the last of the three was sold by the Zweig estate in 1953, meaning it would have formed part of the Zweig collection until the collector's death.

53 *Drei Meister*, p. 171.

54 'Handschriften als schöpferische Dokumente', p. 117.

Marie Antoinette. Like many other writers, Zweig portrayed Napoleon as a figure of genius, a standard of exceptionality by which to compare others. A speech by Robespierre (Zweig MS 182) for the Rosati Society of Arras captures a poetical side to the leader of The Terror. It was precisely the personal aspect of such figures that intrigued Zweig. The speech begins: 'La rose croit pour tous les hommes: mais tous les hommes ne sont pas faits pour sentir ses charmes' – not the political tract one might have expected. Again, the letter from Marie Antoinette to Count Rosenberg (Zweig MS 171) reveals a personal story that would have appealed to Zweig's biographical approach. Indeed, his work on her was built on her intimate correspondence with Count Axel von Fersen (whose father is represented in Zweig MS 145). The collection's letter exposes her lack of interest in her husband, King Louis XVI, when she writes, 'mes gouts [*sic*] ne sont pas les mêmes que ceux du Roi, qui n'a que ceux de la chasse et des ouvrages mécaniques. Vous conviendrez que j'aurais assez mauvaise grâce auprès d'une forge'. The King himself is represented in Zweig's collection with an address to the Legislative Assembly (Zweig MS 169), which Zweig notes as a 'world-historical document'. We might also class the 'Reformatoren Gedenkbuch' (Zweig MS 200) in the same world-historical frame – a document comprising spiritual commentaries by Protestant reformers. Even here we see crossover with Zweig's writing. Martin Luther is the first contributor to the 'Gedenkbuch' and the reformer would act as a counterpoint to Erasmus in Zweig's famous biography, most noted for its unsubtle autobiographical allusions.[55]

Zweig's biographies and essays empathetically animated the lives of his subjects, stylizing the stories to incite a level of interest and compassion in the reader. One contemporary review of *Marie Antoinette: The Portrait of an Average Woman* praised the fact that 'Zweig manages to make her human'.[56] In the collection, too, the same process is at work. Zweig's gathering, preserving, sharing – and ultimately re-animating through essays on manuscripts in his collection – are an attempt to immortalize works and figures by 'making them present' (*Vergegenwärtigung*).[57]

Exile: Pessimism and Refinement

If Zweig's post-war resolve for a 'new idealism' was the spur for a productive period of writing and collecting, the ever-bleaker socio-political landscape in the late 1920s and the beginning of the 1930s led to Zweig's growing pessimism and bouts of depression, which weakened his motivations for both his creative activities. In *The World of Yesterday*, Zweig's productivity is portrayed in the chapter (tellingly) entitled 'Sonnenuntergang' (The Setting Sun), in which Zweig reflected deeply about the nature of his collection and cast his Salzburg residence as a 'European meeting place'.[58] A parallel was thus made between the real world of artistic interaction and the world contained within the autograph collection: 'Many welcome and famous guests visited our

55 *Triumph und Tragik des Erasmus von Rotterdam* (Vienna; Leipzig; Zürich: Herbert Reichner, 1935).

56 H. H., 'Marie Antoinette by Stefan Zweig', *Books Abroad*, 7/4 (October 1933), p. 466.

57 For more on this idea, see Ulrike Vedder, 'Zur Magie der Handschrift. Stefan Zweig als Autographensammler', in *Zweigs England*, ed. Rüdiger Görner and Klemens Renoldner (Würzburg: Königshausen & Neumann, 2014), p. 151.

58 *WoY*, p. 371.

house in those years, but even in the hours when I was alone I was surrounded by a magic circle of distinguished figures from the past whose shades and whose traces I had gradually managed to summon'.[59] Both worlds began to disappear as fascism gained authority. The 1933 book burnings condemned Zweig's works, cutting his ties to the German publishing world, and fundamentally contaminating his relationship to the German language itself. A year later, Austrian government officials searched Zweig's home for weapons. 'I did not like my home any more after that official visit', he later wrote, since 'personal liberty was the most important thing on earth'. He added, '[i]t was the first step to cutting the link between me and my native Austria'.[60] The day after this official visit, Zweig departed for London. Soon afterwards, he made it known to the resident registration office that he had emigrated for good.

The resulting disconnection of Zweig from his country, both physical and psychological, began the process that reshaped the manuscript collection into its present form. Zweig called this process one of refinement.

> But after a while my ambitions as a collector went further. I felt it was no longer enough to have just a gallery of autograph manuscript pages of great literature and music, a reflection of a thousand creative methods. Simply enlarging my collection did not tempt me any more. In my last ten years as a collector I set out to refine it. While it had once been enough for me to own manuscript sheets showing writers or musicians in the process of creation, my efforts now went into finding autographs that would illustrate their work at their most inspired and successful creative moments. So I looked not just for the manuscript of any writer's poems, but for one of his finest, if possible one of those works that begin to form when inspiration first finds earthly expression on the page in ink and pencil, and then go on and on into eternity. Bold and presumptuous it may have been, but I wanted to have those manuscripts – relics of the immortals illustrating what made them immortal in the first place.[61]

Looking back on this final period of collection, Zweig presented it as not so much a reverse dictated by contingent obstacles and personal disaffection, but a progression towards a more focused and sublime artwork. This refinement was achieved through a set of changes implemented by Zweig from the late 1920s onwards, namely: a rebalancing of his acquisitions in favour of music manuscripts; a more international, rather than German-language, focus; the donation of items to cultural institutions; and ultimately the sale of hundreds of manuscripts.

Zweig had spent more and more time abroad in the early 1930s and foreseen his exile. As a result he was reluctant to continue expanding the collection. 'I am actually thinking more about dismantling rather than building, selling off rather than collecting', he wrote in response to an antiquarian's offer of an item in the spring of 1933.[62] While circumstances would lead Zweig towards a large-scale sale, the shape of the collection had already begun to change. Musical manuscripts began to feature more prominently, especially since the 1929 acquisition of his 'Beethoven

59 Ibid., pp. 372–3.
60 Ibid., p. 413.
61 Ibid., p. 374.
62 Zweig to Antiquariat Breslauer, 20 April 1933, cited in *Ich kenne*, p. 52.

Museum'.[63] Although Zweig was more comfortable writing about literary peers – he was no musician himself, despite his father's talent – music had always featured heavily in his life and writing. He counted the likes of Ferruccio Busoni, Arturo Toscanini and Bruno Walter as friends and wrote essays on their creativity. For Zweig, music was always related to the most elevated moments of artistic experience because of its abstraction in comparison to the visual and plastic arts. A growing tendency towards a more abstract beauty was also a result of Zweig's self-distancing from a German language that was becoming increasingly uncomfortable for him. His later Second World War diaries from England testify to this estrangement, 'imprisoned in a language, which I cannot use'.[64] Yet the diaries he wrote during the First World War already hinted at the escapism he experienced in music, in contrast to the personal conflicts he felt in relation to writing. After a concert of Beethoven by the Rosé Quartet, he noted, 'I'm still thinking about it. Music takes away all the grime of the political stuff, the black downpour of events'.[65] Also, after another concert by the same group: 'With the Rosé-Quartett in the evening, where I overcome everything'.[66] The collection's shift towards music is therefore on some level emblematic of an escape from the darkness of a contaminated language and towards a more secure and elevated sphere.

Literary and historical manuscripts were, however, by no means neglected. One of the collection's most remarkable items, acquired by Zweig in 1932, is undoubtedly Adolf Hitler's notes for a speech on foreign policy (Zweig MS 158). Unknown to any of his close friends, this acquisition both represented a collecting triumph in terms of its rarity and incited in Zweig a fear of exposure and a wish to keep his acquisition clandestine. More significantly, alongside Hesse's *Sommer 1933* (Zweig MS 157) manuscript of poems with watercolour illustrations, the Hitler notes are the last of the non-musical acquisitions of German-language items in the present collection. There is no greater contrast within the collection than that between the definitions of land and earth in the delicate poems and landscape watercolours of Hesse's decorative volume designed as a gift, and the hostile evocations of land, blood and earth in Hitler's hurried political sketch. As Zweig organised his collection from exile, many donations from friends also faced expulsion, not out of a 'lack of estimation for his colleagues' but because 'behind the selection of manuscripts to be given up was also the attempt to gain a bit of distance from his life up until now'.[67] That the Hitler manuscript had to – by virtue of its secrecy – survive the cull of many figures of Zweig's generation, adds poignancy to a collection that was shaped, in effect, by circumstances instigated by the rise of the dictator. The manuscript was a reminder of the lasting devastation to Zweig's world of yesterday, both standing for the German-speaking world of the 1930s in the 'world of autograph manuscripts' and forbidding the presence of German and Austrian contemporaries, since their language had long since discomfited Zweig the collector. In *The World of Yesterday*, the long and final description of the manuscript collection in the chapter 'Sonnenuntergang' is tellingly followed by the chapter 'Incipit Hitler'.

63 See Searle, op. cit., for more on the collection of music manuscripts.
64 *Tagebücher*, 3 September 1939, p. 418.
65 Ibid., 27 October 1915, p. 232.
66 Ibid., 25 January 1916, p. 247.
67 *Ich kenne*, p. 60.

In the period 1936–7 a series of auctions was organised through the Viennese antiquarian dealer, Heinrich Hinterberger, to sell off the majority of the Zweig Collection. The Hinterberger auction catalogues betray Zweig's considerable involvement in the process. The introduction to the first lot, for example, includes – by now, much formulated – emphasis on 'the artist in the workshop', where one 'experiences the creative process' in works that 'make the secret condition of creative becoming and emergence visible', as well as a Goethe quotation from *Skizzen zu einer Schilderung Winckelmanns*, that ends, 'in art, like life, it is not completeness that persists, but an infinity in constant movement'.[68] Two auctions in 1936 sold the majority of the selected manuscripts to the Swiss collector Martin Bodmer, in whose Foundation in Coligny-Geneva they remain today. A further auction in 1937 included other items from the Zweig Collection, mostly first and special editions of printed books. Five prestigious printed books and scores remain in the present collection (Zweig MSS 201–205).

The Jewish National and University Library in Jerusalem received thirty-eight items from Zweig's autograph manuscript collection along with a wide range of his correspondence.[69] Included amongst the manuscripts were items by Martin Buber, Alfred Döblin and Karl Emil Franzos. In summer 1937, Zweig decided to donate 101 manuscripts to the Theatersammlung der Nationalbibliothek in Vienna, now the Österreichisches Theatermuseum. This gift consisted predominantly of contemporary German-language authors, which Zweig no longer wanted in his refined collection and that he could not sell since they were gifts to him.[70] A fragment of Kafka's *Amerika*, received through Max Brod, joined esteemed authors such as Thomas, Heinrich and Klaus Mann, Romain Rolland and Franz Werfel in the donation. It may be surprising to see works by Joseph Roth, Arthur Schnitzler or Jules Romains, amongst other close friends of Zweig, in this selection given up to the Theatermuseum. It certainly left him without any examples of the work of those with whom he had spent so much time and whose work he still admired. However, Zweig suggests in his autobiography, regarding his collection, that he 'never considered himself the owner of these things, only their custodian for a certain time'.[71] Thus even these seemingly personal manuscripts could be given away by Zweig to cultural institutions. At the same time, he also imagined that the collection would become a 'mirror and portrait of [his] life's tendencies'.[72] The present collection, shaped by exile and the giving up of the majority of his manuscripts, could then be seen both to reflect and obscure Zweig's life's tendencies. Bereft of much of the personal, the contemporary and the German-language items, the collection might seem a little over-refined and less than a true reflection of its compiler's life. On the other hand,

68 '[...] daß in der Kunst wie im Leben kein Abgeschlossennes beharre, sondern ein Unendliches in Bewegung sei', in *Hinterberger catalogue IX, Eine berühmte Sammlung repräsentativer Handschriften. I. Teil,* British Library Add MS 73183 A.

69 See Mordekhai Nadav, 'Stefan Zweig's Übersendung seiner Privatkorrespondenz an die Jewish National and University Library', in *Bulletin des Leo-Baeck-Instituts* 63 (1982), pp. 66–73.

70 *Ich kenne*, pp. 76–7, and Christiane Mühlegger-Henhapel, '"Etwas wunderbar Substanzloses ...". Die Autographensammlung Stefan Zweig's im Wiener Theatermuseum', in *Stefan Zweig: Abschied von Europa*, ed. Klemens Renoldner (Vienna: Christian Brandstätter Verlag, 2014), pp. 215–38.

71 *WoY*, p. 377.

72 The original reads, 'Spiegel und Bildnis meiner Lebensneigungen', in 'Handschriften als schöpferische Dokumente', p. 117.

the very evident absence of such items may be the truest reflection of a collector whose disaffection with the contemporary and the German language led to more ideal collecting criteria as a form of self-abstraction from what Zweig felt was already lost to him.

Zweig's first wife, while viewing the dispersal of the collection as a 'consequence of his pessimism', suggested that his 'love and understanding of the writer's process' never ceased.[73] Indeed, Zweig's literary collection did expand in his time in England, despite music being the focus of his collecting. The Balzac letter (Zweig MS 134) and the two fragments of 'Monographie de la Presse Parisienne' (Zweig MSS 135, 216) were acquired in 1940, as was the collection's Hans Christian Andersen poem (Zweig MS 132). Yet, it should be borne in mind that by this date the collection had assumed the function of an investment, and a safe and mobile means of securing money in fragile economic conditions.[74] This attitude is evident in the final item that he collected, a letter by Benjamin Franklin (Zweig MS 149), acquired on Zweig's behalf by Heinrich Eisemann in London on 26 August 1941, six months before the collector's death. Zweig never returned to Europe, living temporarily in New York from July 1940 until his departure for Brazil a few months later. It is unlikely that Zweig ever saw his final acquisition.

The last portrait in Zweig's *The World of Yesterday* is reserved for Sigmund Freud, a long-standing friend and fellow exile in England. Zweig gave the address at Freud's funeral on 26 September 1939 in London, in which he lauded 'a moral existence: a heroic life'.[75] In his autobiography, Zweig concluded his ode to his friend: 'And when we, his friends, lowered his coffin into English earth, we knew that we had given that earth the best of our own native land'.[76] Freud's 1924 gift to Zweig of a manuscript of his lecture 'Der Dichter und das Phantasieren' (Zweig MS 150) encapsulates the various aspects of Zweig's collection – friendship and creative interaction; the creative process evident in the haste of Freud's writing and his many corrections, but also as the manuscript's subject matter. In the funeral address, Zweig said: 'This leaving is no end, no final closure, only simply the gentle transition from mortality to immortality'.[77] Zweig's praise for Freud formed part of the process of transition and Zweig's manuscript collection was an attempt to 'make present', to keep alive, and immortalize creative humanity.

The British Library's Stefan Zweig Series of Concerts, Lectures and Exhibitions, which began soon after the donation of this collection over 30 years ago, aimed to 'lend life' to the collection through its programme.[78] This Catalogue of the Zweig Collection's Literary and Historical Manuscripts, along with exhibitions and events past, present and future, aims to fulfil Stefan Zweig's desire that his collection be shared and experienced, and to lend life to the collector and his world of autograph manuscripts.

PARDAAD CHAMSAZ

73 Friderike Maria Zweig, *Stefan Zweig. Eine Bildbiographie* (Munich: Kindler, 1961), p. 92.
74 *Ich kenne*, p. 83.
75 Zweig, 'Worte am Sarge Sigmund Freuds', in *Zeit und Welt*, p. 52.
76 *WoY*, p. 450.
77 'Worte am Sarge Sigmund Freuds', p. 51.
78 In *Music Weekly*, [Michael Oliver visits British Library for Stefan Zweig manuscript exhibition], *BBC Radio 3* (5 December 1986).

The entries are listed in order of British Library Zweig MS number. In a few cases this means that works by the same authors are not listed adjacently in the catalogue as manuscripts came into the British Library at different dates; where this is the case we have cross-referenced between the main and additional entries.

Each entry contains:

1. An identification of the literary or historical work and description of the manuscript.

   The identification is followed by the first and last lines of the main manuscript text. Corrections and annotations which are not autograph are always stated to be by an identified writer, 'in another hand', or 'later'. Where appropriate, the general description of a manuscript is followed by a detailed list of its contents and/or brief details about the work.

2. A description of the physical character of the manuscript (entered in *italic* after the above). This section gives the following:

   (1) Overall measurements, height preceding width. In the case of manuscripts of irregular dimensions the greatest measurements are given.

   (2) The foliation given to the manuscript in the British Library, plus any significant earlier page or folio castings.

The medium, including paper and ink types, and basic structure where this could be gleaned.

   (3) Watermark details are given where possible, but not measurements.

   (4) Binding details.

The information in the remainder of each catalogue entry is given as appropriate under the following headings:

Related manuscripts. Location of known related manuscripts; in some cases, where the manuscript history of a work is particularly complex, reference is made to other published sources which give complete details.

Publication. Editions of the work, in two categories: (a) any edition for which the manuscript is the source or for which it is one among an array of sources, and (b) other editions cited either for comparative descriptive purposes, or to clarify the history of the work.

Reproduced. Details of other partial or complete published reproductions, including the plates in the present volume. All manuscripts, with the exception of those still subject to copyright, can be viewed in full in digital form via the British Library's Digitised Manuscripts website, www.bl.uk/manuscripts.

Exhibited. Details of occasions on which the manuscript has been on public display.

Provenance. Previous known owners in order ending with the date of acquisition by the British Library; where owners are not known, the sales history of the manuscript is given where possible. Sources are given for statements about the provenance of a manuscript; much information comes from Add MSS 73167–73185, the Provenance Papers presented with the Collection, of which a summary list is given below.

Bibliography. Principally lists sources containing references to or descriptions of the manuscript, but full bibliographical details of any other works cited by author or short title in the description, commentary, or elsewhere in the catalogue entry, are also given. Works are cited in chronological order of publication. In some cases where there are entries for more than one manuscript by individual authors, the catalogue entries are preceded by a list of works frequently cited there, with the abbreviations used.

Commentary. An expansion or explanation of material given earlier in the catalogue entry, with any pertinent information which has not otherwise been given in the entry.

In addition the following abbreviations are used throughout the catalogue entries:

Add MS	British Library, Additional MS
BL	London, British Library
f., ff.	folio(s)
vol., vols.	volume(s)

In the bibliographies, the following abbreviations are used for frequently cited works:

BL Programme Book, [Date] Programme book for the Stefan Zweig Series of Concerts, Lectures and Exhibitions (1987–97).

Catalogue of Additions *The British Library Catalogue of Additions to the Manuscripts, New Series, 1986–1990* (London: British Library, 1993). All references to Part I unless otherwise stated.

Frels, *Deutsche Dichterhandschriften* Wilhelm Frels, *Deutsche Dichterhandschriften von 1400 bis 1900. Gesamtkatalog der eigenhändigen Handschriften deutscher Dichter in den Bibliotheken und Archiven Deutschlands, Österreichs, der Schweiz und der CSR*, Bibliographical Publications, Germanic Section, Modern Language Association of America, 2 (Leipzig: Hiersemann, 1934).

75 Musical and Literary Autographs Brochure for the exhibition *75 Musical and Literary Autographs from the Stefan Zweig Collection* (London: British Library, 1986).

The Creative Spirit Brochure for the exhibition *The Creative Spirit in the Nineteenth Century* (London: Christie's, 1987).

Matuschek Oliver Matuschek, *Ich kenne den Zauber der Schrift: Katalog und Geschichte der Autographensammlung Stefan Zweig; mit kommentierten Abdruck von Stefan Zweigs Aufsätzen über das Sammeln von Handschriften* (Vienna: InLibris, 2005).

Essays and books by Stefan Zweig frequently cited throughout are abbreviated as follows:

Die Autographensammlung als Kunstwerk 'Die Autographensammlung als Kunstwerk', in *Deutscher Bibliophilen-Kalender: Jahrbuch für Bücherfreunde und Büchersammler* (1914), pp. 44–50. Separate facsimile included in Matuschek.

Die Sammlung Morrison 'Die Sammlung Morrison', first printed in *Vossische Zeitung* (6 September 1917), (Abendblatt), p. 2. Reprinted in Matuschek, pp. 94–5.

Die unterirdischen Bücher Balzacs 'Die unterirdischen Bücher Balzacs', first printed in *Jahrbuch deutscher Bibliophilen*, 5. Jahrgang (1917), pp. 48–52. Reprinted in Matuschek, pp. 96–9.

Die Welt der Autographen 'Die Welt der Autographen', presentation for the Österreichische Nationalbibliothek, Vienna, first printed in *Neue Freie Presse* (7 November 1923), pp. 1–4. Reprinted in Matuschek, pp. 103–7.

Überschätzung der Lebenden 'Überschätzung der Lebenden', in *Die Autographen-Rundschau*, 7. Jahrgang, Heft 2 (1926), pp. 19–20. Reprinted in Matuschek, pp. 115–16.

Von echten und falschen Autographen 'Von echten und falschen Autographen', first printed in a French version under the title 'Autographes authentiques et faux autographes', in Librairie Simon Kra, *Catalogue No. 14* (Paris, November 1926), pp. 2–3. A German version was published in *Die Autographen Rundschau*, 7. Jahrgang, Heft 8 (Berlin, 8 March 1927), p. 115–16. Reprinted in Matuschek, pp. 118–19.

Meine Autographen-Sammlung 'Meine Autographen-Sammlung' in *Philobiblon*, 3. Jahrgang, Heft 7 (Vienna, September 1930), pp. 279–92. Reprinted in Matuschek, pp. 128–32.

Sinn und Schönheit der Autographen 'Sinn und Schönheit der Autographen', presentation at the *Sunday Times Book Exhibition* in London (15 November 1934). Printed in *Philobiblon*, 8. Jahrgang, Heft 4 (April 1935), 14-page supplement. Reprinted in Matuschek, pp. 136–40.

Drei Meister *Drei Meister. Balzac – Dickens – Dostojewski*, Die Baumeister der Welt, 1 (Leipzig: Insel Verlag, 1920).

Der Kampf mit dem Dämon *Der Kampf mit dem Dämon. Hölderlin – Kleist – Nietzsche*, Die Baumeister der Welt, 2 (Leipzig: Insel Verlag, 1925).

Drei Dichter ihres Lebens *Drei Dichter ihres Lebens: Casanova – Stendhal – Tolstoi*, Die Baumeister der Welt, 3 (Leipzig: Insel Verlag, 1928).

Exhibitions

Manuscripts from the Stefan Zweig Collection were displayed in the small exhibitions mounted annually at the British Library as part of the Stefan Zweig Series of Concerts and Exhibitions between 1987 and 1996. Some have also featured from time to time in the Library's permanent exhibition galleries, and in other temporary exhibitions and displays. These smaller displays have not been listed individually in the catalogue, but major exhibitions within and outside the British Library are cited in full in the relevant entries. References to the following three exhibitions are abbreviated as follows:

London, National Book League, A Thousand Years of French Books, 1948 A Thousand Years of French Books. An Exhibition of Manuscripts, First Editions and Bindings, London, National Book League, 31 September–27 November 1948.

London, BL, 75 Musical and Literary Autographs, 1986 75 Musical and Literary Autographs from the Stefan Zweig Collection, London, British Library, 9 May–29 June 1986.

London, Christies, etc., The Creative Spirit, 1987–8 The Creative Spirit in the Nineteenth Century, London, Christie's, 22 September–2 October 1987 (subsequently shown at the Van Gogh Museum, Amsterdam and Österreichische Nationalbibliothek, Vienna).

Zweig Collection Provenance Papers, Add MSS 73167–73185

Papers concerning the acquisition of many of the manuscripts, and records compiled by Zweig during his ownership, were also presented in 1986 by the Trustees of the Stefan Zweig Collection; these were incorporated in the British Library in 1997 as Additional MSS 73167–73185. They have been used in compiling the accounts of the provenance of the manuscripts in the catalogue entries, with the relevant detailed references given there. The following is a summary list of these provenance papers.

Add MSS 73167–8. Record cards kept by Zweig and mostly in his hand; n.d., relating to items acquired 1908–40. The cards record details of the manuscript concerned and of its acquisition, together with Zweig's comments.

Add MS 73169. Copies of the record cards relating to music manuscripts; n.d., with annotations up to 1955. The copies are mostly not in Zweig's hand, but a number of the early annotations are his.

Add MS 73170. Ten of the large folders in which manuscripts were kept; n.d. The details of the manuscripts on the front covers of the folders are in a number of hands, including that of Zweig.

Add MSS 73171–80. Correspondence and miscellaneous papers; *c.* 1935–55. In addition to correspondence relating to acquisitions and notes on individual items, former wrappers or covers and photographs of manuscripts at various dates before 1986 are included.

Add MSS 73181–2. Card indexes; compiled *c.* 1945–61.

Add MS 73183 A–D. Copies of Heinrich Hinterberger, Vienna, Catalogues IX, XVIII and XX; [1936–7]. The two copies of Catalogue IX are annotated respectively by Zweig and Hinterberger.

Add MS 73184. Index Notebook, partly in Zweig's hand, to his collection of dealers' and auction sale catalogues; n.d. Arranged by names of owners.

Add MS 73185. Portrait photographs of Zweig.

CATALOGUE

Catalogue

List of the Manuscripts Described in the Following Entries

Zweig MSS

Hans Christian Andersen
(1805–1875)

Zweig MS 132.

'Fest-Sang til Landsoldaten', poem: *autograph* fair copy; [1851].

In *Danish*.
Begins: 'Dengang Du drog afsted'.
Ends: 'Hurra, Hurra, Hurra'.
Poem of four stanzas celebrating the return of soldiers from the First Schleswig-Holstein War. Heading 'Fest-Sang til Landsoldaten. Mel. Dengang jeg drog afsted'.
Stanzas 1, 2 and 4 consist of ten lines and Stanza 3 of eleven lines, including the refrain. The symbol :/: appears at both ends of the first lines of Stanzas 1, 2 and 4. Stanza 2, line 2, Stanza 3, line 3 and Stanza 4, line 2 are emphasised by repetition preceded by the word 'Ja'. Written in *Kurrentschrift*. Some words are underlined in the manuscript (for spacing in print). Signed at end 'H. C. Andersen'.

272 x 214mm.
f. 1.
Black ink on pink wove paper.
No watermark.

Related Manuscripts: Two autograph manuscripts of the poem are in the Collin collection of the Royal Library, Copenhagen, Den Collinske Manuscriptsamling 19, 40 nos. 16 and 58. No. 58 is a variant.

Published: *Folkekalender for Danmark* (Copenhagen: Lose & Delbanco, 1852), pp. 55–6; Hans Christian Andersen, *Samlede Skrifter*, 12, 2nd ed. (Copenhagen: C. A. Reitzels Forlag, 1879), pp. 344–5; id., *Samlede digte*, ed. Johan de Mylius (Copenhagen: Aschehoug, 2000), p. 548.

Reproduced: www.bl.uk/manuscripts and Plate 1 below.

Provenance: Purchased by Zweig from Heinrich Eisemann, London, 29 May 1940 (receipted invoice, Add MS 73174, f. 2, and list of purchases f. 17); BL 1986.

Bibliography: Birger Frank Nielsen, *H. C. Andersen Bibliografi* (Copenhagen: H. Hagerup, 1942), no. 592, p. 171; BL Programme Book, 1987; *Catalogue of Additions*, p. 68; Matuschek, p. 165.

Commentary. Andersen's verses were modelled on a song with the title 'Dengang jeg drog af sted' by Peter Christian Frederik Faber (1810–77), which had been written to celebrate the Danish victory at the Battle of Bov on 9 April 1848. Faber's work was set to an existing march tune by the Danish composer Emil Hornemann (1809–70), and the same setting is indicated in the heading to Andersen's poem. The festival at Glorup with which this poem is associated took place at the end of the First Schleswig-Holstein War on 7 July 1851, marking the anniversary of the Danish victory in the Battle of Fredericia on 6 July 1849. Glorup Castle was the home of Gebhard and Adam Gottlob Moltke-Hvidtfeldt, with whom Andersen often stayed. On this occasion, Andersen himself organised the outdoor event for some four hundred people with a triumphal arch, tent and decorations. Andersen's diary for 7 July 1851 describes the feast where he recited his poem to great acclaim.

Zweig also owned a manuscript of the poem 'Was ich liebe' (Andersen's own translation of 'Hvad jeg elsker'), with signature, now held at the Bodmer Foundation, Geneva.

Honoré de Balzac
(1799–1850)

Works frequently cited:
Œuvres complètes: Honoré de Balzac, *Œuvres complètes*, ed. Marcel Bouteron and Henri Longnon (Paris: Louis Conard, 1912–40)

Zweig MS 133.

'Une Ténébreuse Affaire', novel: *printed* proof sheets with very extensive *autograph* corrections and additions; [*c.* 1841].

In *French*.
Begins: 'L'automne de l'année 1803 fut un des plus beaux'.
Ends: 'vous pourrez l'expliquer à madame de Cinq-Cygne, et lui faire comprendre pourquoi Louis XVIII a gardé le silence'.
A tale from *Scènes de la vie politique*, one section of *La Comédie humaine*, Balzac's multi-volume series of interlinked novels and stories about French society during the Restoration and the July Monarchy. The novel is divided into twenty chapters; some are here in duplicate or triplicate, representing successive stages of the text. Interleaved chapter headings, written in a different hand, indicate the contents of each chapter. Corrections and amendments are written in ink on a variety of papers of many shapes and sizes.

Largest sheet 275 x 230mm.
ff. ii + 625.
Black and brown ink and printed text on wove paper.
No watermark.
Tipped into blue quarter shagreen binding with gold-tooling to spine. Gilt-stamped 'H. DE BALZAC / UNE TÉNÉBREUSE AFFAIRE / ÉPREUVES / DONNÉE PAR L'AUTEUR / À / M. DE PEYSSONNEL' on front board. Later British Library gilt-stamping to spine.

Related Manuscript: Bibliothèque nationale de France, Paris, NAF 14318 (a shorter version of 'Une Ténébreuse Affaire' than the present manuscript).
Published: Issued in serial form in *Le Commerce, journal des progrès moraux et matériels*, 14 January–20 February 1841; pirated edition published as Honoré de Balzac, *Une Ténébreuse Affaire: scène de la vie politique* (Brussels: Méline, Cans et Cie, 1841); subsequently edited by Balzac and published with a dedication 'À Monsieur de Margone, son hôte du château de Saché, reconnaissant, H. de Balzac' (Paris: Hippolyte Souverain, 1842); Balzac, *La Comédie humaine*, xii: *Scènes de la vie parisienne et Scènes de la vie politique* (Paris: Furne, 1846); id., *Œuvres complètes*, 26 (1914), pp. 27–275.
Reproduced: Stefan Zweig, *Balzac. Aus dem Nachlass herausgegeben und mit einem Nachwort versehen von Richard Friedenthal* (Stockholm: Bermann-Fischer Verlag, 1946), facing p. 208; *The Creative Spirit*, cover; BL Programme Book, 1988, p. 2; Matuschek, p. 97; www.bl.uk/manuscripts and Plate 2 below.
Exhibited: London, National Book League, A

Thousand Years of French Books, 1948, catalogue no. 127; Paris, Pierre Berès, Exposition commémorative du cent cinquantième anniversaire de Balzac, 1949, catalogue no. 404; Paris, Bibliothèque nationale de France, Honoré de Balzac, Exposition organisée pour commémorer le centenaire de sa mort, 1950, catalogue no. 620; London, BL, 75 Musical and Literary Autographs, 1986; London, Christie's, etc., The Creative Spirit, 1987–8.

Provenance: Presented by Balzac to M. de Peyssonel, 1841?; Auguste Blaizot, bookseller, Paris, early 20th century; acquired by Zweig from Blaizot, 1914; BL 1986.

Bibliography: Stefan Zweig, 'Die unterirdischen Bücher Balzacs'; id., *Drei Meister*; id., 'Meine Autographen-Sammlung'; id., *Balzac* (Stockholm: Bermann-Fischer Verlag, 1946); BL Programme Book, 1987; *Catalogue of Additions*, p. 68; Matuschek, p. 168.

Commentary. Prompted by a constant need for money, Balzac would start a new work by throwing together the first draft of his text with great speed, using subsequent proof stages to carry out all the detailed refinements. Upon completion he was in the habit of collecting together the resulting set of proofs and corrections in order to display the stages of his book's development, sometimes presenting these papers to his closest friends as evidence of his lengthy labours.
Although Zweig already owned a small Balzac manuscript ('La Messe de l'Athée', now held at the Bodmer Foundation, Geneva), he was overjoyed to obtain this tangible evidence of the thought processes behind one of Balzac's major novels, the more so because such Balzac manuscripts were particularly difficult to obtain.

Zweig MS 134.

Autograph letter to Jean Thomassy; [April or May? 1823].

In *French*.
Begins: 'Mon cher Thomassy — j'étais sorti pour aller chercher mon manuscrit de Wann-Chlore'.
Ends: 'Mon père va mieux. Adieu votre dévoué Honoré B'.
Although the primary purpose of the letter was to change the day proposed by Thomassy for a meeting, the young Balzac felt compelled to express indignation about the paltry sum of 600 francs that he was being offered for his novel *Wann-Chlore*, saying that he would rather till the soil with his bare hands than enter into such a scandalous transaction. To add to his woes, the second volume of his novel *La Dernière Fée* was to have twelve leaves, and he would be required to give it a third volume when the second edition was published.

191 x 147mm.
f. 1; 1v blank.
Black ink on laid paper.
Watermark: shield containing orb below clasped hands; knight above.

Related Manuscript: Maison de Balzac, Paris, Inv. 97–26 (an autograph letter to Thomassy, signed 'de Ba', dated Paris, July 1834 and dealing with the novel *Le Médecin de campagne*).

Published: Honoré de Balzac, *Correspondance*, 1, ed. Roger Pierrot (Paris: Garnier, 1960), p. 218.

Reproduced: www.bl.uk/manuscripts and Plate 3 below.

Provenance: Purchased by Zweig from Maggs, London, 14 May 1940; BL 1986.
Bibliography: BL Programme Book, 1987; *Catalogue of Additions*, p. 68; Matuschek, p. 169; see also bibliography for Zweig MS 133 above.

Commentary. Balzac probably met Jean Thomassy (1795–1874) in 1821, when the Paris bookseller G. C. Hubert (publisher of some of Balzac's earliest work) issued Thomassy's book *De la sensation qu'a faite en France la mort de Buonaparte*. Thomassy largely abandoned writing to pursue a legal career, but remained Balzac's close friend and adviser. Despite Balzac's best efforts, *Wann-Chlore* did not appear until 1825, when it was published anonymously in four volumes by Urbain Canel and Delongchamps in Paris. It was subsequently published in two volumes by Hippolyte Souverain in Paris in 1836, under the pseudonym Horace de Saint-Aubin and with the title *Jane la pâle*.

Zweig MS 135.

['Monographie de la Presse Parisienne'], article: *printed* proof sheet with *autograph* corrections; [*c.* 1842].

In *French*.
Begins: 'Le publicisme était un grand miroir concentrique'.
Ends: 'A ce métier, il est difficile qu'un homme ne se fausse pas l'esprit'.
In this satirical article, Balzac set out to offer a complete analysis of the French press. The present sheet, which comes from the section headed 'Le Publiciste', contains the last three lines of the preamble and the opening part of a discussion on the various sorts of journalist. A description of the first type, identified by Balzac as 'Le Directeur-Rédacteur en chef-propriétaire', is followed by the first eight lines of a description of 'Le Ténor'. Printed on one side, with numerous *autograph* corrections, including an extensive passage of nineteen lines, itself somewhat corrected, which has been added on the verso. Numbered '3' in ink in top left-hand corner of the recto (perhaps a page numbering, or possibly referring to the number of the recension).

237 x 160mm.
f. 1.
Printed text with annotations in black ink on wove paper.
No watermark.

Related Manuscripts: BL Zweig MS 216 (see below); Fundação Biblioteca Nacional, Rio de Janeiro, Brazil, 1–7, 7, 13 No 5: a single annotated proof sheet presented by Zweig in 1942 (presentation letter 1–7, 7, 13 No 4); Bibliothèque de l'Institut de France, Paris, MS Lov. A. 154: twelve leaves from the Spoelberch de Lovenjoul library, dated 1843 and described as autograph manuscript fragments from *Monographie de la presse parisienne*.
Published: *La Grande Ville: nouveau tableau de Paris*, ii (Paris: Bureau Central des Publications Nouvelles, 1843), pp. 129–208, and separately as an offprint dated 1842; *Œuvres complètes*, 40 (1940), pp. 553–605.
Reproduced: www.bl.uk/manuscripts and Plate 4 below.
Provenance: Probably purchased by Zweig, together with Zweig MS 216, from Heinrich Eisemann in

London, February 1940; BL 1986. The two proof sheets itemised in the papers relating to this transaction (Add MS 73174, ff. 17–19) offer no indication of content, being described only by their physical characteristics. One clearly matches Zweig MS 216 and the second very probably corresponds to the present leaf. However, Eisemann's identification of the second proof could equally well apply to the other leaf owned formerly by Zweig, now in Rio de Janeiro, which contains an unrelated passage occurring at a much later stage in the article.

Bibliography: BL Programme Book, 1987; *Catalogue of Additions*, p. 68; Matuschek, p. 168; see also bibliography for Zweig MS 133 above.

Commentary. Balzac's unconventional method of working involved the repeated revision of a consecutive series of proofs until he reached a final version. Taken together, this leaf and the leaf of Zweig MS 216 provide a clear illustration of part of this process. Although the texts are more or less continuous, there is overlap, since the lengthy addition at the bottom of the present leaf has been incorporated into the printed text of Zweig MS 216, indicating that the two must come from separate recensions.

The way in which these two leaves together provide direct evidence of Balzac's thought processes when composing the article suggests that Zweig would have found them of particular interest. His other leaf, which he presented to the Biblioteca Nacional in Rio de Janeiro in 1942, did not offer quite the same degree of insight.

Charles Baudelaire
(1821–1867)

Zweig MS 136.

'Fantômes Parisiens', two poems dedicated to Victor Hugo: *autograph* fair copy with a few minor revisions and corrections; [1859].

In *French*.

Contents:

1. ff. 1–2. 'Les sept vieillards', with the heading 'I. Fantômes Parisiens'. Begins: 'Fourmillante cité! Cité pleine de rêves'. Ends: 'Sans mats, sur une mer monstrueuse et sans bords!'.
2. ff. 2–2v. The first part of 'Les petites vieilles', with the heading 'II. Fantômes Parisiens'. Begins: 'Dans les plis sinueux des vieilles capitales'. Ends: 'Pour celui que l'austère Infortune allaita!'.

Two poems of thirteen and eight stanzas respectively, written out for the dedicatee, Victor Hugo. The first poem is complete; the second consists only of the first part of the version published in 1859 (parts two to four are lacking). Both poems are headed 'à Victor Hugo'. After the first dedication is a small mark, apparently added by Hugo to indicate that he had sent a response (Zweig's record card, Add MS 73168, f. 2). At the foot of f. 2 is a note in Baudelaire's hand, 'Le rébus n'est pas de mon invention. Il y a dans le journal de La Mésangère des gravures de mode où le réticule est orné de rébus brodés'. 'V. Hugo' and 'Baudelaire' are pencilled on f. 1.

208 x 265mm.
ff. 2.
Black ink on white wove paper.
Bifolium.
No watermark.

Related Manuscripts: 'Les sept vieillards', designated by Leakey and Pichois as MS 'W', sent to Jean Morel, director of the *Revue française*, early June 1859; 'Les sept vieillards', designated MS 'Y', with a sheet of 'Errata', designated MS 'X', probably sent to Alphonse de Calonne for publication, September 1859; 'Les sept vieillards', including a drawing, designated MS 'Z', probably also sent to Alphonse de Calonne in 1859, and sold at Sotheby's, 27 April 1971, lot 299.

Published: *Revue contemporaine*, 8me année, 2e série, tome 11 (1859), pp. 93–8, with the title 'Fantômes Parisiens' but without the dedication to Victor Hugo; Charles Baudelaire, *Les Fleurs du mal*, 2nd ed. (Paris: Poulet-Malassis et de Broise, 1861), pp. 206–13, in the section 'Tableaux Parisiens', with an additional verse in part one of 'Les petites vieilles' which is not in Zweig MS 136 or the first printed edition.

Reproduced: Stefan Zweig, 'Meine Autographen-Sammlung', p. 130 (original *Philobiblon* publication only); www.bl.uk/manuscripts and Plate 5 below.

Exhibited: London, National Book League, A Thousand Years of French Books, 1948, catalogue no. 142; London, BL, 75 Musical and Literary Autographs, 1986.

Provenance: Purchased by Zweig from Noël Charavay, 23 August 1927; BL 1986.
Bibliography: Stefan Zweig, 'Meine Autographen-Sammlung'; Jean-Bertrand Barrère, *Victor Hugo à l'oeuvre: le poète en exil et en voyage* (Paris: Klincksieck, 1966), p. 41; BL Programme Book, 1987; F. W. Leakey, with Claude Pichois, 'Les sept versions des *Sept Vieillards*', in F. W. Leakey, *Baudelaire: Collected Essays, 1953–88*, ed. Eva Jacobs (Cambridge: Cambridge University Press, 1990), pp. 139–58; *Catalogue of Additions*, p. 68; Matuschek, p. 170.

Commentary. The poems were copied out and sent to Victor Hugo with an accompanying letter, dated [23?] September 1859, in which Baudelaire states that the second poem had been written in imitation of Hugo. It seems, however, that the dedication may have been an afterthought, as the two poems had already been published earlier in the year without it, and it was not to appear in print until the second edition of *Les Fleurs du mal*, in 1861. Zweig, who described the manuscript as 'Aller grösste Seltenheit' (Add MS 73168, f. 2), must have been delighted to acquire such an interesting and prestigious item for his collection. Some fifteen years earlier he had purchased another Baudelaire autograph, 'Note des articles que je puis faire pour Mr. de Calonne', now at the Bodmer Foundation, Geneva.

Arnold Bennett
(1867–1931)

Zweig MS 137.

Autograph draft of a newspaper article in the series 'Books and Persons', including a review of *Conflicts* by Stefan Zweig, written for the London *Evening Standard*; 20 February 1928.

In *English*.
Begins: 'Not long since I saw an advertisement of [deletion] a novel'.
Ends: 'It has sparks of the divine fire'.
The review relates to novels by three European writers newly published in English translation, including Stefan Zweig's *Verwirrung der Gefühle* (Leipzig: Insel Verlag, 1927), part 3 of *Die Kette: Ein Novellenkreis*, translated by Eden and Cedar Paul as *Conflicts: Three Tales* (London: Allen and Unwin, 1928).
Signed at head 'Arnold Bennett'. Many *autograph* deletions and insertions. The names 'RAUCAT' and 'MORAND' entered in the left-hand margins together with crosses and word-counts.

260 x 200mm.
ff. 2; 1v and 2v blank.
Black ink on wove paper.
Watermark: crown above shield.

Related Manuscript: Annotated wrapper in Add MS 73174, ff. 33–4.
Published: *Evening Standard* (London), 23 February 1928, with very few editorial variants.
Reproduced: www.bl.uk/manuscripts and Plate 6 below.

Provenance: Presented to Zweig in 1939 by Charles Archibald Stonehill, London publisher, bookseller and collector (Zweig's record card, Add MS 73168, f. 3). It is not known how it came into Stonehill's possession; BL 1986.
Bibliography: BL Programme Book, 1987; *Catalogue of Additions*, p. 69; Matuschek, p. 172.

Commentary. The novelist Arnold Bennett began writing weekly articles on books for the London *Evening Standard* in 1926 under the heading 'Books and Persons'. The headline in print for this review (not present in the manuscript) is 'New Authors Discovered. A "Genuinely Interesting" French novelist', referring to Thomas Raucat, whose novel *L'Honorable Partie de Campagne*, translated by Leonard Cline as *The Honourable Picnic*, is the main subject. Bennett also discusses Julien Green, *Mont-Cinère*, translated by M. A. Best as *Avarice House*. In the review of Zweig's *Conflicts*, Bennett says that he has never heard of Zweig himself, and castigates the publishers for not providing biographical details about the 'new foreign author'. He compares and contrasts Zweig's tactful approach to the subject of homosexuality with Proust and Gide, and draws parallels with Thomas Mann and Goethe in his 'sententious semi-sentimentality' which is 'characteristic of good German literature'. He concludes, 'But the book is more than respectable. It has sparks of the divine fire.' Bennett was apparently unaware that several of Zweig's works were already published in English by 1928, including *Paul Verlaine* (1913), *Émile Verhaeren* (1914), *Roman Rolland* (1921) and *Jeremiah* (1922). This is the only manuscript in the British Library's Stefan Zweig Collection which refers to Zweig's own work.

George Gordon, 6th Baron Byron
(1788–1824)

Zweig MS 138.

'Note to the lines where Capel Lofft is mentioned', prose note: *autograph* fair copy; [1811].

In *English*.
Begins: 'This well meaning Gentleman has spoilt some excellent Shoemakers, & been accessory to the poetical undoing of many of the industrious poor'.
Ends: 'There is a child, a book, & a dedication, send the girl to her Grace, the volumes to the Grocer, & the Dedication to the D – v – l'.
The prose note explains the allusion to Capel Lofft in Byron's 'Hints from Horace' (1811), lines 693–6: 'Hark to those notes, narcotically soft! / The cobbler-laureats sing to Capel Lofft! / Till, lo! that modern Midas, as he hears, / Adds an ell-growth to his egregious ears!' Byron upbraids men such as Capel Lofft who give patronage to poor poets and encourage the publication of work lacking in merit. On f. 1, 'Staffordshire' was written originally but is struck through, with 'Somersetshire' substituted above. At the end, the words 'Lord Byron's autograph' are in his own hand.

210 x 335mm.
ff. 2.
Black ink on cream wove paper.
Bifolium.
No watermark.

Related Manuscripts: Four complete manuscripts of 'Hints from Horace' survive, along with four incomplete sets of proofs and a number of MS fragments; see *Lord Byron: The Complete Poetical Works*, ed. Jerome J. McGann, pp. 425–6. Those containing Byron's Note are Princeton University Library, Robert H. Taylor Collection MS 207 (the printer's copy manuscript, MS T) and Morgan Library & Museum, Proof M (galley proof set up from MS T late in 1820, containing lines 1–276 and 583–804 with Byron's autograph corrections).
Published: For the detailed publication history of 'Hints from Horace', see McGann, pp. 426–7. Byron made abortive plans to publish in 1811 and 1820–22, each time with corrections and revisions, and it was not until after his death that incomplete versions began to appear in print. *Letters and Journals of Lord Byron*, 1, ed. Thomas Moore (London: John Murray, 1830) appears to be the first publication of the Note; *The Works of Lord Byron*, 5 (London: John Murray, 1831), pp. 273–327, the first publication of the complete text of 'Hints from Horace'; *The Complete Works of Lord Byron* (Paris: Galignani, 1831), p. 727; *Lord Byron: The Complete Poetical Works*, 1, ed. Jerome J. McGann (Oxford: Clarendon Press, 1980), pp. 441–2.
Variants: Zweig MS 138 appears to be the only source in which 'Staffordshire' was first written in error and amended as the location of the Bloomfield brothers. All the printed editions have followed the

corrected reading of 'Somersetshire'. The Zweig MS is close to McGann's 1980 text of the Note except for some variant capitalisation and the lack of the additional paragraph.

Reproduced: www.bl.uk/manuscripts and Plate 7 below.

Provenance: Owned before 1914 by Admiral Julian Alleyne Baker (1845–1922); sold at Sotheby's, 1 May 1914, as lot 352, and purchased by Zweig; BL 1986.

Bibliography: Stefan Zweig, 'Die Autographensammlung als Kunstwerk', p. 5; id., 'Überschätzung der Lebenden'; id., 'Meine Autographen-Sammlung'; id., 'Lord Byron: Das Schauspiel eines großen Lebens' (1924), in *Zeit und Welt* (Stockholm: Bermann-Fischer, 1946), pp. 9–20; BL Programme Book, 1987; *Catalogue of Additions*, p. 69; Matuschek, p. 182.

Commentary. In 'Hints from Horace' Byron imitates freely with contemporary allusions the third book of the *Ars poetica* of the Roman poet Quintus Horatius Flaccus. Byron began the first draft in Athens in March 1811, intending it to be issued with a new edition of *English Bards and Scotch Reviewers*, until he decided to suppress the latter. 'Hints' subsequently underwent many revisions and was not published in the author's lifetime.

In the brief Note to lines 693–6, Byron satirises the patronage of minor, untalented poets. He mentions Capel Lofft (1751–1824), a radical editor and writer whom he had previously criticised for promoting a poem by the self-educated Robert (Bobby) Bloomfield (1766–1823) entitled 'The Farmer's Boy', which was published with his own preface in 1800.

Stefan Zweig described the present manuscript as 'Diese ungemein geistreiche und glühend agressive Prosastelle' (Add MS 73168, f. 4). He also noted, 'Manuskripte Lord Byrons und besonders in sich vollständige wie dieses gehören heute schon zu den allergrössten Seltenheiten und sind fast unauffindbar geworden'. He was particularly pleased to acquire this item because 'andererseits in England die Pietät den grossen Dichtern gegenüber es fast gänzlich unmöglich macht, ein Gedicht von Byron oder Shelley zu erwerben.' ('Die Autographensammlung als Kunstwerk'). By contrast, in America, 'Stevenson wird drüben teurer bezahlt als Lord Byron, eine aktuelle Größe ungemein höher als ein Genius der Vergangenheit.' ('Überschätzung der Lebenden'.) He wrote more than once to Anton Kippenberg encouraging him to promote Byron's works in Germany, and indeed an edition of the poems appeared in 1921 in the Bibliotheca Mundi series published by the Insel Verlag in Leipzig.

Sotheby's catalogue of the sale on 1 May 1914 lists as part of lot 352 a two-page autograph letter with portrait of Teresa, Contessa Guiccioli (1800–73), Lord Byron's mistress in Ravenna. This letter, dated Paris, 6 March 1837, is not now with Zweig MS 138 and has not been traced as ever having been in Zweig's collection.

PAUL CLAUDEL
(1868–1955)

Zweig MS 139.

'L'Annonce faite à Marie', play: signed *autograph* fair copy of the third version; 1911.

In *French*.

Begins with a title page headed 'Incipit', followed by the title 'L'Annonce faite à Marie Mystère en quatre Actes et un Prologue par Paul Claudel'.

Ends: 'Explicit L'Annonce faite à Marie Laus Deo!'.

Written in the style of a medieval mystery play and set at the time of the Crusades, the drama depicts the story of its heroine, Violaine, who contracts leprosy and retires to a life of prayer, leaving her prospective husband to marry her jealous sister Mara. When the couple have a child who dies shortly after birth, Mara appeals to her saintly sister to bring the child back to life.

On f. 145v is the inscription 'Copie terminé à Hostel 18 Juin 1911 (fête Dieu)'.

288 x 230mm.

ff. 145. Paginated 2–144 in black ink. Versos blank.

Black ink on cream wove paper.

No watermark.

Bound in green leather, gold-tooled, by E. A. Enders of Leipzig. Lettered 'PAUL / CLAUDEL / L'ANNONCE / FAITE / A MARIE' on spine.

Related Manuscripts: Bibliothèque nationale de France, Paris, NAF 25662, Achat 94–02 (autograph manuscript of the first version of the play); NAF 28255, Fonds Paul Claudel, Achat 28093 (manuscript of the second version, with documents relating to the third version).

Published: First version with title *La Jeune Fille Violaine* written in 1892 and published in 1926 (Paris: Excelsior); second version with same title published with four other plays in Paul Claudel, *L'Arbre* (Paris: Mercure de France, 1901); heavily revised third version with title *L'Annonce faite à Marie* published in five instalments in the *Nouvelle Revue française*, December 1911–April 1912, and in book form by Éditions de la Nouvelle Revue française in 1912; fourth version, with a reworked fourth act, published 1940 (Paris: Gallimard). Also included in Paul Claudel, *Théâtre*, 2, ed. Jacques Madaule, Bibliothèque de la Pléiade, 73 (Paris: Gallimard, 1947).

Reproduced: Plate 8 below.

Exhibited: London, National Book League, A Thousand Years of French Books, 1948, catalogue no. 178; London, BL, 75 Musical and Literary Autographs, 1986.

Provenance: Apparently purchased by Zweig directly from Claudel for five hundred francs. See letter from Claudel to André Gide, 11 February 1913, printed in Paul Claudel and André Gide, *Correspondance, 1899–1926* (Paris: Gallimard, 1949), pp. 210, 357; BL 1986.

Bibliography: BL Programme Book, 1987; *Catalogue of Additions*, p. 69; Matuschek, p. 187.

Commentary. It was clearly of some importance to Zweig to acquire the manuscript of *L'Annonce faite à Marie* (described on his record card, Add MS 73168, f. 5, as 'Die wundervolle Abschrift des herrlichen Werkes, das heute schon Weltruhm hat'), because he took an active step to purchase the manuscript from the author. Claudel seemed only too willing to let him have it, inscribing the volume 'Offert à M. Stephan [*sic*] Zweig par l'auteur avec mes meilleurs sentiments' (f. 2v). Zweig also owned the autograph manuscript of an Epilogue to *L'Annonce faite à Marie* (now held at the Bodmer Foundation, Geneva) and some autograph notes with ideas for staging the play under the direction of Max Reinhardt (now in a private collection in Switzerland).

Gabriele D'Annunzio
(1863–1938)

Zweig MS 140.

'La laude di Dante', verses: *autograph* fair copy; *c.* 1904.

In *Italian.*
Begins: 'Oceano senza rive infinito d'intorno, e oscuro'.
Ends: 'o tu che odi e vedi e sai, custode alto dei fati, o Dante, noi ti attendiamo!'.
The verses, written in a bold calligraphic hand, sing the praises of the poet Dante, celebrated as one of the great men and heroes of history.
With an additional heading, 'Laudi del Cielo, del Mare, della Terra e degli Eroi'. 'Terra' written diagonally in blue pencil at the beginning of the text. Signed at the end.

Each sheet 232 x 340mm unfolded.
ff. 22.
Black ink on wove paper.
11 folded sheets.
Watermark: 'E MAGNANI' on some sheets. Crown above shield and stag on others.
*Inserted into green linen-covered folder with '*AUTOGRAFI DI G. D'ANNUNZIO */ LAUDE A DANTE' stamped in gold on front board. Green and gold paper on inside boards.*

Related Manuscript: Biblioteca Nazionale Centrale di Roma, ARC.21.32 (autograph leaves from the third book of *Laudi del cielo, del mare, della terra e degli eroi*).
Published: Gabriele D'Annunzio, *Laudi del cielo, del mare, della terra e degli eroi*, 2, *Elettra–Alcyone* (Milan: Fratelli Treves Editori, 1904); *Tutte le opere di Gabriele D'Annunzio*, 6 (Verona: Mondadori, 1928), pp. 4–10.
Reproduced: www.bl.uk/manuscripts and Plate 9 below.
Exhibited: London, BL, 75 Musical and Literary Autographs, 1986.
Provenance: Acquired by Zweig from the bookdealer Paul Gottschalk in Berlin in 1913; BL 1986.
Bibliography: Stefan Zweig, 'Meine Autographen-Sammlung'; BL Programme Book, 1987; *Catalogue of Additions*, p. 69; Matuschek, p. 190.

Commentary. Gabriele D'Annunzio, sometimes known as 'the soldier-poet' because of his military successes, is regarded as an extremely important figure in modern Italian literature. His collection of lyrical verses *Laudi del cielo, del mare, della terra e degli eroi*, composed between 1899 and 1903, contains some of his major poetic achievements. The work was originally designed as a sequence of seven books, each bearing the name of one of the Pleiades, but only the first five volumes appeared in print.

The eulogy to Dante is taken from *Elettra*, the second book, in which D'Annunzio expresses admiration for heroes of the intellectual and artistic world. The somewhat unusual format of this autograph suggests that it may have been intended for presentation, either in its present folder, or possibly in a predecessor.

Charles Darwin
(1809–1882)

Zweig MS 141.

Insectivorous Plants: top half of a page of corrected *autograph* draft; before 1875.

In *English*.
Begins: 'Thus the best plan would have been to puncture the bladders'.
Ends: 'with a few drops of the fluid........chamber and' [page torn, part of last sentence wanting].
The text, headed 'Utricularia', comes from Darwin's account of his experiments on bladderworts, a genus of carnivorous plants that capture their prey in bladder-like traps. On the verso is a single cancelled sentence not included in the printed text, followed by some mathematical calculations relating to meridians made by George Howard Darwin (second son of Charles Darwin), who has identified the fragment in an annotation written in the left-hand margin of the recto at right angles to the text and signed 'G. H. D.' Numbered '21' in top right-hand corner of both recto and verso. Hinterberger catalogue number 'XX/628' in pencil in top left-hand corner.

164 x 200mm.
f. 1.
Black ink on blue wove paper.
No watermark.

Related Manuscripts: Further leaves from the same draft are kept in the following repositories: State and University Library, Aarhus, Denmark, Haandskrift 394A[.1]; Christ's College, Cambridge, Old Library GG.1.25; Cambridge University Library, CUL-DAR 221.128-141.
Published: Charles Darwin, *Insectivorous Plants* (London: John Murray, 1875), p. 413; 2nd ed., revised by Francis Darwin (London: John Murray, 1888); *The Works of Charles Darwin*, 24, ed. Paul H. Barrett and R. B. Freeman (London: William Pickering, 1989), which uses text of the 2nd ed.
Reproduced: www.bl.uk/manuscripts and Plate 10 below.
Provenance: The date of acquisition by Zweig is not known; BL 1986.
Bibliography: Hinterberger catalogue XX, no. 628; BL Programme Book, 1987; *Catalogue of Additions*, p. 69; Matuschek, p. 190.

Commentary. A chance observation of flies caught on the leaf of the common sundew initiated Darwin's investigation of carnivorous plants. He was especially impressed by the fact that the living cells of plants possess a capacity for irritability and response similar to the cells of animals. *Insectivorous Plants* chronicles his experiments with the feeding mechanisms of various plants, in which he tried several methods to stimulate the plants into activating their trap mechanisms. His finding that only the movement of an animal caused the plants to react led him to conclude that this must be an evolutionary adaptation to conserve energy for trapping nutritious prey. He also discovered that some plants have distinct trap-like structures, while others produce sticky fluids to ensnare their prey, a possible example of natural selection pressure resulting in various methods for food capture.

Zweig would have recognised Darwin as one of the most influential scientific figures of the modern world, together with Freud and Einstein. At one time he also owned a fragment of *The Descent of Man*, now held at the Bodmer Foundation, Geneva.

Philippe Desportes
(1546–1606)

Zweig MS 142.

Autograph fair copies of maxims, epigrams and aphorisms; before 1606.

In *French*.
Begins: 'Les mouches Les chiens et les foux'.
Ends: 'Maison faicte et femme a faire'.
Eleven items signed 'D P'. One maxim added to f. 2, in black ink and in a different hand; three maxims and a couplet added at the end of the text (f. 5v), also written in black ink, and in two different hands.

190 x 138mm.
ff. 5.
Brown ink on cream wove paper.
Partial, indistinct watermarks on ff. 1, 3 and 4.

Reproduced: Hinterberger catalogue XVIII, inside back cover; Hinterberger catalogue XX, plate XXI; www.bl.uk/manuscripts and Plate 11 below.
Provenance: The date of acquisition by Zweig is unknown. He offered the manuscript for sale through Heinrich Hinterberger, Vienna, catalogue XVIII, no. 39 [1938]; it remained unsold and was retained in his collection; BL 1986.

Bibliography: Hinterberger catalogue XX, no. 629; BL Programme Book, 1987; Jean-Antoine de Baïf, *Mimes, Enseignemens et Proverbes*, 2, ed. J. Vignes (Paris: Droz, 1992), pp. 113, 455; *Catalogue of Additions*, p. 69; Matuschek, pp. 192–3.

Commentary. Philippe Desportes, who learnt much of his poetic craft in Italy, became a favourite of Henry III of France, his patron from 1574, from whom he received valuable benefices as a reward for the skill of his occasional poems. Excelling primarily in light and elegant verse, he also shared a widespread contemporary interest in collecting maxims and aphorisms, succinct expressions of commonly held beliefs and ideas. Described by Hinterberger as 'ungemein selten', the autograph would have added an interesting dimension to Zweig's collection, both in its contents and in its early date.

Fedor Mikhailovich Dostoevsky
(1821–1881)

Zweig MS 143.

Chapter II of part 3 of the novel *Unizhennye i oskorblennye* [*The Insulted and Injured*]: *autograph* draft; [1861].

In *Russian.*
Begins: 'Онь именно влетель, с каким-то сияющимь лицомь'.
Ends: 'я выскажу все, все!'.
One complete chapter of Dostoevsky's first full-length novel, headed Глава 6 in the manuscript but published as the second chapter in part 3. The chapter describes a tense conversation between Prince Alexei (Alyosha), his father Prince Valkovsky and his lover Natalya Nikolaevna (Natasha) following a visit to Katerina Fedorovna (Katya), whom his father wants Alyosha to marry. Written in Cyrillic script in a small, neat, cursive hand. There are *autograph* corrections and insertions of words or phrases on the manuscript, and ink blots on ff. 1v, 2, and 4. Four-and-a-half lines on f. 3 are struck through for deletion. Paragraphs are indicated in the margin. The leaves are numbered at the top left in the author's hand. Folio 3 was wrongly numbered 2 and is corrected.

287 x 232mm.
ff. 5.
Black ink on cream wove paper.
1 bifolium and 3 single sheets.
No watermark.

Related Manuscript: Dostoevsky had the habit of writing on scraps of paper such as envelopes, forms and newspapers. Zweig MS 143 and a note of seven lines in the State Literary Museum, Moscow, Manuscripts Section, ref. 4828, are the only known surviving manuscripts of *Unizhennye i oskorblennye.*

Published: The novel was first published as a serial in the first seven issues of *Vremya* magazine (January–July 1861); the text in Zweig MS 143 appeared in the third issue (19 March); *F. M. Dostoevskiĭ, Unizhennye i oskorblennye*, 2 vols. (St Petersburg: Pratz, 1861); *F. M. Dostoevskiĭ, Sobranie sochinenii*, 3, ed. L. P. Grossman et al. (Moscow: Gosudarstvennoe Izdatel'stvo, 1956), pp. 7–386; *Polnoe sobranie sochineniĭ: kanonicheskie teksty F. M. Dostoevskiĭ*, 4, ed. V. N. Zakharov (Petrozavodsk: Petrozavodskogo universiteta, 2000); *Polnoe sobranie sochineniĭ F. M. Dostoevskogo v XVIII tomakh*, 4, ed. V. N. Zakharov et al. (Moscow: Voskresene, 2004).

Variants: Variants between Zakharov's text (based on the corrected fifth edition published at St Petersburg in 1879) and Zweig MS 143 (siglum *HP*) are listed on pp. 852–3 of the Petrozavodsk (2000) publication.

Reproduced: *75 Musical and Literary Autographs*, plate 9 (f. 3); www.bl.uk/manuscripts and Plate 12 below.

Exhibited: London, BL, 75 Musical and Literary

Autographs, 1986; London, Christie's, etc., The Creative Spirit, 1987–8 (ff. 2v–3).

Provenance: Acquired by Zweig on 13 September 1912 from the dealer Martin Breslauer of Berlin; BL 1986.

Bibliography: Stefan Zweig, 'Die Autographensammlung als Kunstwerk'; id., *Drei Meister*; id., Foreword to Hans Prager, *Die Weltanschauung Dostoiewskis* (Hildesheim: Borgmeyer, 1925); id., 'Meine Autographen-Sammlung'; V. Nechaeva, *Opisanie rukopiseĭ F. M. Dostoevskogo* (Moscow: Akademiia nauk SSSR, 1957), pp. 119–21; BL Programme Book, 1987; W. J. Leatherbarrow, *Fedor Dostoevsky: a Reference Guide* (Boston, MA: G. K. Hall, *c.* 1990); *Catalogue of Additions*, p. 69; Peter Sekirin, *The Dostoevsky Archive: Firsthand Accounts of the Novelist* (Jefferson, NC; London: McFarland, 1997); Matuschek, p. 194.

Commentary. In his Introduction to the *Drei Meister* publication, Stefan Zweig said that he considered Balzac, Dickens and Dostoevsky the supremely great novelists of the nineteenth century. He went on to claim that no German novelists could be compared with the Russian author. In a letter to Maxim Gorky in March 1928, he spoke of the impact of discovering Tolstoy and Dostoevsky whilst at university.

The present manuscript is apparently the only Dostoevsky autograph that Zweig owned. He described it in his essay 'Die Autographensammlung als Kunstwerk' as 'ein Unikum im Privatbesitz', and declared that he would never part with it (Add MS 74269, ff. 5–5v).

Georges Duhamel
(1884–1966)

Zweig MS 144.

'Le dernier voyage de Candide', short story: *autograph* draft, heavily corrected with numerous deletions and insertions; 1936.

In *French*.
Begins: 'Candide cultivait son jardin depuis bien de années'.
Ends: 'Candide faisait de son mieux pour imaginer le néant'.
The opening line-and-a-half has been struck through.
Duhamel's *Le Dernier Voyage de Candide* is a picaresque continuation of Voltaire's satire *Candide* (1759). In Duhamel's story, the aging Candide embarks optimistically on a voyage to see the 'magnificent world' for one last time. Everywhere he goes, fellow travellers point out innocent-looking places where political opponents and convicts are incarcerated. Disillusioned, Candide wants only to retire to his garden, but he dies when the ship is blown up and is conducted to paradise by a guardian angel. There, too, he hears of dissenters, Lucifer and other agitators, and in the end can only try to imagine nothingness.

303 x 200mm.
ff. 3; 1v and 2v blank. Numbered 2–3.
Black ink on white laid paper.

Published: Georges Duhamel, *Le Dernier Voyage de Candide, suivi d'un choix de nouvelles*, Artisans du Style, 2 (Paris: Fernand Sorlot, 1938), pp. 9–18. The text follows the manuscript as corrected.
Reproduced: Plate 13 below.
Exhibited: London, BL, 75 Musical and Literary Autographs, 1986 (ff. 1 and 2).
Provenance: Presented to Zweig by the author, 21 October 1936 (inscription on f. 1 'pour Stefan Z. Souvenir de Duhamel Octobre 36'). Annotated envelope and separate leaf in Add MS 73174, ff. 50–4. 'Manuscrit de Georges Duhamel recu le de lui même le 21 Oct. 1936 Stefan Zweig'; BL 1986.
Bibliography: Claire Hoch, 'Friendship and Kinship between Georges Duhamel and Stefan Zweig', in Marion Sonnenfeld (ed.), *The World of Yesterday's Humanist Today: Proceedings of the Stefan Zweig Symposium* (Albany: State University of New York Press, 1983), pp. 40–63; BL Programme Book, 1987; *Catalogue of Additions*, p. 70; *Georges Duhamel–Stefan Zweig correspondance: l'anthologie oubliée de Leipzig*, ed. Claudine Delphis, Deutsch-Französische Kulturbibliothek, 18 (Leipzig: Universitätsverlag, 2001); Matuschek, p. 195.

Commentary. Zweig and Duhamel were friends for thirty years. Besides being a doctor, author and founder of a commune for young writers, musicians and painters, Duhamel was a member of the *Académie française* and director of the publishers Mercure de France. Zweig persuaded

Anton Kippenberg to appoint Duhamel editor of the French poetry volume in the Bibliotheca Mundi series, *Anthologie de la poésie lyrique française de la fin du XVe siècle à la fin du XIXe siècle* (Leipzig: Insel Verlag, 1923). He collaborated with Zweig and Maxim Gorky on the production of the *Liber Amicorum* in celebration of Romain Rolland's sixtieth birthday (Erlenbach-Zürich: Rotapfel-Verlag, 1926). In a letter of 22 January 1921, Zweig said of Duhamel, 'au dela de la difference des nos langues, je me sens plus proche de vous que de beaucoup de mes confrères' (*Correspondance* as cited above, p. 83).

The relationship cooled briefly following elections at the International PEN Club meeting in Buenos Aires in September 1936. Duhamel had ambitions to succeed H. G. Wells as President, but Zweig failed to rally to his support and his rival Jules Romains was elected. Zweig knew both candidates personally and admitted his dilemma in a letter to Raoul Auernheimer written on the return voyage on 17 September 1936 (see Stefan Zweig, *Briefe 1932–1942*, ed. Knut Beck and Jeffrey B. Berlin (Frankfurt am Main: S. Fischer, 2005), pp. 165–7). Duhamel's view of Zweig's conduct is reflected in his journal, published as *Le Livre de l'amertume* (Paris: Mercure de France, 1984), p. 258, where he also quotes a conciliatory note from Zweig. The gift of the present manuscript, made in the following month of October, might be seen as a gesture of reconciliation.

Fredrik Axel von Fersen
(1719–1794)

Zweig MS 145.
Autograph signed letter sent with some sealed papers to the Swedish Court of Appeal; 1787.

In *Swedish*.
Begins: 'Min och min frue Grefvinnans År 1776 gjordes Disposition'.
Ends: 'högloflige Kongl. Hof Rättens / ödmjuke Tjänare / Axel Fersen'.
The document is annotated in two different hands; a note at the head of the page by the first records that it was submitted on 25 May 1787, while an annotation by the second, inserted between the formal heading and the text and signed 'Jan A. Sebenius' [Johan Adolph Sebenius, notarial clerk], registers receipt on the same date. The letter starts with a formal address to the President, Vice-President, Assessors and other members of the Court, and requests that two accompanying sealed documents (no longer present) should be deposited with the Court's records until after the death of Fersen and his wife.
Top left is an embossed stamp duty seal for 2 Sch [Schillings]. The amount ('2.SCH') is stamped in black ink above a signature and annotation 'B$^{\underline{TS}}$MED/50.P:C:T:' at right angles to the text (indicating stamp duty paid with a surcharge of 50%). Small original mark in top left-hand corner partly lost through minor damage. Hinterberger catalogue number 'XX/645' in pencil, bottom left-hand corner. On the verso is a pencil note 'Fredrick Axel von Fersen, politist / parchemin, f. 1719 +1794 / (So Hofberg)'. Accompanied by a handwritten draft transcription (f. 2), and a further transcription and German translation (ff. 3–3v), both typewritten.

Largest sheet 317 x 205mm.
ff. 3; 2v blank.
Brown ink on cream laid paper, with annotations in heavier brown ink (f. 1); pencil on cream wove paper (f. 2); typescript with pencil heading on cream wove paper (f. 3).
Unidentified circular watermark (f. 1); partial unidentified watermark (f. 2).

Reproduced: www.bl.uk/manuscripts and Plate 14 below.
Provenance: It is not known when or where Zweig acquired the manuscript; BL 1986.
Bibliography: Hinterberger catalogue XX, no. 645; BL Programme Book, 1987; *Catalogue of Additions*, p. 70; Matuschek, p. 199.

Commentary. Fersen was a Swedish statesman and soldier, probably best identified today as the father of Hans Axel von Fersen, who gained notoriety for his relationship with Marie Antoinette. As leader of the Hattarna ('Hats') party, a Swedish political faction whose name derives from the tricorne hat worn by officers and gentlemen, Fersen defiantly opposed the King and his court until he withdrew from politics in 1789 after being arrested. Zweig's main attraction to this autograph was quite probably the link with Marie Antoinette's lover, but the manuscript is also significant as a piece in its own right, adding international colour and interest to the collection.

GUSTAVE FLAUBERT
(1821–1880)

Zweig MS 146.
'Bibliomanie', short story: *autograph* fair copy; 1836.

In *French*.
Begins: 'Dans une rue étroite et sans soleil'.
Ends: 'Je vous disais bien que c'était le seul en Espagne'.
Flaubert's first published work, written when he was fifteen years old, tells the story of Giacomo, a mad bookseller whose passion for books is so all-consuming that he resorts to murder to thwart another bibliophile's efforts to own a highly prized item. Title page (f. 1) has 'Gv Flaubert' in the top right-hand corner, 'Bibliomanie' in the centre with 'Conte' underneath it, and to the right 'Novembre 1836'.

310 x 200mm.
ff. 14; versos blank. Numbered 1–13.
Blue ink on grey paper.
Title written on first page of a bifolium.
No watermark.

Related Manuscript: Bibliothèque nationale de France, Paris, NAF 14239, acquired 1968 from the collection of Lucien Graux, is a heavily corrected draft of the story. The corrected version corresponds to the fair copy in all but a few minor orthographic details.

Published: *Le Colibri, journal de la littérature, des théâtres, des arts et des modes*, 12 February 1837 (the fair copy matches the published text, with the exception of the title of the book desired in the story, 'La Chronique de Turpin', which appears as 'La Chronique de Turquie' in the printed version); Gustave Flaubert, *Œuvres complètes. Œuvres de jeunesse inédites*, 1 (Paris, Louis Conard, 1910), pp. 132–47; id., *Bibliomanie*, Les Livrets du bibliophile, 7 (Maastricht: A. A. M. Stols, 1926).

Reproduced: Gustave Flaubert, *Bibliomania*, translated by Theodore Wesley Koch (Evanston, IL: Northwestern University Library, 1929), (f. 1); Matuschek, p. 201 (f. 2); www.bl.uk/manuscripts and Plate 15 below.

Exhibited: London, National Book League, A Thousand Years of French Books, 1948, catalogue no. 147; London, BL, 75 Musical and Literary Autographs, 1986.

Provenance: Received from Flaubert's heirs in 1910 by Dr. Paul Zifferer, one of the editors of the 'Nachlass'; acquired by Zweig from Zifferer in 1914; BL 1986.

Bibliography: Stefan Zweig, 'Meine Autographen-Sammlung'; BL Programme Book, 1987; *Catalogue of Additions*, p. 70; Matuschek, p. 200.

Commentary. Only two of Flaubert's early literary works were published in his lifetime, this and 'Une leçon d'histoire naturelle', which also appeared in *Le Colibri*, on 30 March 1837. Others written around the same time were not professionally edited until 1910 when they appeared in Conard's edition of the *Œuvres de jeunesse inédites*.

According to his record card, Zweig knew of no other complete manuscript of Flaubert in private hands when he acquired this one, the others all having been bequeathed to the French Government. Since then the corrected autograph first draft of 'Bibliomanie', now in the Bibliothèque nationale de France, has come to light.

Joseph Fouché
(Duc d'Otrante)
(1759–1820)

Zweig MS 147.

Autograph letter to 'Collègues & amis'; '30 germinal' [19 April 1794].

In *French*.
Begins: 'J'ai retardé le courier dans l'espérance d'obtenir une décision du Comité de salut public'.
Ends: 'Ils abusent, quelque moment, mais tot ou tard ils sont demasqués'.
Signed 'Fouché Je vous embrasse ainsi que nos amis'. Addressed to the 'Commune-Affranchie' [of the city of Lyon], the letter was sent from Paris where Fouché had been summoned by the Committee of Public Safety to account for the massacre of rebels that he had overseen in Lyon. A note in ink in a different hand on the verso of the second leaf reads 'Paris, 3 [*sic*] Germinal an 2e / Fouché à ses collègues à C.^{ne} Aff.^{ie}'. The Hinterberger catalogue number 'XX/051' is pencilled on f. 1, above a semi-legible pencil note of Fouché's name and dates.

309 x 200mm.
ff. 2; 1v and 2 blank.
Brown ink on cream laid paper.
Bifolium.
Watermark: 'J HONIG & ZOONEN' / crown and shield with posthorn 'JH&Z'.

Reproduced: www.bl.uk/manuscripts and Plate 16 below.
Provenance: It is not known when and how Zweig acquired the manuscript, but there is no evidence of its use in the biography of Fouché that he published in 1929, so he may have acquired it after this date; BL 1986.
Bibliography: Stefan Zweig, *Joseph Fouché: Bildnis eines politischen Menschen* (Leipzig: Insel Verlag, 1929); BL Programme Book, 1987; *Catalogue of Additions*, p. 70; Matuschek, p. 203.

Commentary. Joseph Fouché rose to prominence in revolutionary France for his leading role in the brutal and often barbarous mass executions inflicted on nearly two thousand citizens of the city of Lyon, carried out in 1794 as a reprisal for the city's counter-revolutionary movement against the National Convention.

Finding Fouché a fascinating character psychologically, Zweig made a study of him for publication, but his background researches led him to develop something of a revulsion for Fouché's cold-blooded cruelty and lack of feeling. Nevertheless, a document by such an important figure in the French Revolution was a welcome addition to his autograph collection, and at one time he also owned three later letters of Fouché, which are now held at the Bodmer Foundation, Geneva.

‘Anatole France’
(pseudonym of Jacques-Anatole-François Thibault) (1844–1924)

Zweig MS 148.

Letter from ‘M. B.’ in response to an article on orthography by Anatole France, annotated and marked up for printing by France; May 1898.

In *French*.
Begins: ‘Monsieur, Au sujet de votre article de ce matin, “l’Orthographe”’.
Ends: ‘Veuillez, je vous prie’.
The letter is dated 16 May 1898 but probably in error for 17 May, when Anatole France’s first article on orthography and spelling reform was published in the morning daily newspaper *L’Écho de Paris*. The writer, ‘M[onsieur?] B.’, whose signature was deliberately cut off for publication, was an ‘instituteur’ (schoolmaster or tutor). He agreed entirely with France’s view that time spent teaching children orthography could be better spent inculcating social and moral values. Instructions for printing, including type size, have been added in France’s hand with black ink and blue crayon. At the head of f. 1 is the note which introduces the letter, following his second article in *L’Écho de Paris* on 24 May: ‘P.S. J’ai reçu de M. B..., instituteur une lettre dont voici le texte’. On f. 6 are five lines in France’s hand: ‘Cette lettre exprime, ce me semble, les idées les plus [deletion] justes et les plus sages. M. B. souhaite, comme M. Francisque Sarcey, qu’on ne donne pas d’importance à ce qui n’en a pas. A. F.’ These lines are published in the newspaper following the letter. On f. 6v is a fragmentary note or minute in another hand referring to an album. With Hinterberger catalogue number ‘XX/653’ in pencil inside front cover (f. i).

Largest sheet 201 x 158mm.
ff. i + 6, originally numbered 17, 18 and 9.
Sheet of laid paper cut into 4 pieces and mounted on 4 pieces of wove paper (ff. 1, 2, 4, 5). Small piece of tissue paper (f. 3) is mounted on f. 2. Folio 6 wove paper only.
Black and brown ink and blue crayon.
No visible watermark.
Tipped into grey card binding. The inside of the front cover is stamped ‘PETITO’.

Published: The letter with introductory and concluding comments by Anatole France was published on 24 May 1898 on the front page of *L’Écho de Paris*, following the second of France’s two articles on orthography and spelling reform. The only difference from the manuscript is the expansion of ‘2m’ to ‘deuxième’. Anatole France’s first article, which prompted the letter, was published on 17 May 1898 in the same newspaper.
Reproduced: www.bl.uk/manuscripts and Plate 17 below.
Provenance: The date of acquisition by Zweig and the provenance of this item are not known. An annotated envelope in Add MS 73174 states ‘nicht im Katalog’. Offered for sale by Zweig in 1937 through Hinterberger, Vienna, catalogue XX,

no. 653 (Add MS 73183 D); not sold and returned to the collection; BL 1986.
Bibliography: For the background to the controversy over French orthography in the late nineteenth and early twentieth centuries and the role of Anatole France, see the articles by Albert Schinz, 'The Reform of French Orthography' I and II, and 'The Simplification of French Orthography' I and II, in *Modern Language Notes*, 15/8 (Dec 1900), pp. 225–34; 16/3 (March 1901), pp. 80–1; 21/4 (April 1906), pp. 113–17; 21/5 (May 1906), pp. 139–43; BL Programme Book, 1987; *Catalogue of Additions*, p. 70; Matuschek, p. 205.

Commentary. Francisque Sarcey (1827–99), mentioned in France's note, was a French journalist and drama critic who believed that spelling should be ignored in examinations and only syntactical errors penalised.

Zweig also owned a manuscript of 'La Psychologie de la femme moderne' by Anatole France, acquired in 1925 and now held at the Bodmer Foundation, Geneva.

Benjamin Franklin
(1706–1790)

Zweig MS 149.

Autograph signed letter to William Strahan; Philadelphia, 12 February 1744/5.

In *English*.
Begins: 'Sir I receiv'd your Favour p[er] Mr Chew dated Sept. 10. and a Copy via Boston'.
Ends: 'Your obliged humble Servt B Franklin. P.S. Please continue the Political Cabinet'.
Franklin acknowledges receipt from Strahan of 'Mr Middleton's Pieces' and places new orders: a range of pamphlets for friends of different tastes, six sets of Warburton's new edition of Pope if published, a dozen copies of whatever the poet Thomson writes. He expresses the hope that William Caslon will not delay in casting the English fount he wrote for. (Caslon's typeface was to be widely adopted in America, notably for printing the Declaration of Independence.) A postscript by James Read promises a long letter to be sent in duplicate by different ships. Addressed on f. 2v 'To Mr Wm Strahan / Printer in Wine Office / Court Fleetstreet / London via Maryland / P[er] Capt. Harrison.' Post stamp '6 MA'.

330 x 208mm.
ff. 2; 2 blank.
Black ink on white laid paper.
Remains of seal impression in red wax and post stamp on f. 2v.
Watermark: Pro Patria / Crown.

Published: First published with other Franklin letters in 'Unpublished Letters of Franklin to Strahan', ed. S. G. W. Benjamin, in *The Atlantic,* 1 January 1888; published separately as a broadside ([New York]: Museum Press, [1936]); reprinted from *The Atlantic* in *The Papers of Benjamin Franklin,* 3, ed. Leonard W. Labaree (New Haven, CT: Yale University Press, 1961), pp. 13–14.
Reproduced: Facsimile in Add MS 73174, f. 67; www.bl.uk/manuscripts and Plate 18 below.
Provenance: The article in *The Atlantic* states that the letters had been long kept in Strahan's family but were then placed with a London bookdealer for sale and purchased in the summer of 1887 by an American buyer; purchased by Zweig from Heinrich Eisemann, London, 26 August 1941; BL 1986.
Bibliography: BL Programme Book, 1987; *Catalogue of Additions*, p. 70; Matuschek, p. 205.

Commentary. William Strahan (1715–85) was a London printer and publisher, established from 1740 at Wine Office Court in the parish of St Bride's where this letter is addressed. Through contact with the American James Read, he set up a wholesale trade in books to Philadelphia. (For account books and business papers of the Strahan printing house, see BL Add MSS 48800–48918.)

Benjamin Franklin had worked as a journeyman printer in England and was postmaster of Philadelphia before embarking on his career as statesman and diplomat. He maintained a correspondence with William Strahan for many years before Strahan's attitude to the struggles of the American colonists led to friction between them.

The letter was possibly one of Zweig's last purchases, which he may not have seen. He had left for America in July 1940, a year before the date of the invoice, expecting to be back in England in October. However he remained in New York and South America until he came to the decision early in 1941 not to return to live in Europe. The invoice is addressed to him in Bath (both invoice and an annotated envelope are in Add MS 73174, ff. 66–9), but the manuscript was apparently not sent on to him as it was not amongst those he had with him at his death in February 1942.

Sigmund Freud
(1856–1939)

Zweig MS 150.

'Der Dichter und das Phantasieren', lecture: *autograph* draft; [1908].

In *German*.
Begins: 'Ich beabsichtige mich, Ihnen viel Neues zu sagen' (beginning of first three lines, subsequently cancelled).
Ends: 'aber wenigstens auch am Ende unserer heutigen Erörterungen'.
Written in *Kurrentschrift*. Headed 'Der Dichter und das Phantasieren / von Prof Dr Sigm Freud., ~~Wien"~~'. With a paragraph of cancelled text at the beginning and a number of annotations and amendments. 'Korpūs. Cito!:' written in black ink in a different hand above the title on f. 1. '135' pencilled in top left-hand corner of f. 1. 'Spreeberg 153+1' written diagonally in a different hand across top left-hand corner of f. 3. Minor ink stains (f. 1) and two small water stains (f. 5).

400 x 250mm.
ff. 5.
Black ink on cream wove paper.
2 bifolia and one single sheet.
No watermark.

Published: *Neue Revue. Halbmonatschrift für das öffentliche Leben* (Berlin: Verlag der Neuen Revue, 1908), Jahrgang 1, pp. 716–24; Sigmund Freud, *Gesammelte Werke*, ed. Anna Freud and others, 7 (London: Imago Publishing, 1941), pp. 213–23.
Reproduced: BL Programme Book, 1987, p. 15; *The Creative Spirit* (back cover); Matuschek, p. 207; www.bl.uk/manuscripts and Plate 19 below.
Exhibited: London, BL, 75 Musical and Literary Autographs, 1986; London, Christie's, etc., The Creative Spirit, 1987–8.
Provenance: Acquired by Zweig as a gift from Freud, 1924; BL 1986.
Bibliography: Stefan Zweig, *Die Heilung durch den Geist. Mesmer, Mary Baker-Eddy, Freud* (Leipzig: Insel Verlag, 1931); *Catalogue of Additions*, p. 70; Matuschek, p. 206.

Commentary. This autograph draft of Freud's 1907 essay is likely to have been a prized addition to Zweig's collection. Not only does the corrected manuscript illustrate some of Freud's own thought processes in composing it, but the text itself discusses the way in which such creative processes come into being.

The lecture, given informally to a small, random audience in the offices of the publisher Hugo Heller in Vienna, sets out to explain the creative process of writing from the starting point of the analogy of poetic creation and a child's playing. Creative writing is described as an adult substitute for the imaginative play of childhood, both – like dreams – being a means of expressing repressed desires.

Greatly excited by Freud's revolutionary approach to the psyche, Zweig was one of the earliest writers outside the psychoanalytic community to write a study of his work, and he frequently submitted drafts of his own work to Freud for comment. The two became close friends, corresponding continuously from 1908 until Freud's death in 1939, when Zweig delivered the funeral oration.

André Gide
(1869–1951)

Zweig MS 151.
'De l'importance du public', lecture: heavily corrected *autograph* draft; 1903.

In *French*.
Begins: 'Apporter à leurs Altesses, à vous Mesdames et Messieurs la fatigue et l'ennui d'une pesante conférence'.
Ends: 'et puissent leurs Altesses n'en pas trouver trop imparfaite la respectueuse expression'.
In this lecture Gide discusses his movement away from Symbolism and 'Art for Art's sake' towards the need to communicate with a wider public. Headed 'De l'importance du public. Conférence prononcée à la Cour de Weimar le 5 Août 1903', with a dedication 'Au Comte H. Kessler en reconnaissant souvenir'.
Accompanying the text is a signed presentation letter from Gide to Zweig, dated 19 April 1914 (f. 1). The numbers '16' and '6' are pencilled on f. 2, along with some marks (which may be a date), to the right of the heading. Three names have been added in a different hand: on f. 9, at the head of the section beginning 'L'artiste ne peut pas se passer d'un public' is 'M. Verdier'; on f. 16, at the head of the section 'L'art, malgré tout ce qu'il reflète, du ciel', 'M. Roulleau'; on f. 22, at the head of the section 'Quand Joseph était en prison', 'M. Sars'.

Largest sheet 215 x 165 mm.
ff. 24; versos blank except for 18v. Numbered 2–22.
Black ink on cream laid paper. Annotations in pencil and black ink.
One bifolium and 23 single sheets. The letter occupies the recto of the first leaf of the bifolium.
Watermark: partial watermark of stag leaping over a verdant pond / 'POLLERI'.

Published: *L'Ermitage*, 14me année, no. 10 (October 1903), pp. 81–95 (dedicated to Harry Kessler); André Gide, *Nouveaux Prétextes* (Paris: Mercure de France, 1911), pp. 28–44.
Reproduced: Plate 20 below.

Provenance: Presented to Zweig by Gide, 19 April 1914 (accompanying letter, f. 1); BL 1986.
Bibliography: BL Programme Book 1987; *Catalogue of Additions*, p. 70; Matuschek, p. 212.

Commentary. Gide, a longstanding friend of Zweig's, was noted not only for his artistically significant writings but also for his fearless love of truth and his keen psychological insight. Visiting Weimar in August 1903 as the guest of Harry Kessler, diplomat and essayist, he was invited to attend a dinner given by the formidable Grand Duchess of Saxe-Weimar, after which he delivered this lecture in the Belvedere Palace. The present manuscript appears to be the original text as corrected for the printer, although further minor amendments were made before the text was finally published.

The text of the presentation letter, in which Gide explains that he has selected this manuscript from a number of possibilities, suggests that Zweig may originally have approached Gide for a manuscript to add to his collection.

Johann Wolfgang von Goethe
(1749–1832)

Zweig MS 152.

Faust, Part II, Act I, lines 5884–5935: *autograph* fragment; *c.* 1827–8.

In *German.*
Begins: 'Und wenn er zu Mittage schläft'.
Ends: 'Der Bart entflammt und fliegt zurück'.
The extract is taken from the third scene of Act I, 'Weitläufiger Saal mit Nebengemächern', in which Goethe presents a lavish masquerade on the lines of a Florentine carnival, a parable of society with allegorical and mythical figures. Lines 5884–5913 occupy the recto, while lines 5914–35 occupy the top half of the verso.
In a space at the end of the extract is an authentication by Goethe's daughter-in-law, 'Handschrift des Vaters für Franz Grillparzer / von Ottilie von Goethe', written at right angles to the rest of the text.

329 x 200mm.
f. 1.
Black and brown ink and pencil on unbleached paper.
No watermark.

Related Manuscripts: There are many manuscript fragments of *Faust,* Part II known to be, or have been, in circulation; examples include BL Add MS 20273, f. 36 (draft fragment containing lines 9442–53) and Yale University Beinecke Library, YCGL MSS 6 (corrected draft fragment from the William A. Speck collection, containing lines 11043–90).
Published: *Goethe's Werke. Vollständige Ausgabe letzter Hand,* 12 (Stuttgart; Tübingen: J. G. Cotta, 1828). This edition included only the first act of the play; *Goethe's Werke, Vollständige Ausgabe,* 41 (Stuttgart; Tübingen: J. G. Cotta, 1832). This constitutes the first volume of *Goethe's Nachgelassene Werke* with the title page 'Faust, der Tragödie zweyter Theil in fünf Acten (Vollendet im Sommer 1831)'.
Reproduced: BL Programme Book, 1987, p. 26; Matuschek, p. 217; www.bl.uk/manuscripts and Plate 21 below.
Exhibited: Paris, Bibliothèque nationale de France, Goethe, 1749–1832: exposition organisée pour commémorer le centenaire de la mort de Goethe, 1932, catalogue no. 647; Vienna, Albertina, Goethe Gedächtnisausstellung, 1932, catalogue no. 353; London, BL, 75 Musical and Literary Autographs, 1986.
Provenance: Franz Grillparzer: mid-19th century; Josef von Weilen?: late 19th century; Alexander von Weilen: early 20th century; acquired by Zweig from the estate of Alexander von Weilen through the art dealer Gustav Nebehay, 1919; BL 1986.
Bibliography: Frels, *Deutsche Dichterhandschriften,* no. 24a; *Catalogue of Additions,* p. 71; Matuschek, pp. 214–5.

Commentary. The second part of Goethe's *Faust* continues Faust's story after the death of Gretchen in Part I. Goethe began work on it two decades after he finished the first part and there is a marked difference in themes; Faust and Mephistopheles are shown travelling through space and time, interacting with mythological figures, until ultimately Faust overcomes the snares of the devil.

Ottilie von Goethe, who lived in her father-in-law's household for many years, assisted Goethe with the writing of *Faust,* Part II. After its posthumous publication in 1832, she and her sons sometimes took leaves such as this one from the manuscript to give to friends and admirers of the great man.

The recipient of this fragment, the Austrian dramatist Franz Grillparzer (1791–1872), met Goethe for the first time in Weimar in 1826, when he was so overwhelmed to be in the presence of the great author that he found it difficult to control his feelings and struggled to hold back his tears. After Goethe's death he continued to meet Ottilie during her regular visits to Vienna when she was accustomed to spend time with his particular circle of friends. It was probably on one of these visits that Ottilie gave him the Faust fragment.

Zweig owned a total of eighteen manuscripts by Goethe (see Matuschek, pp. 213–9). The poem 'Vorstand und Recht' ('Solang man nüchtern ist'), from the *West-östlicher Diwan*, with a musical setting by Carl Friedrich Zelter, is also in the BL Stefan Zweig Collection (Zweig MS 153); a full description can be found in Arthur Searle, *The British Library Stefan Zweig Collection: Catalogue of the Music Manuscripts* (London: British Library, 1999), p. 157.

Zweig MS 154.

Kammerberg bei Eger: drawing of a landscape with a building on a hill, and figures and rocks in the foreground; [1808].

Inscribed in brown ink in the lower right-hand corner 'Goethes Handzeichnung Gustav Schueler Jena'.

192 x 328mm.
f. 1; 1v blank.
Pen and black ink with monochrome wash over pencil on laid paper.
Watermark: eagle.

Related Manuscripts: A virtually identical drawing (though made from a slightly different perspective), similarly authenticated by Gustav Schueler, is included in the Balthasar Elischer collection of Goethe material in the Hungarian Academy of Sciences, Budapest. A further autograph manuscript in the collection, which describes the Kobes-Mühle near the Kammerberg, bears a similar inscription by Schueler, dated 1841. See Zweig MS 217 for further landscape drawings by Goethe.

Reproduced: Hinterberger catalogue IX, plate XIII; www.bl.uk/manuscripts and Plate 22 below.

Exhibited: Paris, Bibliothèque nationale de France, Goethe, 1749–1832: exposition organisée pour commémorer le centenaire de la mort de Goethe, 1932, catalogue no. 749; Vienna, Albertina, Goethe Gedächtnisausstellung, 1932, catalogue no. 355; London, BL, 75 Musical and Literary Autographs, 1986.

Provenance: Gustav Schueler (1807–55), *c.* 1828–55.

The date of acquisition by Zweig is not known; BL 1986.

Bibliography: 'Der Kammerberg bei Eger 1820', in *Goethe's Werke*, 51 (Stuttgart; Tübingen: J. G. Cotta, 1833), pp. 81–9; Hinterberger catalogue IX, no. 64; *Corpus der Goethezeichungen*, 6b, ed. Gerhard Femmel (Leipzig: E. A. Seemann, 1971), p. 119, no. B86; BL Programme Book, 1987; *Catalogue of Additions*, p. 71; Matuschek, p. 220.

Commentary. This drawing, one in a series, was made in 1808 during Goethe's first visit to the Eger region (modern-day Chleb), an area that he visited nineteen times in all. With his lifelong interest in geology and geological formations, he was particularly moved to investigate the historical origins of the Kammerberg, which is now known to be an extinct prehistoric volcano, tending at first to subscribe to the Vulcanist theory that the source of the rocks was igneous, but later lending his support to the Neptunist theory of aqueous origins. He spent his time there collecting samples, making close observations, taking notes (in preparation for a later published essay) and making drawings.

Gustav Schueler, 'Bergrat' (Minister of mines) and afterwards Professor of Geology in Jena, first met Goethe when he approached him for employment in August 1828. After Schueler's death in 1855 his estate was found to contain a large number of Goethe manuscripts as well as seventeen drawings, all authenticated by the owner. His heirs strove to sell the collection as a group, but it was eventually dispersed.

The present drawing is one of seven Goethe drawings owned by Zweig at various stages of his collecting career. Another two are also in the British Library (see below, Zweig MS 217); for a complete list see Matuschek, pp. 219–20.

Zweig MS 155.

Hair from Goethe's head; [1832?]

Clippings of mixed brown and grey hair, together with a cream envelope bearing the inscription 'Haare des Vaters. Mir von Geh. Hofrath Vogel übergeben' in the hand of Goethe's daughter-in-law Ottilie.

Locks of hair together with envelope in cream wove paper (113 x 175mm).
Hair now housed in a small, sealed transparent pocket.

Related items: Locks of hair had symbolic value, making them popular as tokens of friendship or items to be treasured as a keepsake, and subsequently they became highly prized by collectors. Many examples of Goethe's hair survive; Zweig owned one other, together with a lock of Friedrich Schiller's hair, accompanying the autograph of Goethe's poem 'An Madame Wolf (Erlaubt sey dir in mancherley Gestalten)' and other relics. This is now at the Bodmer Foundation, Geneva (see Matuschek, p. 213, no. 221).

Reproduced: www.bl.uk/manuscripts

Provenance: Remained with the Goethe family until after the deaths of his grandsons Wolfgang (d. 1883) and Walther (d. 1885); purchased by Zweig from Karl Ernst Henrici, Berlin, 19 June 1922, together with a lock of hair from Goethe's granddaughter, Alma. Zweig subsequently gave the latter to Professor Anton Kippenberg for his collection (see Add MS 73170, f. 4); BL 1986.

Commentary. 'Geh. Hofrath Vogel', named on the envelope, was Goethe's private physician, Carl Vogel, who attended him during his last illness. Although not present in the room at the moment of Goethe's death he entered immediately afterwards, and at this moment he could well have cut off some hair at Ottilie's request to provide a keepsake of her father-in-law. That this would not have been an unlikely situation is intimated by Goethe's friend and secretary, Johann Peter Eckermann (1792–1854), in his work *Gespräche mit Goethe* (1836). Concluding with a description of visiting the great man after his death to pay his last respects, he mentions feeling a strong desire to cut a piece of Goethe's hair to take away as a memento (although he refrained from doing so, sensing that it might be considered disrespectful on his part).

Goethe's hair was one of the many highlights of Zweig's collection; his own catalogue notes about it (Add MS 73170, f. 4) start with the words 'kostbare Reliquie', a sentiment that is echoed at the end with the words 'ausserste [*sic*] Kostbarkeit!'. Since it came directly from the family it had an impeccable provenance, and he wondered whether it might perhaps be the only authentic example of its type.

Heinrich Heine
(1797–1856)

Zweig MS 156.

'Die armen Weber', poem: *autograph* draft; [1844].

In *German*.
Begins: 'Im düstern Auge keine Thräne'.
Ends: 'Altdeutschland, wir weben dein Leichentuch! / Wir weben! wir weben!'.
Poem of four stanzas of four lines, written in *Kurrentschrift*, each followed by the refrain 'Wir weben! Wir weben!' Headed originally 'Die schlesischen Weber', the word 'schlesischen' has been deleted and the word 'armen' written above it. Other *autograph* corrections have been made as follows: line 1 of second stanza: 'Verflucht der Gott' cancelled and a new start made on the next line with 'Ein Fluch dem Gotte'; line 2 of second stanza: 'Kl' cancelled before 'kindlichem'; original lines 3, 4 and 5 of fourth stanza, all cancelled: 'Wo Grabesmoder ['Todes' cancelled over 'Grabes'] verpestet die Luft//Wo die Verwesung verpestet die//Wo die ['nur' cancelled above 'die'] Verwesung vergiftet die Luft ['und Moderluft'cancelled above 'die Luft]/ Wir fluchen dir! Fahr hin zur Gruft.' Signature 'Heinrich Heine' following the poem has also been cancelled.

269 x 209mm.
f. 1; 1v blank.
Blue ink on light blue wove paper.
No watermark.

Published: First published, as 'Die armen Weber', in Karl Marx's journal *Vorwärts*, 55 (10 July 1844), and afterwards distributed widely as a leaflet to promote revolutionary propaganda in Prussia. Original version published in *Der Zeitgeist: Beiblatt zum Berliner Tageblatt*, 2 (12 January 1914); Heine subsequently made some small amendments to the wording, adding an extra stanza and reverting to 'Die schlesischen Weber' as his title. This revised version was first published in *Album: Originalpoesieen von George Weerth* [et al.], ed. H. Püttman (Borna: Albert Reich, 1847), pp. 145–6; Heinrich Heine, *Historisch-kritische Gesamtausgabe der Werke*, 2, *Neue Gedichte* (Düsseldorf: Hoffmann und Campe, 1983), p. 150.
Reproduced: Matuschek, p. 234; www.bl.uk/manuscripts and Plate 23 below.
Exhibited: London, BL, 75 Musical and Literary Autographs, 1986; London, Christie's, etc., The Creative Spirit, 1987–8.
Provenance: Purchased by Zweig at Sotheby's sale 30 April / 1 May 1914, lot 400 (described in the Sotheby's catalogue as 'Property of a gentleman'); BL 1986.
Bibliography: BL Programme Book, 1987; *Catalogue of Additions*, p. 71; Matuschek, p. 233.

Commentary. Heine's poem 'Die schlesischen Weber', sometimes called 'Weberlied', is a key example of the political literature of the 'Vormärz' period preceding the 1848 revolution in the states of the German Confederation. It describes the misery of the Silesian weavers after their uprising in 1844 when they took action to express their grievances about exploitation and low wages, a revolt that was unsuccessful but nevertheless exposed some of the inequalities of industrialisation. The poem, which takes a broader approach by criticising the authorities and the general political circumstances as well as complaining about exploitation by the factory owners, was banned by the Prussian Supreme Court because of its rebellious tone.

Zweig also owned the following autograph manuscripts of Heine: the poem 'An Ihn' (1832), now in the Goethe Museum, Anton and Katharina Kippenberg Stiftung, Düsseldorf; a draft fragment of 'Deutschland. Ein Wintermärchen' (1843), and three poems, 'Tragödie I–III', all now at the Bodmer Foundation, Geneva.

Hermann Hesse
(1877–1962)

Zweig MS 157.

'Sommer 1933', collection of poems: *typescript* with watercolour illustrations by the author; 1933.

In German.

The contents are as follows:
1. ff. 2–3. 'Blumen nach einem Gewitter'.
2. ff. 4–5. 'Häuser am Abend'.
3. ff. 6–7. 'Heisser Mittag'.
4. ff. 8–9. 'Höhe des Sommers'.
5. ff. 10–11. 'Sommerglut'.
6. ff. 12–13. 'Gewitter'.
7. ff. 14–15. 'Verwahrloster Park'.
8. f. 16. 'Nächtlicher Regen'.
9. f. 17. 'Rückgedenken'.
10. f. 18. 'Schmetterlinge im August'.
11. f. 19. 'Scheingewitter'.
12. f. 20. 'Sommer ward alt'.
13. f. 21. 'Welkes Blatt'.

With an *autograph* title page (f. 1), *autograph* titles for the first seven poems and seven illustrations (ff. 2, 4, 6, 8, 10, 12, 14). The title page ('Sommer 1933. Gedichte von Hermann Hesse') appears on the first leaf of the initial bifolium with a presentation inscription on the verso, the second leaf remaining blank. In the case of the following seven bifolia the recto of the first leaf is occupied by a drawing above an *autograph* title, whilst the corresponding poem is typed on the recto of the second leaf. The eighth poem (on the single sheet) and the remaining five poems, which all have *typewritten* title headings, occur on rectos, ending on the recto of the first leaf of the eleventh bifolium. A list of abbreviated titles appears on the recto of its second leaf.

157 x 139mm.
ff. 22; versos blank.
Typewritten on grey paper, with drawings in pen and black ink and watercolour. Titles in black ink.
11 bifolia and one single sheet (f. 16).

Related Manuscripts: Hesse was in the habit of putting together small collections of illustrated poems to present to his friends, and many of these are still in existence. A list of fourteen such collections relating to 'Sommer 1933' and very similar to, but apparently not fully identical with, the present manuscript can be found in Mileck's extensive bibliography (part V–C, pp. 474–6) under the heading 'Manuscript Collections of Poems'.
Published: Apparently unpublished as a collection. Publication details for individual poems can be found in Mileck, part V–D.
Reproduced: Plate 24 below.
Exhibited: London, BL, 75 Musical and Literary Autographs, 1986.
Provenance: Gift [1933?] from Hermann Hesse to Zweig (author's presentation inscription, f. 1v); BL 1986.
Bibliography: Joseph Mileck, *Hermann Hesse: Biography and Bibliography* (Berkeley; London: University of California Press, 1977), esp. vol. 1, pp. 445–698, vol. 2, pp. 1041–1125; BL Programme Book, 1987; *Catalogue of Additions*, pp. 71–2; Matuschek, p. 237.

Commentary. Because Hesse produced so many of these small illustrated collections of verses for his friends the manuscript is neither particularly rare, nor does it fulfil Zweig's collecting criterion of demonstrating the thought processes behind the creation of a work of art. Nevertheless it was highly prized by Zweig as a commemoration of his personal friendship with Hesse whom he first met on a visit to Gaienhofen on Lake Constance in 1905. On this occasion Hesse gave him the autograph manuscript of his story *Heumond*, later donated by Zweig to the Österreichisches Theatermuseum, Vienna.

Adolf Hitler
(1889–1945)

Zweig MS 158.
Outline for a speech: *autograph* draft; [1928].

In *German*.
Begins: 'Kritik an der Aussenpolitik'.
Ends: 'Unser Ziel Not vor Glauben'.
A series of headings and subheadings comprising an initial scheme for Hitler's speech on foreign policy, delivered at a rally in the Friedrichshain Rooms in Berlin, 13 July 1928. Note added in pencil at the head of the first page: 'Aufzeichnung Adolf Hitlers [name erased] zu einer Rede am 13 Juli 28 [continuing down right-hand margin] im Friedrichshain (Deutschlands Aussenpolitik) Erst. Vers.' The outline indicates that Hitler intended to speak about the relationship of the population to the country's surface area, the question of possible pacts with Great Britain and Italy and the problem of South Tyrol.

330 x 210mm.
ff. 13 [original numbering]. Versos blank.
Black ink and pencil on cream paper, each sheet punched with two holes along left-hand edge.
Watermark: 'POENSGEN & HEYER PAPIERFABRIK LETMATHE NORMAL 4a'.

Published: Full text of speech printed in *Hitler: Reden, Schriften, Anordnungen*, 3/1, ed. Bärbel Dusik and Klaus A. Lankheit in collaboration with Christian Hartmann (Munich: K. G. Saur, 1993), pp. 11–22.
Reproduced: Matuschek, p. 53 (f. 6); Plate 25 below.
Exhibited: London, BL, 75 Musical and Literary Autographs, 1986.
Provenance: Herr Domeyer of Berlin, Marienfelde; Willi Rossbach of Berlin W 50, Augsburgerstr. 45 (letter confirming legal ownership, Add MS 73174, f. 102); purchased by Zweig through Hellmut, Meyer and Ernst of Berlin, 1933; BL 1986.
Bibliography: BL Programme Book, 1987; Joseph Goebbels, *Tagebücher*, 1/1 (Munich: K. G. Saur, 1987), pp. 242–3, 245; *Catalogue of Additions*, p. 72; Matuschek, pp. 52–5, 239; Thomas Friedrich, *Die missbrauchte Hauptstadt: Hitler und Berlin* (Berlin: Propyläen Verlag, 2007), pp. 189–90.

Commentary. After the failed Munich Putsch of 1923 Hitler was variously barred from public speaking, the ban in Prussia lasting until September 1928. Accordingly his speech of July 1928 was delivered at the closed session of a rally for NSDAP (National Socialist Workers' Party of Germany) members in private rooms in the eastern Berlin district of Friedrichshain. On a blisteringly hot evening the hall, which had an official capacity of 3,500, was reportedly packed with an audience of about 5,000. Hitler spoke for almost three-and-a-half hours with one short break, firstly following the agenda planned in his notes, then turning his attention to the subject of degenerate art. Goebbels reported in his diary that he was received with enormous enthusiasm.

This is something of an unexpected autograph to find in Zweig's collection which otherwise provides little indication that he was interested in contemporary politicians *per se*, although the subjects of some of his biographies show how Zweig was fascinated by strong, powerful figures of authority. One plausible explanation is that his lifelong collecting instincts got the better of him on this occasion. Autographs of Hitler were virtually non-existent since he seldom committed pen to paper, and Zweig's entries on his record card for the manuscript (Add MS 73168, f. 27), where he describes the item as 'das einzige Autograf Adolf Hitlers das je gesehen wurde' and 'Rarissimum', strongly suggest that he regarded it as something of a collecting triumph. Moreover he had been willing to pay quite a considerable sum of money for it (1000 Reichsmark), despite announcing a few months earlier that he was seeking to disperse his collection rather than to add to it (Matuschek, p. 52).

There is another possibility: Zweig's interactions with the National Socialist regime suggest that the acquisition could have been motivated as much by personal reasons as it was by commercial and collecting interests. In the chapter of Zweig's memoirs titled 'Incipit Hitler', he admitted that, even in 1933, after Hitler had become Chancellor, he could still not contemplate the consequences. He wrote, 'it was the high value they set on education that led German intellectuals to go on thinking of Hitler as a mere beer-hall agitator who could never really be dangerous' (*The World of Yesterday*, trans. by Anthea Bell (London: Pushkin, 2009), pp. 383–415). Zweig was well aware of the threat to Jewish authors published in Germany and was later embroiled in an infamous conflict around the performance of his and Richard Strauss's *Die schweigsame Frau*, although he would also joke about the proximity of his Kapuzinerberg home in Salzburg to Hitler's residence in Berchtesgaden just across the border in Bavaria.

Hugo von Hofmannsthal
(1874–1929)

Zweig MS 159.

'Vor Tag', poem: *autograph* fair copy; [1907].

In *German.*
Begins: 'Nun liegt und zuckt am fahlen Himmelsrand'.
Ends: 'Nun geht die Stalltür. Und nun ist auch Tag'.
Thirty-eight lines of blank verse in iambic pentameters. It describes man and nature awaking at daybreak after a storm, a vision of Christ and his mother, and a guilty young man returning to his own room after spending the night with a woman.
Written in *Kurrentschrift.* With *autograph* annotations 'Hofmannsthal' at the top left and 'für die "Morgen"' at the top right (referring to the first publication). There are minor corrections to 'false starts' in lines 17, 29 and 31. On f. 2v is an instruction in pencil in another hand, struck through, 'Bitte in 2 Exemplaren typieren ...'.

290 x 230mm.
ff. 2 [original foliation]; 1v blank.
Black ink and pencil on cream laid paper.
No watermark.

Related Manuscript: Freies Deutsches Hochstift, Frankfurt am Main: FDH 20027 (an autograph draft of 'Vor Tag' dated, possibly retrospectively, 7 August 1907).
Published: *Morgen: Wochenschrift für deutsche Kultur* (Berlin: Marquardt & Co.), 1. Jahrgang, Nr 21 (1 November 1907), p. 664; *Neues Wiener Journal,* 1 November 1907, p. 8; Hugo von Hofmannsthal, *Die Gedichte und kleinen Dramen* (Leipzig: Insel Verlag, 1911), pp. 6–7; id., *Gesammelte Werke in Einzelausgaben. Gedichte und Lyrische Dramen*, ed. Herbert Steiner (Frankfurt am Main: S. Fischer, 1970), pp. 9–10; id., *Sämtliche Werke*, 1, *Gedichte 1*, ed. Eugene Weber (Frankfurt am Main: S. Fischer, 1984), pp. 106–7.
Variants: The editor of the *Sämtliche Werke* (1984) was unaware of Zweig MS 159 and lists variants between the edition (based on the first publication) and the Frankfurt MS. The text of Zweig MS 159 is identical with that of the *Sämtliche Werke*, which means that it differs in certain words and phrases from the other extant manuscript. It is clear from the annotation that the Zweig version was the one prepared for publication.
Reproduced: www.bl.uk/manuscripts and Plate 26 below.
Exhibited: London, BL, 75 Musical and Literary Autographs, 1986.
Provenance: Presented to Zweig by Hofmannsthal in February 1908; BL 1986.
Bibliography: Stefan Zweig, 'Hugo von Hofmannsthal: Gedächtnisrede zur Trauerfeier im Wiener Burgtheater' (1929), in *Zeit und Welt* (Stockholm: Bermann-Fisher Verlag, 1946), pp. 33–48; Eugene M. Weber, 'A Chronology of Hofmannsthal's poems', in *Euphorion*, Band 63, Heft 1/2 (Heidelberg: Carl Winter, 1969), pp. 284–328 ('Vor Tag' is no. 124 on p. 326); Horst

Weber, *Hugo von Hofmannsthal Bibliographie* (Berlin: Walter de Gruyter, 1972), no. 140, pp. 223–4; Hugo von Hofmannsthal, *Briefe an Freunde*, ed. Richard Friedenthal (Frankfurt am Main: S. Fischer, 1984), pp. 17–18; BL Programme Book, 1987; *Catalogue of Additions*, p. 72; Matuschek, p. 245.

Commentary. There is no reason to doubt that 'Vor Tag' was composed on 7 August 1907, as indicated on the Frankfurt manuscript, at Hofmannsthal's home in Rodaun in the Austrian Tirol. Olga, wife of the dramatist Arthur Schnitzler, quoted the whole poem and described the circumstances in which it was written in her memoir *Spiegelbild der Freundschaft* (Salzburg: Residenz Verlag, 1962, p. 76). Hofmannsthal took an evening walk with the Schnitzlers, passing a wayside shrine depicting Christ and Mary. This inspired the vision incorporated into the poem, and its inscription was echoed in the words 'O meine Mutter' and 'Ach mein lieber Sohn'.

Eugene Weber in his *Euphorion* article notes that Hofmannsthal generally only made one draft of his poems, and would produce a fair copy with minimal revision soon afterwards. Zweig MS 159 must therefore have been written in the short space of time between the August draft and the publication on 1 November of the same year. It was too late for inclusion in the 1907 *Gesammelte Gedichte* published by the Insel Verlag, but it was included in subsequent collections.

In a letter of 16 February 1908, Zweig thanks Hofmannsthal for a poem which must be the present manuscript: 'ich danke Ihnen innigst für Ihr schönes Geschenk, das mir doppelt wertvoll ist: als Gedicht und als gütiges Zeichen freundlicher Gesinnung'. He offers in return Spoelberch de Lovenjoul's *Histoire des œuvres de Balzac*, referring modestly to his essay on the French writer in comparison with Hofmannsthal's own.

Zweig's relationship with Hofmannsthal was based on admiration which was not reciprocated. Zweig hoped to emulate the success of the slightly older Viennese Jewish writer and ventured to engage in correspondence with him; letters received by Zweig are preserved in the Jewish National and University Library in Jerusalem. Hofmannsthal did acknowledge the merits of Zweig's Balzac essay (1908), and did make a gesture of friendship in giving him the present manuscript. However he did not regard him as a serious writer, calling him a mere journalist or *littérateur*, and claiming later not to know of his *Novellen*. The fact that both writers published their work through the Insel Verlag may have created professional tensions. In 1906 the young Zweig had shared with others a bursary from the Viennese Bauernfeld Fund. Hofmannsthal disapproved of the arts policy with which the Fund was associated, and was scathing in belittling the recipients of its awards. During the First World War, Hofmannsthal's support for monarchy and his active official role did not accord with Zweig's views, but political differences were not the cause of their personal and intellectual distance. Nevertheless Zweig gave the address at Hofmannsthal's funeral in 1929, and took on his mantle as librettist for Richard Strauss when he wrote the libretto for the opera *Die schweigsame Frau* (Zweig MSS 89–91).

Zweig also owned the following autograph manuscripts of Hofmannsthal: 'Aus einer Alkestis', 'Reiselied' and 'Was die Braut geträumt hat', all now at the Bodmer Foundation, Geneva, and 'Verse zum Gedächtnis des Schauspielers Josef Kainz', now in the Österreichisches Theatermuseum, Vienna.

Friedrich Hölderlin
(1770–1843)

Works frequently cited:
Gedichte: *Friedrich Hölderlin Gedichte*, ed. Franz Zinkernagel (Leipzig: Insel Verlag, 1922)
Stuttgarter Ausgabe: Friedrich Hölderlin, *Sämtliche Werke*, Stuttgarter Ausgabe, ed. Friedrich Beissner (Stuttgart: Kohlhammer, 1943–85)
Frankfurter Ausgabe: Friedrich Hölderlin, *Sämtliche Werke*, ed. D. E. Sattler (Frankfurt am Main: Roter Stern, 1976–2008)
Autenrieth & Kelletat: Johanna Autenrieth and Alfred Kelletat, *Katalog der Hölderlin-Handschriften* (Stuttgart: Kohlhammer, 1961)

Zweig MS 160.

'Stuttgart', poem: *autograph* fair copy; [1800–1].

In *German*.
Begins: 'Wieder ein Glük ist erlebt. Die gefährliche Dürre geneset'.
Ends: 'Aber die größere Lust sparen dem Enkel wir auf'.
An elegy of six stanzas with the title spelt 'Stutgard'. Each strophe is formed of nine distiches in groups of three. The poem reflects the celebration of autumn in a landscape through which a wanderer and his companion pass, considering the role of the gods. They come to his birthplace, which evokes memories of the past and its heroes, and a vision of Stuttgart as priestess. The wanderer appeals to the town and the spirits of the land, recognising that celebrations will end and life is short.
Below the title is the autograph dedication 'An Siegfried Schmidt'. F. 1 bears annotations in various hands which have been identified and interpreted by Autenrieth and Kelletat. The *autograph* title is deleted and the alternative 'Herbstfeyer' inserted in ink (top centre). At the top left 'steht schon in der Sam̃lung' is written and at the top right '(in Sekendorfs Musenalm. gedrukt.)', both in ink. There are two annotations in red crayon, 'p. 99' and 'Creutze zu vergleichen', and at the top right are the figures '41/99' in ink and 'Nr. 98' in pencil, the latter overwritten with the figure 5 in ink. At the bottom are '8 C' over 'W' on the left in pencil, possibly a dealer's mark, and on the right 'Hölderlin' in very faint pencil.

248 x 205mm.
ff. 3. The second half of the outer bifolium is blank on recto and verso.
Brown ink and red crayon on cream laid paper.
Two bifolia, originally interleaved but now separated.
Watermark: 'J WHATMAN 1794'.

Related Manuscripts: Württembergische Landesbibliothek, Stuttgart. Part of Stuttgart Cod. poet. et philol. fol. 63, bound as Faszikel I,5 page 5: lines 104–108. A bifolium with lines 1–103 missing; Stadtbibliothek Homburg vor der Höhe, Hessen. Homburger Folioheft-Homburg.F, pages 11–15. Lines 41–59 and 66–8 transposed. There are few variants between the three manuscripts, mainly in punctuation.

Published: *Musenalmanach für das Jahr 1807*, ed. Leo Freiherr von Seckendorf (Regensburg: Montag- und Weißischen Buchhandlung, 1807), pp. 3–12, based on the Homburg text or a derivative and with title 'Die Herbstfeier'; Gedichte, pp. 291–6; Stuttgarter Ausgabe, 2.1, pp. 86–9 (text), 2.2, pp. 584–91 (critical commentary, listing variants); Frankfurter Ausgabe, 6, pp. 181–201 (includes text and facsimiles of the Homburg and Stuttgart MSS, text of the 1807 printing, and a reconstructed text).

Reproduced: Christian Waas, *Siegfried Schmid aus Friedberg in der Wetterau, der Freund Hölderlins*, in *Hessische Volksbücher*, 66–9 (Darmstadt: W. Diehl, 1928), following p. 310 (not showing annotations at the top of the leaf); Friedrich Hölderlin, *Stutgard. Originalgetreue Wiedergabe der Londoner Handschrift*, erläuterungen von Cyrus Hamlin, Schriften der Hölderlin-Gesellschaft, 8 (Tübingen: Hölderlin-Gesellschaft, 1970), containing a full facsimile, text and details of variants, with introduction, notes and structural analysis; www.bl.uk/manuscripts and Plate 27 below.

Exhibited: London, BL, 75 Musical and Literary Autographs, 1986.

Provenance: The manuscript was apparently amongst Hölderlin's papers when the first collection of his poems was made about 1820 (see notes to Hölderlin-Gesellschaft facsimile). It may subsequently have belonged to Carl Künzel, the autograph collector (1808–77), and then to his nephew Wilhelm Künzel (d. 1896). Sold by Leo Liepmannssohn of Berlin, auction 22, 7–8 March 1898, lot 446; sold again by Liepmannssohn, auction 48, 21 October 1926, lot 437, and purchased by Zweig through Heinrich Rosenberg; BL 1986.

Bibliography: Stefan Zweig, *Der Kampf mit dem Dämon*, pp. 23–151; id., 'Meine Autographen-Sammlung'; Frels, *Deutsche Dichterhandschriften*, pp. 134–5; Autenrieth & Kelletat, p. 126, no. 443; BL Programme Book, 1987; *Catalogue of Additions*, p. 72; Matuschek, p. 243.

Commentary. D. E. Sattler believes that Hölderlin started writing the present poem in Stuttgart in September 1800 at the earliest. The composition may have continued through the winter and even into the New Year of 1801. On 3 February Siegfried Schmid wrote a letter of thanks to Hölderlin, but not necessarily relating to this poem (see Stuttgarter Ausgabe, 2.2, p. 584). Schmid (1774–1859) was a writer and a cadet in the Imperial army. He first met Hölderlin in Frankfurt in 1797 and they became part of the same circle of friends in Homburg. Hölderlin dedicated 'Stuttgart' to him to welcome him back from the war, but Zweig MS 160 may not be the copy he sent to his friend. Hölderlin was able to make amendments to the Homburg manuscript, possibly in spring 1804, but when the time came for publication in the *Musenalmanach* he was already insane, and his friends Isaac von Sinclair and Leo Freiherr von Seckendorf saw it into print. It is not clear who made the decision to change the title to 'Die Herbstfeier'. Zweig thought the alternative title written on the MS, identified by Autenrieth and Kelletat as written by Justus Kerner, was in Sinclair's hand (see record card at Add MS 73168, f. 1). However he was not confident of his opinion, as he also suggested and deleted the names of Seckendorf and Mörike.

In his essay 'Handschriften als schöpferische Dokumente', Zweig gave as an example of a manuscript which sparked his schoolboy interest in collecting 'ein Wahnsinnsgedicht Hölderlins mit seinem wirr durcheinander fahrenden Zeilen'. He was sufficiently fascinated by the poet to include him in the second volume of his 'Baumeister der Welt' series, alongside Kleist and Nietzsche. He wrote here of Hölderlin's perfecting lyrical form and creating heroic rhythm, and of his habit of excessive revision, creating new versions of poems in several layers on the same manuscript (as evidenced by the Homburg MS). He spoke of thousands of pages destroyed and of a lack of recognition from a whole generation, but concluded that despite his weakness as an artist and incompetence for life, Hölderlin triumphed through singleness of purpose and the music of his words.

The Zweig provenance papers (Add MS 73174) include two letters from the Hölderlin Archiv in Stuttgart to Dr. M. Altmann (ff. 108, 109) relating to the inclusion of the poems in Beissner's Stuttgarter Ausgabe (April and August 1947), and a draft physical description (f. 110) prepared by Dr. Friedenthal for the same edition.

Zweig's record card (Add MS 73168, f. 31) notes: 'Prachtstück ersten Ranges! Nie gelangte ein Gedicht Hölderlins von [deletion] ähnlichem Umfang zum Verkauf'. He also owned fourteen other autograph manuscripts of Hölderlin; with the exception of BL Zweig MS 161, all are now at the Bodmer Foundation, Geneva (see Matuschek pp. 239–43).

Zweig MS 161.

'An die Deutschen' and 'Die scheinheiligen Dichter', two poems: *autograph* drafts; *c.* 1798.

In *German.*
1. f. 1. 'An die Deutschen'. Begins: 'Spottet ja nicht des Kinds, wenn es mit Peitsch' und Sporn'. Ends: 'Daß ich büße die Lästerung'.
2. f. 1v. 'Die scheinheiligen Dichter'. Begins: 'Ihr kalten Heuchler, sprecht von den Göttern nicht!' Ends: 'Und ist ein großes Wort vonnöthen', with the missing final line 'Mutter Natur so denkt man deiner' added in pencil in the margin by another hand.
Two of the twelve epigrammatic odes that Hölderlin prepared for publication in 1798, both of eight lines in two stanzas. 'An die Deutschen' is a call to action for Germans who, like a child playing on a wooden horse, are more inclined to thoughts than deeds. This is the first version of a poem that Hölderlin later expanded. 'Die scheinheiligen Dichter' criticises hypocritical poets, who must not speak of gods in whom they have no belief – the gods are manifest in Nature.
There is an erased pencil note in an unidentified hand at the head of f. 1. In line 1 of 'An die Deutschen', the 'K' of 'Kinds'and the 'e' of 'Peitsch' overwrite an erroneous 'D' and 's' respectively. The word 'glüklich' in line 2 is deleted. Signed at the foot of the recto (the corresponding signature on the verso is cut away).

158 x 121mm.
f. 1. The bottom edge is cut away with loss of one line of text on the verso.
Partial watermark: 'BRENN [ER & COMP IN] BA [SEL]'.
Brown and black ink and pencil on cream laid paper.

(See Add MS 73174, f. 111 for the draft physical description prepared by Dr. Friedenthal in 1947 for Beissner's edition of the works.)

Related Manuscripts: See Stuttgarter Ausgabe, 1.2, pp. 570–2 and Autenrieth & Kelletat, nos. 421, 442 and 456. The strip cut from the bottom of Zweig MS 161, bearing the last line of 'Die scheinheiligen Dichter' on the verso with the signature, and blank on the recto, was sold by Liepmannssohn of Berlin, auction 36, 17–20 November 1906, lot 908, to the artist Marie Paquet-Steinhausen of Frankfurt am Main (1881–1958); see Autenrieth & Kelletat, p. 126, no. 421.

Published: Both poems appeared in the *Taschenbuch für Frauenzimmer von Bildung*, ed. C. L. Neuffer (Stuttgart: Steinkopf), 'An die Deutschen' in the edition for 1799, p. 68, and 'Die scheinheiligen Dichter' in the edition for 1800, p. 280; Gedichte, pp. 132, 185–7; Stuttgarter Ausgabe, 1.1, pp. 256, 257 (text), 1.2, pp. 570–2 and 2.2 pp. 1002–3 (commentary); Frankfurter Ausgabe, 4, pp. 78–81 (texts and reproductions), 5, pp. 525–38 (commentary).

Variants: Variants from the published texts are very minor (see Stuttgarter Ausgabe, 1.2, pp. 571, 572 and Frankfurter Ausgabe, 5, pp. 526, 538). The strip removed from the manuscript differs from the text added in the margin in having an exclamation mark after 'Natur' and 'gedenkt' for 'denkt'.

Reproduced: Frankfurter Ausgabe, 4, pp. 79 and 80. In the facsimile of 'Die scheinheiligen Dichter' on p. 80, the separated slip is reproduced in position at the foot of the leaf. According to Zweig's record card (Add MS 73168, f. 30), the present manuscript came from Gustav Könnecke's collection, and 'An die Deutschen' was reproduced in his *Bilderatlas*. However, it is not in the editions of 1887, 1895 or 1912, which have instead facsimiles of Hölderlin's poem 'Maennerjubel'. It is possible that Zweig confused the two poems, as the manuscript of 'Maennerjubel' was apparently also owned by Könnecke, but it was not in the auction catalogue of his collection in 1926 and is now lost; www.bl.uk/manuscripts and Plate 28 below.

Provenance: Auctioned by Liepmannssohn, 7 June 1886, lot 370; purchased by Zweig from Karl Ernst Henrici of Berlin, 22 February 1926, auction 107, the sale of Gustav Könnecke's collection, lot 276 (see record card); BL 1986.

Bibliography: Stefan Zweig, 'Meine Autographen-Sammlung'; Frels, *Deutsche Dichterhandschriften*, pp. 134–5; Autenrieth & Kelletat, p. 126; BL Programme Book, 1987; *Catalogue of Additions*, p. 72; Matuschek, p. 239.

Commentary. Hölderlin expanded 'An die Deutschen' to fourteen stanzas around 1800, and developed the opening of the separate poem 'Rousseau' from lines 44 and following of this version (see Stuttgarter Ausgabe, 2.1, pp. 9–11 and 2.2, pp. 396–403).

On Zweig's interest in Hölderlin and the other autograph manuscripts of Hölderlin that he owned, see the description of Zweig MS 160 above.

Henrik Ibsen
(1828–1906)

Zweig MS 162.

'En Udflugt til Abydos', article: *autograph* draft fragment; [1869].

In *Norwegian.*
Begins: 'Mandagen den 8de November dampede vi paa "Ferous" nedover Nilen'.
The article describes Ibsen's visit to the ruins of Abydos in Egypt on his way to the ceremony for the opening of the Suez Canal in 1869. The manuscript contains notes describing the journey by steamship from Quenneh in Nubia and the activities of those on board.
Apart from the title and first line, the manuscript appears to be a quick first draft of incomplete phrases, with corrections and additions. 'Ibsen' is pencilled in another hand at the top left of f. 1, and the Hinterberger catalogue number '20/707' at the bottom. The Hinterberger catalogue describes it as a 'Flüchtige erste Niederschrift. Die Schriftzüge weichen stark von den bekannten regelmässigen Zügen der Reinschriften ab'. Ibsen uses the large capitals for nouns and double consonants after short vowels characteristic of his orthography in the period 1865–70. A single leaf written closely on both sides across the whole width. Interlineations and additions at the head and in the left margin on the recto.

216 x 138mm.
f. 1.
Black ink on brown wove paper.
No watermark.

Related Manuscripts: Four manuscripts survive including BL Zweig MS 162. The others are Nasjonalbiblioteket, Oslo, NBO Ms.8° 1216a–b: two manuscripts bound together (1216a, autograph working manuscript of four bifolia, 1216b, autograph fair copy with some corrections on four bifolia); Nasjonalbiblioteket, Oslo, NBO Ms.8° 1933: autograph draft on one side of a single leaf of part of the text copied in Ms.8° 1216b.
Published: *Samtiden*, ed. Gerhard Gran (Kristiania [Oslo]: Aschehoug), 2, 1908, pp. 108–116; Henrik Ibsen, *Efterladte skrifter*, 1, ed. Halvdan Koht and Julius Elias (Kristiania [Oslo]: Gyldendal, 1909), pp. 288–98. Variant readings are given in vol. 3, pp. 359–63; *Henrik Ibsens Samlede Verker,* Hundreårsutgave, 15, ed. F. Bull, H. Koht, D. Arup Seip (Oslo: Gyldendal, 1930), pp. 340–51; *Henrik Ibsens Skrifter,* 16, *Sakprosa* (Oslo: Universitet i Oslo, 2010), text volume, pp. 430–50 and 451–72 (two versions), description of the manuscripts, pp. 545–9; commentary volume, pp. 565–84.
Reproduced: Matuschek, p. 249; www.bl.uk/manuscripts and Plate 29 below.
Exhibited: London, BL, 75 Musical and Literary Autographs, 1986.
Provenance: Purchased by Zweig from Antiquariat Ignaz Schwarz, Vienna, auction 11, 9 April 1924; offered for sale by Zweig in 1937 through Hinterberger, Vienna, catalogue XX, no. 707 but returned to the collection unsold; BL 1986.

Bibliography: BL Programme Book, 1987; *Catalogue of Additions*, p. 72; Matuschek, pp. 248–9. For Ibsen's attitude to Egypt, see Elisabeth Oxfeldt, *Nordic Orientalism: Paris and the Cosmopolitan Imagination, 1800–1900* (Copenhagen: Museum Tusculanum Press, 2005), pp. 153–4, 157–8.

Commentary. In the summer of 1869, the Khedive of Egypt invited representatives from European countries to attend ceremonies marking the opening of the Suez Canal. Two Norwegians were nominated, the Egyptologist Jens Daniel Carolus Lieblein (1827–1911) and Ibsen, who had made reference to Egypt in the fourth act of *Peer Gynt* but may simply have been chosen as his country's foremost contemporary author. Before the official opening on 17 November, the European party left Cairo on 22 October on the steamship Ferous for a cruise up the River Nile, visiting ancient sites including Abydos, a ruined city between Luxor and Aswan, once the most powerful after Thebes and the necropolis of the early pharaohs.

Ibsen told Frederik Hegel in a letter of 14 December 1869 that he had kept a diary during the tour which would provide material for publication, and the 'Abydos' article may have been intended as part of a fuller account for *Morgenbladet* or a similar periodical. This did not materialise, though Ibsen did produce a piece entitled 'Suezkanalen' for Nordahl Rolfsen's *Laesebog* (1894) and reflected his experiences in Egypt in two poems.

An index card relating to this manuscript is in private hands in Switzerland. Zweig also owned a manuscript of 'Verbrannte Schiffe', Ibsen's translation into German of his own poem 'Braendte Skibe', now at the Bodmer Foundation, Geneva.

John Keats
(1795–1821)

Zweig MS 163.

'I stood tip-toe upon a little hill', poem: *autograph* fragment of first draft; [1816].

In *English*.
Begins: 'Sometimes Gold-finches one by one will drop'.
Ends: 'To bow for gratitude before Jove's Throne'.
Fifty-seven lines (including deletions) from the fourth leaf of the poem. The whole work consists of 242 lines in rhyming couplets, drafted on ten leaves. Lines 87–106 of the final version are drafted on the recto, and lines 123–50 on the verso of this fragment. The gap between is accounted for by fragments at Harvard and in New York Public Library (see below under Related Manuscripts).
The complete poem reflects, partly through observation and partly in visions, the power of nature to inspire the poet. At the end, Keats's first use of the Endymion theme emerges. The recto of the present fragment describes a real flight of goldfinches evoking the vision of a maiden moving through a field; the verso marks the opening of an extended address to the moon.
The rough draft is characterised by the deletion of ten lines or part lines and displays its hasty composition in the alterations, flowing script and lack of punctuation. Line numbers are confused: lines 120, 136, 150 are numbered in the margin, but the first does not correspond to the published editions. There are pen trials in the left-hand margin and at the top of the recto. 'John Keates' [*sic*] has been added in another hand.

194 x 121mm.
f. 1.
Black ink on wove paper.
No watermark.

Related Manuscripts: For the manuscript tradition, reconstruction of the draft fragments and details of published transcriptions, see *The Poetical Works of John Keats*, ed. H. W. Garrod, 2nd ed. (Oxford: Clarendon Press, 1958), pp. lxxxiv–lxxxviii; Jack Stillinger, *The Texts of Keats's Poems* (Cambridge, MA: Harvard University Press, 1974), pp. 122–4; id., *The Poems of John Keats* (London: Heinemann, 1978), pp. 556–9, an excellent reconstruction leaf by leaf but without knowledge of the Zweig fragment which is said to be missing; *Index of English Literary Manuscripts*, 4/2, ed. Barbara Rosenbaum (London: Mansell, 1990), pp. 361–3.
The rough draft, of which Zweig 163 is part, was given by Keats to Charles Cowden Clarke, who cut it into thirteen fragments which he presented to various friends. These fragments contain twenty-two sections of the poem (on rectos and versos), a total of 193 of the 242 lines plus ten cancelled lines. The known whereabouts of the other pieces is as follows: Harvard University, Houghton Library, Cambridge, MA, five pieces, MS Keats 2.8.1–2.8.4 and 2.5 (1st

leaf, lines 1–6 and 19–23, 7–10 and 24–7; 2nd leaf, lines 38–48 and 53–60 with 107–10; 3rd leaf, lines 111–12, 113–14 (cancelled) and 61–4; 9th leaf, lines 231–5); New York Public Library, Berg Collection (3rd leaf, lines 70–80 and 116–23); Scottish National Portrait Gallery, Edinburgh, SPD 345 (3rd leaf, four additional lines to follow line 122 and lines 81–6); Morgan Library & Museum, New York, MA 658.1 (5th leaf, lines 25–8 revised and 151–9); anonymous owner (6th leaf, lines 157–72, with parts of 173, 174 and 181–92 with cancelled 193–5) – a digital copy, deposited under Export Licence regulations, is available for consultation at the British Library, reference RP 10067; Free Library of Philadelphia, AMS (8th leaf, lines 215–30); Harvard University, Houghton Library, MS Keats 2.9 (complete autograph fair copy, given by Keats to the painter Benjamin Robert Haydon); Harvard University, Houghton Library, MS Keats 3.8 (transcript by Tom Keats, younger brother of John, thought to have been based on a lost manuscript of later date than the autograph fair copy).

Published: First published, prepared by Keats himself, in *Poems* (London: printed for Charles and James Ollier, 1817), the first poem in the collection; *The Poetical Works of John Keats*, ed. H. W. Garrod, 2nd ed., op. cit., pp. 3–11 (text with variants in footnotes) and Introduction, pp. lxxxiv–lxxxviii, for a note on the first version of this poem; *The Poems of John Keats*, ed. Jack Stillinger, op. cit., pp. 79–88 (text and apparatus), pp. 556–9 (notes and reconstruction); John Keats, *Complete Poems*, ed. Jack Stillinger (Cambridge, MA: Harvard University Press, 1982), pp. 47–53, with notes pp. 425–6.

Reproduced: Stefan Zweig, 'Meine Autographen-Sammlung' (original *Philobiblon* publication only), p. 285; *Hampstead & Highgate Express*, 16 May 1986, p. 97; *75 Musical and Literary Autographs*, plate 4; Add MS 73175, ff. 7–8; *Index of English Literary Manuscripts*, 4/2, op. cit., facsimiles 6a and b; BL Programme Book, 1990, p. 11 (recto of the leaf); Stephen Hebron, *John Keats: A Poet and his Manuscripts* (London: British Library, 2009), pp. 51–2, with commentary on p. 50; www.bl.uk/manuscripts and Plate 30 below.

Exhibited: Paris, Bibliothèque nationale de France, Le Livre Anglais, 1951–2, catalogue no. 192 (indemnity form in Add MS 73175, f. 13); London, BL, 75 Musical and Literary Autographs, 1986; London, Christie's, etc., The Creative Spirit, 1987–8; Grasmere, Dove Cottage, John Keats. A Bicentenary Exhibition, 1995–6; London, BL, The Writer in the Garden, 2004–5.

Provenance: In 1816 Keats gave the draft manuscript to Charles Cowden Clarke, who cut up and dispersed it as described above; purchased by Zweig in February 1924 from Leo Liepmannssohn in Berlin, noting that it came 'Aus grosser deutscher Privatsammlung' (record card Add MS 73168, f. 32). The German collector has not been identified. The history is confused by a further statement on the record card 'Hinweis auf den Erwerb in beiliegenden Ausschnitt aus amerik. Kat.' but this has been deleted and must be presumed erroneous. See also the correspondence, invoice and related papers in Add MS 73175, ff. 4–14. The cutting here which refers to a letter and poem as lot 90 does not relate to the present manuscript; BL 1986.

Bibliography: Stefan Zweig, 'Meine Autographen-Sammlung'; BL Programme Book, 1987; *Catalogue of Additions*, p. 72; Matuschek, p. 255.

Commentary. Keats had published his first poem 'O Solitude' in *The Examiner* in May 1816, and this gave the impetus to further composition throughout the rest of that year. According to Leigh Hunt's biography of Lord Byron, an account treated with scepticism by some critics, 'I stood tip-toe' was inspired by the view on a summer day from a gate near the Battery on Hampstead Heath leading to a field by Caen Wood. Keats may have begun to write the poem at Margate in July, in which case he must have set it aside before completing it in December, the date documented on the draft, fair copy and Tom Keats's transcription.

Stefan Zweig felt a particular affinity with Keats, naming him in his explanation of how autographs enable us to connect through our memories with the creative writer: 'Ein Gedichtblatt Keats' bleibt solange nichts als ein armes Blatt Papier, sofern in uns nicht schon bei der bloßen Anrufung dieses Namens ehrfürchtige Erinnerung aufklingt an heilig schöne Verse, die wir von ihm gelesen haben und die unserer Seele so wirklich und gegenwärtig sind wie jedes Haus dieser Stadt und der Himmel darüber und die Wolken und das Meer.' ('Sinn und Schönheit der Autographen'.) On his record card (Add MS 73168, f. 32), he noted that this fragment '[Geh]ört zu den allergrössten Seltenheiten der Welliteratur [*sic*]. Durch die Schönheit des Gedichtes noch kostbarer'. On 11 March 1924, he wrote to the Paris manuscript dealer Simon Kra that he wanted to keep this Keats manuscript, acquired the previous month, as it was quite expensive and he did not expect to see another for sale, except in America, where they were bought for hundreds of dollars (Add MS 74269, ff. 10–11v).

Heinrich von Kleist
(1777–1811)

Zweig MS 164.

'Germania an ihre Kinder', 'An Franz den Ersten, Kaiser von Österreich' and 'Kriegslied der Deutschen', three patriotic poems: *autograph* fair copy; [1809].

In *German.*

1. ff. 1–3v. 'Germania an ihre Kinder'. Begins: 'Die des Maines Regionen'. Ends: 'Oder unser Grabmal sein!'.

Poem of six stanzas of eight lines, each followed by a chorus of four lines. Lines 1–8 rhyme alternately, lines 9–12 in couplets. With subtitle 'eine Ode von Heinrich von Kleist.' written in a space at the top right of f. 1 and marked for insertion.

2. ff. 4–4v. 'An Franz den Ersten, Kaiser von Österreich'. Begins: 'O Herr, du trittst [above deletion], der Welt ein Retter'. Ends: 'Und dein der Lorbeer sein!'.

Poem of three stanzas of five lines. Line 2 rhymes with 5 and 3 with 4. With subtitle 'gesungen von Heinrich von Kleist, Dreßden, d 9[t] Aprill 1809'.

3. ff. 5–5v. 'Kriegslied der Deutschen'. Begins: 'Zottelbär und Pantherthier'. Ends: 'Daß er gleichfalls weiche'.

Poem of six stanzas of four lines, rhyming alternately. Author's name below the title 'von Heinrich von Kleist'. This manuscript lacks the place and date 'Dresden, im März 1809' which is found in the Hanover manuscript and in the editions.

Written in *Kurrentschrift.* A note at the foot of f. 1 reads, 'Diese drei Lieder überlässt der Verf. jedem, der sie drucken will, und wünscht weiter nichts, als daß sie einzeln erscheinen und schnell verbreitet werden. H. v. Kl.' 'An Franz den Ersten' begins on second leaf of second bifolium. 'Kriegslied' occupies the separate leaf.

211 x 168mm.
ff. 5.
Brown ink on cream laid paper.
2 bifolia and 1 single sheet.
Watermarks: [TANNENBERG ?] and shield.

Related Manuscripts: During his lifetime, Kleist made many autograph copies of his poems for friends. The early printed editions are important sources of variant readings where manuscripts are lost. For full details of the sources, both manuscript and printed, their relationships and variants, see the works by Sembdner and the editions cited in the bibliography.

'Germania an ihre Kinder': Landesarchiv, Berlin: A Rep. 021–04. Nr. 62, Kleist's autograph with Tieck's confirmation and date 'Dresden 1808'; Stadtarchiv Dresden from Körner family papers, autograph manuscript. Facsimile in *Zeitschrift für Bücherfreunde*, January 1917, p. 249.

'An Franz den Ersten': Russian National Library, St Petersburg: F 964 No. t II N 4.

'Kriegslied der Deutschen': Stadtarchiv, Hanover: 1199. Facsimile in *Schriften der Kleist-Gesellschaft,* Band 13/14 (Jahrbuch 1931–2), between pp. 110–11.

Published: 'Germania an ihre Kinder' was the only one of the three poems originally published separately, edited by Ernst von Pfuel (Berlin: J. E. Hitzigs Druckerei, 1813). 'Germania an ihre Kinder' and 'Kriegslied der Deutschen' were both printed in *Rußlands Triumph*, Heft 3 (Deutschland [i.e. Berlin: Werckmeister?], 1813), pp. 1–4; *Heinrich von Kleists hinterlassene Schriften*, ed. Ludwig Tieck (Berlin: G. Reimer, [1821]): the first publication of 'An Franz den Ersten' and the first time the three poems appeared together: 'Germania an ihre Kinder', pp. 288–90, 'An Franz den Ersten', p. 285, 'Kriegslied der Deutschen', pp. 281–2; *Heinrich von Kleist's Gesammelte Schriften*, ed. Ludwig Tieck (Berlin: G. Reimer, 1826): 'Germania an ihre Kinder', pp. 338–40, 'An Franz den Ersten', p. 336, 'Kriegslied der Deutschen', p. 332; *H. v. Kleists Werke*, 4, ed. Erich Schmidt with Georg Minde-Pouet and Reinhold Steig (Leipzig; Vienna: Bibliographisches Institut, 1904), pp. 30–4 (text), pp. 242–3 (notes); Heinrich von Kleist, *Sämtliche Werke und Briefe*, 1, ed. Helmut Sembdner, 2nd revised ed. (Munich: Carl Hanser Verlag, 1961), pp. 25–9 (text), pp. 911–13 (notes); id., *Sämtliche Werke*, Brandenburger Kleist-Ausgabe, 3, ed. Peter Staengle and Roland Reuss (Basel; Frankfurt am Main: Stroemfeld; Roter Stern, 2005), pp. 77–160 (texts, commentaries and facsimiles).

Variants: Zweig was aware of the existence of a second version of 'Germania' (see the record card at Add MS 73168, f. 33 where he refers to sale catalogues of Henrici, Boerner und Breslauer). See Sembdner for a detailed comparison of all the variants. In the other two poems, Sembdner modernises spelling and some punctuation in a similar fashion but otherwise follows the Zweig manuscript. Tieck's main deviations in 'An Franz den Ersten' are his dating to 1 March 1809, whereas the manuscript has 9 April, and 'Und dem' for 'Und dein' in the last line.

Reproduced: 'Germania an ihre Kinder' is reproduced in full in *Zeitschrift für Bücherfreunde,* Jahrgang 11, Band 1 (1907/8), ed. Fedor von Zobeltitz (Bielefeld; Leipzig: Velhagen & Klasing, [1908]), between pages 44 and 45; Karl Strecker, *Heinrich von Kleist* (Bielefeld; Leipzig: Velhagen & Klasing, 1912), pp. 20–3; *Sämtliche Werke*, 3, op. cit., pp. 84–94 (Germania), 130–2 (An Franz den Ersten), 144–7 (Kriegslied), all with transcripts and with other manuscripts for comparison; www.bl.uk/manuscripts and Plate 31 below.

Exhibited: London, BL, 75 Musical and Literary Autographs, 1986 (f. 1).

Provenance: Owned in 1885 by Carl Meinert, autograph collector, of Dessau; sold as part of Alexander Meyer-Cohn Collection by Stargardt, Berlin, October 1905, no. 1705 in sale catalogue; auctioned by Boerner of Leipzig (catalogue no. 212) in 1907 and purchased by 'an antiquarian' (i.e. Adolf Weigel of Leipzig on behalf of Viktor Mannheimer); no. 307 in the Henrici catalogue XV for sale on 19 May 1913; purchased by Zweig from Mannheimer in January 1914 (1915 according to the

Brandenburger Ausgabe); BL 1986.

Bibliography: Stefan Zweig, *Der Kampf mit dem Dämon*, pp. 153–229; id., 'Meine Autographen-Sammlung'; Frels, *Deutsche Dichterhandschriften*, pp. 160–1; Eva Rothe and Helmut Sembdner, 'Kleists Handschriften und ihr Verbleib', in *Jahrbuch der deutschen Schiller-Gesellschaft*, 8. Jahrgang (Stuttgart: Alfred Kröner, 1964), pp. 324–43; Helmut Sembdner, *Kleist-Bibliographie, 1803–1862* (Stuttgart: Fritz Eggert, 1966); Hans Joachim Kreutzer, 'Über die Geschicke der Kleist-Handschriften und Kleists Handschrift', in *Kleist-Jahrbuch 1981/2* (Berlin: Erich Schmidt Verlag, 1983), pp. 66–85; BL Programme Book, 1987; *Catalogue of Additions*, p. 73; Helmut Sembdner, 'Kleists Kriegslyrik in unbekannten Fassungen', in *In Sachen Kleist: Beiträge zur Forschung*, 3rd expanded ed. (Munich; Vienna: Carl Hanser, 1994), pp. 88–98; Matuschek, pp. 258–9.

Commentary. The present manuscript cannot pre-date 1809 on the evidence of the subtitle to 'An Franz den Ersten' on f. 4. The *Catalogue of Additions* was in error in attributing it to 1806. There is a discrepancy in Tieck's dating of 1 March for that poem, and 9 April in the manuscript. Tieck thought 'Germania', not dated in the manuscript, was composed at Dresden in 1808, but Zobeltitz places it in the spring of 1809, when French troops under Napoleon were approaching the Danube. In those circumstances the patriotic tone would have been particularly appropriate, although the poem was not published immediately.

Kleist himself sent the three poems to Heinrich Josef von Collin in Vienna on 20 April 1809, telling him to give them to J. V. Degen, the court printer, or anyone else who would print them (see footnote on f. 1). He stressed that they should only be published separately, to allow their later re-use in a collected edition. In the event, they did not appear in print until after his death.

In his study of Kleist in *Der Kampf mit dem Dämon*, Zweig focused on his plays and novels, and compared Kleist to Dostoevsky. He argued that Kleist, in contrast to Hölderlin, Novalis and Goethe, used the German language as a weapon or plough, rather than a harp, and described him burning his papers before his death. Zweig was sufficiently impressed by 'Kriegslied der Deutschen' to recommend it to Hans Feigl for reproduction in the *Bibliophilen Kalender* (see Matuschek, p. 21). His record card (Add MS 73168, f. 33) describes the manuscript as 'Kostbarkeit aller ersten Ranges!'

Zweig also owned the following autograph manuscripts of Kleist: 'An die Königin von Preußen', 'An Friedrich Wilhelm den Dritten', 'An Wilhelmine von Zenge' and 'Die Bedingung des Gärtners', all now at the Bodmer Foundation, Geneva, and a fragment of the play *Der zerbrochene Krug*, now in the Staatsbibliothek zu Berlin.

Jean de La Fontaine
(1621–1695)

Zweig MS 165.

Autograph fair copy of five occasional verses, with a few corrections; 1660.

In *French*.

Contents:

1. f. 1. 'Madrigal. Au Roy, et a l'Infante'. Begins: 'Héureux couple d'amans, race de mille Roys'. Ends: 'que par celles de la fortune'. Six lines, probably written in January 1660, immediately before the marriage of Louis XIV and Maria Theresa of Spain.
2. f. 1. 'Autre Pour le Roy'. Begins: 'Que dites vous du coeur d'Alcandre'. Ends: 'Il n'a rien perdu pour attendre'. Four lines.
3. f. 1. 'Autre Sur le mesme suiect'. Begins: 'Dez que l'heure est venue Amour parle en vainqueur'. Ends: 'Et iamais a ces yeux on n'a rien refusé'. Six lines.
4. f. 1v. 'Épigramme. A Monseigneur le surintendant qui ne s'estoit pas contententé [*sic*] de trois madrigaux a la derniere St Jean'. Begins: 'Trois madrigaux ce n'est pas vostre conte'. Ends: 'Et tant plustost on s'en doit contenter'. Ten lines, addressed to Nicolas Fouquet, Finance Minister in the early years of Louis XIV's reign, to whom Jean de La Fontaine had been introduced and whose protégé he had become, receiving an income for the verses that he undertook to deliver every quarter.
5. f. 1v. 'Autre Pour l'Infante'. Begins: 'Ils sont partis, les ieux, les ris, les graces'. Ends: 'que nostre Reyne en merite sans faute'. Eleven lines. Written in January 1660.

To the right of the heading of the first verse is an original numbering, '6', and a note reading 'Par le même La Fontaine', to which has been added in a lighter ink 'et de Sa main'.

226 x 169mm.
f. 1.
Black ink on laid paper.
Bifolium.
No watermark.

Published: First verse in Jean de La Fontaine, *Œuvres diverses*, 3 (Paris: Barbou, 1729), p. 295; second verse in Mathieu Marais, *Histoire de la vie et des ouvrages de M. de La Fontaine* (Paris: Renouard, 1811), pp. 124–5; third and fourth verses in *Ouvrages de prose et de poësie. Des Srs de Maucroy, et de La Fontaine*, 1 (Paris: Claude Barbin, 1685), pp. 118, 119–20; fifth verse in La Fontaine, *Fables, nouvelles, et autres poësies* (Paris: Denys Thierry, 1671), p. 85. All published in id., *Œuvres completes*, 2, *Œuvres diverses*, ed. Pierre Clarac (Paris: Gallimard, 1958), pp. 499, 500, 508.

Reproduced: Lithograph copy of the fourth verse, 'Épigramme', reproduced as an example of La Fontaine's handwriting in Antoine Charles Marie Robert, *Fables inédites des XIIe, XIIIe et XIVe siècles*

et fables de La Fontaine, I (Paris: Étienne Cabin, 1825), p. xlii; www.bl.uk/manuscripts and Plate 32 below.
Exhibited: London, BL, 75 Musical and Literary Autographs, 1986.
Provenance: Apparently owned by Henri Fatio, early 20th century. Although Zweig originally notes the acquisition of the autograph at the Fatio sale, Noël Charavay, Paris, in 1932, he has subsequently changed the date to 1930 (Add MS 73168, f. 34); BL 1986.
Bibliography: Stefan Zweig, 'Von echten und falschen Autographen'; BL Programme Book, 1987; *Catalogue of Additions*, p. 73; Matuschek, p. 261.

Commentary. One of the foremost men of letters in seventeenth-century France, La Fontaine was particularly admired for his mastery of the nuances of the French language. Although remembered above all for his fables, he also wrote some very successful tales and verses. Possibly appearing slight in comparison with his other works, the verses nevertheless played an important role in his life, since they earned him a regular income for several years.

Both in his 1927 article on genuine and forged autographs and on his record card for the present autograph, Zweig mentions the fact that there are many examples of forged La Fontaine verses in circulation. In this instance, however, he was confident of the authenticity of his own acquisition.

Jean Henri Latude
(1725–1805)

Zweig MS 166.

'vingtieme Cahier de la copie du Memoire pour Monsieur de Sartine Conseiller d'Etat lieutenant général de police Envoyé du donjon de vincennes le 1 9bre 1770 a une heure du soir', *autograph* manuscript; 1770.

In *French*.
Begins: 'Grand dieu aye pitié de moy'.
Ends: 'je te conjure ... de supplier Mr de Sartine de lire au moins ce dernier cahier. fini le premier de novembre 1770'.
Part twenty of the *Mémoire* sent by Latude from prison in Vincennes to M. de Sartine, Lieutenant-General of the Police. Signed on f. 24v with both Latude's assumed names, 'Danry ou mieux Henri Masers secretaire'. The notebook also includes a dedication (ff. 3v–4) dated Paris, 1 January 1789 to 'Monsieur le Comte', an etched portrait of the author (f. 2) and an authentication by F.[?] Decaïeu (f. 1). Latude complains in a repetitious manner of his treatment in prison, the searching of his room and the refusal to send him a confessor. He alleges that the notebooks he has previously sent to M. Sartine have not been delivered or read, because Sartine has been bewitched by the Marquis de Marigny. He can make second copies from memory and begs Sartine to read the *Mémoire*.

Largest sheet 156 x 88mm.
ff. 24. With original numbering 413–452 (the last leaf has 443 and 444 deleted).
Black ink on unbleached rag paper.
No watermark.
Bound notebook.
Marbled paper covers, loosely inserted in a portfolio of matching paper-covered boards, half bound in red morocco and gold-tooled.

Related Manuscripts: Latude wrote and re-wrote accounts of his imprisonment in many forms, and unauthorised versions and forgeries have contributed to the complexity of the tradition. For sources see Claude Quétel, *Les Évasions de Latude* (Paris: Denoël, 1986), pp. 203–4. The whereabouts of the other nineteen manuscripts of the *Mémoire* of which this is part twenty is not clear. No other manuscript copy of the present notebook has been identified.
Published: Latude's *Mémoires* were edited and published from various sources and translated into English and German at an early date, though these editions were not explicitly based on Zweig MS 166. See Quétel, op. cit.
Reproduced: www.bl.uk/manuscripts and Plate 33 below.
Provenance: Purchased by Zweig from Maggs, June

1931, catalogue 560, no. 566. The sale catalogue also mentions a translation which is not present; BL 1986.

Bibliography: BL Programme Book, 1987; *Catalogue of Additions*, p. 73; Matuschek, p. 262. For biographical details, see Quétel, op. cit. and Franz Funck-Brentano, *Légendes et Archives de la Bastille* (Paris: Hachette, 1948), pp. 135–212.

Commentary. The author of the *Mémoire* was an illegitimate child, known simply as Jean Henri until he adopted the name Danry and later the title Viscount Masers de Latude. Imprisoned initially on account of an imaginary plot to poison Madame de Pompadour with a booby-trapped parcel, he was sent to the Bastille on 1 May 1749. For the next twenty-eight years he was effectively a prisoner of the state. In his confinement, Latude was constantly engaged in writing and re-writing his memoirs, which became increasingly confused and exaggerated. Over the years he made numerous appeals to the Lieutenant General of Police of Paris, Antoine de Sartine, comte d'Alby, but these were apparently intercepted by the warders and not delivered. Eventually, in March 1771, the confessor Latude had repeatedly requested arrived. In a clear reference to the present Zweig MS 166, Latude wrote of the meeting: '...je lui dis que le 1er novembre de l'année dernière 1770, je lui avais envoyé un grand mémoire à ce sujet, et que je croyais qu'il avait été étouffé.' See *Mémoires authentiques de Latude*, ed. F. Funck-Brentano (Paris: Arthème Fayard, [1911]), p. 118. Latude continued to send letters in vain to Sartine and his successor, and only gained his release in 1784 after thirty-five years in prison. During the Revolution he was regarded as a victim of tyranny, a view which Zweig seemed to share.

Giacomo Leopardi
(1798–1837)

Zweig MS 167.

'XXXVIII. Dal greco di Simonide', verses: *autograph* draft, with a few major amendments; 1823–4.

In *Italian*.
Begins: 'Ogni mondano evento'.
Ends: 'Ed al mal proprio suo cotanto amore'.
Free translation of a Greek poem by Semonides of Amorgos (thought by Leopardi to be Simonides of Ceos), with a few major amendments. 'G. Leopardi' written at foot of f. 1v in a different hand with a lighter shade of ink. An authentication note in German on the verso of the second leaf reads 'Handschrift von Giac / Leopardi von Reca / nati – berühmter / moderner dichter / nach Niebuhr erster / Philolog in Italien. Von [?Doct] Schulz erhalten'.

133 x 97mm.
ff. 2.
Black and brown ink on laid paper.
Bifolium.
Watermark: partial dove in circle.

Related Manuscripts: Biblioteca Nazionale di Napoli, C.L., X, 1, 2a, ff. 3–3v; Biblioteca Nazionale di Napoli, C.L., X, 1, 2b. The present manuscript, which bears the page numbers 35 and 36, appears to have been taken from this volume, which lacks 'Ogni mondano evento'.
Published: First published in the posthumous edition of *Canti*, ed. Antonio Ranieri in *Opere di Giacomo Leopardi*, 1 (Florence: Felice le Monnier, 1845); *Tutte le Opere di Giacomo Leopardi*, ed. Francesco Flora, 'Le Poesie e le Prose', 1 (Milan: Mondadori, 1945), p. 135.
Reproduced: www.bl.uk/manuscripts and Plate 34 below.
Provenance: Apparently owned by Heinrich Wilhelm Schulz, art historian and museum director, Dresden, before 1855; purchased by Zweig through Eugen Wolbe at the sale of S. Martin Fraenkel, Berlin, 29 May 1922, lot 256; BL 1986.
Bibliography: Stefan Zweig, 'Meine Autographen-Sammlung'; BL Programme Book, 1987; *Catalogue of Additions*, p. 73; Matuschek, p. 268; Lorenzo Abbate, 'Un autografo leopardiano sconosciuto di "Ogni mondano evento" (Canti, XL)', in *Cognitive Philology*, 7 (2014).

Commentary. Leopardi made a series of translations from some of the Greek poets in 1823 and 1824, considering them to be 'Versi morali' rather than 'Canti'. They do not seem to have been published in Leopardi's lifetime, but two translations from Simonides (the present one included) were ultimately added with other fragmentary material to Ranieri's posthumous edition of the *Canti* in 1845.

Zweig must have been delighted to acquire this autograph, described in the Fraenkel sale catalogue as 'selten'. Not only does it illustrate Leopardi's thought processes through its corrections, but it also makes an important contribution to widening the international range of his collection.

John Locke
(1632–1704)

Zweig MS 168.

Epitaph on René Descartes: *autograph* fair copy of the inscription on a memorial tablet; [1670s?].

In *Latin*.
Begins: 'VIR SUPRA TITULOS OMNIUM RETRO PHILOSOPHORUM'.
Ends: 'I NUNC VIATOR / ET DIVINITATIS IMMORTALITATISQUE ANIMAE / MAXIMUM ET CLARUM ASSERTOREM / AUT IAM CREDE FAELICEM AUT PRECIBUS REDDE'.
The verse of twenty-eight lines, written in capital letters on vellum, is pasted down as f. 4 on a sheet of paper (f. 1) which also includes an engraving of Descartes (f. 2) and annotations by subsequent owners (f. 3). The Descartes portrait is engraved by Jean-Baptiste de Grateloup (1735–1817), after a painting by Frans Hals. The dates indicate that the epitaph and portrait were not brought together by Locke himself but by a subsequent owner.
The annotations are as follows:
On the portrait 'p 312' in pencil.
On f. 3 in ink 'Epitaph of Descartes, in the hand-writing of Locke, from whom it descended to Lord King, his Biographer, & was by his Lordship given to Jno. Whishaw Esq., & by him to me D. T.' Another hand has expanded 'urner' in pencil to identify Dawson Turner, and repeated 'p 312'.
On f. 4, top left-hand corner, 'Parisus in ecclesia Ste Genev[i]eve'.
The Hinterberger catalogue number 'XVIII/145' is written in pencil on the support sheet (f. 1) with 'RRZ· John Locke'.
a/c RZZ

Support sheet (f. 1) 271 x 212mm; engraving (f. 2) 103 x 72mm; epitaph (f. 4) 94 x 75mm.
ff. 4 (rectos only visible).
Epitaph copied in black ink on white vellum.
No watermark visible.

Published: Epitaph published from the tablet by Ellis Veryard, *An Account of Divers Choice Remarks* (London: S. Smith and B. Walford, 1701), p. 63. This published version is very close to Zweig MS 168, which suggests that both were copied carefully from the inscription. In line 13, Locke gives Descartes's age correctly as 54, whereas Veryard has printed 45. Locke then omits the next line 'Tandem post septem & decem annos', evidently his error. Also transcribed in Awnsham Churchill and Jean Barbot, *A Collection of Voyages and Travels*, 6 (London: John Walthoe, 1732), p. 94. The version here contains several misreadings as compared with Locke's MS and Veryard, but Descartes's age at 54 is correct.
Reproduced: www.bl.uk/manuscripts and Plate 35 below.
Provenance: Bequeathed by Locke to Peter King, 1st Baron King (1669–1734); given by King to John

Whishaw (1764/5–1840); given by Whishaw to the antiquary Dawson Turner (1775–1858); sold as part of Turner's collection by Puttick and Simpson, 6–10 June 1859; the date and immediate source of acquisition by Zweig are not known; offered for sale by Zweig in 1937 through Hinterberger, Vienna, catalogue XVIII, no. 145 (Add MS 73183 C); not sold and returned to the collection; BL 1986.

Bibliography: BL Programme Book, 1987; *Catalogue of Additions*, p. 73; Matuschek, p. 273.

Commentary. René Descartes (1596–1650), French mathematician and philosopher, had travelled as tutor to Queen Christina of Sweden to Stockholm where he died on 11 February 1650. After initial burial there, his remains were transferred in 1667 to the Church of Sainte-Geneviève-du-Mont in Paris, where they remained until that church fell into disuse during the French Revolution. In 1793 they were reinterred temporarily in the Jardin Elysée des Monuments Français, before finally coming to rest in the Abbey of Saint-Germain-des-Près.

Desmond M. Clarke, *Descartes: A Biography* (Cambridge: Cambridge University Press, 2006), says 'Clerselier provided a suitable epitaph, which was inscribed on a marble stone to mark the place where Descartes was buried in the nave of the church [of Ste. Geneviève-du-Mont].' Claude Clerselier (1614–84) was the editor and translator of Descartes who inherited his papers. Ellis Veryard described the memorial tablet as 'a small Marble in the Wall near the place where the late famous Renatus Cartesius lies buried'.

Locke is believed to have begun reading mechanical philosophy and the works of Descartes whilst at Oxford in the early 1660s. He spent a few weeks in Paris in the autumn of 1672 and was again in France, first in Montpellier and then in Paris as tutor to the son of Sir John Banks, from 1675 to 1679. It is likely that he copied the inscription at Ste. Geneviève-du-Mont during the 1670s.

Louis XVI, King of France
(1754–1793)

Zweig MS 169.

'a l'Assemblee Nationale', *signed* address to the Legislative [National] Assembly, notifying members of his response to the Holy Roman Emperor's protest at the ultimatum delivered to the Elector of Trier; 31 December 1791.

In *French.*
Begins: 'J'ai charge le Ministre des affaires etrangeres, MM, de vous communiquer l'office que l'Empereur a fait remettre a l'Ambassadeur de France a Vienne'.
Ends: 'je regarderai toujours le maintien de sa dignité et de sa sureté comme le plus essentiel de mes devoirs. Louis'.
Louis had asked the Minister of Foreign Affairs to communicate to the Assembly the protest delivered by the Emperor to the French Ambassador at Vienna. The protest was a surprise, because the Emperor was considered an ally, but he may have believed mistakenly that the Elector of Trier was meeting his obligations as a good neighbour. Louis assures the Assembly that in his answer to the Emperor he stated that he made only reasonable demands to the Elector, reiterating the French desire for peace, but warning that if the émigrés were not dispersed by the deadline, military force would be used. He says that if the ultimatum does not have the desired effect, he will make the whole of Europe aware that the French cause is just, and he will uphold the dignity and security of the nation. Aside from the pencil annotation 'Luis XVI' [*sic*], f. 2 is blank.

230 x 187mm.
ff. 2; 2v blank.
Black ink on white laid paper.
Bifolium.
Partial watermark at centre fold.

Published: *Gazette nationale ou Le Moniteur universal*, 1 December 1792, p. 5.
Reproduced: www.bl.uk/manuscripts and Plate 36 below.
Provenance: Purchased by Zweig at Sotheby's sale, London, 29 July 1930, lot 368, via Maggs. The provenance is not given. The BL Department of Manuscripts' copy of the sale catalogue is annotated in the margin 'Maggs £ 41'. Annotated envelope in Add MS 73175, ff. 41–2. Record card Add MS 73168, f. 38. Zweig noted 'Welthistorisches Dokument'. 'Der berühmte eigenhändige Erlass an die Assemblé Legislative, Ankündigung des Ultimatum an das deutsche Reich'. He mistakenly transcribed the date, written 31 Xbre 1791, as 31 Okt 1791; BL 1986.
Bibliography: BL Programme Book, 1987; *Catalogue of Additions*, p. 73; Matuschek, p. 274.

Commentary. Although addressed to the National Assembly, this document would have been received by the Legislative Assembly which had succeeded the disbanded National Constituent Assembly on 1 October 1791. The issue under discussion was the perceived threat to France from émigrés, mostly nobles unsympathetic to the Revolution, who had moved out to the Austrian Netherlands and German states. On 9 November the Legislative Assembly had decreed that émigrés who did not return would be considered traitors and would face the death penalty. However, Louis had vetoed the decree. By the end of November, Louis was under pressure to demand that the rulers of the neighbouring territories expel the émigrés. He issued an ultimatum to the Elector of Trier, threatening military action if the expulsions were not carried out by 15 January, and wrote to the Emperor seeking his continued support. The ultimatum apparently caused the Emperor to lodge a protest with the French Ambassador. In consequence, Louis was obliged to reiterate and justify to the Assembly, in the present document, the terms of the ultimatum. The Elector of Trier began to take action to disperse the émigrés early in January 1792. Louis himself was deposed and arrested on 13 August 1792 and guillotined on 21 January 1793.

Stefan Zweig also owned a marriage treaty signed by four French kings, including Louis XVI. He acquired it in 1932 but its present whereabouts is unknown (see Matuschek, p. 205).

Stéphane Mallarmé
(1842–1898)

Zweig MS 170.

Signed *autograph* fair copy of an untitled sonnet; [*c.* 1887].

In *French.*
Begins: 'La chevelure vol d'une flamme à l'extrême'.
Ends: 'Ainsi qu'une joyeuse et tutélaire torche'.
Headed 'Sonnet', starred with a reference to a footnote 'Sur le rythme de la Renaissance anglaise'. Superficially the sonnet is a celebration of a woman whose magnificent golden-red hair encapsulates the essence of her inner beauty which needs no further embellishment. The poem occupies fourteen lines, without punctuation apart from the brackets in the third line, arranged in the form of a traditional Shakespearean sonnet of three quatrains with alternating rhyme and a rhyming couplet.

195 x 153mm.
f. 1; 1v blank.
Black ink on laid paper.
Watermark: lion and crown above 'ORIGINAL STAIRS MILL'.

Published: Published as part of the prose poem 'La Déclaration foraine', written for the ladies' journal *L'Art et la mode*, 37 (12 August 1887), pp. 440–2. Published as a separate poem (untitled) in *Les Poésies de S. Mallarmé* (Brussels: Edmond Deman, 1899), pp. 71–2.
Reproduced: www.bl.uk/manuscripts and Plate 37 below.

Provenance: Acquired by Zweig in June 1926 from Simon Kra, Paris; BL 1986.
Bibliography: Austin Gill, *Mallarmé's Poem 'La chevelure vol d'une flamme...'* (Glasgow: University of Glasgow, 1971); BL Programme Book, 1987; *Catalogue of Additions*, pp. 73–4; Matuschek, p. 275.

Commentary. Writing the sonnet for publication in a piece in a ladies' journal, Mallarmé may well have received the inspiration for its subject from a potential reader of that journal, his muse Méry Laurent, a lady of the Parisian demi-monde, with whom he was very preoccupied at the time. The literal meaning of the sonnet is of little consequence, however, as the piece is open to many layers of subtle symbolic interpretation which have been widely discussed.

Zweig regarded this manuscript (which he described as 'sehr selten') as a particularly important acquisition, because to the best of his knowledge there was no other literary manuscript by Mallarmé in a private collection (record card Add MS 73168, f. 40).

Marie Antoinette, Queen of France
(1755–1793)

Zweig MS 171.

Autograph letter from Marie Antoinette to Count [Xavier] von Rosenberg; 17 April [1775].

In *French*.
Begins: 'le plaisir que j'ai eu a causer avec vous'.
Ends: 'du plaisir que j'aurai a recevoir de vos lettres, j'y compte'.
Letter, signed 'Antoinette', in which Marie Antoinette speaks frankly and somewhat indiscreetly of her lack of compatibility with the King and her disillusionment with life at court. Corresponding vertical and horizontal creases on the two leaves and a small red wax seal below the address 'A Monsieur le comte de Rosenberg' on the second leaf provide an indication of the format of the letter as it was sent.

189 x 136mm.
ff. 2.
Brown ink on laid paper, written on recto and verso of first leaf only.
Bifolium. Wax seal stamped with Queen's arms on f. 2v.
Watermark: shield with posthorn above 'D&CBLAUW'.

Published: *Maria Theresia und Marie Antoinette: Ihr Briefwechsel*, ed. Alfred Ritter von Arneth, 2nd augmented ed. (Leipzig: Köhler, 1866), pp. 144–5. Zweig's record card for the manuscript (Add MS 73168, f. 41) states erroneously that 1867 was the date of the first publication by Arneth. *Marie-Antoinette: correspondance secrète entre Marie-Thérèse et le Cte de Mercy-Argenteau*, 2 (Paris: Librairie de Firmin Didot Frères, 1874), pp. 361–2.
Reproduced: Matuschek, p. 279; www.bl.uk/manuscripts and Plate 38 below.

Exhibited: London, BL, 75 Musical and Literary Autographs, 1986.
Provenance: Zweig acquired the manuscript in May 1933 from Countess Anna Orsini Rosenberg (Zweig's pencil note, f. 2). Two letters from the Countess confirm that the letter had remained with the Rosenberg family throughout the centuries (Add MS 53175, ff. 44–7); BL 1986.
Bibliography: Stefan Zweig, *Marie-Antoinette: Bildnis eines mittleren Charakters* (Leipzig: Insel Verlag, 1932); BL Programme Book, 1987; *Catalogue of Additions*, p. 74; Matuschek, p. 279.

Commentary. Zweig was fascinated by the figure of Marie Antoinette, and in 1932 published a highly successful biography of her, based chiefly on the correspondence with her mother and with her great love, Count Axel von Fersen. While carrying out the research for this biography, Zweig came across many Marie Antoinette letters that were clearly of dubious authenticity, so it must have been particularly pleasing for him to acquire the present letter for his collection, not only on account of its revealing and characteristic contents, but also because it possessed an absolutely impeccable provenance.

Thomas Moore
(1779–1852)

Zweig MS 172.

''Tis the last rose of summer', poem: *autograph* fair copy; 1805–13.

In *English*.
Begins: ''Tis the last rose of summer / Left blooming alone'.
Ends: 'O! who would inhabit / This blaek [for bleak] world alone?'.
Poem of three eight-line stanzas from Moore's *Irish Melodies*.
With 'Thomas Moore' at the end in a different hand and ink, and with Zweig's annotation 'Sein berühmtes Gedicht' in pencil (f. 2).

199 x 165mm.
ff. 2; 2v blank.
Black ink on laid paper.
Bifolium.
No watermark.

Related Manuscripts: The British Library holds a setting of the poem with piano accompaniment in the hand of and probably by Johann Nepomuk Hummel, *c.* 1829, in Add MS 32189, f. 108v, and a nineteenth-century copy in MS Mus. 1038, f. 37.

Published: Published in many editions. Among the earliest are: *A Selection of Irish Melodies with Symphonies and Accompaniments by Sir John Stevenson ... Words by Thomas Moore* (London; Dublin: J. Power, [1813]), pp. 14–15; *The Works of Thomas Moore Esq ... never before published without the accompanying music*, 4 (Paris: Galignani, 1819), pp. 121–2.

Reproduced: Both folios in the BL Programme book, 1988, p. 36; f. 1 in Matuschek, p. 289; www.bl.uk/manuscripts and Plate 39 below.

Provenance: Purchased by Zweig at auction, Hellmut Meyer [& Ernst], Berlin, 14 February 1930; BL 1986.

Bibliography: *A Catalogue of Vocal Music by Thomas Moore Esq and Sir John Stevenson, Mus. Doc. printed for J. Power* (London: printed by Conway and Rayer, 1815); BL Programme Books, 1987 and 1988; *Catalogue of Additions*, p. 74; Matuschek, pp. 288–9.

Commentary. The Irish poet Thomas Moore composed this poem in 1805 at Jenkinstown Park in Kilkenny. It became, in Zweig's opinion, 'einer der populärsten der englischen Sprache' (Add MS 73168, f. 44). Originally sung to the air 'Castle Hyde' or 'Groves of Blarney', the version published in *Irish Melodies* in 1813 was set by Sir John Stevenson (1762–1833), who collaborated with Moore on several works for the same series. Other composers including Beethoven, Mendelssohn, Friedrich von Flotow and Benjamin Britten arranged or wrote variations on it. Zweig also owned Moore's autograph poem 'Returning from America after a Storm', now at the Bodmer Foundation, Geneva.

Joachim Murat
(1767–1815)

Zweig MS 173.

Autograph letter as King of Naples to General Augustin Daniel Belliard; Naples, 18 May [1809].

In *French*.

Begins: 'Mon cher Belliard On est entré à Vienne le 9, l'Empereur fait des merveilles à son ordinaire'.

Ends: 'Adieu, reviens, tu connais mon amitié'.

The letter reflects Murat's reaction to events in the European war and Napoleon's entry into Vienna on 9 May 1809. Murat himself is in Naples prepared for the enemy to disembark. The letter is annotated at the head of f. 1, 'Naples 18 Mai' in ink in another hand (the day and month are given in autograph at the end). 'Moody's L', '18' and 'Murat' are written in pencil at the top left of f. 1, and at the top right is the instruction in ink 'faire une Copie'.

248 x 200mm.
ff. 2.
Black ink on cream wove paper.
Bifolium.
Watermark: partial, indistinct watermark in lower right-hand corner of f. 1.

Related Manuscripts: The Murat family archives are in the private sector of the Archives Nationales de France. For the history of the family papers, see Paul le Brethon's Introduction, cited below. The present letter has apparently not survived in the correspondence registers of the King of Naples or the special personal register mentioned by Le Brethon on p. xxxiii.

Published: Alphonse Wyatt Thibaudeau, *Catalogue of the Collection of Autograph Letters and Historical Documents formed between 1865 and 1882 by Alfred Morrison*, 4 [letter M] (London: Printed for private circulation, 1890), p. 326; *Lettres et documents pour servir à l'histoire de Joachim Murat*, 7, introduction and notes by Paul le Brethon (Paris: Librairie Plon, 1913), pp. 231–2.

Reproduced: www.bl.uk/manuscripts and Plate 40 below.

Provenance: From the collection of Alfred Morrison and sold at Sotheby's, 15 April 1918, as lot 850 in the second sale; purchased by F. Sabin for £4 5s od. It is likely that Zweig bought the manuscript subsequently through another dealer or auction. Zweig himself did not buy at the Morrison sale, but he had seen the Thibaudeau catalogue briefly at the Bibliothèque nationale in Paris, as described in his essay 'Die Sammlung Morrisson'; BL 1986.

Bibliography: BL Programme Book, 1987; *Catalogue of Additions*, p. 74; Matuschek, p. 290. For background to the events of May–June 1809 in Naples, see Hubert Cole, *The Betrayers: Joachim and Caroline Murat* (London: Eyre Methuen, 1972), pp. 117–23.

Commentary. Joachim Murat was Duke of Cleves and Berg, 1806–8, then from 1 August 1808 King of Naples and Sicily under the Italianised name of Gioacchino-Napoleone. He was the brother-in-law of Napoleon Bonaparte. At the time of writing, he was in Naples, eager to join forces with Napoleon in Austria but ordered by him to remain in Italy, and facing the immediate threat of a British landing from ships arriving off the coast from Sicily. His correspondent, the French general Augustin Daniel Belliard, Comte Belliard (1769–1832), was serving in Spain, where he was to be appointed Governor of Madrid in July 1809.

Benito Mussolini
(1883–1945)

Zweig MS 174.

'Responsibilità', article: *autograph* fair copy; 1921.

In *Italian.*
Begins: 'Piu volte in articoli e in discorsi abbiamo precisato il carattere, definito il "tipo" della violenza fascista'.
Ends: 'I fascisti di tutta Italia si tengano serrati e pronti a tutti gli eventi'.
The article openly proclaims the violent nature of fascism. Signed at the end. It is written on scrap paper bearing signs of earlier use. F. 2 is the bottom half of a sheet of flimsy paper torn from a carbon copy of a previous document, of which five typewritten lines remain on the verso; f. 3v contains part of a typed letter sent from the office of Ugo Lombardi, Milan, dated 25 February 1921; f. 4v contains a printed text in French, beginning 'Les deux cent milles réfugiés bulgares de la Thrace' and ending 'l'anéantissement systématique des populations slaves recommença par le fer et le feu'.

Largest sheet 233 x 215mm.
ff. 4.
Black ink on wove paper.

Published: First appeared as the leader article in *Il Popolo d'Italia*, 51 (1 March 1921) (copy of the published article kept with the provenance papers, Add MS 73175, f. 61); *Opera Omnia di Benito Mussolini*, 16, ed. Edoardo and Duilio Susmel (Venice: La Fenice, 1955), pp. 189–90.
Reproduced: www.bl.uk/manuscripts and Plate 41 below.

Provenance: Purchased by Zweig on 9 October 1926 from the bookseller Rudolf Geering in Basel; BL 1986.
Bibliography: Zweig, 'Meine Autographen-Sammlung'; BL Programme Book, 1987; *Catalogue of Additions*, p. 74; Matuschek, p. 291.

Commentary. The newspaper *Il Popolo d'Italia*, founded by Mussolini after his split from the Italian Socialist Party in 1914 and in circulation from 15 November 1914 until 24 July 1943, became the foundation for the Fascist movement in Italy after the First World War. The inclusion of this item in Zweig's collection may in the first place have had something to do with his fascination for strong, powerful figures, although above all it seems to have been added for its importance as a piece of writing of great historical significance, '[ein] ungemein wichtiger, ja historischer Aufsatz' (Zweig's record card, Add MS 73168, f. 45). In *The World of Yesterday* Zweig does, however, describe a personal link to the dictator, since Mussolini responded positively 'to the first request I ever made of a statesman' (p. 368). Zweig was called upon by the wife of a doctor –

imprisoned for his association with the murdered socialist Giacomo Matteoti – to reach out to influential acquaintances, who might be able to convince Mussolini to reduce the sentence. Unsuccessful, he wrote directly to the leader, who was incidentally an enthusiastic reader of Zweig's work. Four days later, Zweig received a letter accepting his requests and the doctor ultimately received a full pardon. He notes, 'No letter in my life has ever given me so much delight and satisfaction, and if I ever think of my own literary success, it is this instance of it that I remember with especial gratitude' (*The World of Yesterday*, trans. by Anthea Bell (London: Pushkin, 2009), p. 370).

Friedrich Nietzsche
(1844–1900)

Zweig MS 175.

'Die Geburt des tragischen Gedankens', treatise: *autograph* fair copy; June 1870.

In *German.*

Begins: 'Die Griechen, die die Geheimlehren ihrer Weltanschauung in ihren Göttern aussprechen und zugleich verschweigen'.

Ends: 'Der Kampf beider Erscheinungsformen des Willens hatte ein ausserordentliches Ziel, eine *höhere Möglichkeit des Daseins* zu schaffen und auch in dieser zu einer noch *höheren Verherrlichung* – durch die Kunst – zu kommen'.

In roman script with a few alterations and underlining for emphasis. Signed on the title page. An early version of Nietzsche's first major work, *Die Geburt der Tragödie*, closely related to the essay of the same period entitled *Die Dionysische Weltanschauung*. The argument revolves around the creative tension between Apollonian and Dionysian views of the world, Apollo representing control and reason as opposed to Dionysus's spontaneity and rapture. Balancing these forces enables a higher level of existence to be experienced through art, of which Greek tragedy is the ultimate expression.

An *autograph* note at the foot of f. 1 states the date of composition as 'Aus dem Juni des Jahres 1870'. The manuscript is thought to be a fair copy, written out later that year as a Christmas gift. Stefan Zweig's inscription in pencil on the verso of f. i reads: 'Die Geburt der Tragödie. Für Cosima Wagner abgeschrieben, frühe und bis 1931 unbekannte Fassung. Stammt aus dem Besitz der Frau Thode, Cosimas Tochter. Stefan Zweig'.

Binding 230 x 192mm. Leaves 222 x 190mm.
ff. i + 30; versos blank.
Black ink on cream wove paper.
No watermark.
Contemporary binding of brown cloth. Glossy flyleaves.

Related Manuscripts: See Hans Joachim Mette, *Der handschriftliche Nachlaß Friedrich Nietzsches*, Jahresgabe der Gesellschaft der Freunde des Nietzsche-Archivs, 6 (Leipzig: Richard Hadl, 1932, reprint Nendeln: Kraus, 1975); *Nietzsche Werke Kritische Gesamtausgabe*, III, 5/1 and 2, ed. G. Colli and M. Montinari (Berlin: Walter de Gruyter, 1997), here cited as *KGW*. Most of the surviving Nietzsche manuscripts are held by the Klassik Stiftung Weimar, housed in the Goethe- und Schiller- Archiv (GSA). The connections and sequence of the plans, drafts, notes and fragments eventually developed into *Die Geburt der Tragödie* is very complex, but the principal manuscript sources in GSA are: U I 2 (GSA 71/104b). Contains autograph preparatory work for *Die Geburt der Tragödie*, including the essay 'Die

Dionysische Weltanschauung'. See Mette, p. 41 and *KGW* III, 5/2, pp. 1332–3; Mp-XII-1a-d (GSA 71/228). Autograph preparatory work for *Die Geburt der Tragödie*, 1871. See Mette, pp. 51–2 and *KGW* III, 5/2, pp. 1295–7; D 3 (GSA 71/3). Autograph printer's copy for *Sokrates und die griechische Tragoedie*, 1871, and *Die Geburt der Tragödie aus dem Geiste der Musik*, 1872. See Mette, pp. 4, 7 and *KGW* III, 5/2, pp. 1279–83.

Published: The developed treatise, for which Zweig MS 175 represents early first thoughts, was published as *Die Geburt der Tragödie aus dem Geiste der Musik* (Leipzig: E. W. Fritzsch, 1872); the first publication of the present manuscript was in *KGW* III/2, *Nachgelassene Schriften, 1870–1873* (Berlin: Walter de Gruyter, 1973), pp. 71–91, where it is identified as GG. The manuscript is almost identical with the published *Dionysische Weltanschauung*, but lacks the ending on pp. 30–41 and also displays minor variants.

Reproduced: The title page is reproduced in *KGW* III/2, p. 72; www.bl.uk/manuscripts and Plate 42 below.

Exhibited: London, BL, 75 Musical and Literary Autographs, 1986; London, Christie's, etc., The Creative Spirit, 1987–8.

Provenance: Presented by Nietzsche to Cosima Wagner, 1870; after Cosima's death, her daughter Daniela Thode entrusted the manuscript to Hugo Helbing, art and book dealer, who agreed an exchange with Zweig, though it is not clear what he received in return. The record card in Add MS 73168, f. 48 reads 'Nie ein Mcpt. Nietzsches in diesem Umfang aufgetaucht'. Zweig described it as an 'Erste Fassung', unknown before 1931; BL 1986.

Bibliography: Stefan Zweig, *Der Kampf mit dem Dämon*, pp. 231–322; id., 'Meine Autographen-Sammlung'; Frels, *Deutsche Dichterhandschriften*, pp. 216–17; BL Programme Book, 1987; *Catalogue of Additions*, p. 74; Matuschek, p. 294.

Commentary. Already in 1870, Nietzsche had delivered two lectures at the museum in Basel on subjects related in content to the present manuscript: 'Das griechische Musikdrama' on 18 January and 'Sokrates und die Tragödie' on 1 February. He was also developing the ideas in the 'Dionysische Weltanschauung' which he finished in mid-August. In this context, 'Die Geburt des tragischen Gedankens' is another working of the same material, not intended for immediate publication, though he was sufficiently confident of its worth to give away a fair copy as a gift to Cosima Wagner, daughter of Franz Liszt and second wife of Richard Wagner, for Christmas 1870.

Zweig visited the Nietzsche Archiv in Weimar with Romain Rolland in 1925, as he reported in a letter to Friderike Zweig on 10 June: '[wir] waren gestern im Nietzsche-Archiv, wo die uralte Frau Foerster-Nietzsche sich wie ein Kind über Rollands Besuch freute und zu mir über mein Buch ganz gegen meine Erwartung *rührend* und dankbar war'. Elisabeth Foerster-Nietzsche (1846–1935) was the philosopher's sister who established the archive housing his papers in Naumburg in 1894. Two years later it was transferred to Weimar, still in her care. The papers are now held by the Klassik Stiftung Weimar and housed in the Goethe- und Schiller-Archiv.

Zweig's book referred to in the letter was his study of Nietzsche, together with Hölderlin and Kleist, in vol. 2 of the 'Baumeister der Welt' series. He compared Nietzsche with Dostoevsky in his overcoming adversity through creative will, and in his excessive sensibility. He described his style in a musical metaphor: 'His German reads like an orchestral score, a prose sometimes written for a small band of players and at other times for a considerable company. An artist in language finds as much delight in the study of Nietzsche's polyphony as a musician in examining the score of a master composer.' (Quoted from the translation by Eden and Cedar Paul, *Hölderlin, Kleist und Nietzsche: The Struggle with the Daemon* (reissue New Brunswick: Transaction Publishers, 2011), p. 508).

Zweig also owned the following autograph manuscripts of Nietzsche: a piano duet 'Nachklang einer Sylvesternacht', British Library Zweig MS 71, described in Arthur Searle, *The British Library Stefan Zweig Collection: Catalogue of the Music Manuscripts* (London: British Library, 1999), p. 87; 'An Goethe', poem, now in the Goethe Museum, Dusseldorf; 'Euphorion', 'Heimkehr', three poems from 'Lieder des Prinzen Vogelfrei', and 'Briefmanifest an Ferdinand Avenarius', all now held at the Bodmer Foundation, Geneva. In 'Meine Autographen-Sammlung' Zweig mentioned three further Nietzsche manuscripts as being in his possession in 1930.

'Novalis'
(pseudonym of Georg Philipp Friedrich von Hardenberg)
(1772–1801)

Zweig MS 176.

Astralis poem from 'Die Erfüllung', part of the novel *Heinrich von Ofterdingen*: *autograph* draft; [1800].

In *German*.

Heading: 'Heinrich von Afterdingen. / Ein Roman / von / Novalis. / 2ter Theil. / Die Erfüllung. / Das Kloster, oder der Vorhof. [inserted] / [deletion] Astralis.'

Begins: 'An einen Sommermorgen ward ich jung'.

Ends: 'Das Herz, als Asche, niederfällt'.

The second part of *Heinrich von Ofterdingen,* entitled 'Die Erfüllung', opens with a verse prologue of ninety lines in four or five foot iambics, assigned to Astralis. This mysterious spirit of the stars describes his creation through the first kiss exchanged between Heinrich the hero and his lover Mathilde. 'Afterdingen' as written here was changed to 'Ofterdingen' before publication. The line setting the scene beginning 'Das Kloster' appears to be in a different ink and may have been added later by Novalis himself or possibly by his editor Ludwig Tieck. The word deleted before 'Astralis' has been read by Sophia Vietor as 'Genius', which would indicate a significant change of mind about the nature of the speaker.

The text is heavily corrected, especially on f. 2 where a block of six lines is deleted and alternatives are written in the margin. Written in *Kurrentschrift*, but the words 'Mathilde' and 'Genius' (if the reading is correct) are in roman script, which Novalis sometimes used for proper names.

244 x 197mm.
ff. 2.
Brown ink on cream laid paper.
No watermark.

Related Manuscripts: British Library Zweig MS 176 is the only extant manuscript of the Astralis poem. Other extant fragments of the novel include: a draft of the first leaf of Part I, counterpart to the first leaf of Part II in Zweig MS 176, acquired in 2011 by the Freie Deutsche Hochstift, Frankfurt am Main; Goethe- und Schiller- Archiv, Weimar, NFG 96/1065: eight bifolia from Chapter 1 of Part II; Bodmer Foundation, Geneva: the ninth bifolium from the preceding manuscript (formerly in Zweig's possession), containing the last section of the unfinished Part II; Bodmer Foundation: 'Die Vermählung der Jahreszeiten' (also formerly in Zweig's possession), intended as the final poem in the work; Freies Deutsche Hochstift, Frankfurt am Main, FDH Nr. 9616–19: 'Lied der Todten', intended for Part II; Biblioteka Jagiellonska, Cracow: the Berlin Papers or Paralipomena, formerly in the Preußische Staatsbibliothek, Berlin, consisting of notes for Part II. For a fuller though not up-to-date account of the extant MS fragments of the novel and its publication history, see Richard Samuel, *Novalis: Der handschriftliche Nachlaß des Dichters* (Hildesheim: Gerstenberg, 1973).

Published: *Heinrich von Ofterdingen: Ein nachgelassener Roman von Novalis*, ed. Friedrich Schlegel and Ludwig Tieck (Berlin: Buchhandlung der Realschule, 1802), a special edition of Part I issued prior to the two-volume *Schriften* later that year; *Novalis Schriften*, ed. Schlegel and Tieck, 2 vols. (Berlin: Buchhandlung der Realschule, 1802). Part I of *Heinrich von Ofterdingen* occupies vol. 1. The Astralis poem is printed as a separate prologue in vol. 2, pp. 1–8, followed by the rest of Part II on pp. 9–50, and Tieck's *Fortsetzungsbericht* based on the Paralipomena on pp. 50–78; *Novalis Schriften*, ed. Schlegel and Tieck, 2nd ed., 2 vols. (Berlin: Buchhandlung der Realschule, 1805 [recte 1806]). All the material relating to *Heinrich von Ofterdingen* is brought together in vol. 1; Novalis, *Heinrich von Ofterdingen*, ed. Julian Schmidt (Leipzig: Brockhaus, 1876); *Novalis Schriften*, 1, *Das dichterische Werk*, ed. Paul Kluckhohn and Richard Samuel, 3rd revised ed. (Stuttgart: Kohlhammer, 1977), with text of Astralis on pp. 317–19, notes pp. 643–4 (the standard critical edition of Novalis's work, hereafter *HKA*); Sophia Vietor, *Astralis von Novalis: Handschrift – Text – Werk*, Stiftung für Romantikforschung, 15 (Würzburg: Königshausen & Neumann, 2001), with a line-by-line transcription and analysis of the Astralis text, pp. 93–103, print copy for critical edition, pp. 129–31.

Variants: Vietor, op. cit., pp. 79–81 tabulates the variants, mainly in orthography and punctuation, between the Zweig manuscript, Tieck's first edition, the Boerner sale catalogue, Kluckhohn's 1929 edition, and *HKA* 1977. The autograph amendments in the Zweig manuscript are discussed on pp. 111–24.

Reproduced: Samuel, *Novalis: Der handschriftliche Nachlaß*, op. cit. (f. 3, incorrectly captioned 'Atlantis' and described as 'verschollen'); *HKA*, 1, facing p. 321 (f. 3); Vietor, op. cit. (a facsimile of the whole Zweig manuscript is included as an insert, with an enlargement of the deleted word 'Genius'); www.bl.uk/manuscripts and Plate 43 below.

Exhibited: London, BL, 75 Musical and Literary Autographs, 1986.

Provenance: Following Novalis's death in March 1801, his younger brother, Karl von Hardenberg, sent the present two leaves to Ludwig Tieck in June 1801. Zweig purchased them at the Geibel-Hertenried sale, 3–6 May 1911, catalogue CIV, lot 396, p. 85. Their whereabouts in the intervening period is not recorded in the sale catalogue, *Autographen Sammlungen Dr. Carl Geibel Leipzig Carl Herz v. Hertenried Wien*, and remains unclear. Carl Geibel (1806–84), a book dealer and publisher working in Budapest and Leipzig, possibly obtained them directly from Julie von Podmaniczky, Novalis's former fiancée. Geibel's son gave his father's collection to C. G. Boerner for auction. The annotated envelope in Add MS 73175, ff. 79–80 notes (erroneously) 'Heinrich von Ofterdingen erster Teil.' However, the record card (Add MS 73168, f. 49) recognises that this fragment is from Part II: 'Das herrliche Gedicht "Astralis" das den Anfang des zweiten Teiles bildet, Vorklang zu dem ganzen zweiten Teil des Romans'. Also designated 'Unikum in Privatbesitz'; BL 1986.

Bibliography: Stefan Zweig, 'Meine Autographen-Sammlung'; Frels, *Deutsche Dichterhandschriften*, pp. 134–5; BL Programme Book, 1987; *Catalogue of Additions*, p. 74; Matuschek, p. 296.

Commentary. The novel *Heinrich von Ofterdingen*, which is unfinished and fragmentary in the second part, portrays the poetic education of Heinrich, a medieval Minnesinger figure, and, in parallel, the apotheosis of poetry itself in the imagination of the Romatic era. The dates of composition of the components of the novel are uncertain, but Novalis first noted ideas for Part II in 1799. He then completed Part I and returned to Part II in the summer or early autumn of 1800. (Vietor has identified four periods of activity through handwriting analysis.) Preparation of the first part for printing began during Novalis's lifetime, but the editorial decisions were Tieck's, most notably the change of name in the title from 'Afterdingen' to 'Ofterdingen'. Samuel, *Novalis: Der handschriftliche Nachlaß*, op. cit., attempts to reconstruct the passage of the manuscripts between the Hardenberg family, the Schlegels, Tieck and von Bülow as the various editions of the novel were produced. Some sections were eventually given away to friends by Tieck and von Bülow.

Stefan Zweig strongly supported Hugo von Hofmannsthal's suggestion that works of Novalis be included in the 'Bibliotheca Mundi' series of the 'Inselbücherei', which needed the addition of a Geman poet. In a letter to Hofmannsthal, dated 17 March 1920, Zweig recommended that a representative selection of Novalis's writing should encompass more than just the Fragments. Unfortunately the publication did not materialise. Another ultimately unrealised idea was Zweig's plan for a new volume in the 'Drei Meister' series, featuring Shelley, Novalis and Leopardi and with the title 'Die Dichter des Elements'.

Zweig also owned a fragment of the end of Part II of *Heinrich von Ofterdingen* and four other manuscripts of Novalis: 'An ihrem Busen weih ich mich', 'In stiller Treue sieht man gerne ihn walten', 'Die Vermählung der Jahreszeiten' and 'Der Fremdling'. All are now at the Bodmer Foundation, Geneva, with the exception of the last, which passed to Robert Ammann, Aarau, Switzerland in 1936. Its current location is unknown.

Alexander Pope
(1688–1744)

Zweig MS 177.

'To the Right Honourable The Earl of Oxford Upon a piece of News in Mist', poem: *autograph* fair copy; *c.* 1728.

In *English*.
Begins: 'Wesley, if Wesley tis they mean'.
Ends: 'The Lord of Oxford knows'.
Three four-line stanzas. The complete heading reads: 'To the Right Honourable / The Earl of Oxford. / Upon a piece of News in Mist, that the / Rev. Mr W. refus'd to write against Mr Pope / because his best Patron had a Friendship / for the said P.' Addressed on f. 2 'To the Right Honble the Earl of Oxford in Dover Street'. With confirmation of authenticity, in the hand of James Dowland and signed: 'These Lines in the hand writing of Pope were communicated by me to the Editor of the Gentleman's Magazine and a facsimile of them appears in that work for July 1809. p. 609'.

f. 1: 369 x 194mm; f. 2: 114 x 103mm; f. 3: 201 x 166mm.
ff. 3.
Black ink on laid paper.
Two sheets of paper (ff. 2, 3) mounted on one support sheet (f. 1).
No watermark.

Published: First published as an engraved facsimile in *The Gentleman's Magazine*, July 1809; printed in Sotheby's sale catalogue for 1 July 1930, pp. 53–4, with misreading 'Orford' for 'Oxford'; *The Twickenham Edition of the Works of Alexander Pope*, 6, 'Minor Poems', ed. Norman Ault and John Butt (revised reprint London: Routledge, 1993), pp. 294–5. The text in this edition is identical with the manuscript.
Reproduced: Engraved facsimile in *The Gentleman's Magazine*, July 1809, plate 11; facsimile in *English Poetical Autographs*, ed. Desmond Flower and A. N. L. Munby (London: Cassell, 1938), no. 14, with acknowledgement of Zweig's ownership; www.bl.uk/manuscripts and Plate 44 below.
Exhibited: London, BL, 75 Musical and Literary Autographs, 1986.
Provenance: Sold at Sotheby's, 1 July 1930, lot 363 as the property of Mrs Hamilton Gell of Winslade, Exeter; purchased by Maggs for £29 (annotations in BL MSS copy of sale catalogue); purchased by Zweig through Maggs; BL 1986.
Bibliography: BL Programme Book, 1987; *Catalogue of Additions*, p. 74; Matuschek, p. 301.

Commentary. The notes in the Twickenham edition explain in detail the situation that arose as a consequence of Pope's ridiculing other authors in the recently-published *Dunciad*. The editors suggest that Pope himself might have been responsible for the 'News in Mist', an epistle in his defence which was printed in *Mist's Weekly Journal*, 164 (8 June 1728), above the initials of James Moore Smythe. 'The Rev. Mr W.' is identified as Samuel Wesley the younger, who had complained about the allusion to his father in the *Dunciad*. 'Father Francis' is Francis Atterbury, Bishop of Rochester, then in exile, and 'Earl Edward' is Edward Harley, 2nd Earl of Oxford, both friends of Pope, who withdrew the reference to Wesley senior in later issues of his poem.

The author of the authentication on f. 2 has not been identified, but a James Dowland was involved with *The Gentleman's Magazine* in the early nineteenth century, publishing a masonic manuscript there in 1815. Autograph letters and documents collected by a Kaye Dowland were sold in the same Sotheby's sale as Zweig MS 177, also the property of Mrs Hamilton Gell, though there is no evidence of a family connection.

Zweig describes this manuscript on his record card (in Add MS 73168, f. 50) as 'von äußerster Seltenheit'. He also owned a signature of Pope on a printed receipt for two guineas for the translation of Homer's *Iliad*, to be delivered in quires, purchased with the present manuscript as part of lot 363 in Sotheby's sale and now held at the Bodmer Foundation, Geneva.

Pierre-Joseph Proudhon
(1809–1865)

Zweig MS 178.

'A Propos de Louis Blanc', article: *autograph* draft, heavily corrected and annotated; 1849.

In *French*.
Begins: 'Je m'étais dit; Que ferons-nous de Louis Blanc?'.
Ends: 'La Suite demain'.
Newspaper article for *La Voix du peuple,* subtitled 'De l'Utilité présente, et de la Possibilité future de l'Etat'. Eighteen irregular fragments of text with paragraphs numbered in margin 1–17, plus a pastedown. The manuscript displays many deletions and insertions, above the line and in the margins. Italics are indicated by single underlining, and capitals by double underlining.

Largest sheet 351 x 228mm.
ff. 7.
Brown ink on cream wove paper.
Sheets of various sizes cut and stuck onto larger sheets.
No watermark.
Limp paper binding, stitched and with red tape on spine.

Related Manuscripts: The main corpus of Proudhon's manuscripts is in the Bibliothèque d'Étude et de Conservation, Besançon, France. No other copies of this manuscript have been traced.
Published: *La Voix du peuple*, 87 (26 and 27 December 1849); *Œuvres complètes de P. J. Proudhon*, 19, *Mélanges, iii: Articles de journaux, 1848–1852* (Paris: A. Lacroix, Verboeckhoven et Cie, 1870), pp. 41–7. This is the first article on the subject of Louis Blanc. The printed edition also includes seven others, originally published between 1849 and 1850. The text in this edition follows the author's final intentions in the manuscript with a few variant spellings and capitalisations and later word changes or omissions.
Reproduced: www.bl.uk/manuscripts and Plate 45 below.
Provenance: Purchased by Zweig on 13 May 1939 from Pierre Berès, Paris, catalogue 22. The invoice from Berès, marked 'bezahlt durch New Trading', with a sheet and envelope, is at Add MS 73175, ff. 86–9. Record card with long annotation by Zweig is Add MS 73168, f. 52. The date is wrongly entered there as '1929'; BL 1986.
Bibliography: BL Programme Book, 1987; *Catalogue of Additions*, p. 75; Matuschek, p. 302. For background, see Leo A. Loubère, *Louis Blanc: his Life and his Contribution to the Rise of French Jacobin-Socialism* (Evanston, IL: Northwestern University Press, 1961).

Commentary. Pierre-Joseph Proudhon was a French politician, economist and socialist, the first self-styled 'anarchist'. Rejecting both capitalism and communism, he favoured a philosophy of 'mutualism' in which the means of production is controlled by the workers, organised in a federation of free communes, and social revolution is achieved by peaceful means. He was particularly critical of authoritarian socialists like Louis Blanc, who wanted to effect change through the established government. Influential as a journalist during the Second Republic, he contributed articles to the *Voix du peuple* from September 1849 to May 1850. Louis Jean Joseph Charles Blanc (1811–82) was a French politician, historian and socialist reformer. A member of the Provisional Government in 1848, he was appointed President of the Luxembourg Commission with the remit to investigate labour problems. In this role, he instigated the setting up of co-operative National Workshops, financed by the railway system. Proudhon condemned the Commission's financial management and the controlling influence of Blanc, who bore the blame for the failure of the Workshops within a year.

RAINER MARIA RILKE
(1875–1926)

Zweig MS 179.

'Die Weise von Liebe und Tod des Cornets Otto Rilke (Geschrieben 1899)', poetic tale: *autograph* fair copy of the second version; August 1904.

In *German.*
Begins: 'Appel von Rilke, Herr auf Langenau, Gränitz, Greussen u.s.f.'.
Ends: 'Aber man kennt den Namen der Gräfin nicht und nicht den Namen des Sohns, den sie bald in anderen friedsamen Landen gebar'.
The tale is a romantic tribute to a young soldier fighting in the Austro-Turkish war of the early 1660s, whom Rilke erroneously believed to be one of his ancestors.
After the unnumbered title page and preface the text is divided into sections numbered I–XXVIII.
With two corrections ('fühlt' amended to 'versteht' on f. 5; 'Aufseufzung' amended to 'Athemholung' on f. 13) and two deletions (ff. 14, 24).

Binding 200 x 142mm. Largest sheet 191 x 133mm.
ff. i + 27; versos blank. Original foliation 1–25.
Black ink on white squared paper.
Bound in gold-tooled brown morocco by E. A. Enders of Leipzig, with green marbled end-papers and the remains of a green silk ribbon bookmark. 'RAINER MARIA RILKE – DIE WEISE VON LIEBE UND TOD' is gold-tooled on the spine.

Related Manuscripts: Rilke-Archiv MS 269, an autograph manuscript of the earliest version of the text, written in autumn 1899; University of Nottingham Library, MS 43, a copy, made by an unidentified transcriber sometime between 1906 and 1947, of what is thought to be an unknown early version.
Published: First version published in a limited edition facsimile of the manuscript by Anton Kippenberg (Leipzig: Sinsel, 1927); second version published in Prague as 'Die Weise von Liebe und Tod des Kornets Otto Rilke' in *Deutsche Arbeit. Monatschrift für das geistige Leben des deutschen in Böhmen* (Prague), Jahrgang 4/1, (1904), pp. 60–5; third version published as *Die Weise von Liebe und Tod des Kornets Christoph Rilke* (Berlin; Leipzig; Stuttgart: Axel Juncker Verlag, 1906). The protagonist's name was changed from Otto to Christoph at Juncker's request; republished as the first volume in the 'Inselbücherei' series (Leipzig: Insel Verlag, 1912); Rainer Maria Rilke, *Die Weise von Liebe und Tod: Texte und Dokumente*, ed. W. Simon (Frankfurt am Main: Suhrkamp, 1974). Includes all three versions; the second version on pp. 23–38 with notes on the text on pp. 72–3.
Reproduced: Matuschek, p. 18 (f. 3); www.bl.uk/manuscripts and Plate 46 below.
Exhibited: London, BL, 75 Musical and Literary Autographs, 1986.
Provenance: Given to Zweig in Paris by Rilke, spring 1913 (note by Zweig, f. i); BL 1986.
Bibliography: Stefan Zweig, 'Meine Autographen-Sammlung'; BL Programme Book, 1987; *Catalogue of Additions*, p. 75; Matuschek, pp. 19–20, 34, 117, 306.

Commentary. In a letter to Hermann Pongs in 1924 Rilke claimed that he wrote the *Cornet* in a single night in 1899. The text went through a number of revisions and publications without achieving any notable success until, in 1912, at the suggestion of Stefan Zweig, the Insel Verlag in Leipzig re-issued it as Volume 1 in its ground-breaking new series of small books, reasonably priced but well designed with superior typography and distinctive decorative covers, a series that was to prove so popular that it is still in production today. In this new format Rilke's work suddenly became an instant success, a bestseller quickly achieving cult status. Because of its subject matter it was particularly popular among the front-line soldiers in the two World Wars, many of whom carried a copy with them. The first edition sold out within weeks, and for many years it was reprinted on a regular basis, selling more than 200,000 copies in Rilke's own lifetime.

Although this fair copy falls short of fulfilling Zweig's usual criteria for showing the development of thought behind the composition of the work, he was extremely proud to include it in his collection because of his great admiration for the writer.

Zweig MS 180.

Letter to A[lfred] Wolfenstein: *autograph*, signed; 23 November 1920.

In *German.*
Begins: 'Lieber Herr Wolfenstein. Sie hatten alles Recht, von mir zu erwarten, dass ich die Insel auf Ihr Manuscript aufmerksam machen'.
Ends: 'In immer gleicher Gesinnung grüßt Sie, lieber Herr Wolfenstein, Ihr R M Rilke'.
In the letter Rilke explains the reasons for his tardiness in reading a manuscript by Wolfenstein before passing it on to the Insel Verlag, for whom Rilke worked as a reader from 1917. He explains that the delay has not been entirely of his own making, and reassures Wolfenstein that Stefan Zweig will understand the situation as soon as he knows that the manuscript had been awaiting Rilke's scrutiny before submission. He is expecting to receive a direct response from Professor Kippenberg, Director of the Insel Verlag, who has promised him a visit, and he concludes with a greeting for Wolfenstein's wife (the poet Henriette Hardenberg) and his young son, Frank.

175 x 135mm.
ff. 2; f. 2v blank.
Black ink on grey paper.
Bifolium.

Reproduced: www.bl.uk/manuscripts and Plate 47 below.
Provenance: It is not known how and when Zweig acquired this letter, although it is not impossible that it could have been given to him by Wolfenstein; BL 1986.

Bibliography: Paul Verlaine, *Gesammelte Werke*, 1, ed. Stefan Zweig (Leipzig: Insel Verlag, 1922), pp. 81, 128, 160; BL Programme Book, 1987; *Catalogue of Additions*, p. 75; Matuschek, p. 306.

Commentary. Alfred Wolfenstein (1883–1945), an Expressionist poet, dramatist and translator, published his first collection of poems *Die gottlosen Jahre* in 1914 with the support of Rilke and Robert Musil, and was later well-known for his translations of Rimbaud and other French poets. The 'manuscript' mentioned in the letter presumably contained his German versions of three Verlaine poems, 'Die harte Prüfung...' ('La dure épreuve va finir' from the collection *La bonne chanson*, 1872), 'Es glänzten...' ('Les faux beaux jours...' from the collection *Sagesse*, 1881) and 'Des menschlichen Körpers...' ('La tristesse, la langueur du corps humain', also from *Sagesse*), published in 1922 in a two-volume edition of German translations of Verlaine's works which Stefan Zweig edited for the Insel Verlag.

Arthur Rimbaud
(1854–1891)

Zweig MS 181.

Poésies: *autograph* fair copies of the twenty-two poems of the 'Recueil Demeny'; 1870.

In *French*.
Composed between 1869 and 1870 when Rimbaud was aged fifteen to sixteen, and as he explored a range of subject matter and verse forms. Each poem is signed at the end, and some are also dated, although these may be dates of copying rather than of composition. Each poem is preceded by a leaf bearing the title, stamped in blue ink.
In many cases, other autograph manuscripts of the poems exist, most notably in letters sent to his schoolteacher, Georges Izambard. In the contents list below, those related manuscripts are noted, together with references to dates of first publication.
1. ff. 2–3v. 'Les reparties de Nina'; [dated 15 August 1870 in Izambard's manuscript]. An earlier autograph now in a private collection, with title 'Ce qui retient Nina', was almost certainly sent to Izambard in a letter of 25 August 1870. This manuscript has two additional stanzas but lacks lines 61–4 in the Zweig manuscript. Published in Arthur Rimbaud, *Reliquaire. Poésies* (Paris: L. Genonceaux, 1891).
2. f. 5. 'Venus Anadyomène'; [dated 27 July 1870 in Izambard's manuscript]. An earlier autograph, in which lines 7 and 8 are transposed, exists in a private collection, having been sent to Izambard in a letter of 25 August 1870. Published in the *Mercure de France*, 1 November 1891.
3. f. 5v. 'Un français de soixante dix'; dated Mazas, 3 September 1870, although Izambard claimed it was composed on 17 July and sent to him the next day. Published in *Reliquaire*, 1891.
4. ff. 7–7v. 'Première Soirée'; [composed June / July 1870]. Two earlier autograph manuscripts existed; one, now in a private collection, sent to Izambard with the title 'Comédie en trois baisers' and a second, now lost, with the title 'Trois baisers'. There are only minor variants in the texts. Published in *La Charge*, 13 August 1870, from the lost manuscript.
5. f. 7v. 'Sensation'; dated March 1870. An autograph manuscript, now in the Bibliothèque littéraire de Jacques-Doucet, was sent in a letter to Théodore de Banville on 24 May 1870. The poem there was dated 20 April. Variants in the text as first published suggest the existence of a third version. Published in *La Revue indépendante*, January–February 1889.
6. ff. 9–9v. 'Bal des pendus'; [composed February or April 1870?]. Published in the *Mercure de France*, 1 November 1891.
7. ff. 11–11v. 'Les Effarés'; dated 20 September 1870. An autograph manuscript, now in the collection of François-Marie Banier, with variant final stanza, was sent to Jean Aicard in a letter of 20 June 1871. Two copies were made by Paul Verlaine early in 1872, one of which is now in the Bibliothèque nationale de France, NAF 18895. Published in *The Gentleman's Magazine*, January 1878 under the title 'Petits Pauvres', from an unidentified manuscript.

8. ff. 13–13v. 'Roman'; dated 29 September 1870 but possibly composed in June 1870. Published in *Reliquaire*, 1891.
9. f. 15. 'Rages de Césars'; [composed and written in September 1870 in the aftermath of the Battle of Sedan]. Published in *Reliquaire*, 1891.
10. f. 17. 'Le Mal'; [composed August 1870?]. Published in *La Revue indépendante*, January–February 1889. Differs from Zweig MS 181 in orthography and punctuation.
11. ff. 19–19v. 'Ophélie'; [15 May 1870 or earlier?]. There are two earlier autograph manuscripts which differ significantly from Zweig MS 181: one sent to Izambard and one, now in the Bibliothèque littéraire de Jacques-Doucet, in a letter of 24 May 1870 to Théodore de Banville. The latter is dated 15 May 1870, but the date of composition may be earlier. Published in *Reliquaire*, 1891.
12. f. 21. 'Le châtiment de Tartufe'; [1870?]. Published in *La Revue indépendante,* January–February 1889.
13. ff. 23–23v. 'À la Musique'; [composed July / August 1870?]. An earlier autograph manuscript with many variants, now in the Musée-bibliothèque Arthur Rimbaud at Charleville, was sent to Izambard. Published in *La Revue indépendante*, January–February 1889.
14. ff. 25–28. 'Le Forgeron'; [date of composition unknown]. An earlier autograph manuscript, wanting the text from line 157 onwards and now in a private collection, was sent to Izambard. That manuscript bears the subtitle 'vers le 20 juin 1792', whilst Zweig MS 181 has 'Palais des Tuileries vers le 10 août 92' as the setting. Published in *Reliquaire*, 1891.
15. ff. 30–32v. 'Soleil et Chair'; dated May 1870. An earlier autograph manuscript of a longer version of the poem, now in the Bibliothèque littéraire de Jacques-Doucet, was sent in a letter to Théodore de Banville on 24 May 1870. It bears the title 'Credo in Unam' and the date 29 April 1870, and it differs very significantly from Zweig MS 181. It is reasonable to suppose that the composition was finished at the end of April 1870, as this date implies. Rimbaud appears to have given Demeny the first leaf of Zweig MS 181, which is blank on the verso, before he had finished copying the rest for him. The pencilled note at the end indicates that he left the remaining two leaves for collection on 26 September. The missing lines 81–116 may have been deliberately suppressed in this copy, or a page may be lost. Published in *Reliquaire*, 1891.
16. f. 35. 'Le Dormeur du Val'; dated October 1870. Possibly published in the journal *Le Progrès des Ardennes*, November 1870; published in *L'Anthologie des poètes français du XIXe siècle*, 4 (Paris: Alphonse Lemerre, 1888).
17. f. 37. 'Au Cabaret-Vert, cinq heures du soir'; dated October 1870. Published in *La Revue d'aujourd'hui*, 15 March 1890.
18. f. 39. 'La Maline'; dated Charleroi, October 1870. Published in *Reliquaire*, 1891.
19. f. 41. 'L'éclatante victoire de Sarrebrück'; dated October 1870. Published in *Reliquaire*, 1891.
20. f. 43. 'Rêvé Pour l'Hiver'; dated 'En Wagon, le 7 octobre 70'. Published in *Reliquaire*, 1891.
21. f. 45. 'Le buffet'; dated October 1870. Published in *L'Anthologie des poètes français du XIXe siècle*, 4 (Paris: Alphonse Lemerre, 1888).
22. f. 47. 'Ma Bohème' 'Fantaisie' (added); [probably end September or October 1870]. Published in *La Revue indépendante*, January–February 1889.

The first cahier (ff. 1–34), which Rimbaud is thought to have written out in September 1870, is written on both sides of the leaves. The second cahier (ff. 35–47) on the smaller leaves, written out in October, is on one side only, as by that stage the manuscript was intended for printer's copy. The differences in the ink between the first and second parts show that the transcription was not continuous.

Binding 325 x 218mm. Largest sheet 312 x 200mm.
ff. 47.
Brown and black ink on wove and laid paper. Annotations in pencil and red crayon. Titles printed in blue ink on wove paper.
No watermark.
Red cloth binding with gilt-stamped spine. Marbled end-papers. 'ARTHUR RIMBAUD / POESIES' in gilt on front board.

Related Manuscripts: See above, and Murphy, 1, pp. 43–7, which describes and indicates the accessibility of primary sources and reproductions for the whole of Rimbaud's poetic *oeuvre.*

Published: Arthur Rimbaud, *Reliquaire. Poésies* (Paris: L. Genonceaux, 1891), pp. 1–62 (contains texts of all twenty-two poems from Zweig MS 181 in the same order as the manuscript); id., *Poésies complètes,* with preface by Paul Verlaine (Paris: Léon Vanier, 1895); id., *Poésies. Édition critique*, ed. Henry de Bouillane de Lacoste (Paris: Mercure de France, 1939); id., *Oeuvres complètes*, ed. Rolland de Renéville and Jules Mouquet (Paris: Gallimard, 1946), pp. 40–69 (first edition of complete works); id., *Oeuvres complètes*, 1, ed. Steve Murphy, *Poésies,* 4, *Fac-similés*, Textes de Littérature Moderne et Contemporaine, 36 and 66 (Paris: Honoré Champion, 1999 and 2002); id., *Oeuvres complètes*, ed. André Guyaux, Bibliothèque de la Pléiade ([Paris]: Gallimard, 2009). Both Murphy and Guyaux print texts which are faithful to Zweig MS 181 together with other versions and commentaries on the variants.

Reproduced: Arthur Rimbaud, *Poésies,* notice de Paterne Berrichon, Les manuscrits des maîtres (Paris: Albert Messein, 1919). Contains reproductions of all twenty-two poems from Zweig MS 181 but arranged in what Berrichon believed to be chronological sequence, not in the same order as the manuscript. Followed by nineteen other Rimbaud poems from 1871 and 1872. Murphy, op. cit., 4, *Fac-similés,* pp. 191–243. New reproductions of all twenty-two Zweig MS 181 poems in a slightly different order, with the related manuscripts *passim.* Explanatory notes are at pp. 513–26; www.bl.uk/manuscripts and Plate 48 below.

Exhibited: London, National Book League, A Thousand Years of French Books, 1948, catalogue no. 156, but wrongly described as 'Les Illuminations' (see also Add MS 73175, f. 100 and card in Add MS 73182); Paris, Bibliothèque nationale de France, Arthur Rimbaud. Exposition organisée pour le centième anniversaire de sa naissance, 1954–5, catalogue no. 74; London, BL, 75 Musical and Literary Autographs, 1986 (f. 35); London, Christie's, etc., The Creative Spirit, 1987–8 (f. 17); Paris, Bibliothèque nationale, Le Printemps des Génies, 1993; La Casa Encendida, Madrid, then Fundación Garcia Lorca, Granada, Vida y Hechos de Arthur Rimbaud, 2007 (f. 47); Paris, Grand Palais, Bohèmes. De Léonard de Vinci à Picasso, 2012–13, catalogue no. 153 (f. 47).

Provenance: Rimbaud transcribed the twenty-two poems in Zweig MS 181 and gave them to Paul

Demeny at Douai in the autumn of 1870. Demeny sold them to Rodolphe Darzens as he prepared his preface to the *Reliquaire*. He passed them to Léon Genonceaux, his editor, who compiled and published the *Reliquaire* without further consultation, and who, during the ensuing dispute, took the manuscripts entrusted to him to Belgium and England. (See Pierre Petitfils, 'Les manuscrits de Rimbaud', in *Etudes rimbaldiennes*, 2 (1970), pp. 41–144.) They eventually came into the hands of Pierre Dauze, pseudonym of the bibliophile Paul Louis Dreyfus-Bing (1852–1913). Stefan Zweig purchased the volume on 29 May 1914 at the auction of his collection by Auguste Blaizot, Paris. The sale also included first editions and letters of Rimbaud; see the *Catalogue de la Bibliothèque de Feu M. Pierre Dauze* (Paris: Leclerc / Blaizot, 1914), Premier partie. Manuscrits M–Z, lot 1896, pp. 176–7. The catalogue refers to the forthcoming Messein publication. Record card in Add MS 73168, f. 56: 'Kostbarkeit aller ersten Ranges! da Manuskripte Rimbauds überhaupt nicht mehr auffindbar sind'. See also Add MS 73175, ff. 95–100; BL 1986.

Bibliography: Stefan Zweig, 'Meine Autographen-Sammlung'; Georges Izambard, *Rimbaud tel que je l'ai connu* (Paris: Mercure de France, 1946); Pierre Petitfils, 'Les manuscrits de Rimbaud', in *Etudes rimbaldiennes,* 2 (1970), pp. 41–144. See pp. 145–57 for a chronological table of publications, and the history of the related manuscripts, though the Zweig MS is mislocated; BL Programme Books, 1987 and 1992; *Catalogue of Additions*, p. 75; Matuschek, p. 307. See Guyaux's edition for bibliographies of the individual poems.

Commentary. The poems were composed before the autumn of 1870, probably mostly between March and October of that year. As an adolescent studying at the Collège de Charleville, Rimbaud was encouraged to develop his literary talent by his rhetoric teacher Georges Izambard, to whom he gave copies of his work. In August 1870, his formal education disrupted by the Franco-Prussian War, Rimbaud ran away to Paris, and was detained in the Mazas prison for fare evasion and vagrancy. The poem entitled 'Un français de soixante dix' was purportedly written in the Mazas, although this may be a conceit, just as 'Rêvé pour l'Hiver' was probably not written 'en wagon'.

Izambard secured Rimbaud's release from prison in September and sent him to stay with his own family at Douai, where he began to assemble a collection of his verses. This collection was in two parts, the first consisting of fifteen poems written out in September, and a second section of seven poems compiled the following month. Possibly with publication in mind, Rimbaud gave his copies to Paul Demeny, a young acquaintance of Izambard who had just published his own collection of poems *Les Glaneuses* in the Librairie Artistique de Paris. However, on 10 June 1871, Rimbaud wrote to Demeny asking him to burn the poems, as he felt them outdated and could no longer identify with them. Demeny did not comply, and indeed within a few days Rimbaud had sent another copy of 'Les effarés' to Jean Aicard, showing that he was not after all intent on destruction.

The collection became known as the 'Recueil Demeny', the 'Recueil de Douai' or the 'Cahier(s) de Douai' (although according to Izambard the poems were on loose leaves at this stage, and were only bound up later for Pierre Dauze). When Rimbaud left Europe on his travels in 1876, Rodolphe Darzens acquired the manuscripts, apparently by purchase from Demeny. It is not clear why Demeny had failed to publish the poems whilst he held them, or why Izambard had passed his copies on to Paul Verlaine; both men may have had scruples about the content, or they may have intended to follow Rimbaud's own wishes. Darzens arranged first publication of some poems in periodicals, but they appeared for the first time as a collection in 1891 in the *Reliquaire*. Darzens had written the preface before handing the source materials to his editor, Léon Genonceaux. The edition was certainly based on the manuscripts and preserved the order of the Recueil Demeny but was marred by misprints. It was issued around the time of Rimbaud's death.

The proper order of the collection has been much disputed by subsequent editors. An analysis and a table comparing the order in the different editions are provided by Steve Murphy in 'Autour des "cahiers Demeny" de Rimbaud' in *Studi Francesi*, 103 (Anno XXXV), Fascicolo I (Turin: Rosenberg & Sellier, 1991). pp. 78–86. Zweig MS 181 is not necessarily in the order in which the poems were composed or copied.

Stefan Zweig was clearly delighted to own this manuscript of Rimbaud's early poetry. He wrote 'Es sind darinnen enthalten die berühmten Gedichte Ma Boheme, Sensation, Reve pour l'hiver, Roman, Les effaree [all sic.] und viele andere Kostbarkeiten. Eine Sammlung von Gedichten besitzt sonst nur der Ministerpraesident Barthou in seiner Sammlung und den Wert dieser Verse kennzeichnet am besten die Tatsache, dass das vorliegende Manuskript in der Kollektion "Les manuscrits des maîtres" (bei Messein) reproduziert wurde' (Add MS 73168, f. 56). He called the poem 'Sensation' 'das schönste deutsche Gedicht der französischen Sprache' and translated it for an anthology in Reclams Universalbibliothek in 1904.

Zweig also wrote the introduction to K. L. Ammer [Karl Klammer], *Arthur Rimbaud: Leben und Dichtung* (Leipzig: Insel Verlag, 1907), the first German translation of Rimbaud's poems with a biography based on Berrichon. His essay was reprinted in *Begegnungen mit Menschen Büchern, Städten* (Vienna: Reichner, 1937). In it he spoke of 'ein rein instinktives Leben inmitten der Moralsphären' and 'ein Heros innerer Freiheit in unseren Tagen. Ein Desperado des Instinktes.'

Zweig also owned an autograph manuscript of two poems from Rimbaud's *Illuminations,* acquired in 1924 and now at the Bodmer Foundation, Geneva; the autograph manuscript of three poems from the Jeunesse cycle in *Illuminations*, acquired from Albert Messein in exchange for permission to make a facsimile of Verlaine's 'Fêtes Galantes', now also at the Bodmer Foundation; and a printed edition of *Une Saison en Enfer* (Brussels: Alliance Typographique, 1873), now in the British Library as Zweig MS 202. Zweig MS 181 was one of the manuscripts with which Zweig said he would never part (Add MS 74269, ff. 5–5v).

Maximilien de Robespierre
(1758–1794)

Zweig MS 182.

['Eloge de la Rose']: *autograph* draft of Robespierre's acceptance speech to La Société des Rosati on being admitted as a member; 1786.

In *French*.
Begins: 'La Rose croit pour tous les hommes'.
Ends: 'In his duobus tota lex est'.
The text is heavily corrected, with many deletions and insertions. The name 'ROBESPIERRE' has been added in pencil at the head of the text on f. 1.

302 x 194mm.
ff. 7.
Brown ink on laid paper.
Three bifolia and one single leaf.
Watermark: 'L M HOMO'.

Published: Lucien Peise, *Quelques vers de Maximilien Robespierre* (Paris: Lucien Gougy, 1909), pp. 35–45; *Œuvres complètes de Maximilien Robespierre*, 1, ed. Eugène Desprez (Paris: Ernest Leroux, 1910), pp. 185–94.
Reproduced: www.bl.uk/manuscripts and Plate 49 below.
Exhibited: London, BL, 75 Musical and Literary Autographs, 1986.
Provenance: Agricol Moureau, maternal grandfather of Lucien Peise, received the manuscript from Robespierre's sister Charlotte (d. 1834) as a reminder of her brother (see Add MS 73168, f. 58). Lucien Peise may have inherited the manuscript by 1909, or it may possibly have been owned by one of Moureau's other descendants. Acquired by Zweig on 11 May 1927 through Charles Vellay, Paris; BL 1986.
Bibliography: Stefan Zweig, 'Meine Autographen-Sammlung'; BL Programme Book, 1987; *Catalogue of Additions*, p. 76; Matuschek, pp. 307–8.

Commentary. The Rosati Society of Arras (the name is an anagram of Artois) was formed of a group of wealthy young men who gathered together every summer from 1778 until about 1787 to indulge in the delights of poetry, pastoral rituals and conviviality. Robespierre was admitted as a member on 21 June 1786, composing a special poem for the occasion.

Although this address to the Rosati is somewhat trivial by comparison with the more significant, political speeches made by Robespierre, the manuscript was recorded by Zweig as 'Seltenheit 1. Ranges' (Add MS 73168, f. 58) on account of its numerous amendments and corrections, which provide a particularly revealing insight into the mind of its author at work. Zweig also owned a fragment of Robespierre's *Affaire de Chabot*, now held at the Bodmer Foundation, Geneva.

Jeanne-Marie Roland de la Platière
(1754–1793)

Zweig MS 183.

'Rêveries, Philosophiques, ou Folles', etc.: *autograph* manuscripts; 1777, 1782.

In *French*.
A composite volume containing:

1. ff. 1–11v. 'Rêveries, Philosophiques, ou folles, comme l'on voudra'. Mainly thoughts on religion and philosophy. A separate piece entitled 'De l'observation' follows on ff. 10v–11v.
2. ff. 13–21v. Letters 'à Madame D' [incorrectly Madame P on the record card at Add MS 73168, f. 59 and in the *Catalogue of Additions*]. Four items, not genuine letters, but a format adopted by Mme Roland to record her ideas – see the note on f. 16 beginning 'Ces lettres sont factices'.
3. ff. 23–25v. 'Pensées détachées'. A series of short disconnected thoughts of a few lines each, separated by drawn lines.
4. ff. 27–32v. Letter to M. Neret fils, 25 October 1782 from Jean-Marie Roland de la Platière, with note of seven lines (f. 27v) and numerous corrections in the hand of Mme Roland.

Interleaved (ff. 12, 22 and 26) with inserted titles and notes in the hand of Claude Perroud, editor of Mme Roland's memoir and letters, numbered XXIII, XXIV and XXV. The first four-and-a-half pages are struck through by Luc Antoine Champagneux, her executor and editor of the *Œuvres,* whose note (inserted as f. 4) explains that some thoughts are not for publication, as Mme Roland changed her opinions, especially about religion. Champagneux has also inserted below the heading on f. 1 'tirées du manuscrit contenant les ouvrages composés par la C[me] Roland en 1777'. The date 'janvier 1777' is written at the top left of f. 1. F. 13 is marked '74' in ink at the top right. The fictitious letters on ff. 13–21v appear to be in a different hand, but may be examples of Mme Roland's juvenile writing. Ff. 27–32v are mainly in Jean-Marie Roland's hand. Stefan Zweig's entry in pencil on f. i, 'Madame Roland (einziges erhaltenes Manuscript von ihrer Hand)' is in error in stating that the manuscript is a unique survival. At f. ii is an engraved portrait by an unidentified artist of the author above a tribunal scene. It shows Mme Roland at a younger age than in the portrait published in the 1800 edition of her *Œuvres*. The two-and-a-half-page autograph letter to Monsieur de Boismorel, Paris, 16 February 1776, signed 'Phlipon', which is mentioned in Sotheby's sale catalogue, is not present (see Commentary below).

Largest sheet 226 x 177mm.
ff. ii + 32; 12v, 22v and 26v blank.
Black ink on laid and wove paper.
Single and bifolium sheets.
No watermark.
Bound in gold-tooled red morocco by Rivière and Son, Bath.

Published: 'De l'observation' was published as an enclosure in a letter of 1 May 1777 to Henriette Cannet in *Lettres de Madame Roland,* nouvelle série, 2, ed. Claude Perroud (Paris: Imprimerie Nationale, 1915), pp. 69–70. The present draft lacks the final four paragraphs of the printed letter. The other manuscripts in this volume were said in Sotheby's 1927 sale catalogue to be unpublished, and no editions published after that date have been found.

Reproduced: www.bl.uk/manuscripts and Plate 50 below.

Provenance: The Roland family kept the papers for nearly a century at their Château de Rosières near Bourgoin, France. The main archive was transferred to the Bibliothèque nationale de France in 1888, but apparently some items were given to Claude Perroud, and the presence of his annotations suggests that the contents of the present volume were among them. The manuscripts, already bound together and including the missing letter to M. Boismorel, were offered for sale at Sotheby's on 31 May 1927 under the heading of 'Other properties', as lot 446; purchased by Zweig via Maggs; BL 1986.

Bibliography: *Œuvres de J. M. PH. Roland, Femme de l'ex-ministre de l'intérieur*, ed. L. A. Champagneux (Paris: Bidault, 1800); *Mémoires de Madame Roland*, ed. Claude Perroud (Paris: Librarie Plon, 1905); *Lettres de Madame Roland*, ed. Claude Perroud (Paris: Imprimerie Nationale, 1900–15); BL Programme Book, 1987; *Catalogue of Additions*, p. 76; Matuschek, p. 310; Siân Reynolds, *Marriage and Revolution: Monsieur and Madame Roland* (Oxford: Oxford University Press, 2012).

Commentary. Madame Roland was born Marie-Jeanne Phlippon in Paris in 1754. She developed a broad range of intellectual interests, though largely self-taught, reading widely as shown in her correspondence with M. Boismorel who supplied her with books. She was still young and unmarried when she recorded the 'Rêveries' and 'Pensées' in Zweig MS 183. In 1780 she married Jean-Marie Roland de la Platière, himself a writer and rising revolutionary politician. Madame Roland supported him in these activities, and the couple became the focus of a circle of influential Girondins in Paris. After the king's surrender, her husband was appointed Minister of the Interior, but lost popularity by rejecting revolutionary extremism and allowing his wife influence in public affairs. In June 1793 both were arrested for treason. Her husband escaped but Madame Roland was guillotined on 8 November 1793.

Jean-Marie Roland's letter to M. Néret fils of St Quentin is preceded by a note stating that it was written on 25 October 1782, addressed to his château at Séry near Crépy-en-Valois. The letter should be read in the order ff. 27v, 28r, 28v, 29v, 29r, 31r top half, 30r inserted, 31r bottom half, 31v, 32r, 32v. The reply to Roland's letter has not survived, but on 6 November 1782 his wife alluded to it when she wrote, 'Je suis bien aise de la réponse de M. Néret et de la petite correspondance qui en résulte; la première pièce n'est pas une perle jetée à des pourceaux.' (*Lettres de Madame Roland*, 1, pp. 204–7).

The letter to Monsieur de Boismorel mentioned in the 1927 sale catalogue was seemingly removed, perhaps for separate sale, between the compilation of the catalogue and Zweig's purchase of the volume. Zweig knew it was missing when he wrote on the folder 'dabei ursprünglich noch ein Brief'.

Zweig's interest in the French Revolution is demonstrated by his literary portraits of Marie Antoinette and Joseph Fouché, and the manuscripts he collected from this period, represented in the British Library by Zweig MSS 147, 169, 171, 182, 183 and 187.

Romain Rolland
(1866–1944)

Zweig MSS 184, 185.

'L'Aube Nouvelle', the final volume of Rolland's ten-volume novel *Jean-Christophe*: *autograph* draft, corrected; 1911–12.

In *French*.
A dedication on f. 1 of Zweig MS 184 reads: 'Aux âme libres – de toutes les nations – qui souffrent, qui luttent, qui vaincront'. This is followed by a preface, signed 'RR' and dated 17 January 1912 (f. 2), and a title page bearing the words 'L'Aube Nouvelle' (f. 3).
Text begins: 'La vie passe. Le corps et l'âme s'écoulent comme un flot'.
Ends: 'Sous la main de sa raison harmonieuse'.
Zweig MS 185 has a title page bearing the words 'L'Aube Nouvelle' (suite)' (f. 1).
Text begins: 'Malheureusement, il ne dépend pas de nous'.
Ends: 'Je suis la jour qui va naître'.
At the foot of f. 108 is written 'Baveno, mardi 18 juin 1912 / Romain Rolland'.
Instructions for spacing are incorporated intermittently.

220 x 177mm.
ff. 111, 108. Numbered 3–110 and 111–217 respectively.
Black ink on wove paper, largely on rectos only. Annotations in pencil and blue ink.
Two volumes.
No watermark.
Blue and brown card bindings with canvas tape along spines.

Published: *Cahiers de la Quinzaine*, Series XIV, No. 2, 3 (1912). *Jean-Christophe* was serialised in the journal between 1904 and 1912.
Reproduced: BL Programme Book, 1988, p. 25 (f. 2); BL Programme Book, 1996, p. 11 (f. 2); www.bl.uk/manuscripts and Plate 51 below.
Exhibited: London, BL, 75 Musical and Literary Autographs, 1986.
Provenance: Presented to Stefan Zweig by the author, December 1912; BL 1986.
Bibliography: Stefan Zweig, 'Die Autographensammlung als Kunstwerk'; id., *Romain Rolland: Der Mann und das Werk* (Frankfurt am Main: Rütten & Loening, 1921); id., 'Meine Autographen-Sammlung'; BL Programme Book, 1987; *Catalogue of Additions*, p. 76; Matuschek, p. 310.

Commentary. It was largely on account of his masterpiece *Jean-Christophe*, which explores the power of art to bridge cultural differences through the development of its eponymous hero, that Romain Rolland received the Nobel Prize in Literature in 1915. In a letter of 17 February 1912 Zweig reminded Rolland that he had requested, and been promised, part of *Jean-Christophe* for his collection of manuscripts of his favourite authors, telling him that it will be in the good company of a novel by Balzac and another by Flaubert.

Zweig MS 186.

Two *autograph* essays; 1917, 1919.

In *French*.
1. ff. 1–17. 'La Jeunesse Suisse [Une Discussion sur l'Impérialisme, à Zofingue]'.
Begins 'On connaîtrait fort mal l'esprit public en Suisse'.
Ends: 'pareilles à d'orgueilleux, "gratte-ciel", à la carcasse noircie'.
Corrected draft, signed at the end and dated June 1917. A discussion prompted by views expressed in the *Feuille centrale de la Societé de Zofingue*, journal of the oldest and largest student fraternity in Switzerland, the *Zofingerverein*. First page has a green 'Demain' stamp in the top left-hand corner, and is marked up for printing in blue pencil. The Hinterberger catalogue number 'XX/802' is pencilled at the top of the page.
2. f. 18. 'Déclaration de l'Indépendance de l'Esprit'.
Begins: 'Travailleurs de l'esprit, compagnons, dispersés à travers le monde'.
Ends: 'l'Esprit libre, un et multiple, éternel'.
Fair copy, signed at the end and dated March 1919. Manifesto written to express the view of intellectuals after the First World War.

274 x 210mm.
ff. 18; versos blank except for 3v and 18v. With original numbering 2–15 (first folio unnumbered and extra leaf, numbered '3bis', inserted between 3 and 4). ff. 5 and 6 are a single sheet that has been cut into two pieces horizontally.
Black ink on wove paper.
Watermark: 'Sihl Mills for TYPEWRITER'.

Published: 'La Jeunesse suisse' published in *Demain*, 14 (June 1917), pp. 69–81; 'Déclaration de l'indépendence de l'Esprit' published in *L'Humanité*, 26 June 1919, appearing over the names of supporting intellectuals including that of Stefan Zweig; both reprinted in Romain Rolland, *Les Précurseurs* (Paris: Éditions de "L'Humanité", 1919).
Reproduced: Fold-out facsimile of 'Déclaration de l'Indépendence de l'Esprit' in Stefan Zweig, *Romain Rolland*, facing p. 256; www.bl.uk/manuscripts and Plate 52 below.
Provenance: It is not known when or where Stefan Zweig acquired this manuscript; BL 1986.
Bibliography: Stefan Zweig, *Romain Rolland: der Mann und das Werk* (Frankfurt am Main: Rütten & Loening, 1921); Hinterberger catalogue XX, no. 807; BL Programme Book, 1987; *Catalogue of Additions*, p. 76; Matuschek, p. 311.

Commentary. Romain Rolland, a lifelong pacifist with international values, found a sympathetic supporter in Stefan Zweig, who was proud to count Rolland among his closest friends. Having published a biography of Rolland in 1921, he describes their friendship in some detail in *Die Welt von Gestern*, the memoir of his own life published in 1944.

In addition to the present manuscript and the precious autograph volumes of *Jean-Christophe* (Zweig MSS 184, 185), Zweig also owned a typescript of *Clérambault*, signed and with autograph corrections, now held in the Österreichisches Theatermuseum, Vienna.

Louis-Antoine de Saint-Just
(1767–1794)

Zweig MS 187.

Draft decree concerning the creation of censorship; *autograph* manuscript [1794].

In *French*.

Begins: 'La convention N^lle^, considerant que Le gouvernement revolutionaire a pour but La repression prompte De tous Les crimes'.

Ends: 'L'indemnité des censeurs est fixée à 6000 livres'.

Outline in fourteen paragraphs of a decree that censors of public officials be appointed in each district and army of the Republic until peace is established. Frequent deletions and insertions suggest that this is the first draft. The most significant change is the substitution of the word 'fonctionnaires' for 'magistrats' in line eleven of the first page. On f. 1 are the annotations 'Copié', at the top left in ink, 'Saint-Just', in pencil (twice in different hands) and a figure [50?] at the top left in ink.

250 x 195mm.
ff. 2.
Black ink on grey laid paper.
Bifolium.

Related Manuscripts: Two manuscripts in Saint-Just's autograph in the Bibliothèque nationale de France, Paris, NAF 24136, ff. 1–59 and NAF 24158, ff. 7–13, contain texts from the *Fragments sur les institutions républicaines,* but not the decree on censorship. NAF 24158, ff. 62–84 is a manuscript copy in another hand from the 1800 edition of the *Fragments*, which includes a version of the decree on censorship on f. 81.

Published: Sixteenth fragment in Saint-Just, *Fragments sur les institutions républicaines* (Paris: Fayolle, [1800?]), assembled by Pierre-Joseph Briot (this contains a preliminary passage not included in Zweig MS 187, and there are also differences in wording and paragraph order); *Œuvres complètes de Saint-Just*, 2, ed. Charles Vellay (Paris: Charpentier et Fasquelle, 1908), pp. 538–9; Saint-Just, *Œuvres complètes*, 4, *Œuvres inachevées. Fragments divers*, ed. Michèle Duval (Paris: Éditions Gérard Lebovici, 1984), pp. 958–9.

Reproduced: www.bl.uk/manuscripts and Plate 53 below.

Provenance: Vellay (op. cit., p. 537) indicates that 'ce projet de décret fut trouvé, après le 9 thermidor, dans les papiers saisis chez Saint-Just'. The present manuscript is singled out for special mention in the *Inventaire des autographes et des documens historiques composant la collection de M. Benjamin Fillon* (Paris: Étienne Charavay, 1877), no. 627, as found at the end of a dossier of fifty fragments of the *Institutions républicaines* in the hand of Saint-Just. It is stated here that the fragments were collected by Briot and belonged subsequently to Gateau, the friend of Saint-Just. Benjamin Fillon (1819–1881) was a Republican judge and collector of manuscripts, art and antiquities. Series 4 of his collection, the French Revolutionary documents, was sold on 21 April 1877. Zweig's record card (Add MS 73168, f. 60) notes that he acquired the manuscript from Charles Vellay on 5 May 1927, and refers to their correspondence. Vellay (1876–1953) must have obtained it for the 1908 edition, but it is not clear who was the previous owner or where the rest of the dossier described in the Charavay inventory was dispersed. Zweig notes that it was once in the Fillon collection and continues (unaware of the existence of the other fragments) 'Große Seltenheit da fast nur Unterschriften St Just vorkommen'. Annotated envelope in Add MS 73175, ff. 105–6, 'nicht im Katalog'; BL 1986.

Bibliography: Stefan Zweig, 'Meine Autographen-Sammlung', p. 130; BL Programme Book, 1987; *Catalogue of Additions*, p. 76; Matuschek, p. 315.

Commentary. Louis-Antoine de Saint-Just began his career as the youngest deputy in the National Convention and rose to be its President in February 1794. He was a member of the Committee of Public Safety and drafted the radical Constitution of 1793. In the last year of his life, he was preparing legislation based on republican ideals and suppression of dissent. Proposals for civil censorship had already been put forward by others but none had been implemented. Early in 1794, the Committee of Public Safety commissioned Saint-Just to prepare a decree to create censors in the districts and army, but it had not progressed beyond this draft when its author was prevented from speaking in the Assembly in defence of his friend Robespierre on 27 July. He was immediately arrested, and guillotined the next day with Robespierre and others. Saint-Just's unpublished proposals for republican society were collected by his supporters and published posthumously as the *Fragmens sur les institutions républicaines.*

In Add MS 74269, ff. 28–29v, Stefan Zweig recommends another Saint-Just manuscript to Simon Kra as a potential purchase, saying that he himself already owns one.

Percy Bysshe Shelley
(1792–1822)

Zweig MS 188.

'Lines to —', a sonnet to Lord Byron: *autograph* fair copy; headed 'Jan 22.' [composed 1821 or 1822].

In *English*.
Begins: 'If I esteemed you less, Envy would kill / Pleasure'.
Ends: 'The worm beneath the sod / May lift itself in worship to the God'.
A sonnet of fourteen lines, divided into two stanzas of eight and six lines. The addressee or subject of the sonnet was first publicly identified as Lord Byron by Thomas Medwin in 1833. This poem should be distinguished from another entitled 'Lord Byron'.
The poem acknowledges Byron's genius and reflects Shelley's own sense of inferiority. The introductory prose line 'I am afraid these verses will not please you, but', which appears before Shelley's rough draft in Bodleian MS Shelley adds. e. 17, is lacking in the present fair copy, which suggests that Shelley did not intend it to be included in the final version. The number '200' is written on the verso.

165 x 122mm.
f. 1; 1v blank.
Black ink on wove paper.
No watermark.

Related Manuscripts: Bodleian Library, Oxford, MS. Shelley adds. e 7: a notebook containing on p. 228 reversed three-and-a-half opening lines of the poem, pencilled, in Shelley's autograph; Bodleian Library, MS. Shelley adds. e. 17: a notebook containing on p. 94 reversed Shelley's autograph rough draft of the prose introductory line and first eleven lines, with the final line on the stub of p. 73 reversed. The paper of Zweig MS 188 is possibly the same as that of Bod. adds. e. 17 and may have come from that notebook (see Crook, p. 131 and Reiman 1997, p. 247, cited below). However, Zweig MS 188 is trimmed to the edge of the written space on left and right edges, so no evidence of extraction remains; Bodleian Library, MS. Shelley adds. d. 7: a notebook containing on pp. 95–6 a copy of the poem made by Mary Shelley from the fair copy manuscript which is now Zweig MS 188.

Published: First published by Thomas Medwin, Shelley's cousin, seven lines only, in his 'Memoir of Shelley' in the *Athenaeum* (London: J. Francis), issue 248, 28 July 1832, p. 489; Medwin reprinted the lines unchanged in *The Shelley Papers* (London: Whittaker, Treacher & Co., 1833), p. 37, and with corrections and four additional lines in *The Life of Percy Bysshe Shelley*, ii (London: Thomas Cautley Newby, 1847), pp. 35 and 162; *The Poetical Works of Percy Bysshe Shelley*, ii, ed. William Michael Rossetti (London: E. Moxon, 1870), p. 362, note p. 585, fourteen lines published, with the first printing of the introductory prose line; *The Life of Percy Bysshe Shelley by Thomas Medwin,* ed. H. Buxton

Forman, amended and extended ed. (London: Humphrey Milford / Oxford University Press, 1913), where a version of the poem in twelve lines from Medwin's 1847 *Life* is on p. 258; Sotheby's sale catalogue, 16 December 1931, lot 713, p. 93, the fourteen lines of Zweig MS 188 quoted; *Fair-Copy Manuscripts of Shelley's Poems in European and American Libraries. The Manuscripts of the Younger Romantics. Percy Bysshe Shelley*, 7, ed. Donald H. Reiman and Michael O'Neill (New York; London: Garland, 1997), containing a thorough physical and textual analysis of Zweig MS 188, with reference to the publication history and related manuscripts, pp. 246–53.

Reproduced: Sotheby's sale catalogue (1931), facing p. 93, and Reiman and O'Neill (1997), p. 250; reproduced from Sotheby's catalogue in *The 'Charles the First' Draft Notebook. A facsimile of Bodleian MS Shelley adds. e. 17.*, The Bodleian Shelley Manuscripts, 12, ed. Nora Crook (New York; London: Garland, 1991), p. 132; www.bl.uk/manuscripts and Plate 54 below.

Exhibited: Paris, Bibliothèque nationale de France, Le Livre Anglais, 1951–2, catalogue no. 192 (see indemnity form in Add MS 73175, f. 13 and envelope at Add MS 73175, f. 111).

Provenance: The present manuscript was owned by Mary Shelley who, after copying, gave it to her acquaintance Charlotte Murchison sometime between 1831 and 1833; sold at Sotheby's in 1931 as the property of Sir Kenneth Murchison, of Hargrave Hall, Huntingdonshire, from the collection of Sir Roderick Murchison; purchased by Zweig at Sotheby's sale, 16 December 1931, lot 713, through Maggs; BL 1986.

Bibliography: William J. Burling, 'New light on Shelley's "Lines to —"', *Keats–Shelley Journal* (New York: Keats–Shelley Association of America, 1986), 35, pp. 20–3; BL Programme Book, 1987; *Catalogue of Additions*, p. 76; Matuschek, p. 327.

Commentary. The date of composition of the sonnet is disputed. Zweig noted January 1822 on his record card (Add MS 73168, f. 61), and the evidence of Mary Shelley's headnote and social events in Italy at the start of the year would support this. From the jottings in the Hellas notebook, and the association of the autograph draft with the Charles the First manuscript, Robinson argues that it might have been begun in November 1821 and finalised in the following January. If Crook's theory about the matching paper is correct, there is no need for a long gestation, as the fair copy could have been written immediately after the draft, on one of the following pages of the notebook, which was then torn out.

In Thomas Medwin's *Life of Shelley*, as revised by H. Buxton Forman in 1913, there is a reconstruction, possibly imagined, of the circumstances in which this sonnet was composed when both Shelley and Byron were staying in Pisa. It is suggested that Shelley was inspired by reading Byron's *Corsair*, and wrote the poem the very next day. Crook and Reiman demonstrate from other sources that Byron's work was familiar to the circle at Pisa at the start of 1822. Medwin claimed that Byron himself never saw the poem, though, if true, it is not clear whether the reason was Shelley's premature death by drowning in July, or because friends advised him that the tone was too self-effacing.

Zweig described this manuscript on his record card as 'eines der wichtigsten Documente aus der Heroenzeit der englischen Literatur'.

‘Stendhal’
(pseudonym of Marie-Henri Beyle)
(1783–1842)

Zweig MS 189.

‘Testament de M Henry Beyle’: *autograph* will with multiple signatures, sent to Stendhal’s cousin and executor, Romain Colomb; Paris, 8 June 1836.

In *French*.
Begins: ‘Je desire être transporté directement et sans frais au Cimetière’.
Ends: ‘Je lègue mes livres de Rome à M. le Prince Don Filippo Caetani. H. Beyle’.
The will states Stendhal’s instructions for his burial and his bequests. It is addressed (f. 2v) to ‘Monsieur R Colomb, n°. 35 rue Godot de Mauroy. Paris’. ‘Testament de M Henry Beyle’ written in the left-hand margin of f. 1 with signature. Annotated in pencil (f. 1, top left) ‘Testament Stendhals’ in Zweig’s hand, ‘1[8?]17’ and (top right) the figure ‘9’ in pencil in the same hand. Endorsed twice on f. 2v: ‘Testament de M. H. Beyle’.

335 x 234mm.
ff. 2; 1v and 2 blank. Address and endorsements on 2v.
Brown ink on cream wove paper.
Traces of seal in brown wax on f. 2v.
Bifolium.
Watermark: ‘L S V’.

Related Manuscripts: Stendhal wrote multiple wills. Thirty-seven had been counted by 1997 (see Y. J. Montrozier, cited below). Most of Stendhal’s papers were left to Louis Crozet, whose widow presented them to the Bibliothèque de Grenoble, France in 1861. See *Catalogue du Fonds Stendhal. Deuxième partie. Manuscrits*, ed. V. del Litto and Paul Hamon (Grenoble: Bibliothèques Municipales de Grenoble, 1995). According to Colomb, only the wills of 27 September 1837 and 28/29 September 1840 were formally filed and registered at the Tribunal de la Seine (now in the Archives de Paris). They were endorsed by the Tribunal and by the family notary M. Yver in May and June 1842. A final will of 1841, which Abraham Constantin claimed in a letter of 22 November 1844 to have found, is now lost (see *Correspondance*, vi, no. 3272).

Published: Auguste Cordier, *Comment a vécu Stendhal* (Paris: Villerelle, 1900). This edition contains the first publication of the three main wills, with details of all fourteen identified at the time. The text of Zweig MS 189, with a detailed physical description, is on pp. 67–8. *Stendhal Correspondance Générale*, ed. V. Del Litto et al. (Paris: Librairie Honoré Champion, 1999). Zweig MS 189 is printed in vol. 5 (1834–6) as no. 2728, pp. 741–2, but the source is Cordier’s edition, not the manuscript (see also vol. 6 for letters of the executor and friends concerning events following Stendhal’s death and the execution of the will).
Reproduced: Stefan Zweig, ‘Meine Autographen-Sammlung’, p. 282 (original *Philobiblon* publication only); www.bl.uk/manuscripts and Plate 55 below.
Provenance: The documents held by Colomb as

executor were passed to Auguste Cordier for his edition and then to Casimir Stryienski (1853–1912), who wrote a preface for Cordier and edited Stendhal's unpublished works. Purchased by Zweig at the sale of P. A. Chéramy's collection, auctioned by Noël Charavay, Paris, 23 April 1913, lot 22. Zweig bought three Stendhal manuscripts at this sale. [Auguste] Paul Arthur Chéramy (1840–1912) was a collector of literary manuscripts and art who owned some two hundred letters of Stendhal. Seventeen Stendhal items were sold at the Charavay sale. (See the Charavay journal, *L'amateur d'autographes*, nouvelle série, année 46 (1913), p. 133 for the list of items sold with prices.) Sheet and annotated envelope in Add MS 73175, ff. 112–4. Record card Add MS 73168, f. 62 describes the manuscript as 'Kostbarkeit ersten Ranges' but refers incorrectly to Raymond [for Romain] Colomb.

Bibliography: Stefan Zweig, 'Die Autographensammlung als Kunstwerk'; id., *Drei Dichter ihres Lebens*, pp. 123–228; id., 'Meine Autographen-Sammlung'; BL Programme Book, 1987; *Catalogue of Additions*, p. 77; Yves Jocteur Montrozier, 'Le fonds Stendhal de la bibliothèque municipale de Grenoble', in *Bulletin des bibliothèques de France* (Paris: Direction des bibliothèques de France, 1997), T. 42, n° 2, pp. 22–7; Matuschek, p. 330.

Commentary. After 1814, Stendhal spent most of his life in Italy. Suffering from poor health, partly the result of harsh treatment for syphilis, he developed a will-writing habit, despite his maxim 'Puisque la mort est inévitable, évitons d'y penser'. He wrote the present will when on leave in Paris in June 1836, and he was again in Paris when he died during the night of 22/23 March 1842. The penultimate will of 27 September 1837 (*Correspondance*, vi, no. 2814) was the one which Colomb decided should be proved, as reflecting most accurately his cousin's last wishes.

Stefan Zweig owned three Stendhal manuscripts and declared in Add MS 74269, ff. 5–5v that they were autographs he would never relinquish. He purchased all three at the Charavay sale in April 1913, the other two being 'Fin de l'amour et de l'ambition' and 'Préface pour une édition d'Helvetius', both now held at the Bodmer Foundation, Geneva. For Zweig's efforts to build a relationship with Charavay, see his diary entries for 15 March and 15 April 1913 and Matuschek, p. 19.

As an outcome of his interest in Stendhal, Zweig included his biography in *Drei Dichter ihres Lebens*. He considered him a master craftsman in the art of deception, and described his death, gravestone and the distribution of his books and papers in a way that showed familiarity with events reflected in the wills and correspondence. In one vivid scene, he portrayed Stendhal writing a will when on the point of suicide in 1828, the year he produced four wills between August and December. Zweig suggested that the crisis was only averted when Stendhal was encouraged to develop his ideas for the novel *Le rouge et le noir.*

Sully Prudhomme
(1839–1907)

Zweig MS 190.

'Le vase brisé', poem enclosed with a signed letter to Monsieur —: signed *autograph* fair copy; Paris, 17 February 1888.

In *French*.
Begins: 'Le vase où meurt cette verveine'.
Ends: 'Il est brisé: n'y touchez pas'.
In the letter (f. 1), Prudhomme thanks the unnamed addressee for his letter, and for a magnificent volume left by Captain Coèût during Prudhomme's absence from home on the previous day, in which his poem 'La grande ourse' is reproduced with some flattering comments. Touched by this interest in his work, he appends a fair copy of 'Le vase brisé', separately signed, as a mark of his gratitude (f. 2). The poem of five four-line stanzas, in which is depicted the gradual weakening of a cracked vase, damaged by a light tap from a lady's fan, provides an elegant metaphor for the heartbreak accompanying an unhappy love affair. Signed at the end 'Sully Prudhomme'.

180 x 112mm.
ff. 2; 2v blank.
Black ink on cream laid paper.
Bifolium.
Partial watermark along lower edge.

Related Manuscripts: Signed autograph copy of the poem, written on the canepin leaf of a fan, included in the sale of the Fan Collection of Madame Goran-Hurtez, Christie's, London, 25 May 1999, lot 32; a signed autograph copy of the poem, together with a letter of authentication written by Sully Prudhomme's secretary, J. Bourgeois, and dated 20 January 1903, was offered for sale by Ader of Paris, 27 June 2013, lot 151. Sully Prudhomme was apparently fond of distributing signed fair copies of his best-known poems, and there are almost certainly a number of other signed copies of 'Le vase brisé' in circulation that have not been traced.
Published: *Stances et poëmes* (Paris: Achille Faure, 1865), p. 9. The text is identical to that in Zweig MS 190 except that the printed edition includes the dedication 'A Albert Decrais' after the title.
Reproduced: www.bl.uk/manuscripts and Plate 56 below.
Provenance: Acquired in London by Zweig, 1938 (see Add MS 73186, f. 51); BL 1986.
Bibliography: *Catalogue of Additions*, p. 77; Matuschek, p. 333.

Commentary. Sully Prudhomme's most famous poem, composed in or before 1865 while the poet was still a young man, was originally dedicated to his friend Albert Decrais, a young lawyer in Paris who later became an eminent diplomat and politician. Having originally studied to become an engineer, Sully Prudhomme turned to philosophy and later to poetry, abandoning the latter after 1888 in order to write essays on aesthetics and philosophy. A particularly influential figure in the European literary world, he was the first ever winner of the Nobel Prize in Literature in 1901, awarded 'in special recognition of his poetic composition, which gives evidence of lofty idealism, artistic perfection and a rare combination of the qualities of both heart and intellect'.

Zweig's admiration and his pride in ownership are intimated in the entry on his record card for this manuscript (Add MS 73186, f. 1), on which he notes that 'Le vase brisé' is 'Eines der berühmtesten Gedichte der französischen Lyrik (in jeder Anthologie)'.

Zweig also owned a signed autograph manuscript of Sully Prudhomme's poem 'Les Danaïdes', acquired in 1912 from Maggs and now held at the Bodmer Foundation, Geneva.

Leo Tolstoy
(1828-1910)

Zweig MS 191.

Kreĭtserova sonata [*The Kreutzer Sonata*], short story: *autograph* draft of three chapters; [1889].

In *Russian.*
Begins: 'В хнашемъ мире образованных европейских [struck through] В нашем мире происходит одно [struck through] Неужели она такая стерва? Или может быть нечаянно. Совпадение?'.
Ends: 'И два яда слились в моем сердце'.
The central character of the story reveals, in the course of a conversation about love, marriage and divorce, how he was driven by jealousy to murder his wife because of her infidelity with a violinist. Beethoven's Kreutzer Sonata, performed by the lovers together, engenders the violent emotions which underpin the action. This bifolium, removed from the manuscript now held as MS N 13 in the Tolstoy Archive at the State Russian Library, comprises the end of Chapter 23, Chapter 24 and the beginning of Chapter 25.
Deletions in the draft show that Tolstoy was still developing the character of the musician, whom he first conceived as an artist or poet. The evolution of the work is complex, but Zweig's claim that this is the 'erste Urschrift' (Add MS 73168, f. 63) is mistaken.
Annotated in another hand: f. 1: 'Автограф гр. Льва Тостого (из его Крейцеровой сонаты!) получен в марте 91 г.' [= Autograph of Count Leo Tolstoy (from his Kreutzer Sonata!) received in March 91].
f. 1v: 'Получено от гр. Татьяны Львовны Толстой, в апр. 91 г., удостоверяю Николай Богушевский' [= Received from countess Tat'iana L'vovna Tolstaia in April 91, confirmed by Nikolai Bogushevskii].

221 x 176mm.
ff. 2.
Black and brown ink on cream wove paper.
Bifolium.
No watermark.

Related Manuscripts: Because of Tolstoy's habit of constant revision and the way the novella was circulated, initially by recitation and then in a clandestine lithograph, at least nine versions were produced. Sixteen related manuscripts in total survive in Moscow: the State Tolstoy Museum, main collection, folder 27 and the V. Cherktov collection, folder 14; the Tolstoy Archive in the State Russian Library (folders 54 and 55). Manuscript N 13, dated 28 August 1889, is the one from which the bifolium, now Zweig MS 191, was extracted. Manuscript N 13 reflects Version 7, and together with manuscripts NN 10, 11, 12 and 14 forms Version 8 of the text, which was the basis for the so-called 'lithograph edition'.

Published: For a comprehensive overview of the variants and the history of creation and publication of *The Kreutzer Sonata*, see the work by N. K. Gudzii cited below, pp. 563–624. The story was first heard in a public recitation at the home of Tatiana Kuzminskaia, Tolstoy's sister-in-law, on 29 October 1889. A further recitation was given in Vladimir Chertkov's publishing house in St Petersburg in November 1889. Immediately afterwards, a clandestine edition of three hundred lithographed copies was distributed, made against Tolstoy's will, from the recitation copy (manuscript 15). The British Library holds one of the lithographed copies at shelfmark RB.23b.6954. *Sochineniia grafa L. N.Tolstogo*, 13, *Proizvedeniia poslednikh godov* (Moscow: I. N. Kushnerev, 1891); *L. N. Tolstoi, Polnoe sobranie sochinenii*, 27, *Proizvedeniia 1889–1890* (Moscow: Gosudarstvennoe izdatel'stvo, 1933), text of chapters 23–5, pp. 402–5, commentaries and variants, pp. 264–432.

Variants: See 'Varianty k Kreizerovoi sonate', in *L. N. Tolstoi, Polnoe sobranie sochinenii,* 27 (Moscow: Gosudarstvennoe izdatel'stvo, 1933), pp. 389–415.

Reproduced: Stefan Zweig, 'Meine Autographen-Sammlung' (original *Philobiblon* publication only), p. 289 (bottom third of f. 2 reproduced); British Library Programme Books, 1988, p. 30 and 1996, p. 15 (f. 1 reproduced in both); www.bl.uk/manuscripts and Plate 57 below.

Exhibited: London, BL, 75 Musical and Literary Autographs, 1986; London, Christie's, etc., The Creative Spirit, 1987–8 (ff. 1v–2).

Provenance: The annotations on ff. 1 and 1v indicate that in 1891 the bifolium was already separate from the rest of the manuscript and was in the possession of Countess Tatiana Tolstoy (1864–1950), the author's eldest daughter. She passed it to the archaeologist and manuscript collector Nikolai Bogushevsky (1851–91). He died soon after receiving the manuscript, and his sister Olga inherited his collection; sold by Liepmannssohn, Berlin, auction 36, 17–20 November 1906, lot 944; acquired by Zweig 20 April 1921 from Dr. Kurt von Oerthel of Kolberg (?) [or Pertel as on the record card at Add MS 73168, f. 63]; BL 1986.

Bibliography: Stefan Zweig, *Drei Dichter ihres Lebens*, pp. 229–378; id., 'Meine Autographen-Sammlung'; N. K. Gudzii, 'Istoriia pisaniia I pechataniia Krei tzerovoi sonaty', in L. N. Tolstoi, *Polnoe sobranie sochinenii*, 27, *Proizvedeniia 1889–1890* (Moscow: Gosudarstvennoe izdatel'stvo, 1933), pp. 620–1; Stefan Zweig, 'Tolstoi als religiöser und sozialer Denker' (1937), printed in *Zeit und Welt*, ed. Richard Friedenthal (Stockholm: Bermann-Fischer Verlag, 1946), pp. 65–88; *Catalogue of Additions*, p. 77; Matuschek, pp. 335–6; L. N. Tolstoy, S. A. Tolstaya, L. L. Tolstoy, *Kreitserova sonata. Chia vina? Pesnia bez slov. Preliudiia Shopena* (Moscow: Tolstoy Museum, 2010).

Commentary. In the 1880s Tolstoy had concentrated mainly on writing non-fiction, and this short story is one of his few works of fiction from that period. It was first conceived about 1887. In 1889 Tolstoy wrote of his intention to re-write the novella as it was 'a little roughshod, unsatisfactory and uncorrected'. The present bifolium can be dated to 1889 from the date written on the manuscript from which it was extracted. The Kreutzer Sonata of the title is Beethoven's Sonata No. 9, Op. 47 for piano and violin.

Stefan Zweig said that he discovered Russian authors whilst at university, but it is not clear to what extent he was familiar with the language. In a letter to Maxim Gorky on 29 August 1923, he claimed to have obtained his Dostoevsky and Tolstoy manuscripts before the First World War 'mit viel Geld und Mühe', although he only acquired the Tolstoy autograph in 1921. He also said that he would never give up the latter (Add MS 74269, ff. 5–5v).

In his essay on Tolstoy in the 'Baumeister der Welt' series, Zweig noted that 'The original texts of his works show that Leo Tolstoy was not a man to whom writing came easily. He was one of the most painstaking and diligent of penmen; his literary frescoes were mosaics, laboriously pieced together out of millions upon millions of details, out of countless minute and particular observations.'

Perhaps as a result of this publication, Zweig was invited to represent Austrian writers at the Tolstoy Centenary celebrations in Moscow in September 1928. In a letter to Friderike Zweig he described how he delivered an unprepared speech on 'Tolstoi und das Ausland', attended the opening of the Tolstoy house, visited the Tolstoy Museum and saw 'mein Tolstoibuch ... an allen Straßenecken für 25 Kopeken verkauft'.

One of Zweig's final letters to Friderike, sent from Petropolis on 4 February 1942, mentions the comfort to be gained from favourite authors: 'Reading is my best help and only reading good old, if I may say, *proved* books, Balzac, Goethe, Tolstoy'.

Lope de Vega
(1562–1635)

Zweig MS 192.

La Corona de Ungría y la Injusta Vengança, play in three acts: signed and dated fair copy with *autograph* revisions, rubrics and numberings; 1633 (date corrected from 1623).

In Spanish.
Begins: 'Rey çeloso de la guerra voy / no puedo decirte mas'.
Ends: 'que la Corona de Ungria / da fin al serviçio vuestro'.
Play in three acts based on the universally popular tale of a wife wrongly suspected of infidelity and later vindicated, here played out in the setting of Hungarian history. A censor's endorsement of the play, signed by Pedro de Varga Machuca and dated 1 January 1634, appears at the end (f. 55). The title page and some of the annotations are written in a different hand. A detailed analysis of the various hands and other complex features of the manuscript can be found in Tyler, p. 20.

Binding 222 x 160mm. Largest sheet 220 x 152mm.
ff. ii + 55. Each act has its own autograph foliation.
Brown ink on cream laid paper.
No watermark.
Bound in brown leather, with decorative panel on front and back boards. Gold-tooling consisting of a simple decorative motif on the spine and, in the panel on the front board, the title 'LA CORONA DE UNGRIA / Y / LA INJUSTA VENGANZA / COMEDIA AUTÓGRAFA DE LOPE DE VEGA' with 'DE LA LIBRERIA DE S. DE OLOZAGA' in the lower left-hand corner.

Related manuscript: Biblioteca Nacional, Madrid, MS 15108: copy made by D. Salustiano de Olózaga, 20 December 1830 (omitting lines 345–428 and 1460–87).
Published: *Obras de Lope de Vega*, 2, ed. Cotarelo y Mori (Madrid: Real Academia Española, 1916), pp. 29–56, based on Olózaga's copy, and with the same omissions; Richard W. Tyler, *A Critical Edition of Lope de Vega's 'La corona de Hungría'*, Estudios de hispanófila, 20 ([Chapel Hill, NC]: University of North Carolina, 1972), based on a set of photocopies of the manuscript (see below).
Reproduced: Add MS 73180 (Zweig provenance papers) contains a set of photocopies of the manuscript; a facsimile of the entire manuscript made from another set of photocopies, formerly belonging to Dr. Courtney Bruerton, is included in Tyler's edition; Griswold Morley and Bruerton, p. 51; Presotto, pp. 160, 161; Matuschek, p. 340; www.bl.uk/manuscripts and Plate 58 below.
Exhibited: Madrid, Biblioteca Nacional, Exposición Bibliográfica de Lope de Vega, 1935, catalogue no. 11 (the exhibit was a photocopy of the manuscript acquired by the Biblioteca Nacional from Professor Ludwig Karl of Graz); London, BL, 75 Musical and Literary Autographs, 1986.
Provenance: Archives of the Marqués de Astorga, before 19th century; S. de Olózaga, early 19th

century (see Add MS 73168, f. 37); Lady Esthope [i.e. Easthope] 1851 (presentation inscription on f. 2v; Tyler suggests that the date might have been intended as 1831); purchased by Zweig from Maggs, February 1935; BL 1986.

Bibliography: Ludwig Karl, 'Un manuscrito de Lope de Vega, "La corona de Hungría y la injusta venganza"', in *Revista de Filología Española*, 22 (1935), pp. 399–406; S. Griswold Morley and C. Bruerton, 'Addenda to the Chronology of Lope de Vegas Comedias', in *Hispanic Review* 15 (1947), pp. 49–71; BL Programme Book, 1987; *Catalogue of Additions*, p. 77; Marco Presotto, *Le commedie autografe di Lope de Vega: catalogo e studio*, Teatro del Siglo de Oro. Bibliografías y catálogos, 25 (Kassel: Edition Reichenberger, 2000), pp. 155–61; Matuschek, p. 339.

Commentary. The change of date from 1623 to 1633 at the end of the manuscript indicates that the play was probably written earlier than 1633; certainly a drama with the same title is thought to have been performed in Valencia in 1628. If this is the same play, the original censor's endorsement must either have been lost, or was for some reason intentionally replaced in 1634.

Lope de Vega, one of the key figures in the Spanish Golden Age of Baroque literature, may be regarded as one of the greatest dramatists in Western literature. As an author he was enormously prolific, producing about five hundred plays as well as poetry and novels. The autograph manuscript of one of his plays, never before published in its entirety, would have been a very significant acquisition for Zweig's collection. After Zweig's death the manuscript was thought to have disappeared, so the first full critical edition in 1972 was made from one of several sets of photocopies in circulation at the time.

Émile Verhaeren
(1855–1916)

Zweig MS 193.

'Admirez vous les uns les autres': *autograph* drafts of the collection of poems published as *La Multiple Splendeur*; 1906.

In *French*.

A first attempt to assemble the collection published in 1906 as *La Multiple Splendeur*. The draft title page (f. 2) does not reflect the order of either the manuscript or the edition, and bears deletions and alterations. The poems themselves show many variants, corrections, insertions and deletions. Amendments are often written vertically on the outer edge of the page or on paste-downs. The order towards the end differs from that of the publication. Some poems are identified by their first lines, suggesting that titles had not yet been decided. Includes two *printed* proof sheets with *autograph* corrections (ff. 57–58, 62–63v). Ff. 33–4, 79–80*v and 83 are in the hand of Verhaeren's wife Marthe Massin, with his corrections. Accents are generally omitted.

Contents:

1. ff. 3–8. 'Le monde est fait avec des astres & des hommes'.
2. ff. 9–13. 'Le chant' (published title 'Le verbe').
3. ff. 14–26. 'Les vieux empires'.
4. ff. 27–32v. 'Les Mages'.
5. ff. 33–34. 'A la Gloire des Cieux'.
6. ff. 35–36. 'La louange du corps humain'.
7. ff. 37–43. Untitled, begins 'Pour vivre clair' (published title 'Autour de ma maison').
8. ff. 44–47. Untitled, begins 'O ces îles' (published title 'Les rêves').
9. ff. 48–51v. 'Les souffrances' (f. 51v contains a variant of first four lines).
10. ff. 52–56v. Untitled, begins 'Le monde est trepidant de trains & de navires' (published title 'La conquête').
11. ff. 57–58. 'Plus loin que les gares, le Soir'.
12. ff. 59–61. 'Les plus forts' (published title 'Les élus').
13. ff. 62–63v. 'A la gloire du vent'.
14. ff. 64–67. 'La joie'.
15. ff. 68–73v. 'L'arbre'.
16. ff. 74–80*. 'L'Europe'.
17. f. 80*v. First seven lines of 'Les penseurs' (see below, f. 83).
18. ff. 81–82. 'La lutte' (published title 'La vie').
19. ff. 83–91. 'Les penseurs'.
20. ff. 92–96. 'L'effort'; here entitled 'Le travail'.
21. ff. 97–98. 'La Ferveur'; here untitled, with a different title deleted.

Two further poems, 'La mort' and 'Les idées', were included in the published edition but are not represented in this manuscript.

Largest sheet 315 x 204mm. Some leaves are made up of several pieces glued together and with paste-downs.
ff. 98. Mostly written on rectos only, but some leaves have notes or rough drafts on the verso.
Black, blue and red ink, printed black ink and pencil, on paper of various types and sheet composition.
Formerly housed in a box 250 x 205mm made to resemble a bound volume in dark red leather with green silk lining and ribbon. Marbled fore-edges and gold-stamped title and date. The box is stored separately.

Published: Émile Verhaeren, *La Multiple Splendeur* (Paris: Mercure de France, 1906). Limited edition of 26 copies in 18mo. Significant changes were made for the octavo edition. See André Fontaine, *Verhaeren et son œuvre* (Paris: Mercure de France, 1929), pp. 191–2. Émile Verhaeren, *Œuvres*, 5 (Paris: Mercure de France, 1928), pp. 1–108.
Reproduced: www.bl.uk/manuscripts and Plate 59 below.
Provenance: The manuscript bears Zweig's note recording presentation by the author, dated 26 June 1909 (f. 1). The record card in Add MS 73168, f. 65 has the same information and is annotated 'London' in pencil and 'Kostbarkeit aller ersten Ranges'; BL 1986.
Bibliography: Stefan Zweig, *Émile Verhaeren* (Leipzig: Insel Verlag, 1910); id., 'Die Autographensammlung als Kunstwerk'; id., *Erinnerungen an Emile Verhaeren* (Leipzig: Selbstverlag, 1917 and 1927); id., 'Meine Autographen-Sammlung'; Jean-Marie Culot, *Bibliographie de Émile Verhaeren* (Brussels: Palais des Académies, 1954); BL Programme Book, 1987; *Catalogue of Additions*, p. 77; Matuschek, p. 339.

Commentary. Zweig first encountered Verhaeren's work as a schoolboy, and was immediately struck by the contrast with the poetry being produced in contemporary Vienna. He began to prepare his own German translations, and in 1898 sought Verhaeren's permission to publish these early efforts. A friendship between them developed after Zweig published his translations in the first edition of the *Ausgewählte Gedichte* in 1904, and dedicated his *Verlaine* to Verhaeren and gave him a copy of the manuscript. Zweig promoted Verhaeren's works in German-speaking countries through translations, publications, conferences and public readings, in all translating and publishing sixty-five of Verhaeren's poems, as well as plays and essays. For details see *Verhaeren–Zweig correspondence*, ed. Fabrice van de Kerckhove (Brussels: A. M. L. Éditions, 1996), pp. 531–4 and 551–3. Zweig also wrote a biography of his friend and, following his death, the privately printed *Erinnerungen an Emile Verhaeren.*

The present manuscript is one that Zweig said he would never give up (Add MS 74269, ff. 5–5v). Zweig also owned autograph manuscripts of Verhaeren's 'Les vergers de mai', acquired in 1908 and now held at the Bodmer Foundation, Geneva, and 'Le Meunier', acquired in 1908 and now BL Zweig MS 194. Both were gifts of the author.

Zweig MS 194.

'Le Meunier', poem: signed *autograph* draft, heavily corrected with deletions and substitions; [1895?].

In *French*.
Begins: 'Le vieux meunier du moulin noir'.
Ends: 'Comme seules elles avaient illimité sa vie'.
Poem of ninety-nine lines divided into irregular sections with varying rhyme patterns. Title and sheet numbers have been added in lead pencil; with an insertion (f. 1) and signature (f. 5) in blue pencil; some amendments in a paler ink.

Largest sheet 227 x 219mm.
ff. 5; versos blank.
Black ink and blue crayon on flimsy cream paper.
No watermark.

Published: A different poem with the title 'Le Meunier' had appeared in Émile Verhaeren, *Les Villages illusoires* (Brussels: Edmond Deman, 1895), pp. 21–3. First verified publication of the present poem is *Le Coq rouge. Revue littéraire*, 11–12 (March–April 1896), pp. 518–21. There are some textual differences, and the poem there has the title 'Le moulin vide'. Émile Verhaeren, *Poésie complète*, 4, ed. Michel Otten (Brussels: A. M. L. Éditions, 2005), pp. 66–73.
Reproduced: www.bl.uk/manuscripts and Plate 60 below.
Provenance: Presented to Zweig by the author; see the paper folder annotated by Zweig at Add MS 73170, f. 10: 'Von Emile Verhaeren, Caillou qui bique, Sommer 1908'. Offered for sale by Zweig in 1937 through Hinterberger, Vienna, catalogue XX, no. 851 (Add MS 73183 D); not sold and returned to the collection; BL 1986.
Bibliography: André Fontaine, *Verhaeren et son œuvre: d'après des documents inédits* (Paris: Mercure de France, 1929); BL Programme Book, 1987; *Catalogue of Additions*, p. 77; *Émile et Marthe Verhaeren–Stefan Zweig (1900–1926): correspondance générale,* ed. Fabrice van de Kerckhove (Brussels: Labor, 1996); Matuschek, p. 339.

Commentary. On a paper folder in which he enclosed the manuscript, now separated as Add MS 73170, ff. 10–11v, Stefan Zweig wrote the following annotations:
f. 10 'Verhaeren Emile (1854–1915)
Gedicht a. s.
„ Le meunier" Erste Fassung, wie sie zuerst in »La Belgique artistique et litteraire" erschien, in Buchform (1892) und später stark verändert'
[in pencil] 'XX/851'
f. 11v [in pencil, struck through] 'Verhaeren / Gedicht / nicht im Katalog / Hinterberger 20 851'.

Apart from the error in Verhaeren's date of death, other details in this note may be incorrect. There is no evidence of a publication of the poem in book form in 1892, and the work has not been located in the periodical *La Belgique artistique et littéraire* which appeared from October 1905 to July 1914.

Zweig translated the poem into German and included it in his collection of 'Nachdichtungen', *Emile Verhaeren, Ausgewählte Gedichte* (Leipzig: Insel Verlag, 1904). For more on the friendship between Zweig and Verhaeren and the other gifts of manuscripts, see Commentary to Zweig MS 193.

Paul Verlaine
(1844–1896)

Zweig MS 195.

'Fêtes Galantes', poems: *autograph* drafts with numerous corrections, and two *printed* proof sheets corrected by the author; 1869.

In *French*.
The poems are preceded by a calligraphically written title page (f. 1), apparently in a different hand, and an *autograph* list of the poems, with the number of lines in each (f. 2).

Contents (*autograph* unless stated otherwise):
1. ff. 3–5. 'Clair de lune' (printed proof with corrections), numbered '1'.
2. f. 6. 'Pantomine', numbered '2'.
3. f. 7. 'Sur l'herbe', numbered '3'.
4. f. 8. 'L'allée', numbered '4'.
5. f. 9. 'Dans la grotte', numbered '6'.
6. f. 10. 'Les Ingénus', numbered '7'.
7. f. 11. 'Cortège', numbered '8'.
8. f. 12. 'Les coquillages', numbered '9'.
9. ff. 13–14. 'En patinant', numbered '10'.
10. f. 15. 'Fantoches', numbered '11'.
11. f. 16. 'Cythère', numbered '12'.
12. f. 17. 'En bateau', numbered '13'.
13. f. 18. 'Le Faune', numbered '14'.
14. ff. 19–21. 'Mandoline' (printed proof with corrections), numbered '15'.
15. ff. 22–23. 'À Clymène', numbered '16'.
16. ff. 24–25. 'Lettre', numbered '17'.
17. f. 26. 'Les Indolents', numbered '18'.
18. ff. 27–27v. 'Colombine', numbered '19'.
19. f. 28. 'L'Amour par terre', numbered '20'.
20. f. 29. 'En sourdine', numbered '21'.
21. ff. 30–31. 'Colloque sentimental', numbered '22'.

Binding 217 x 158mm. Largest sheet 211 x 132mm.
ff. 31.
Black and brown ink and black printed text on laid and wove paper of differing sizes, the proof sheets stuck down on support sheets. Some proof sheets bear substantial autograph corrections, on pieces of paper pasted down over text.
Binding of red morocco by E. A. Enders of Leipzig with gold-tooling. Author's name and the title 'Paul Verlaine Fêtes Galantes' on spine. Pale blue end-papers. Integral bookmark of pale blue ribbon.

Published: Collection published as *Fêtes galantes* (Paris: Alphonse Lemerre, 1869).
Poems published individually as follows:
'Clair de lune', with the title 'Fêtes Galantes', and 'Mandoline', with the title 'Trumeau', in *La Gazette rimée*, 1, 20 February 1867, pp. 11–12; 'Clair de lune', 'L'allée', 'Sur l'herbe', 'Mandoline', 'Pantomime', 'Le Faune' in *L'Artiste*, 1 January 1868, under the heading 'Fêtes galantes'; 'À la promenade', 'Dans la grotte', 'Les ingénus', 'À Clymène', 'En sourdine', 'Colloque sentimental' in *L'Artiste*, 1 July 1868, under the heading 'Nouvelles Fêtes galantes'; 'Cortège', 'L'Amour par terre' in *L'Artiste*, 1 March 1869, under the heading 'Poésie'.
Reproduced: Facsimile of the present manuscript published in the series *Les Manuscrits des maîtres* as Paul Verlaine, *Fêtes galantes* (Paris: Albert Messein, 1920); BL Programme Book, 1987, p. 31 (f. 30); BL Programme Book, 1988, p. 27 (f. 29); www.bl.uk/manuscripts and Plate 61 below.
Exhibited: London, Christie's, etc., The Creative Spirit, 1987–8.
Provenance: Purchased by Zweig from Noël Charavay, Paris, 12 March 1913; BL 1986.
Bibliography: Stefan Zweig, *Paul Verlaine*, authorised translation by O. F. Theis (Boston; Dublin: Luce; Maunsel and Co., 1913); id., 'Meine Autographen-Sammlung'; BL Programme Books, 1987, 1988; *Catalogue of Additions*, p. 78; Matuschek, pp. 341–2.

Commentary. Zweig's fascination with Verlaine started at a very early age. Not only did he publish a monograph on the French poet while he was still only twenty-three, but at an early date he also published an anthology of translations of Verlaine's poetry and was the editor of Paul Verlaine, *Gesammelte Werke*, published in two volumes by the Insel Verlag in 1922.

The poems in *Fêtes galantes* are among the best-known of Verlaine's works, not least because they have often been set to music, notably by Debussy. It was a tremendous triumph for Zweig to secure the present, very important manuscript, which he had actively been seeking for his collection. He made no secret of the fact that he was intending to acquire it at the Charavay sale no matter what the cost, although in the event he had to pay less than he expected.

'À la promenade', the fifth poem in the list on f. 2, was seemingly never part of the manuscript Zweig acquired and was typewritten in the 1920 reproduction of *Fêtes galantes*.

Zweig MS 196.

Fragment from a chapter intended for inclusion in the prose work *Voyage en France par un français*: *autograph* draft; [1880].

In *French*.
Begins: 'qui ne serait rien qu'un tout petit malheur littéraire'.
Ends: 'la très humble queue de ce serpent hydrocéphale!'.
Heavily corrected *autograph* draft fragment, with a footnote below the text beginning 'mon nom et à mon rôle' and ending 'le sang versé pour nous par notre Seigneur Jesus Christ'. Inscribed 'Autographe de Verlaine offert à M. Stefan Zweig. Ernest Delahaye' in the top left-hand corner. With the Hinterberger catalogue number 'XX/852' in pencil.

220 x 175mm.
f. 1.
Black ink on cream lined paper.
No watermark.

Published: Ernest Delahaye, *Documents relatifs à Paul Verlaine* (Paris: Maison du Livre, 1919), pp. 57–9; Paul Verlaine, *Œuvres en prose complètes*, ed. Jacques Borel (Paris: Gallimard, 1972), pp. 1043–6.
Reproduced: www.bl.uk/manuscripts and Plate 62 below.

Provenance: Acquired by Zweig from Ernest Delahaye after 1919 (note of presentation, f. 1); BL 1986.
Bibliography: Hinterberger catalogue XX, no. 852; BL Programme Book, 1987; *Catalogue of Additions*, p. 78; Matuschek, p. 342.

Commentary. The extract forms part of a projected eighth chapter of *Voyage en France par un français*, entitled 'Le Théâtre, l'Art et les Femmes', but it was not incorporated when the work was first published in 1907. In the footnote, Verlaine responds to a comment by Émile Zola that Verlaine has ruined his life by imitating Baudelaire, an allegation that Verlaine refutes, suggesting that his life has been ruined in other ways.

This is one of several Verlaine autographs formerly owned by Zweig. As well as the 'Fêtes galantes' manuscript (Zweig MS 195), his collection included a signed manuscript of the poem 'Balanide II' from the collection *Hombres* (now held at the Bodmer Foundation, Geneva), and manuscripts of the poems 'Vigo Street! rêve de ma tristesse et mon sort' and 'Pour le Roi des Belges', both now in a private collection in Switzerland.

Jules Verne
(1828–1905)

Zweig MS 197.

Autograph letter to Charles Carter, Captain of the 'Mayfly'; Le Tréport, 24 August [1881].

In *French*.
Begins: 'M^{r} Ch. Carter, capitaine du Mayfly, Saint Malo, poste restante. Je reçois capitaine la note de reparation de votre canot'.
Ends: 'Je vous prie de me croire Votre devoué Jules Verne'.
The letter relates to a repair bill received by Verne for damage to the Mayfly's dinghy during an incident occurring on 12 July 1881 in adverse conditions. Verne reminds Captain Carter, commander of the Mayfly, that it is customary in France for costs resulting from damage caused by 'force majeure' to be shared by the two parties. Hinterberger catalogue number 'XX, 854' pencilled in bottom left-hand corner of f. 1. Top left-hand corner has '9A' in pencil. 'Jules Verne' is written in pencil in an unidentified hand on f. 2 below his signature.

134 x 104mm.
ff. 2. Versos blank.
Brown ink on cream laid paper.
Bifolium.
No watermark.

Published: Ian Thompson and Philippe Valetoux, 'Dramatic Incident of the Saint-Michel III at Saint Malo, 1881', in *Extraordinary Voyages* (newsletter of the North American Jules Verne Society), 14/2 (2007), pp. 1–4.
Reproduced: www.bl.uk/manuscripts and Plate 63 below.

Provenance: Date of acquisition by Zweig unknown; BL 1986.
Bibliography: Hinterberger catalogue XX, no. 854 (Add MS 73183 D); BL Programme Book, 1987; *Catalogue of Additions*, p. 78; Matuschek, p. 342; discussed in detail in Thompson and Valetoux, op. cit.

Commentary. Arriving at Saint-Malo en route from Dieppe to Nantes, Verne's yacht, the Saint-Michel III, under the command of Captain Ollive, was prevented from entering port by the shallowness of the water at low tide. Moored in Dinard Bay on the advice of the pilot who had been taken on board, the yacht dragged her anchor in the strong currents and drifted, narrowly avoiding a direct collision with the Mayfly and causing her dinghy to smash into the dinghy of the other vessel. The Saint-Michel III finally regained her mooring in the treacherous waters after several attempts and with the assistance of her steam engine. Despite the perilous conditions, it appears that Captain Ollive may well have been at fault, since initially he used only a single anchor, contrary to the guidance given in the *Instructions Nautiques* for the treacherous Dinard moorings.

Zweig also owned a signed manuscript of Verne's article 'Souvenirs d'enfance et de jeunesse', acquired in 1931 and now held at the Bodmer Foundation, Geneva.

'Charles Vildrac'
(pseudonym of Charles Messager)
(1882–1971)

Zweig MS 198.

'Le Paquebot Tenacity', three-act play: heavily corrected *autograph* fragment of the first draft of Act II, Scene 1; [*c.* 1919].

In *French.*
Begins: 'Segard et Therese. Ils sont près d'une table, au premier plan à droite'.
Ends: 'Et je suis bien avec tout le monde; et je rends des services, on pourra te le dire'.
The play was first performed at Jacques Copeau's Théatre de Vieux-Colombier, Paris in 1920. A white label on the front cover of the manuscript bears the inscription 'Le Paquebot Tenacity – Acte II Premier tableau – Premier état' in black ink in Vildrac's hand. Inside the front cover Vildrac has written '"Le Paquebot Tenacity" Act II – Premier tableau – premier manuscrit. Souvenir offert à Stefan Zweig avec la solide poignie de main d'amitié de Charles Vildrac'. There are rough drawings of several male faces (possibly intended to portray the characters) in the left-hand margin of f. 4v, and one on the inside back cover (f. 10), while a female face is sketched in the margin of f. 8.

170 x 220mm.
ff. 10.
Brown and blue ink in a school exercise book with lined paper and pink covers.

Published: Charles Vildrac, *Le Paquebot Tenacity* (Geneva: Éditions du Sablier, 1919), with woodcut illustrations by Frans Masereel; id., *Le Paquebot Tenacity* (Paris: Nouvelle Revue française, 1920).
Reproduced: Plate 64 below.

Provenance: Presented to Zweig by the author, probably *c.* 1919; BL 1986.
Bibliography: BL Programme Book, 1987; *Catalogue of Additions*, p. 78; Matuschek, pp. 342–3.

Commentary. *Le Paquebot Tenacity* tells the story of two young friends, recently discharged from the army and on their way to the freedom of a new life in Canada, whose very different personalities are revealed through the train of events arising when their ship, the Tenacity, is delayed in port by a breakdown of its boiler. During a convivial evening both fall for the barmaid, one of them seducing and subsequently marrying her and staying, while the other – betrayed – continues his journey. Simple in action and economical of language, the play comes from the *Théâtre de l'Inexprimé*, a genre in which silence and a special kind of understatement were used to suggest intimate thoughts and emotions. The play was very successful in its day, and in 1934 was adapted to become a popular black and white film, *SS Tenacity*, directed by Julien Duvivier, with a script by Duvivier and Vildrac.

Vildrac, together with the writer Georges Duhamel (later his brother-in-law) and others, was a founder member of 'L'Abbaye', a community of young artists and writers who, from 1906 to 1907, lived together in the Paris suburb of Créteil. Zweig was introduced to Vildrac and Duhamel by a poet and writer close to the 'Abbaye' members, Jules Romains, whom he had met through Émile Verhaeren.

OSCAR WILDE
(1854–1900)

Zweig MS 199.

'In the Gold Room. A Harmony', poem: *autograph* draft with numerous *autograph* amendments; [1881].

In *English*.
Begins: 'Her ivory hands on the ivory keys'.
Ends: 'With the spilt-out blood of the rose-red wine'.
The poem consists of three six-line stanzas. The manuscript is unsigned but Zweig has written 'Oscar Wilde' in pencil in the top left-hand corner.

260 x 206mm.
f. 1; 1v blank.
Black ink on cream laid paper.
No watermark.

Published: Oscar Wilde, *Poems* (London: David Bogue, 1881), pp. 150–1; republished with two minor revisions under a new heading 'Flowers of Gold' in the 1882 editions of *Poems* (London: David Bogue), pp. 148–9; *The Collected Works of Oscar Wilde*, 9, *Poems*, ed. Robert Ross (London: Methuen, 1908), p. 159; *The Complete Works of Oscar Wilde*, 1, *Poems and Poems in Prose*, ed. Bobby Fong and Karl Beckson (Oxford: Oxford University Press, 2000), pp. 153–4.
Reproduced: BL Programme Book, 1987, p. 22; *The Creative Spirit*; Matuschek, p. 349; www.bl.uk/manuscripts and Plate 65 below.
Exhibited: London, BL, 75 Musical and Literary Autographs, 1986; London, Christie's, etc., The Creative Spirit, 1987–8; Moscow, State Pushkin Museum of Fine Arts, Oscar Wilde and Aubrey Beardsley – A Russian Perspective, 2014.
Provenance: Owned by Frederick Garland Burmester (*c.* 1840–1930), whose collection was sold by Puttick & Simpson, London, 7 January 1931. Lot 203, the present manuscript, was purchased by Zweig through Maggs; BL 1986.
Bibliography: See the Editorial Introduction in *The Complete Works*, ed. Fong and Beckson for publication history and ranking of sources; Stuart Mason *pseud.* [i.e. Christopher Millard], *A Bibliography of the Poems of Oscar Wilde* (London: E. Grant Richards, 1907), p. 41; id., *Bibliography of Oscar Wilde*, new ed. (London: Bertram Rota, 1967), pp. 307–8 (refers to the unamended original wording in 'a manuscript version' which must be Zweig MS 199); *Catalogue of Additions*, p. 78; Matuschek, pp. 348–9.

Commentary. Oscar Wilde began his writing career with poems. Between 1877 and 1881 he produced about forty, some of which were first published in periodicals. His first published collection of poetry, issued at his own expense, appeared in 1881. Two further editions were published in the same year, and a fourth and fifth edition in 1882. All were published by David Bogue, in print runs of two hundred and fifty copies. Unsold copies of the fifth edition with artwork by Charles Ricketts were reissued in 1892 by Elkin Matthews and John Lane following Bogue's bankruptcy. The textual tradition of the early poems relies on the collected editions, as Wilde's literary manuscripts were dispersed at auction in the mid 1890s during his imprisonment. After 1882, he published only single poems.

On his record card, Add MS 73168, f. 69, Zweig describes the MS as 'eines seiner bekanntesten Gedichte!' He notes the title incorrectly as 'In a golden room'. Zweig owned two other Wilde manuscripts, 'Impression du soir' and 'Five aphorisms on art' from *Intentions*, both acquired in 1928 and both now held at the Bodmer Foundation, Geneva. Zweig's regard for Wilde as a significant author is shown in a letter to Anton Kippenberg of 16 March 1919, in which he speaks of expanding the 'Inselbücherei' to include not just German but other European authors and names Flaubert, Wilde and Swinburne as potential candidates in three or four years' time.

'Reformatoren-Gedenkbuch'

Zweig MS 200.

Collection of scriptural commentaries by Protestant Reformers, the so-called 'Reformatoren-Gedenkbuch'; 1542.

In *German* and *Latin*.
Leaves containing signed notes on passages from the Scriptures by well-known Reformers and their associates.
The contributors are: Martin Luther (1483–1546), Johannes Bugenhagen (1485–1558), Philipp Melanchthon (1497–1560), Caspar Creutziger (1504–48), Georg Rörer (1492–1557), Hieronymus Noppus (d. 1551), Georg Helt (*c.* 1485–1545), Georg Major (1502–74), Leonhard Bayer [Reiff] (*c.* 1495–1552), Johannes Göbel (1515–51) and Paul von Rode (1489–1562).
At f. 5 is a letter dated 20 March 1554 from Philipp Melanchthon to Theodor Fabricius, Superintendent at Zerbst (reversed), inviting the recipient's endorsement of 'Augustinus', son of the Pastor in Cosswik [Coswig], whom the elderly Pastor of Wertlo [Wertlau] in the Zerbst district wishes to be his successor.
This letter is listed in a 19th-century index of contents (f. 2), headed 'Reformatoren-Gedenkbuch' and bearing the stamp of the Library of the Counts of Stolberg-Wernigerode, written on the recto of the second leaf of a paper bifolium, the first having been pasted down on the inside of the front cover to form an end-paper. An equivalent leaf has been used as an end-paper on the back cover.

Paper covers 340 x 235mm. Largest sheet 342 x 233mm.
ff. i + 9.
Black and brown ink on laid paper.
In original paper covers, slightly soiled and marked with small areas of water staining. The Stolberg-Wernigerode library pressmark Zm 25, written in black ink on a slip of cream paper, has been added to the lower left-hand corner. The pressmark has also been added in pencil on f. 2 in the upper right-hand corner. The leaves have been re-sewn directly into these covers, having been formerly attached with linen strips, removed for conservation reasons. These are now kept with the manuscript in a clear protective housing, as are the remains of the original sewing threads.
A binding of blue-green linen-covered boards added in the 20th century (presumably after 1927, since the facsimile published in that year mentions only the paper covers) and its flyleaves have also been detached for conservation reasons and are kept separately with the manuscript. The Stolberg-Wernigerode library pressmark Zm 25 has similarly been added to the later binding.
Indistinct watermarks.

Related Manuscripts: See commentary.

Published: *Stammbuch eines Wittenberger Studenten 1542, nach dem Original in der Stolbergischen Bibliothek zu Wernigerode in Faksimiledruck herausgegeben*, ed. Wilhelm Herse (Berlin: Woelbing Verlag, 1927); Melanchthon's letter printed in *Zeitschrift des Harz-Vereins fur Geschichte und Alterthumskunde*, ed. Jacobs (Wernigerode: Harzverein, 1869), Heft 2, p. 66; also in H. E. Bindseil, *P Melanchthonis Epistolae, Judicia, Consilia, Testimonia aliorumque ad eum epistolae quae in corpore reformatorum desiderantur* (Halle: Schwetschke, 1874) p. 356.

Reproduced: Matuschek, p. 305 (f. 3); www.bl.uk/manuscripts and Plates 66–7 below.

Provenance: 'Nicolas Reinhold of Zwickau' (almost certainly erroneous), 1542; ?Theodor Fabricius (1501–70), Superintendent at Zerbst and recipient of the enclosed letter, 1554; 'Johann Schröder' (name written inside the back paper cover), late 17th/early 18th century; owned by the Counts of Stolberg-Wernigerode, before 1890 (library stamp on f. 2 and notes of library pressmark on binding, inner paper cover and on f. 2); purchased by Zweig from J. Halle, Munich, March 1931 (Zweig's record card, Add MS 73168, f. 54); BL 1986.

Bibliography: Bernhard Bess, 'Stammbuch eines Wittenberger Studenten, 1542', *Zentralblatt für Bibliothekswesen*, 46 (1929), pp. 572–3 (review of 1927 facsimile); BL Programme Book, 1987; Wolfgang Klose, *Corpus Alborum Amicorum* (Stuttgart: Hiersemann, 1988), pp. XV–XVI; *Catalogue of Additions*, pp. 78–9; Matuschek, p. 304.

Commentary. Until comparatively recently the volume was thought to represent the earliest example of an *album amicorum* or *Stammbuch*, ownership being attributed to the Wittenberg student Nicolaus Reinhold of Zwickau, but there is no evidence to support this attribution. The likelihood of a false assumption about the nature of the book is reinforced by the fact that the contents of the volume consist solely of scriptural material, bearing none of the personal characteristics of the entries typically found in an *album amicorum*. A more plausible suggestion has been made that the leaves originally belonged to a Bible, subsequently being detached and bound up separately. A few surviving copies of the Luther Bible printed by Hans Lufft in 1541, including one in the British Library (shelfmark 679.i.15–16), are known to contain similar pages, giving credence to this notion.

Miguel de Cervantes Saavedra
(1547–1616)

Zweig MS 201.

El ingenioso hidalgo don Quixote de la Mancha (Madrid: por Iuan de la Cuesta. Vendese en casa de Francisco de Robles, 1605): *printed* book.

In *Spanish*.
Second edition of the first part. Includes the Privilege dated 26 September and the *Tassa* dated 20 December 1604, together with the Privilege for Portugal dated 9 February 1605.

196 x 136mm. 208 x 150mm.
ff. [12] + 316 + [iv].
Bound in vellum, stamped with 'Camperdown Library' ownership mark in gold on front board.

Reproduced: www.bl.uk/manuscripts and Plate 68 below.
Provenance: From the library of the Countess of Buckingham; sold at auction, by Dowells Ltd., Edinburgh, to Heinrich Eisemann (presumably on behalf of Zweig), 1941; purchased by Zweig from Heinrich Eisemann, London, June 1941 (see Add MS 73174); BL 1986.

Bibliography: [Uncredited], 'An Early "Don Quixote"', in *Times Literary Supplement*, 9 August 1941; Luis Andrés Murillo, *Don Quijote de la Mancha: bibliografía fundamental*, Clásicos Castalia, 79 (Madrid: Castalia, 1978); BL Programme Book, 1987; *Catalogue of Additions*, p. 79; *El Quijote: Biografía de un Libro* (Madrid: Biblioteca Nacional, 2005).

Commentary. Not until the nineteenth century were the first and second editions of Cervantes's *Don Quixote* correctly identified (see Vincent Salvá, *A Catalogue of Spanish and Portugiese Books, with Occasional Literary and Bibliograhical Remarks*, part 1 (London: M. Calero, 1826), pp. 233–4). The book in the Zweig Collection is a second edition printed by Juan de la Cuesta, in which some of the errors of the first edition (1605) have been corrected. Subsequent imprints are based on this edition. Between the first edition produced by Juan de la Cuesta and the second, other printers gained licences to publish the book outside of Madrid. Two versions appeared in Lisbon before Cuesta received the privilege covering Portugal and the areas of Aragón and Castile. As the *TLS* article has it, this still did not 'prevent the subsequent appearance, still in 1605, of an edition with a Valencia imprint.' Zweig's copy, thus recognisable by the imprint 'Con Privilegio de Castilla, Aragon y Portugal. En Madrid, por Iuan de la Cuesta,' is almost as rare as the first edition.

It appears that Zweig had also purchased a 1608 edition of the book a year earlier, also from Eisemann, for which – the receipt shows – he paid significantly less than he did for the 1605 second edition. Cervantes was for Zweig a master, against whom he compared many of his biographical protagonists. Zweig suggests Cervantes's *Novelas ejemplares*, with 'ihr selig leichtes Verraten, ihr spitzbübisches Schalten mit Versteck und Geheimnis' (*Der Kampf mit dem Dämon*), were a model for the work of Heinrich von Kleist. Zweig often portrayed his historical characters in conflict with their surroundings in order to enhance their struggle towards achievement. Cervantes, too, was an archetype in this respect, when Zweig notes, 'Den Don Quichotte verdanken wir den öden Kerkerjahren des Cervantes' (*Drei Dichter ihres Lebens*). The most comprehensive exposition of Zweig's thoughts on Cervantes comes again through a comparison, this time between Don Quixote himself and Miguel Servet, the Spanish humanist: 'Nicht nur bildmäßig hat dieser schmächtige, fahle, spitzbärtige Aragonier Ahnlichkeit mit dem hagern und magern Helden de la Mancha; auch innerlich ist er verbrannt von der gleichen großartigen und grotesken Leidenschaft, für das Absurde zu Kämpfen und in blindwütigem Idealismus gegen alle Widerstände der Realität anzurennen' (*Castellio gegen Calvin*, published Vienna: Reichner, 1936).

Arthur Rimbaud
(1854–1891)

Zweig MS 202.

Une Saison en enfer (Brussels: Alliance typographique (M.-J. Poot et Compagnie), 1873): *printed* book.

In *French*.
Written on the inside of the original box, in Zweig's hand: 'Arthur Rimbaud "Une saison en enfer" Originalausgabe. Die gesammte Auflage wurde bis auf ungefähr sieben Exemplare vom Verfasser vernichtet: dies eines der erhaltenen *Rarissimum* der französischen Literatur'. The fact that all but about seven copies were destroyed is erroneous.
Pencil notes on the inside of the original box refer to the book's location in Zweig's library: 'Bl Tisch links. 2. Schließfach links'.

180 x 120mm.
pp. 53.
Binding of brown morocco, gold-tooled, by E. A. Enders of Leipzig. Green and brown morocco on spine, with gold-tooled 'RIMBAUD – UNE SAISON EN ENFER'. Marbled end-papers. Red fore-edging. Green silk bookmark.

Reproduced: www.bl.uk/manuscripts and Plate 69 below.
Exhibited: London, National Book League, A Thousand Years of French Books, 1948; London, National Book League, England: Her Friends and Visitors, July 1956.
Provenance: Léon Losseau bought the entire stock of the *Alliance typographique*, amongst which were over two hundred and fifty copies of *Une Saison en enfer*. Some copies of this first edition were distributed to writers. Zweig received his copy from a mutual friend of his and Émile Verhaeren's, O. Van den Daele. Gifted with the following dedication: 'A Monsieur Stefan Zweig, en souvenir des journées passées avec E Verhaeren au Caillou & à Angre. Mons, le 8. X '08. Bien cordialement, O. Van den Daele'.
Bibliography: BL Programme Book, 1987; Chris Michaelides, 'Stefan Zweig's copy of Rimbaud, *Une Saison en enfer* (1873)', in *The British Library Journal*, 14/2 (1988), pp. 199–203; *Catalogue of Additions*, p. 79.

Commentary. *Une Saison en enfer* was the only work to be published by Rimbaud himself. The accepted view until 1914 understood the majority of the print-run to have been burnt by the author, who renounced literature and did indeed burn copies in his possession as well as his manuscripts before his death. After 1914, two conflicting accounts emerged explaining the circumstances of the discovery of some 425 remaining copies. Léon Losseau, a lawyer from Mons, suggested in 1914 that his discovery was based on checking the printer's account books, and establishing Rimbaud's inability to settle the account, which meant that the author only received a dozen of the five hundred printed copies. Losseau claimed to have made this discovery in 1901, waiting until he would host the next meeting of the *Société des bibliophiles belges séant à Mons* to present the copies to his fellow members, while some were distributed in secret to esteemed authors such as Émile Verhaeren, Maurice Maeterlinck and Stefan Zweig. This meeting, however, was not to take place until November 1912, a delay which casts doubt on Losseau's story. Louis Piérard, the Belgian journalist, poet and art critic, contests Losseau, suggesting the lawyer bought up the stock without knowing exactly what it contained. Not until Piérard and a friend searched the archive in 1912 were the remaining copies discovered. While Piérard's version of events fits more closely with the timing of the announcement, Zweig's dedication shows that the books must have been discovered in or before October 1908. Whatever the actual sequence of events, Michaelides writes, 'Piérard's claim is borne out by the signature "O. Van den Daele" in Zweig's copy. Van den Daele was Piérard's teacher and friend' (see Michaelides for a comprehensive account of the facts surrounding the discovery and donation of *Une Saison en enfer*).

In Zweig's 1907 essay 'Arthur Rimbaud', he reiterates the common acceptance of *Une Saison en enfer*'s destruction by the author, before comparing Rimbaud's style in the work to that of Nietzsche: 'kaum gibt es eine merkwürdigere Stilähnlichkeit des Zufalles als die beiden fast gleichzeitigen Bücher der einsam Gewordenen, von der Welt Befreiten, als "Une saison d' [en] enfer" und "Zarathustra". Rimbauds Wortkraft wird allmählich phänomenal, die Worte schwellen an unter seiner Hand: das graue Gallert der Begriffe saugt sich vampirhaft mit Blut an und schillert nun, von Farben bis zum Bersten geschwellt, in nie gesehenen Licht.' Rimbaud also acts as a poetic model to compare other great poets to, as, for instance, Hugo von Hofmannsthal could only ever be compared to John Keats and Rimbaud, sharing their 'Unfehlbarkeit in der Bemeisterung der Sprache' (*Die Welt von Gestern*). Zweig also owned the manuscript of Rimbaud's collection of poems entitled *Poésies* (see Zweig MS 181).

Hans Holbein
(1497–1543)

Zweig MS 203.

Les simulachres & historiees faces de la mort, autant elegammēt pourtraictes, que artificiellement imaginées (Lyon: [Melchior et Gaspar Trechsel], 1538): *printed* book.

In *French* and *Latin*.
Contains woodcuts by Hans Holbein for the 'Dance of Death' series, executed by Holbein's collaborator Hans Lützelburger. With a Biblical passage in Latin above each image and a quatrain in French below. The French verses are attributed in the Sotheby's auction catalogue to Gilles Corrozet (see Add MS 73174), while they are elsewhere attributed to Jean de Vauzelles (see Hofer).
Bookplate: 'From the library of John Charrington, The Grange, Shenley.' An inscription inside the cover in an unknown hand reads 'Ces 41 images continues dans ce livre sont de Hans Holbein, et sont de la première impression'.

165 x 120mm.
Letterpress text and woodcut illustrations.
ff. 1 + 53. Gatherings of four leaves with signatures A to N. Gii and Giii are transposed.
Binding of brown leather, gold-tooled on spine.
Marbled end-papers.

Reproduced: www.bl.uk/manuscripts and Plate 70 below.
Provenance: John Charrington, Shenley (bookplate); purchased by Zweig at Sotheby's auction, London, *Valuable books, manuscripts and autograph letters*, which included 'The Valuable Library of the late John Charrington, Esq', 18 December 1939, lot 237; BL 1986.
Bibliography: James M. Clark, *The Dance of Death in the Middle Ages and the Renaissance* (Glasgow: Jackson, Son & Co., 1950); Werner L. Gundersheimer, Introduction in *The Dance of Death by Hans Holbein the Younger: A Complete Facsimile of the Original 1538 Edition of* Les simulachres & historiées faces de la mort (New York: Dover, 1971); *The Dance of Death. Les simulachres & historiées faces de la mort. Designed by Hans Holbein, and cut in wood by Hans Lützelburger.* Introductory essays by Philip Hofer and Amy Turner Montague (Boston, MA: Cygnet Press, 1974); BL Programme Book, 1987; *Catalogue of Additions*, p. 79.

Commentary. Holbein did not cut the woodblocks himself, leaving the cutting to his 'most gifted woodcutter Hans Lützelburger, also from Augsburg' (see Hofer's essay in *The Dance of Death* (1974)). The first forty-one woodcuts were made before 1526 and the woodblocks were printed from many times thereafter. Not until 1538 did they appear together in series in the Lyon edition.

By the 1562 edition the number of woodcuts had risen to fifty-eight. It is presumed that some of the additional woodcuts were not originally conceived as part of the *Dance of Death* series, as they are of a different spirit, namely the four woodcuts depicting children (Hofer). Arguing that the work is not a pure 'Dance of Death' series with 'alternating series of living forms and cadavers or skeletons', Gundersheimer suggests Holbein's work synthesized two strands of representation, 'placing the familiar social types of the Dance of the Dead into individual vignettes of the "Memento mori" type'. The latter mode of representation often depicts a single individual in the company of a figure of death. By depicting human mortality, 'the cuts, as well as the text, were meant to lead the reader to a virtuous life so that he might die well' (Montague).

Contained within Add MS 73177 is a German facsimile edition of Holbein's *Todtentanz* (Munich: Georg Hirth, 1884), in which is inserted a note written by Zweig in English to his second wife describing the first edition: 'First Edition of Holbein[']s "Danse [*sic*] of death" Lyon 1531 [1538], one of the capital works of illustrated books, extremely rare and nearly unrecorded in such a perfect copy'. Matuschek writes of Zweig's later foray into collecting artworks, mentioning the Holbein acquisition, and argues that 'wurde auch hier der angenehme Kunstgenuß mit der nützlichen Sicherung des Kapitals verbunden'. In other words, this element of his collection was informed as much by his intention to invest in safe and valuable assets, as by a taste for artworks. That said, Holbein played an important role in one of Zweig's most significant works, *Triumph und Tragik des Erasmus von Rotterdam*. Holbein's portrait of the humanist Erasmus was, for Zweig, a masterpiece, and the definitive image of a figure, in whom Zweig in exile and desperation saw himself reflected and in whom he sought inspiration: 'Unvergleichlich, unvergeßlich darum das Bild Holbeins, das Erasmus im heiligsten Augenblick, in der schöpferischen Sekunde der Arbeit darstellt, dieses Meisterwerk seiner Meisterwerke und vielleicht schlechthin die vollkommenste malerische Darstellung eines Schriftstellers, dem das erlebte Wort sich magisch umsetzt in die Sichtbarkeit der Schrift'.

Giorgio Vasari
(1511–1574)

Zweig MS 206.

Part of Vasari's account of the life of the painter Luca Signorelli: contemporary manuscript *copy* in an unidentified hand; [after 1550]. With supplementary *typewritten* and *printed* materials.

In *Italian*.
Begins: 'Chi ci nasce di bona natura, nō ha bisogno nelle cose del vivere di alchuno artificio'.
Ends [mid sentence]: 'capella di palazzo nella quale tanti begli i gegni'.
The narrative breaks off where Pope Sisto sends for Signorelli to work in the chapel of his palace. Contemporary manuscript *copy* (ff. 1–2v) of approximately three quarters of the Life of Signorelli as published in part 2 of the 1550 edition of *Le Vite dei più Eccellente Architetti, Pittori, Scultori e Architettori Italiani*. With a *typewritten* English translation (ff. 3–7), made from the manuscript, ending in the same place and indicating lacunae where the original is damaged. Followed (ff. 8v–11) by pages 525–30 of the printed edition of 1568, where the text is prefaced by a head-and-shoulders portrait of Signorelli. The 1568 edition was substantially revised, and so contains passages with more details of Signorelli's works not found in the present manuscript. These are marked in the margin with the word 'fehlt' in ink, apparently not in Zweig's hand.

Largest size 292 x 218mm.
ff. 11; 11–11v blank.
Brown ink on cream laid paper; bifolium (ff. 1–2), typewritten text on cream paper (ff. 3–7); letterpress with woodcut and corrections in blue ink on cream laid paper (ff. 8–10).
Watermark: Paschal lamb (f. 1).
Loss to text around some edges.

Related Manuscript: There are apparently no other extant manuscripts of Vasari's *Vite* except for an annotated leaf in a copyist's hand of the Vita di Raffaele discovered in 1998 by Piero Scapecchi in the Biblioteca Nazionale Centrale in Florence (BNCF Nuove Accessioni, 1396). The copyist's hand is not the same as that in Zweig MS 206.
Published: Giorgio Vasari, *Le Vite de' piú Eccellenti Architetti, Pittori, et Scultori Italiani* ... (Florence: [Lorenzo Torrentino], 1550), pp. 520–4; second revised ed., *Le Vite de' piú Eccellenti Architetti, Pittori, et Scultori Italiani* (Florence: Appresso i Giunti, 1568), pp. 526–[30]; *Le Vite de' piú Eccellenti Architetti, Pittori, et Scultori Italiani* ... ed. Luciano Bellosi and Aldo Rossi (Turin: Einaudi, 1986), pp. 504–8, with text from the 1550 edition, plus explanatory footnotes.
Reproduced: www.bl.uk/manuscripts and Plate 71 below.
Provenance: From the collection of Alfred Morrison; sold at Sotheby's, 16 April 1918 as lot 1164, and described in the sale catalogue as autograph; purchased by Maggs and sold as an autograph draft in July 1923, catalogue 439, no. 1151, when purchased by Zweig; presented to the British Library by the Trustees of the Stefan Zweig Collection, 27 September 1989, supplementing the earlier donation.

Bibliography: Recorded but not transcribed in Alphonse Wyatt Thibaudeau, *Catalogue of the Collection of Autograph Letters and Historical Documents formed between 1865 and 1882 by Alfred Morrison*, 6 [letters S–Z] (London: Printed for private circulation, 1892), p. 301; Stefan Zweig, 'Meine Autographen-Sammlung'; *Catalogue of Additions*, Part II, p. 515; Sara Nair James, 'Vasari on Signorelli: The Origins of the 'Grand Manner of Painting', in A. B. Barriault et al. (eds.), *Reading Vasari* (London: Philip Wilson, 2005). pp. 75–87; Matuschek, p. 339.

Commentary. Luca Signorelli, also known as Luca d'Egidio di Ventura or Luca di Cortona (*c.*1441–1523), was renowned for his frescoes, especially those of the Apocalypse and Last Judgment in Orvieto Cathedral. He was a cousin of Vasari, whose artistic talent he encouraged, recommending him as a pupil to the stained glass painter Guglielmo da Marsiglia. Vasari himself, a practising architect and painter, compiled biographies of Italian artists in four genres, in encyclopaedic format, combining facts with anecdote. His *Vite* was dedicated to Grand Duke Cosimo I de Medici. The first edition was partly rewritten and enlarged in 1568 with the addition of woodcut portraits.

Zweig MS 206 was once thought to be Vasari's autograph but comparison with Add MS 23139, ff. 20–35 and Egerton MS 1977, f. 27 shows Vasari's hand to be smaller, more cursive and less disciplined, with a distinctive letter 'v'. Based on the description in Maggs's sale catalogue, Zweig initially wrote that the manuscript was 'zweifellos eine erste Urschrift' (Add MS 73168, f. 64), believing that it was autograph and unaware that it was almost identical with the first edition. He later came to the conclusion that the manuscript was in fact a copy: an index card in Add MS 73182 is annotated by him 'MS, wahrscheinlich Kopie', and 'Untersucht nicht echt'. Provenance papers in Add MS 73175, ff. 113–25 include a card and letter in Italian from Luigi Banzi to Heinrich Eisemann dated 12 February 1957, with German translation of a letter concerning the hand of the MS, photocopies of Vasari's hand, and an envelope annotated 'Doubtful Manuscript!'

It seems likely that Zweig MS 206 is a contemporary copy, rather than a forgery, possibly made from the first printed edition, to which it is textually very close, with very occasional omission or transposition of words, abbreviations, single letters for double and 'bona' for 'buona' in the first line. Folio 1 displays a typical copyist's mistake in anticipating, and then deleting, the words 'il virtu'. Zweig, as a collector, made clear his own definitions of genuine and false in his essay 'Von echten und falschen Autographen', published as a Foreword to *Basler Bücherfreund*, Jahrgang 3, Heft 1, April 1927 (reprinted in Matuschek, pp. 118–19).

Honoré de Balzac
(1799–1850)

Zweig MS 216.

['Monographie de la Presse Parisienne'], article: *printed* proof sheet with *autograph* corrections; [*c.* 1842].

In *French.*

Printed text begins: 'Il ne suffit pas d'une centaine de mille francs'.

Ends: 'et se rendent encore plus médiocres à ce travail fasti-'.

Part of a satirical article in which Balzac sets out to offer a complete analysis of the French press. The text, which comes from the first part of the article in a section headed 'Le Publiciste', contains the beginning of a discussion of various types of editor. It partly duplicates and continues the text found in Zweig MS 135. Printed on one side with numerous *autograph* corrections in black ink, including a lengthy insert consisting of seven lines added at the bottom of the printed text and continuing into another three lines on the verso. The recto is numbered '4' in ink at the top, while the number '10737', encircled and in pencil, appears diagonally in the top left-hand corner with 'Balzac' below it, also in pencil and apparently in Zweig's hand.

Frame 292 x 167mm. Sheet 263 x 140mm.
f. 1. Printed text with annotations in black ink on wove paper.
In a black frame, glazed on recto and verso.

Related Manuscripts: BL Zweig MS 135 (see entry above for this and for a description of other related manuscripts).

Published: See entry for Zweig MS 135.

Reproduced: www.bl.uk/manuscripts and Plate 72 below.

Exhibited: Paris, Pierre Berès, Exposition commémorative du cent cinquantième anniversaire de Balzac, 1949, catalogue no. 408; Paris, Bibliothèque nationale de France, Honoré de Balzac, Exposition organisée pour commémorer le centenaire de sa mort, 1950, catalogue no. 596.

Provenance: Zweig purchased the leaf from Heinrich Eisemann in London in February 1940, together with a further leaf from the same manuscript (probably Zweig MS 135); BL 2009 (formerly on deposit as Loan 95/12).

Bibliography: See bibliography for Zweig MS 133 above.

Commentary. See entry for Zweig MS 135.

Johann Wolfgang von Goethe
(1749–1832)

Zweig MS 217.

Drawing of a landscape, with a building in the distance, probably depicting the area around Jena, with a landscape pencil sketch on verso; [probably about 1808].

Inscribed in black ink in top left-hand corner of verso 'Handzeichnung von Joh. Wolfg. Göthe. Empfangen von Hrn. Chrn Schuchardt, Vorsteher d. Grossherzogl. Museums zu Weimar, welcher die Aechtheit derselben verbürgt'.

Frame 169 x 245mm. Sheet 102 x 165mm.
Pen and black ink with monochrome wash over pencil (f. 1).
Black ink and pencil (f. 1v).
On a blue laid paper mount, with openings on both sides, both with washline mounts. In a metal frame, glazed on both sides.

Related Manuscript: See Zweig MS 154 for another landscape drawing by Goethe.
Reproduced: *Corpus der Goethezeichungen*, 6b, plates 135, 138 Rs.; Stargardt, Berlin sale catalogue, 327 (1931), Tafel 1, 2; Stargardt, Berlin, sale catalogue 337 (1933), p. 12, no. 257; Otto Kletzl, 'Goethes Rotes Reisebüchlein', *Germanoslavica*, 1 (1931), between pp. 460 and 461; Ludwig Münz, *Goethes Zeichnungen und Radierungen* (Vienna: Österreichische Staatsdruckerei, 1949), Abb. 135; www.bl.uk/manuscripts and Plate 73 below.
Provenance: Johann Christian Schuchardt, mid 19th century; purchased by Zweig from Stargardt, probably in 1933 (see Zweig's record card, Add MS 73168, f. 14); BL 2009 (formerly on deposit as Loan 95/13).

Bibliography: Liepmannssohn, Berlin, auction catalogue 58 (1929), p. 5, no. 1; id., catalogue 59 (1930), p. 79, no. 567; Fr. Meyer catalogue, Leipzig, 2 (1927), p. 26, no. 207; Stargardt, Berlin, sale catalogue 327 (1931), p. 8, no. 33; Otto Kletzl, 'Goethes Rotes Reisebüchlein', *Germanoslavica*, 1 (1931), between pp. 453–61; Stargardt, Berlin, sale catalogue 337 (1933), p. 12, no. 257; *Corpus der Goethezeichungen*, 6b, ed. Gerhard Femmel (Leipzig: E. A Seemann, 1971), p. 51, no. 138; Nicholas Boyle, 'Goethe's Later Cycles of Drawings', in *Goethe und das Zeitalter der Romantik*, ed. Walter Hinderer (Würzburg: Königshausen und Neumann, 2002), pp. 281–306; Matuschek, p. 220.

Commentary. The views in these drawings have never been formally identified, but it seems likely that they are taken from the countryside near Jena, a town for which Goethe had a special affection, regarding it almost as his second home. The river landscape in the smaller drawing seems to bear quite a strong resemblance to the valley of the Saale, while the ruined castle in the larger drawing may perhaps be the Lobdeburg, a twelfth-century fortress above Jena whose medieval owners were credited with the founding of the town, and which fell into decay around the end of the sixteenth century. For many years Goethe was accustomed to stay with his friends, the von Ziegesar family, in Drackendorf, an area of Jena just below the Lobdeburg, and the ruins were a favourite destination for walks with Sylvie, the young daughter of the house, one in particular delighting him so much that he celebrated by composing the poem 'Bergschloss' in 1802.

The dimensions of the leaf suggest that the drawings could have been intended for an album, perhaps Goethe's so-called 'Rotes Reisebüchlein', an album made in 1808 for eighteen-year-old Wilhelmine Herzlieb.

Johann Christian Schuchardt, who authenticated the smaller drawing, acted as one of Goethe's secretaries from 1825 onwards and became Head of the Grand Ducal Museum in Weimar. In 1848–9 he published *Goethe's Kunstsammlungen* (3 vols.), an inventory of Goethe's own art collection that was then in his care.

The present drawings are two of the seven Goethe drawings owned by Zweig at various stages of his collecting career. Another is also in the British Library (see above, Zweig MS 154): for a complete list see Matuschek, pp. 219–20.

Maurice Maeterlinck
(1862–1949)

Zweig MS 218.
'Le Trésor des Humbles', essays: corrected *printed* proofs with extensive *autograph* manuscript in the second half of the volume; [*c.* 1896].

In *French*.
A combination of printed articles and book sections and manuscript sheets, all cut and pasted onto pages of a larger book. Manuscript insertions are stuck two to a page and numbered by the author as separate pages. With a table of contents on f. 95. Minor corrections throughout but little variation from the final version.

1. ff. 2–5. 'Le Reveil de l'Ame'.
2. ff. 5v–7v. 'Le Silence'.
3. ff. 8–10v. 'Les Avertis'.
4. ff. 11–13. 'La Morale Mystique'.
5. ff. 13–16. 'Sur les femmes'.
6. ff. 17–28. 'Ruysbroeck l'Admirable'.
7. ff. 29–35v. 'Emerson'.
8. ff. 36–43v. 'Novalis'.
9. ff. 44–50v. 'Le tragique quotidien'.
10. ff. 50v–58v. 'L'Etoile'.
11. ff. 58v–68v. 'La Bonté invisible'.
12. ff. 68v–81v. 'La Vie profonde'.
13. ff. 81v–94. 'La beauté intérieure'.

Overall size 271 x 206mm.
ff. 95, with various early numberings throughout.
Black, brown and blue ink, blue and red crayon, pencil and black printed text on a variety of paper types and sizes. Manuscript sections in black ink on lined cream paper.
Slip-case with green and brown marbling. Book bound in green morocco, with gold-tooling on spine, 'MAETERLINCK / LE TRÉSOR / DES / HUMBLES'. Gold-tooling to front and back boards. Cloth and marbled end-papers. Yellow, red and green cloth bookmark. Bottom of inside front cover bears the name 'E. CARAYON' in gold. Émile Carayon (1843–1909) was a notable decorative binder with the distinctive style evident in this volume.

Published: Many of the essays were first published individually in journals between 1894–6, predominantly in *La nouvelle revue*, namely, essays 1, 4, 5, 11, 12, 13 from the list above, while 'Novalis' is cut from a copy of Maeterlinck's own introduction to his 1895 translation of Novalis's *Die Lehrlinge zu Saïs* (*Les Disciples à Saïs*) (see Lecat). First published as a collection in Maurice Maeterlinck, *Le Trésor des humbles* (Paris: Mercure de France, 1896). The published version begins with the essay 'Le Silence' before 'Le Reveil de l'Âme'. Republished in Maurice Maeterlinck, *Œuvres,* 1 (Paris: Mercure de France, 1913). A special edition illustrated with woodcuts by Frans Masereel appeared in 1921 (Geneva: Éditions du Sablier). Some essays were published in Maurice Maeterlinck, *Œuvres: édition établie et présentée par Paul Gorceix*, 1, *Le Reveil de l'Âme* (Brussels: A. Versaille, 2010).

Reproduced: www.bl.uk/manuscripts and Plate 74 below.

Provenance: Acquired by Zweig through Auguste Blaizot, from the Auction Pierre Dauze, Paris, 29 May 1914; BL 2009 (formerly on deposit as Loan 95/19).

Bibliography: Maurice Lecat, *Bibliographie de Maurice Maeterlinck* (Brussels: Librairie Castaigne, 1939); Stefan Zweig, *Erinnerungen an Émile Verhaeren* (1917), reprinted in *Begegnungen mit Menschen, Büchern, Städten* (Berlin; Frankfurt am Main: S. Fischer, 1955).

Commentary. The winner of the 1911 Nobel Prize in Literature, Maurice Maeterlinck wrote on a wide range of topics in his essays, including entomology, metapsychology and mysticism, while being perhaps better known for his symbolist poetry and drama. *Le Trésor des humbles* shows the author's interest in Germanic sources, which was emblematic more generally of the group of Flemish authors writing in French in the late 1890s, including Émile Verhaeren, Georges Eekhoud and Georges Rodenbach. In particular, the German Romantic thinker Friedrich von Hardenberg (pseudonym Novalis), was key in shaping Maeterlinck's mysticism, hence his inclusion in this volume. Maeterlinck writes, after Novalis, 'Nous ne sommes qu'un mystère et ce que nous savons n'est pas intéressant', which might represent his continuous interest in the mysterious and the inexplicable aspects of life.

Zweig already owned one Novalis manuscript (now BL Zweig MS 176), possibly more, at the time of acquiring *Le Trésor des humbles*, and the connection would have formed a small part of his attraction to the item. However, Zweig was already drawn, early in his literary career, to Flandrian writing, particularly that of his long-time collaborator and friend, Émile Verhaeren. It is likely that Zweig would have nominated his friend rather than Maeterlinck for the Nobel Prize in 1911. In his *Erinnerungen an Émile Verhaeren*, Zweig writes about Verhaeren's patience in awaiting literary recognition, while Maeterlinck, ten years his junior, already enjoyed worldwide fame. Zweig calls the present item 'das bekannte philosophische Meisterwerk von Maurice Maeterlinck' on his catalogue card (Add MS 73618), but concentrates mainly on the rarity of the object, since the author began composing his works by typewriter soon after, rendering manuscripts from his early period more select. Zweig's further note on numerous 'Abweichungen und Aenderungen gegen den gedruckten Text' is a slight overstatement for a text with only minor corrections.

List of Manuscripts by Stefan Zweig's Date of Acquisition

Date acquired	Reference	Author and Work
1908	Zweig MS 159	Hugo von Hofmannsthal: 'Vor Tag'; [1907].
1908	Zweig MS 194	Émile Verhaeren: 'Le Meunier'; [1895?]
1909	Zweig MS 193	Émile Verhaeren: 'Admirez vous les uns les autres'; 1906.
1911	Zweig MS 139	Paul Claudel: 'L'annonce faite à Marie'; 1911.
1911	Zweig MS 176	'Novalis': 'Die Erfüllung'; [1800].
1912	Zweig MS 143	Fedor Mikhailovich Dostoevsky: 'The Insulted and Injured'; [1861].
1912	Zweig MSS 184–5	Romain Rolland: 'L'aube nouvelle'; 1911–12.
1913	Zweig MS 140	Gabriele D'Annunzio: 'La Laude di Dante'; [*c.* 1904].
1913	Zweig MS 179	Rainer Maria Rilke: 'Die Weise von Liebe und Tod des Cornets Otto Rilke'; 1904.
1913	Zweig MS 189	'Stendhal': Will sent to Romain Colomb; 1836.
1913	Zweig MS 195	Paul Verlaine: 'Fêtes Galantes'; 1869.
1914	Zweig MS 133	Honoré de Balzac: 'Une Ténébreuse Affaire'; [*c.* 1841].
1914	Zweig MS 138	George Gordon, 6th Baron Byron: 'Note to the lines where Capel Lofft is mentioned'; [*c.* 1811].
1914	Zweig MS 146	Gustave Flaubert: 'Bibliomanie'; 1836.
1914	Zweig MS 151	André Gide: 'De l'importance du public'; 1903.
1914	Zweig MS 156	Heinrich Heine: 'Die armen Weber'; [1844].
1914	Zweig MS 164	Heinrich von Kleist: 'Germania an ihre Kinder', 'An Franz den Ersten, Kaiser von Österreich' and 'Kriegslied der Deutschen'; [1809].
1914	Zweig MS 181	Arthur Rimbaud: 'Poésies'; 1870.
1914	Zweig MS 218	Maurice Maeterlinck: 'Le trésor des humbles'; [*c.* 1896].
1919	Zweig MS 152	Johann Wolfgang von Goethe: 'Faust', Part II, Act I; [*c.* 1827–8].
after 1919	Zweig MS 196	Paul Verlaine: 'Voyage en France par un français'; [1880].
after 1919	Zweig MS 198	'Charles Vildrac': 'Le Paquebot Tenacity'; [*c.* 1919?].
1921	Zweig MS 191	Leo Tolstoy: 'The Kreutzer Sonata'; [1889].
1922	Zweig MS 155	Johann Wolfgang von Goethe: Hair from Goethe's head; [1832?].
1922	Zweig MS 167	Giacomo Leopardi: Verses headed 'XXXVIII. Dal greco di Simonide'; 1823–4.
1923	Zweig MS 206	Giorgio Vasari: Account of the life of the painter Luca Signorelli; [after 1550].

1924	Zweig MS 150	Sigmund Freud: 'Der Dichter und das Phantasieren'; [1908].
1924	Zweig MS 162	Henrik Ibsen: article 'En udflugt til Abydos'; [1869].
1924	Zweig MS 163	John Keats: 'I stood tiptoe upon a little hill'; [1816].
1926	Zweig MS 160	Friedrich Hölderlin: 'Stuttgart'; [1800–1].
1926	Zweig MS 161	Friedrich Hölderlin: 'An die Deutschen' and 'Die scheinheiligen Dichter'; [*c.* 1798].
1926	Zweig MS 170	Stéphane Mallarmé: 'La chevelure vol d'une flamme à l'extrême'; [*c.*1887].
1926	Zweig MS 174	Benito Mussolini: 'Responsibilità', 1921.
1927	Zweig MS 136	Charles Baudelaire: 'Les sept vieillards' and 'Les petites vieilles'; [1859].
1927	Zweig MS 182	Maximilien de Robespierre: 'La rose croît pour tous les hommes'; 1786.
1927	Zweig MS 183	Jeanne-Marie Roland de la Platière: 'Rêveries Philosophiques ou Folles', etc.; 1777, 1782.
1927	Zweig MS 187	Louis-Antoine de Saint-Just: Draft decree concerning the creation of censorship; [1794].
1930	Zweig MS 165	Jean de la Fontaine: Five occasional verses; 1660.
1930	Zweig MS 169	Louis XVI: Decree to the Legislative Assembly; 1791.
1930	Zweig MS 172	Thomas Moore: ''Tis the Last Rose of Summer'; [1805–13].
1930	Zweig MS 177	Alexander Pope: 'To the Earl of Oxford upon a Piece of News...'; [*c.* 1728].
1931	Zweig MS 166	Jean-Henri Latude: Mémoire sent from Vincennes to M. de Sartine, Lieutenant-General of the Police; 1770.
1931	Zweig MS 175	Friedrich Nietzsche: 'Die Geburt des tragischen Gedankens'; 1870.
1931	Zweig MS 188	Percy Bysshe Shelley: 'Lines to —', a sonnet to Lord Byron; [1821 or 1822].
1931	Zweig MS 199	Oscar Wilde: 'In the Gold Room. A Harmony'; [1881].
1931	Zweig MS 200	Reformatoren-Gedenkbuch; 1542.
1933?	Zweig MS 157	Hermann Hesse: 'Sommer 1933'; 1933.
1933	Zweig MS 158	Adolf Hitler: Outline for a speech; [1928].
1933	Zweig MS 171	Marie Antoinette: letter to Count [Xavier] von Rosenberg; [1775].
1933?	Zweig MS 217	Johann Wolfgang von Goethe: Two landscape drawings; [*c.* 1808?].
1935	Zweig MS 192	Lope de Vega: 'La Corona de Ungría y la Injusta Vengança'; 1633.
1936	Zweig MS 144	Georges Duhamel: 'Le dernier voyage de Candide'; 1936.
before 1938	Zweig MS 142	Philippe Desportes: Maxims, epigrams and aphorisms; before 1606.
1938	Zweig MS 190	Sully Prudhomme: 'Le vase brisé'; 1888.
1939	Zweig MS 137	Arnold Bennett: 'Books and Persons', including review of 'Conflicts' by Stefan Zweig; 1928.

1939	Zweig MS 178	Pierre-Joseph Proudhon: 'A propos de Louis Blanc'; 1849.
1940	Zweig MS 132	Hans Christian Andersen: 'Fest-Sang til Landsoldaten'; [1851].
1940	Zweig MS 134	Honoré de Balzac: letter to Jean Thomassy; [1823].
1940?	Zweig MS 135	Honoré de Balzac: 'Monographie de la Presse Parisienne'; [*c.* 1842].
1940?	Zweig MS 216	Honoré de Balzac: 'Monographie de la Presse Parisienne'; [*c.* 1842].
1941	Zweig MS 149	Benjamin Franklin: Letter to William Strahan; 1744/5.
unknown	Zweig MS 141	Charles Darwin: 'Insectivorous Plants'; bef. 1875.
unknown	Zweig MS 145	Fredrik Axel von Fersen: Letter sent to the Swedish Court of Appeal; 1787.
unknown	Zweig MS 147	Joseph Fouché: Letter to 'Collègues & amis'; [1794].
unknown	Zweig MS 148	'Anatole France': Letter from 'M. B.' concerning an article on orthography; 1898.
unknown	Zweig MS 154	Johann Wolfgang von Goethe: Drawing of the Kammerberg bei Eger; [1808].
unknown	Zweig MS 168	John Locke: Latin epitaph to Descartes; [1670s?].
unknown	Zweig MS 173	Joachim Murat: Letter as King of Naples; [1809].
unknown	Zweig MS 180	Rainer Maria Rilke: Letter to A. Wolfenstein; 1920.
unknown	Zweig MS 186	Romain Rolland: 'La jeunesse suisse'; 1917; 'Déclaration de l 'indépendence de l'esprit'; 1919.
unknown	Zweig MS 197	Jules Verne: Letter to Charles Carter; [1881].

THE PLATES

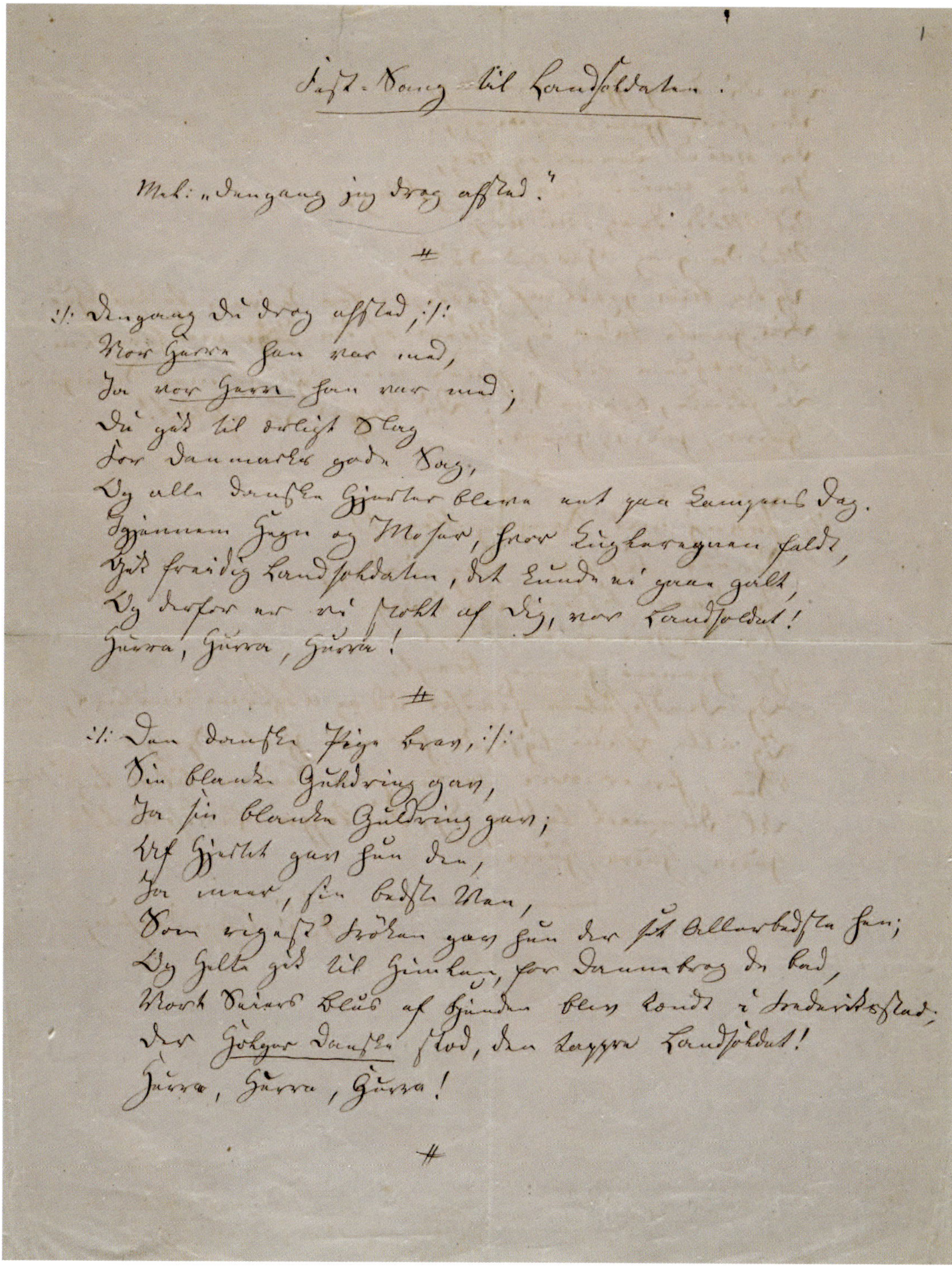
1

Fest-Sang til Landsoldaten.

Mel: „Dengang jeg drog afsted."

#

:/: Dengang du drog afsted, :/:
Vor Herre han var med,
Ja vor Herre han var med;
Du gik til ærligt Slag
For Danmarks gode Sag,
Og alle danske Hjerter bleve med paa Langveis Dag.
Igjennem Skov og Moser, hvor Kuglerne faldt,
Gik freidig Landsoldaten, det kunde ei gaae galt,
Og derfor ere vi stolte af Dig, vor Landsoldat!
Hurra, Hurra, Hurra!

#

:/: Den danske Pige brav, :/:
Sin blanke Guldring gav,
Ja sin blanke Guldring gav;
Sit Hjerte gav hun den,
Ja mere, sin bedste Ven,
Som eneste Sønnen gav hun der sit allerbedste har;
Og Helte gik til Himlen, for Danmark de bad,
Mod Seirens Blod af Fjenden blev vundet i Frederiksstad,
der Sønner danske stod, den tappre Landsoldat!
Hurra, Hurra, Hurra!

#

Plate 1 Hans Christian Andersen: Zweig MS 132, f. 1r

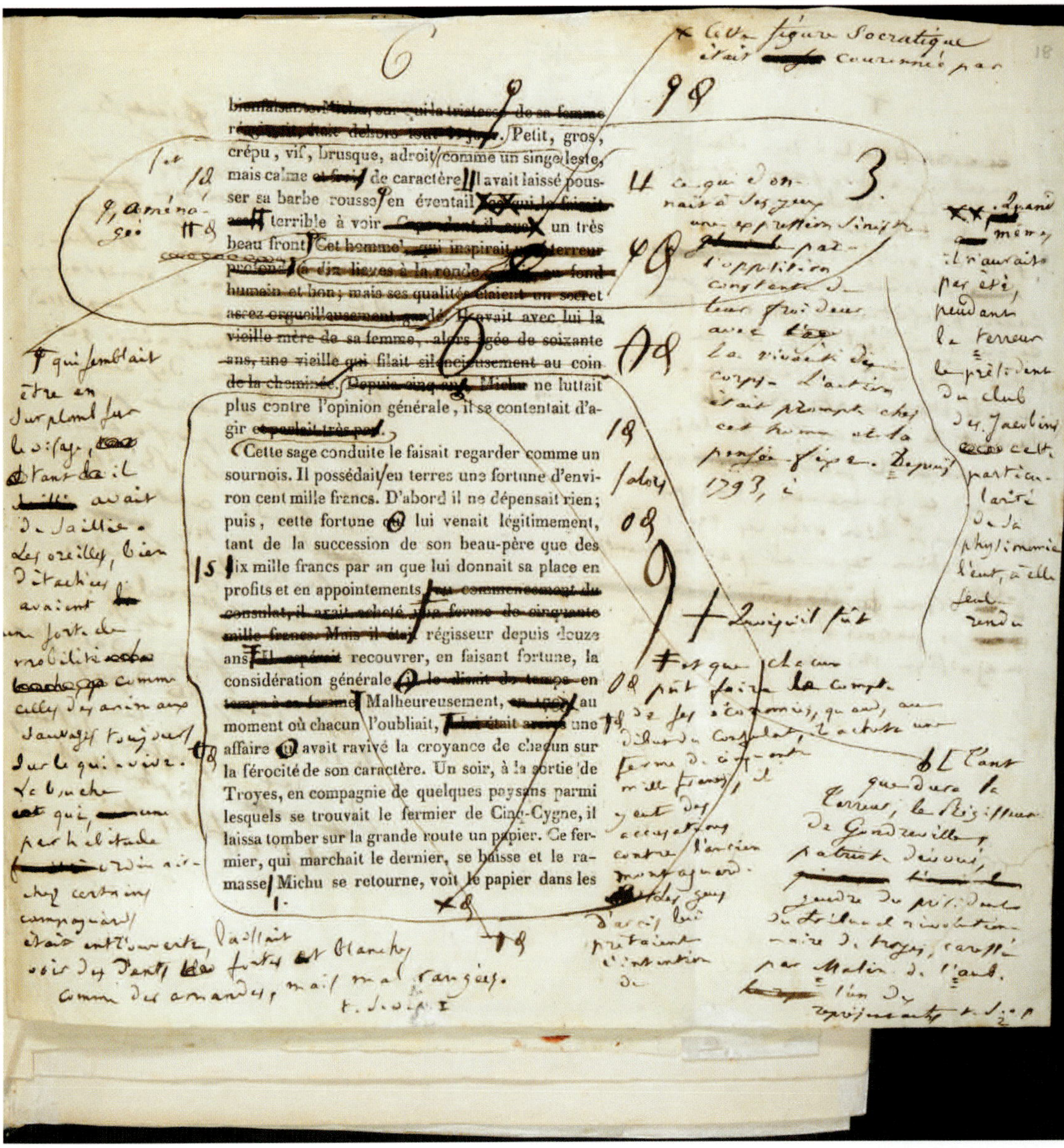

Plate 2 Honoré de Balzac: Zweig MS 133, f. 18r

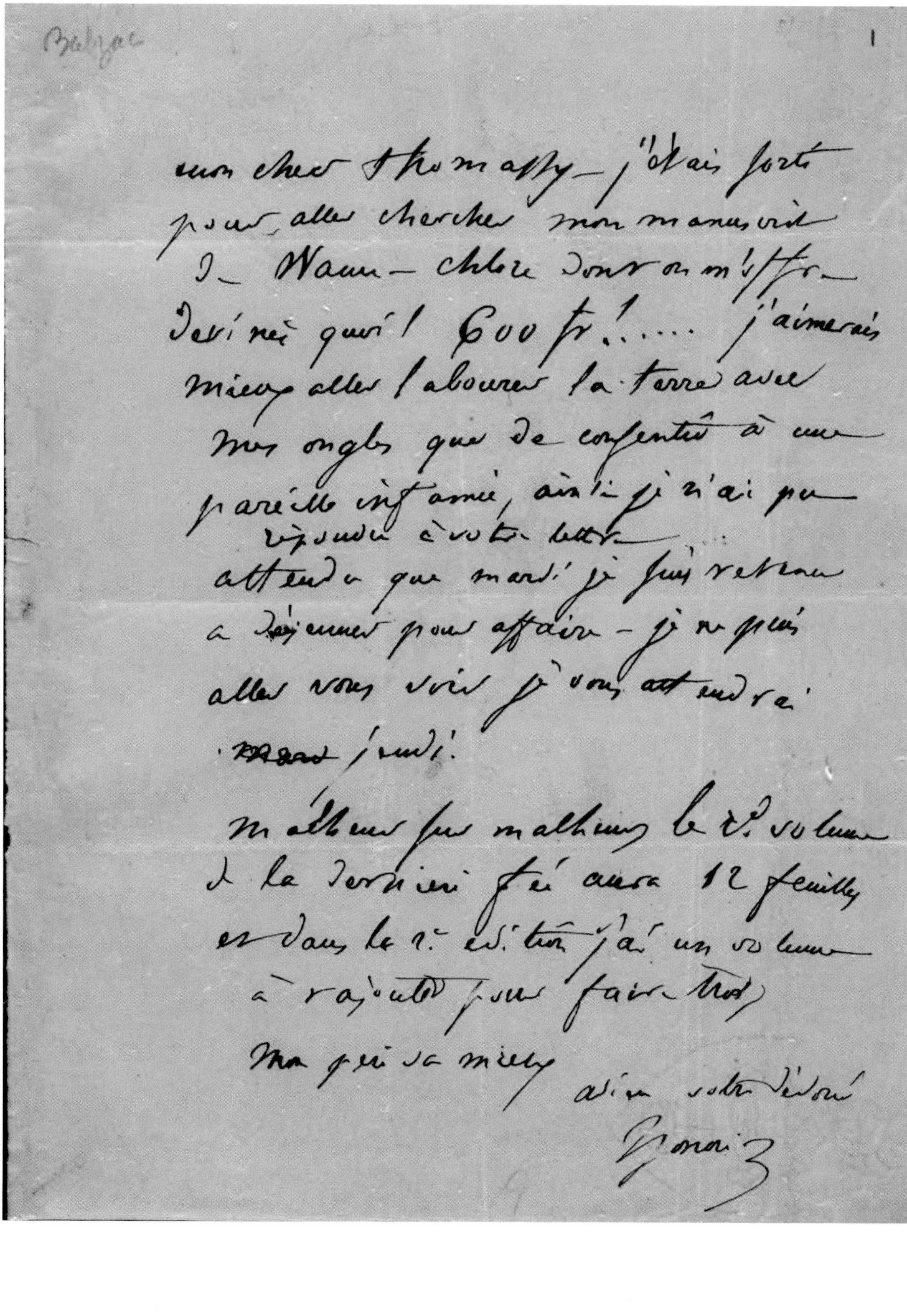
Balzac

1

mon cher Thomassy — j'étais sorti
pour aller chercher mon manuscrit
de Wann-Chlore dont on m'offre
devinez quoi! 600 fr!..... j'aimerais
mieux aller labourer la terre avec
mes ongles que de consentir à une
pareille infamie, ainsi je n'ai pu
répondre à votre lettre
attendu que mardi je suis retenu
à déjeuner pour affaire — je ne puis
aller vous voir je vous attendrai
~~[illegible]~~ jeudi.

malheur sur malheur le 2d volume
de la dernière qui aura 12 feuilles
et dans la 1re édition j'ai un volume
à rajouter pour faire trois

Mon père va mieux

adieu votre dévoué

Honoré B

Plate 3 Honoré de Balzac: Zweig MS 134, f. 1r

3.

Le publicisme était un grand miroir concentrique : les publicistes d'aujourd'hui l'ont mis en pièces et en ont tous un morceau. Ces différents morceaux les voici :

A. LE JOURNALISTE.

CINQ VARIÉTÉS : 1° *le Rédacteur en chef-propriétaire* ; 2° *le Ténor* ; 3° *le Faiseur d'articles* ; 4° ~~*l'Homme du journal*~~ ; 5° *les Camarillistes*.

PREMIÈRE VARIÉTÉ. *Le directeur-rédacteur en chef-propriétaire*. Cette belle espèce est le marquis de Tuffière du journalisme. Publiciste pour ce qu'il n'écrit pas, comme les autres sont publicistes pour ce qu'ils écrivent, il tient du propriétaire, de l'épicier, du spéculateur, et comme il n'est propre à rien, il se trouve propre à tout. Les rédacteurs font de ce propriétaire ambitieux un homme énorme : il veut être et il devient quelquefois préfet, conseiller d'état, receveur-général, directeur de théâtre, quand il n'a pas le bon sens de rester ce qu'il est : le portier de la gloire, de la spéculation et de l'électorat. ~~Ne fait-il pas~~ passer les articles ou les laisse se morfondre sur le marbre de l'imprimerie, il peut pousser un livre, une affaire et un homme ; il peut quelquefois ruiner l'homme, l'affaire et le livre, selon les circonstances. Ce Bertrand de tous les Ratons du journal, se donne comme l'âme de la feuille, et nécessairement on traite avec lui. A force de causer avec les rédacteurs, il se frotte d'idées, il a l'air d'avoir de grandes vues et se carre comme un vrai personnage. C'est ou un homme fort ou un homme habile qui se résume par une danseuse, par une actrice ou par une cantatrice, la vraie puissance occulte, ~~et qui~~ est le gouvernail de la feuille. Il n'y a eu (il est mort) qu'un seul directeur de journal, dans la véritable acception de ce mot. Cet homme était savant, il avait une forte tête, il n'écrivait rien, ses rédacteurs venaient prendre chez lui, tous les matins, le mot d'ordre, il leur imposait le sens des articles. Ce personnage fut sans ambition, il fit des pairs, des ministres, des académiciens et une royauté, sans rien vouloir, il refusa même la visite d'un roi. Vieillard, il était passionné ; journaliste, il n'était pas toujours *in petto* de l'avis de son journal. Tous les journaux d'aujourd'hui, mis ensemble, propriétaires et rédacteurs, ne sont ~~même~~ pas la monnaie de cette tête-là.

DEUXIÈME VARIÉTÉ. *Le Ténor*. On appelle premiers-Paris, la tartine qui doit se trouver en tête de toutes les feuilles publiques, tous les jours, et sans laquelle il paraît que, faute de cette nourriture, l'intelligence des abonnés maigrirait ~~en quelque sorte~~. Le rédacteur des premiers-Paris est donc le ténor du journal, il est ou se croit l'*ut* de poitrine qui fait l'abonnement, comme le ténor fait la recette au théâtre.

A ce métier, il est difficile qu'un homme ne se fausse pas l'esprit

Plate 4 Honoré de Balzac: Zweig MS 135, f. 1r

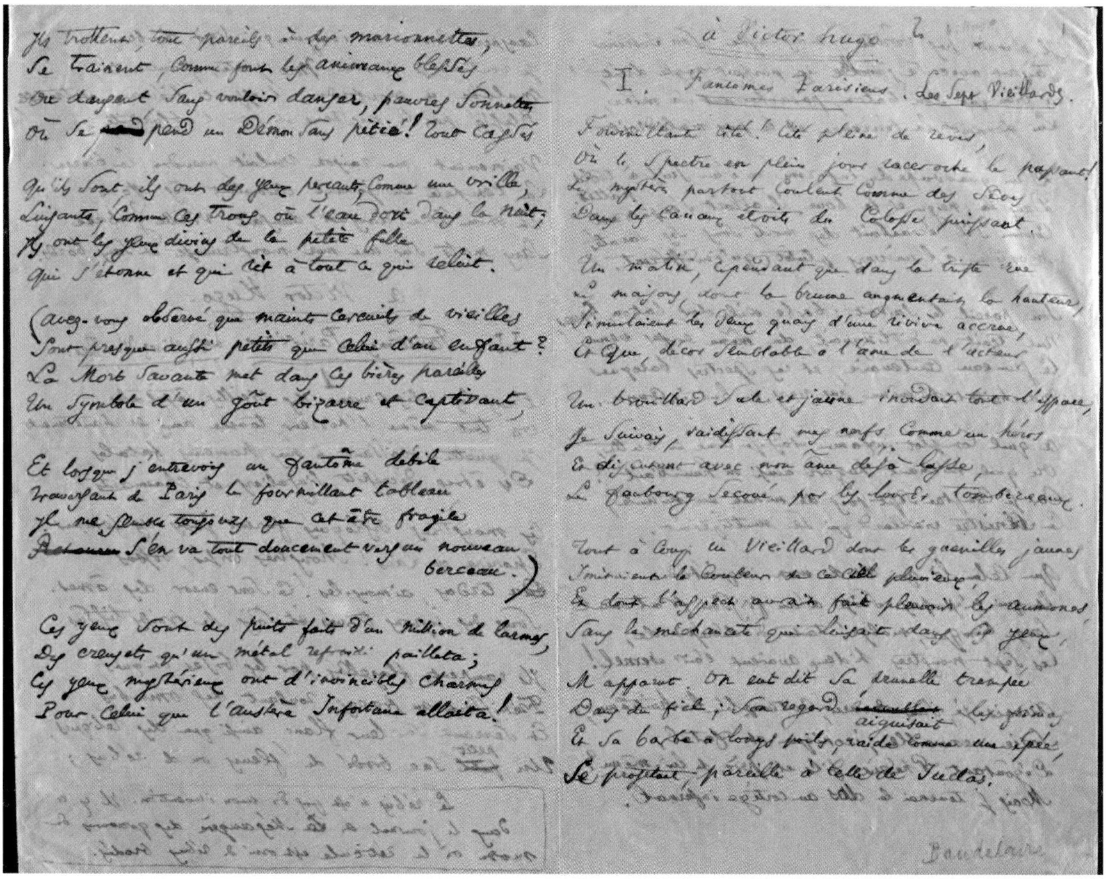

Plate 5 Charles Baudelaire: Zweig MS 136, ff. 1r and 2v

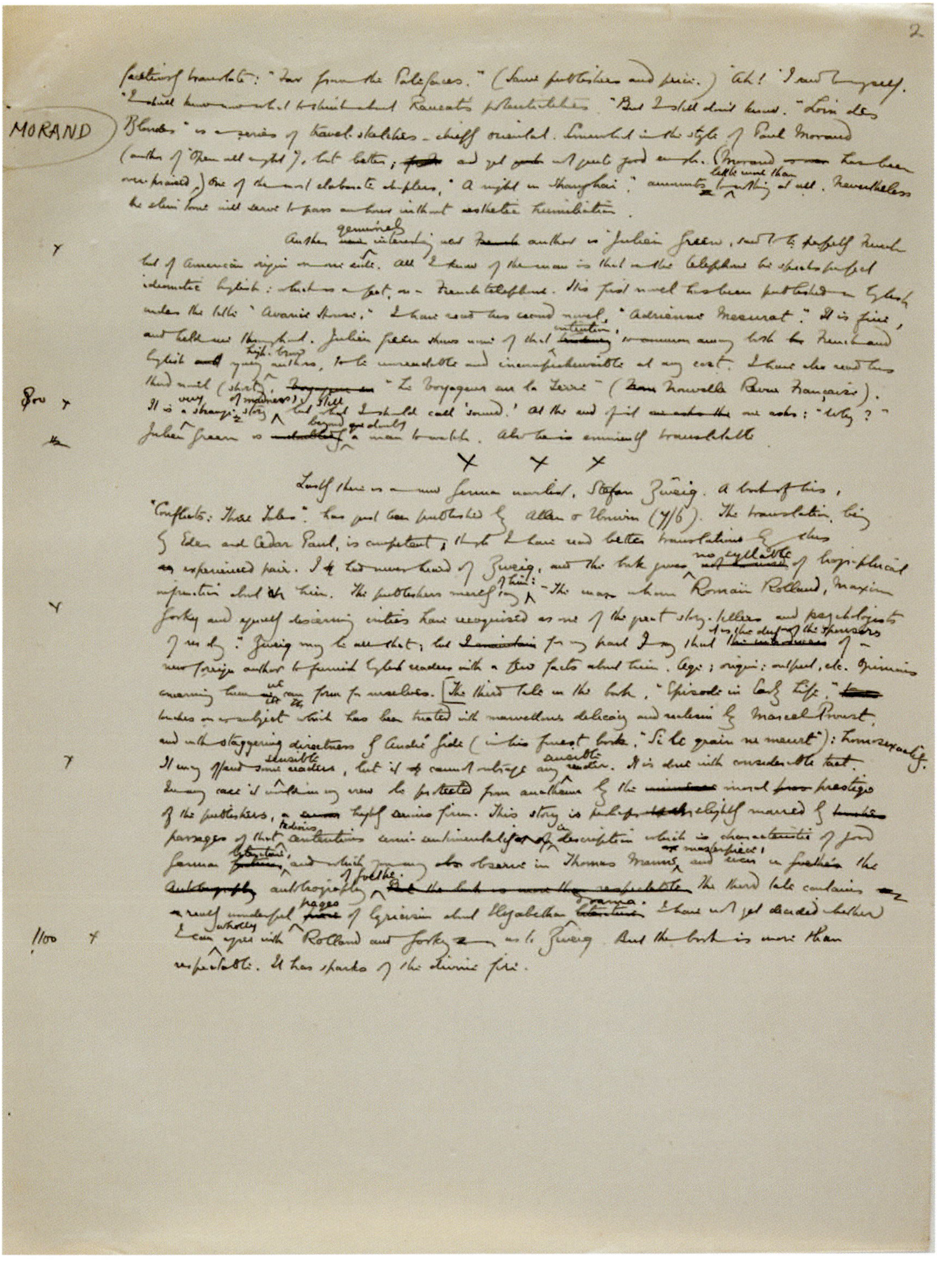

2

faithfully translate: "Far from the Palefaces." (Same publishers and price.) "Ah!" I said to myself. "I shall know [illegible] about Rancati's potentialities." But I still don't know. "Loin des Blondes" is a series of travel-sketches – chiefly oriental – [illegible] in the style of Paul Morand (author of "Open all night"), but better; and yet not quite good enough. (Morand has been over-praised.) One of the most elaborate chapters, "A night in Shanghai," amounts to little more than nothing at all. Nevertheless the slim book will serve to pass an hour without aesthetic humiliation.

MORAND

Another genuinely interesting and [illegible] author is Julien Green, said to be perfectly French but of American origin on one side. All I know of the man is that on the telephone he speaks perfect idiomatic English: such is a fact, on a French telephone. His first novel has been published in English under the title "Avarice House." I have read his second novel, "Adrienne Mesurat." It is fine, and [illegible] throughout. Julien Green shows none of that intention, so common among both the French and English high-brow young authors, to be unreadable and incomprehensible at any cost. I have also read his third novel (short), "Le Voyageur sur la Terre" (Nouvelle Revue Française). It is a very strange story (of madness); still, but that I should call 'sound.' At the end of it one asks: "Why?" Julien Green is beyond any doubt a man to watch. Also he is eminently translatable.

800

X X X

Lastly there is a new German novelist, Stefan Zweig. A book of his, "Conflicts: Three Tales" has just been published by Allen & Unwin (7/6). The translation, by Eden and Cedar Paul, is competent, though I have read better translations by this experienced pair. I had never heard of Zweig, and the book gives no syllable of biographical information about him. The publishers merely say of him: "The man whom Romain Rolland, Maxim Gorky and equally discerning critics have recognised as one of the great story-tellers and psychologists of our day." Zweig may be all that, but for my part I say that it is the duty of the sponsors of a new foreign author to furnish English readers with a few facts about him. Age; origin; output, etc. Opinions concerning him we can form for ourselves. [The third tale in the book, "Episode in Early Life," touches on a subject which has been treated with marvellous delicacy and realism by Marcel Proust, and with staggering directness by André Gide (in his finest book, "Si le grain ne meurt"): homosexuality. It may offend some sensible readers, but it cannot outrage any sensible reader. It is dealt with considerable tact. In any case it [illegible] in my view be protected from anathema by the moral prestige of the publishers, a highly serious firm. This story is perhaps slightly marred by passages of that tedious semi-sentimentality in description which is characteristic of good German literature, and which may be observed in Thomas Mann's masterpiece, and even in Goethe's autobiography. The third tale contains really wonderful pages of lyricism about Elizabethan drama. I have not yet decided whether I can agree wholly with Rolland and Gorky as to Zweig. But the book is more than respectable. It has sparks of the divine fire.

1100

Plate 6 Arnold Bennett: Zweig MS 137, f. 2r

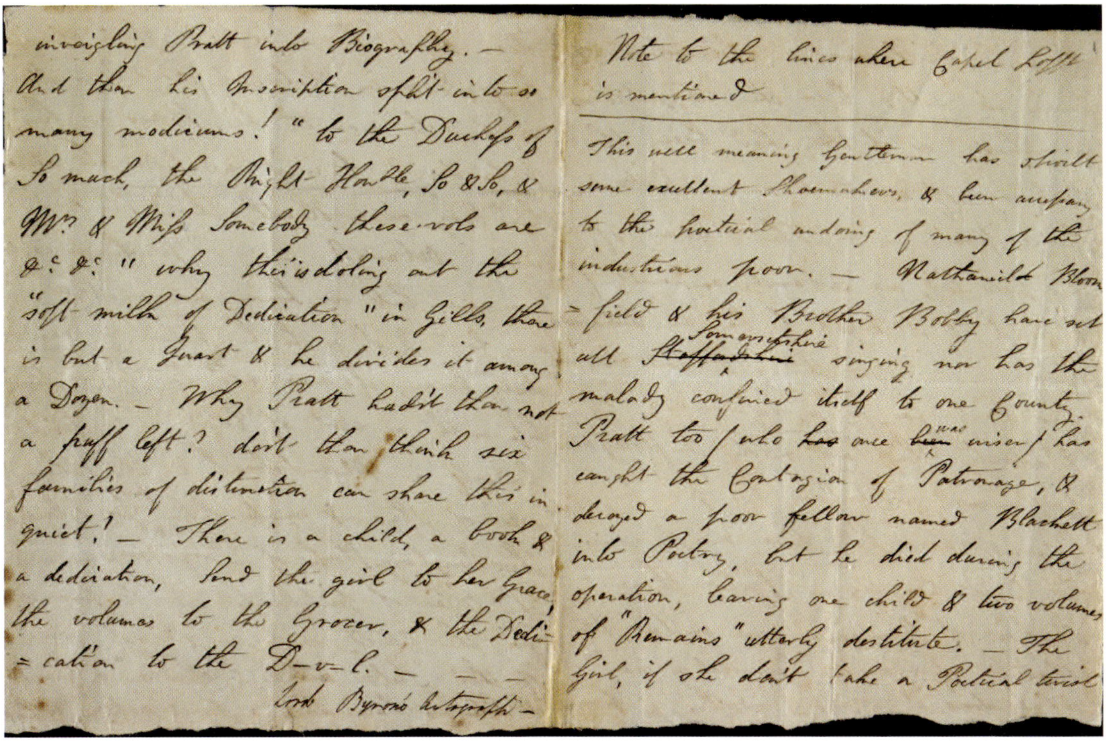

inveigling Pratt into Biography. —
And then his Inscription split into so
many modicums! "to the Duchess of
So much, the Right Honble. So & So, &
Mrs. & Miss Somebody these vols are
&c. &c." why this is doling out the
"soft milk of Dedication" in Gills, there
is but a Quart & he divides it among
a Dozen. — Why Pratt hadst thou not
a puff left? dost thou think six
families of distinction can share this in
quiet! — There is a child, a book &
a dedication, send the girl to her Grace
the volumes to the Grocer, & the Dedi-
-cation to the D—v—l. — —
Lord Byron's Autograph —

Note to the lines where Capel Lofft
is mentioned

This well meaning Gentleman has spoilt
some excellent Shoemakers, & been accessary
to the poetical undoing of many of the
industrious poor. — Nathaniel Bloom-
-field & his Brother Bobby have set
all ~~Staffordshire~~ [Somersetshire] singing nor has the
malady confined itself to one County.
Pratt too (who ~~has~~ once ~~been~~ [was] wiser) has
caught the Contagion of Patronage, &
decoyed a poor fellow named Blackett
into Poetry, but he died during the
operation, leaving one child & two volumes
of "Remains" utterly destitute. — The
Girl, if she don't take a Poetical twist

Plate 7 George Gordon, 6th Baron Byron: Zweig MS 138, ff. 1r and 2v

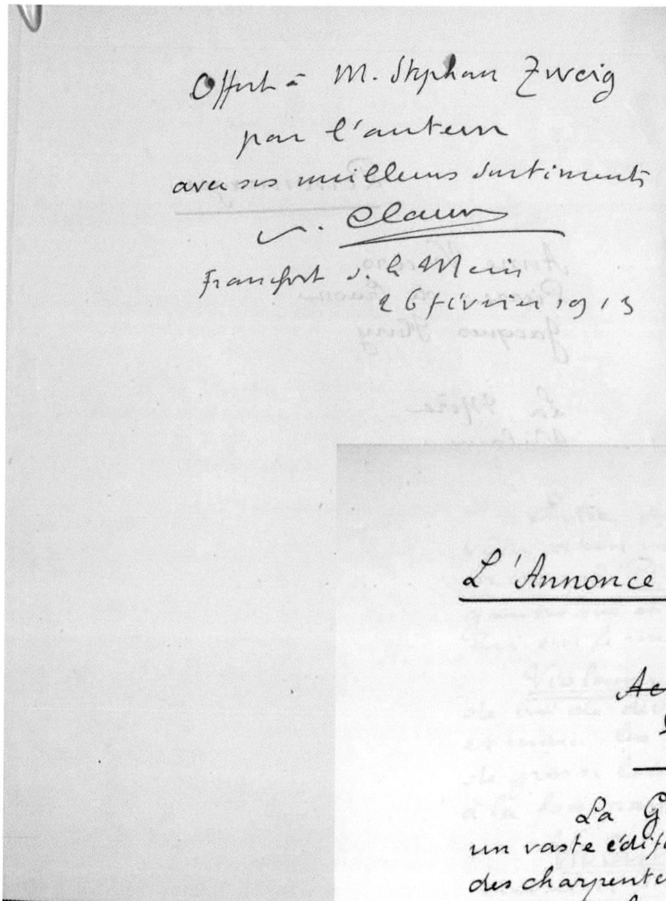

Offert à M. Stephan Zweig
par l'auteur
avec ses meilleurs sentiments
P. Claudel
Francfort s. le Main
26 février 1913

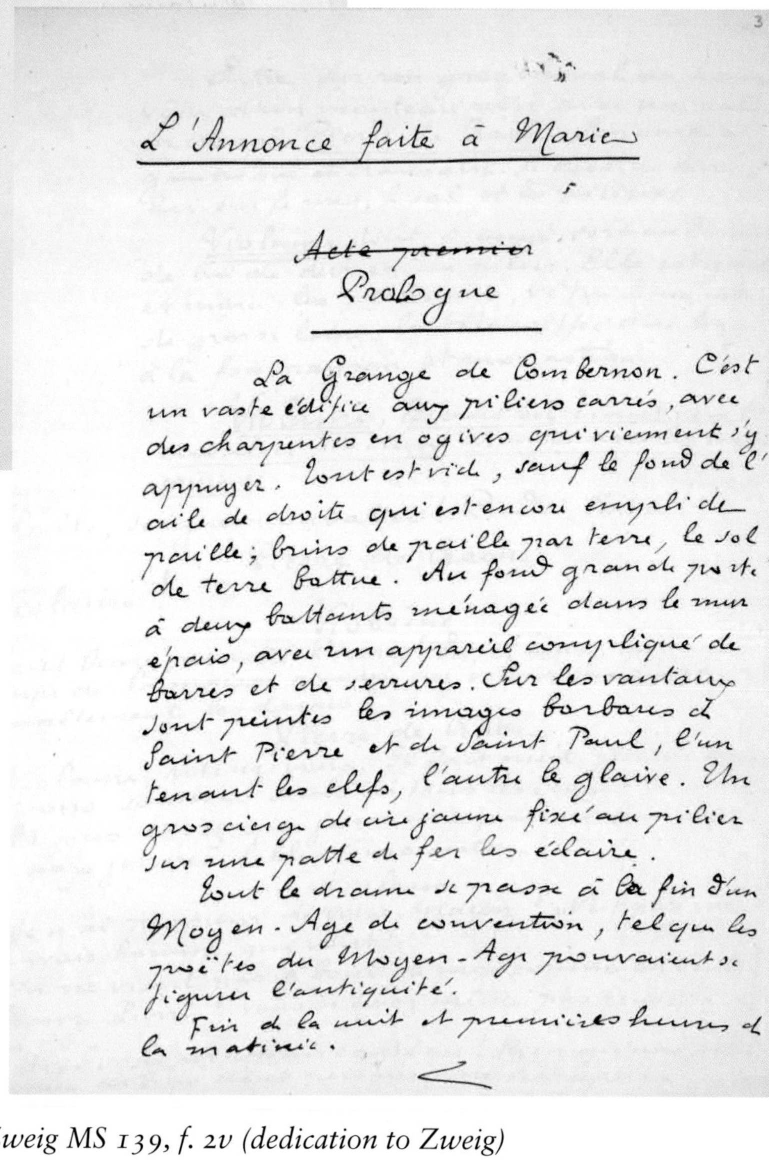

3

L'Annonce faite à Marie

~~Acte premier~~

Prologue

La Grange de Combernon. C'est un vaste édifice aux piliers carrés, avec des charpentes en ogives qui viennent s'y appuyer. Tout est vide, sauf le fond de l'aile de droite qui est encore empli de paille; brins de paille par terre, le sol de terre battue. Au fond grande porte à deux battants ménagée dans le mur épais, avec un appareil compliqué de barres et de serrures. Sur les vantaux sont peintes les images barbares de Saint Pierre et de Saint Paul, l'un tenant les clefs, l'autre le glaive. Un gros cierge de cire jaune fixé au pilier sur une patte de fer les éclaire.

Tout le drame se passe à la fin d'un Moyen-Age de convention, tel que les poètes du Moyen-Age pouvaient se figurer l'antiquité.

Fin de la nuit et premières heures de la matinée.

Plate 8 (a) Paul Claudel: Zweig MS 139, f. 2v (dedication to Zweig)

Plate 8 (b) Paul Claudel: Zweig MS 139, f. 3r

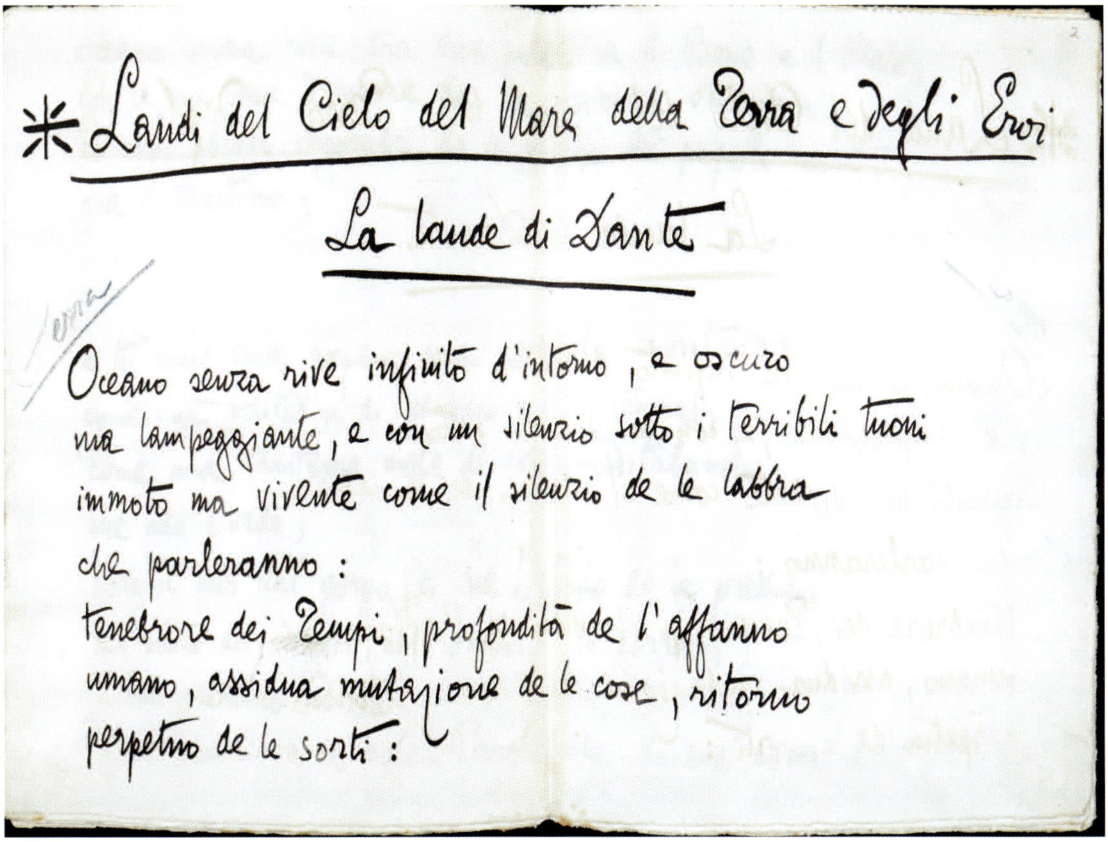

2

* Laudi del Cielo del Mare della Terra e degli Eroi

La laude di Dante

Terra

Oceano senza rive infinito d'intorno, e oscuro
ma lampeggiante, e con un silenzio sotto i terribili tuoni
immoto ma vivente come il silenzio de le labbra
che parleranno:
tenebrore dei Tempi, profondità de l'affanno
umano, assidua mutazione de le cose, ritorno
perpetuo de le sorti:

Plate 9 Gabriele D'Annunzio: Zweig MS 140, ff. 1v–2r

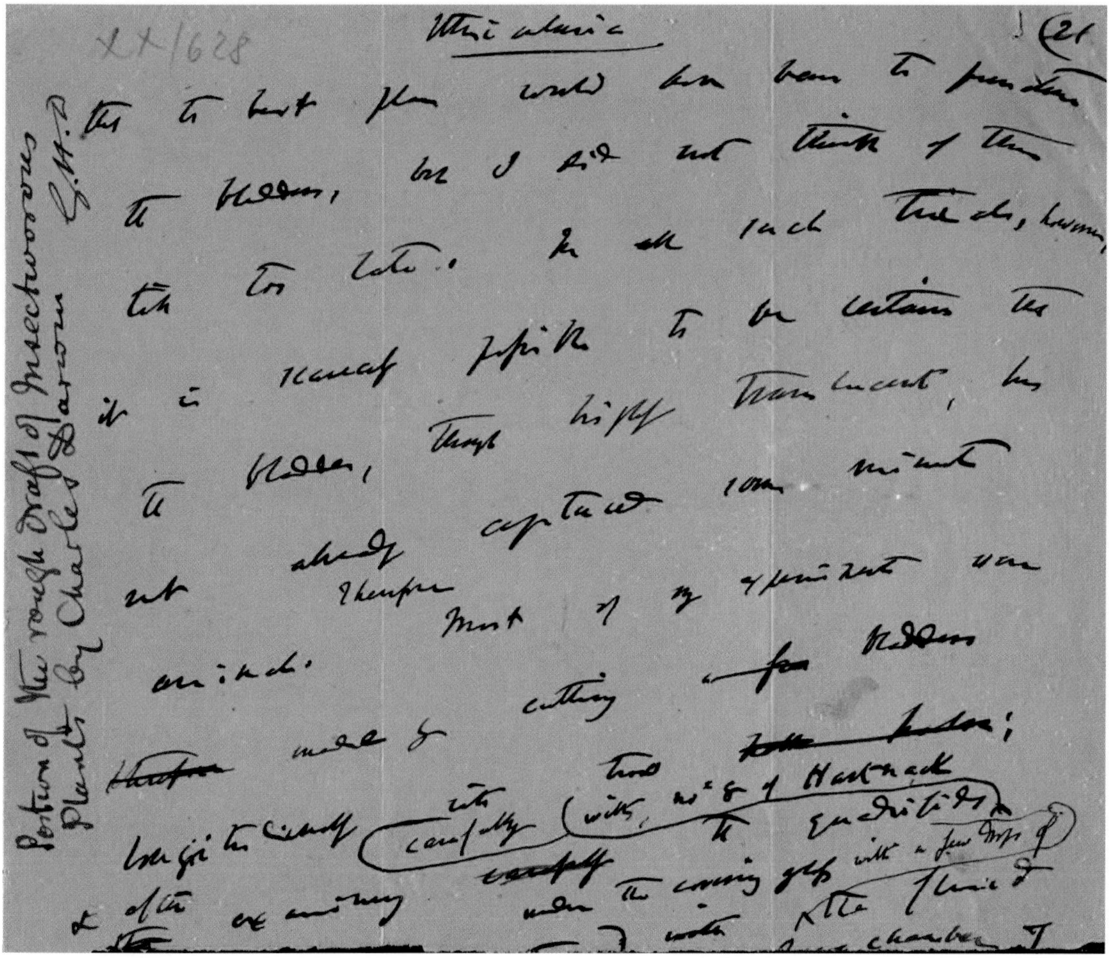

Plate 10 Charles Darwin: Zweig MS 141, f. 1r

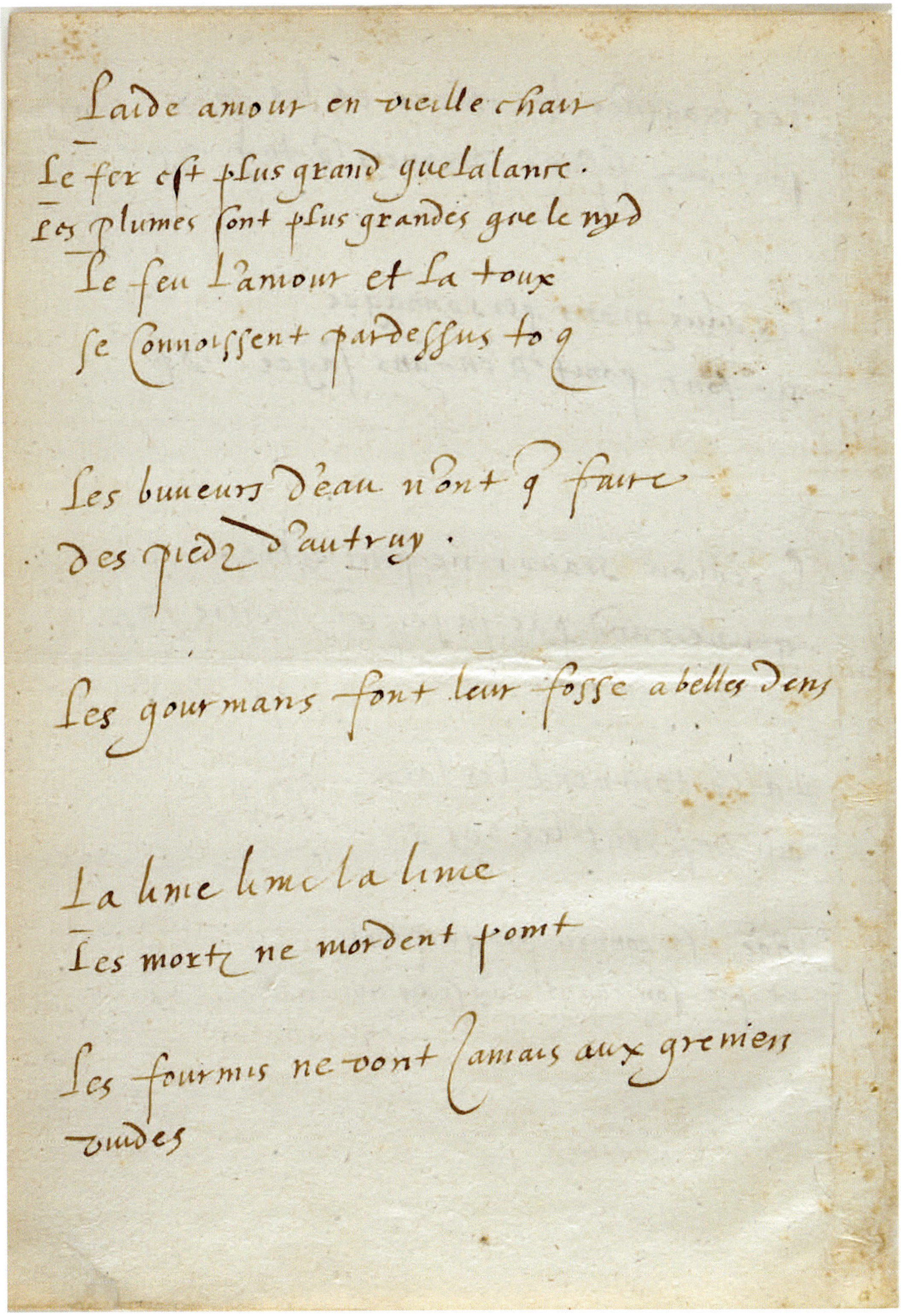

Laide amour en vieille chair

Le fer est plus grand que la lance.
Les plumes sont plus grandes que le nyd
Le feu l'amour et la toux
se connoissent pardessus tous

Les buveurs d'eau n'ont que faire
des piedz d'autruy.

Les gourmans font leur fosse a belles dens

La lime lime la lime
Les mortz ne mordent point

Les fourmis ne vont jamais aux greniers
vuides

Plate 11 Philippe Desportes: Zweig MS 142, f. 1v

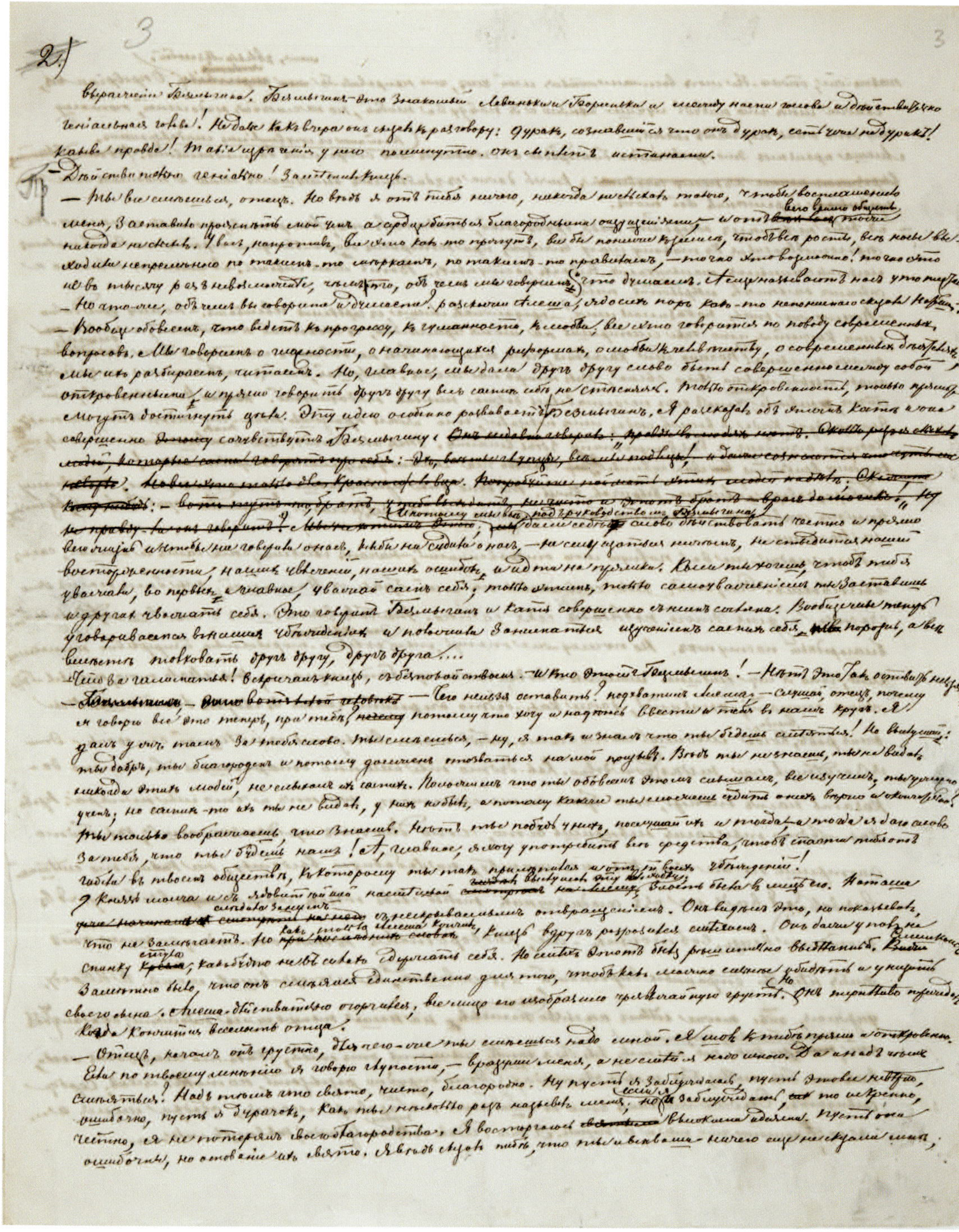

Plate 12 Fedor Mikhailovich Dostoevsky: Zweig MS 143, f. 3r

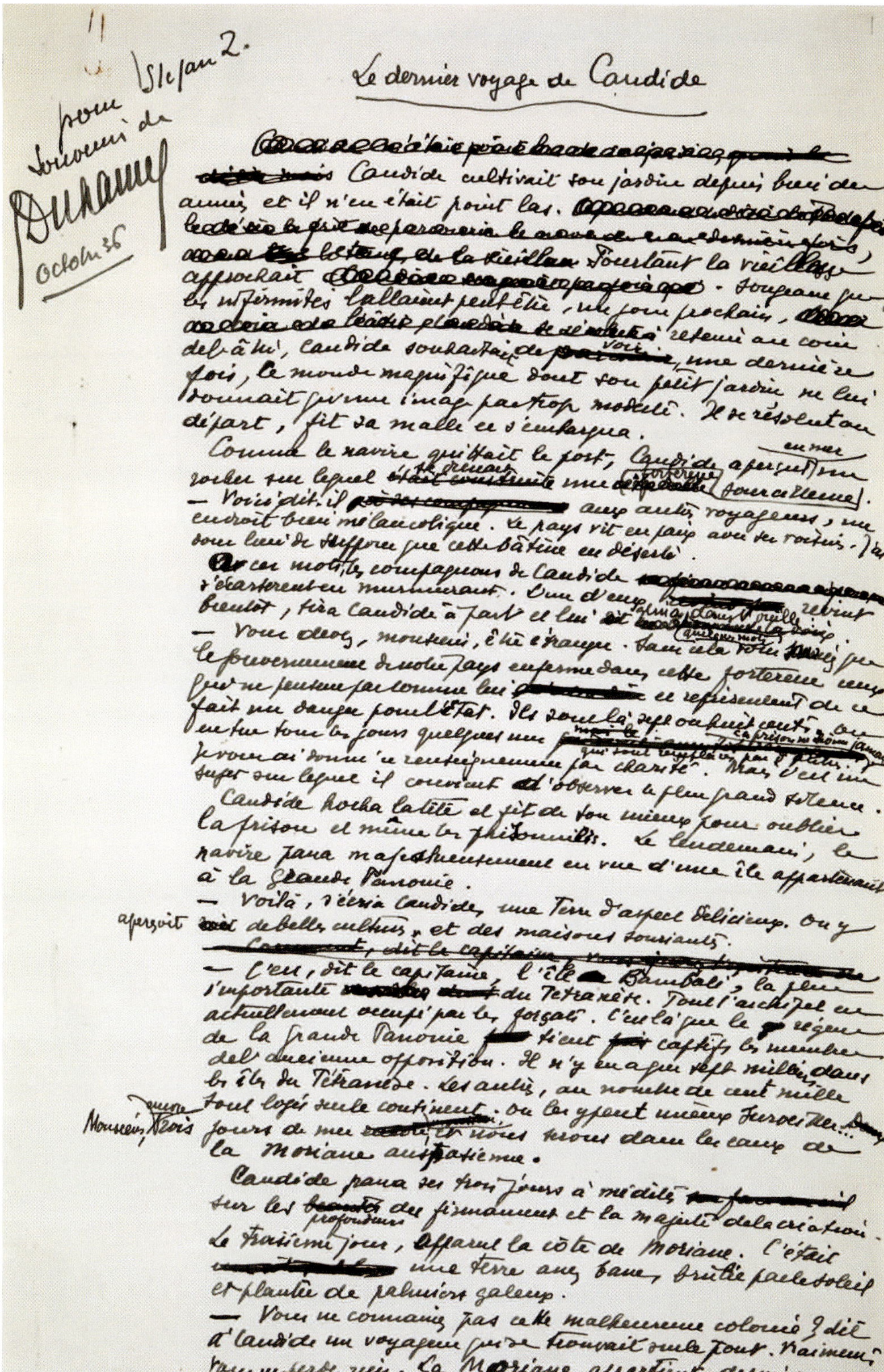

11

pour Stefan Z.
souvenir de
Duhamel
Octobre 36

Le dernier voyage de Candide

Candide cultivait son jardin depuis bien des années, et il n'en était point las. Pourtant la vieillesse approchait. Songeant que les infirmités l'allaient peut-être, un jour prochain, retenir au coin de l'âtre, Candide souhaita de voir, une dernière fois, le monde magnifique dont son petit jardin ne lui donnait qu'une image par trop modeste. Il se résolut au départ, fit sa malle et s'embarqua.

Comme le navire quittait le port, Candide aperçut en mer un rocher sur lequel se dressait une forteresse sourcilleuse.

— Voici, dit-il aux autres voyageurs, un endroit bien mélancolique. Le pays vit en paix avec ses voisins. J'ai lieu de supposer que cette bâtisse est déserte.

À ces mots, les compagnons de Candide s'écartèrent en murmurant. L'un d'eux revint bientôt, tira Candide à part et lui dit

— Vous devez, monsieur, être étranger. Sans cela vous sauriez que le gouvernement de notre pays enferme dans cette forteresse ceux qui ne pensent pas comme lui et représentent de ce fait un danger pour l'État. Ils sont là sept ou huit cents. On en tue tous les jours quelques-uns. Je vous ai donné ce renseignement par charité. Mais c'est un sujet sur lequel il convient d'observer le plus grand silence.

Candide hocha la tête et fit de son mieux pour oublier la prison et même les prisonniers. Le lendemain, le navire passa majestueusement en vue d'une île appartenant à la Grande Panonie.

— Voilà, s'écria Candide, une terre d'aspect délicieux. On y aperçoit de belles cultures et des maisons souriantes.

— C'est, dit le capitaine, l'île Bambali, la plus importante du Tétranèse. Tout l'archipel est actuellement occupé par les forçats. C'est là que le régime de la Grande Panonie tient captifs les membres de l'ancienne opposition. Il n'y en a que sept mille dans les îles du Tétranèse. Les autres, au nombre de cent mille, sont logés sur le continent. On les y peut mieux surveiller. Encore deux jours de mer, Monsieur, et nous serons dans les eaux de la Moriane aussi...

Candide passa ses trois jours à méditer sur les profondeurs du firmament et la majesté de la création.

Le troisième jour, apparut la côte de Moriane. C'était une terre aux bancs brûlés par le soleil et plantée de palmiers galeux.

— Vous ne connaissez pas cette malheureuse colonie ? dit à Candide un voyageur qui se trouvait sur le pont. Vraiment vous ne perdez rien. La Moriane appartient, depuis un

Plate 13 Georges Duhamel: Zweig MS 144, f. 1r

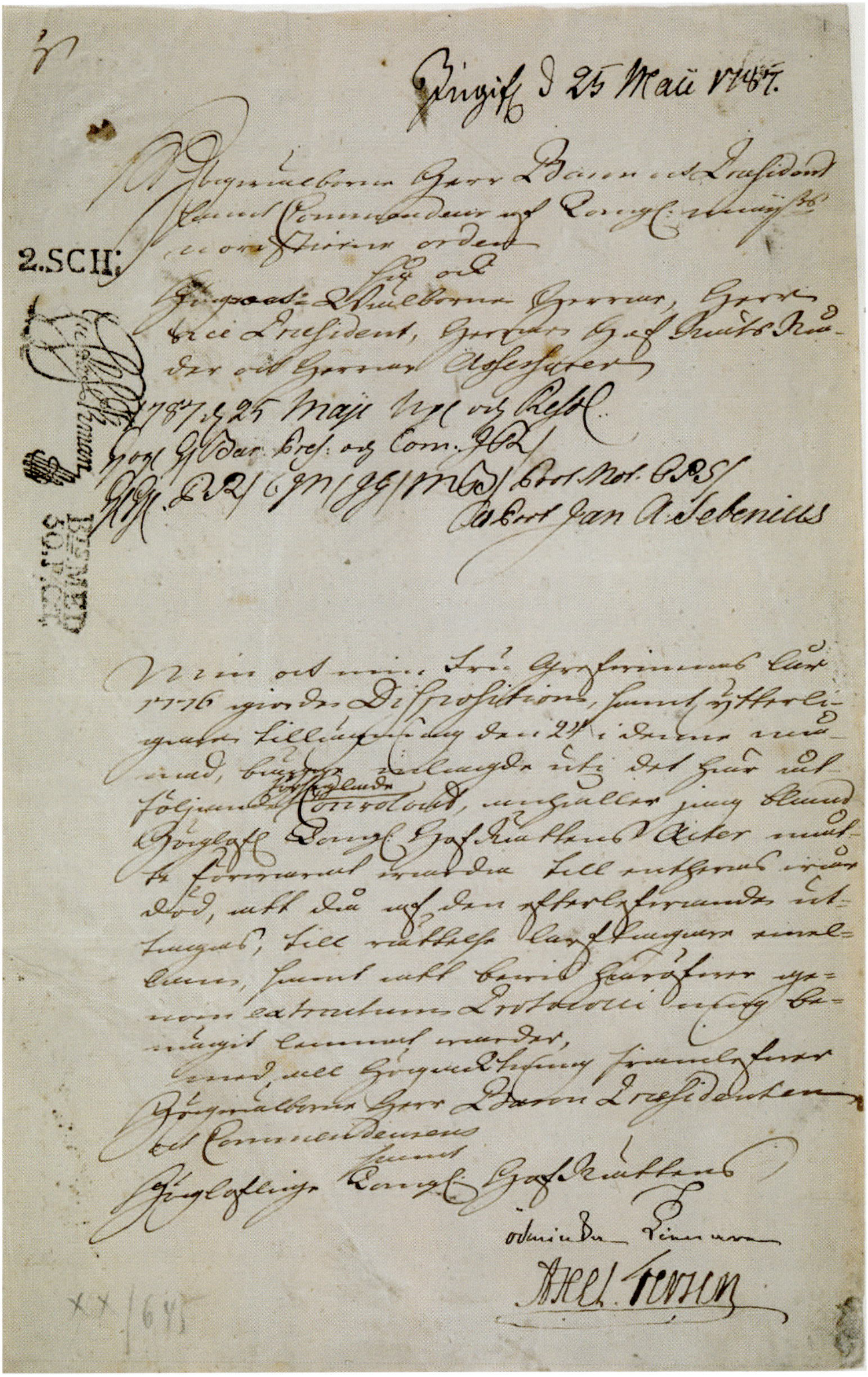
d 25 Maii 1787.

Högwälborne Herr Baron och President
samt Commendeur af Kongl. Nordstierne Orden
och
Högwälborne Herrar, Herr Vice President, Herrar Hof Rätts Råder och Herrar Assessorer

1776

Högwälborne Herr Baron Presidenten
och Commendeurens
samt
Högloflige Kongl. Hof Rättens
ödmiuke Tienare
Axel Fersen

Plate 14 Fredrik Axel von Fersen: Zweig MS 145, f. 1r

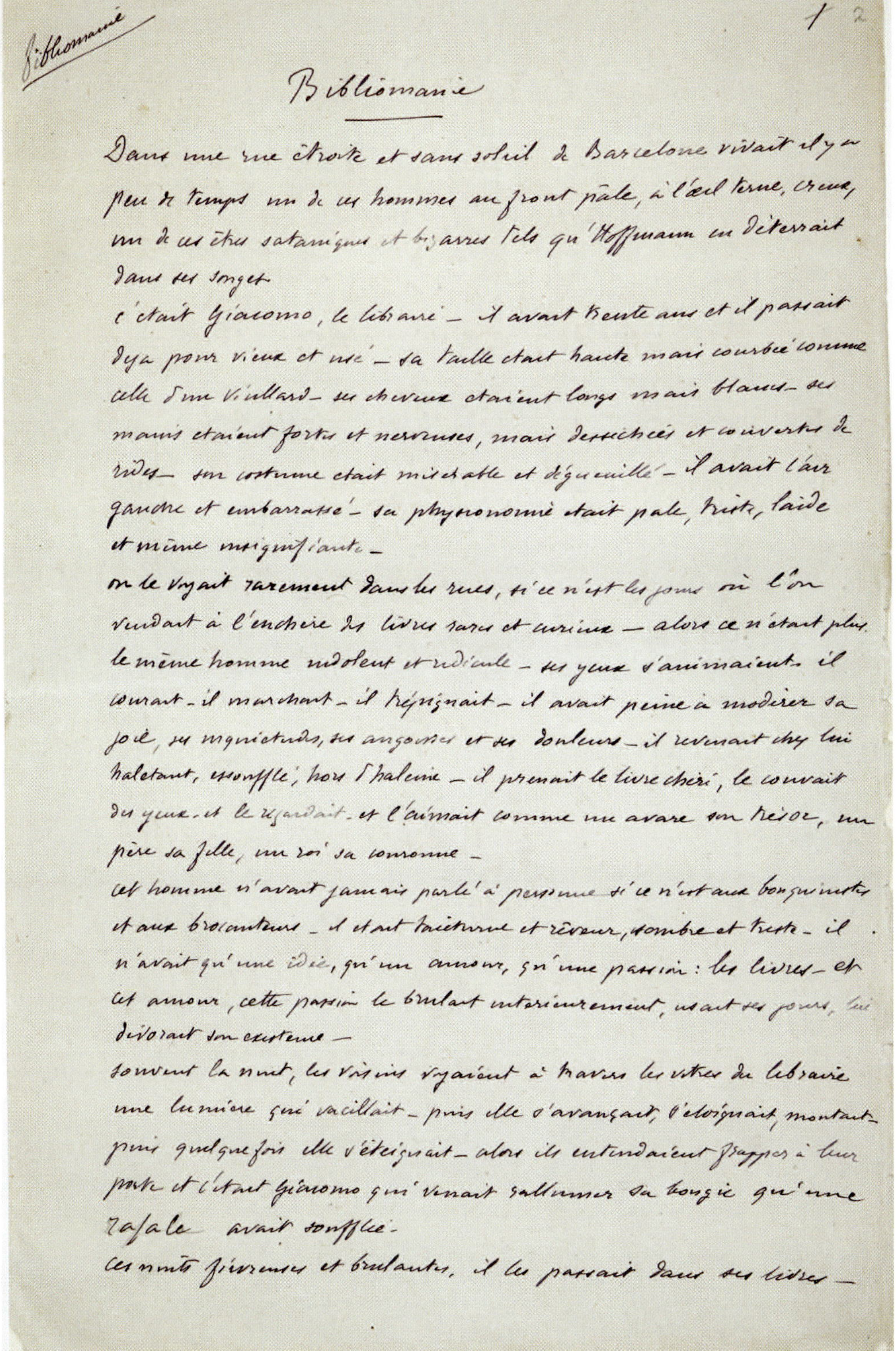

Bibliomanie

1 2

Bibliomanie

Dans une rue étroite et sans soleil de Barcelone vivait il y a peu de temps un de ces hommes au front pâle, à l'œil terne, creux, un de ces êtres sataniques et bizarres tels qu'Hoffmann en déterrait dans ses songes.

c'était Giacomo, le libraire — il avait trente ans et il passait déjà pour vieux et usé — sa taille était haute mais courbée comme celle d'un vieillard — ses cheveux étaient longs mais blancs — ses mains étaient fortes et nerveuses, mais desséchées et couvertes de rides — son costume était misérable et déguenillé — il avait l'air gauche et embarrassé — sa physionomie était pâle, triste, laide et même insignifiante —

on le voyait rarement dans les rues, si ce n'est les jours où l'on vendait à l'enchère des livres rares et curieux — alors ce n'était plus le même homme indolent et ridicule — ses yeux s'animaient — il courait — il marchait — il trépignait — il avait peine à modérer sa joie, ses inquiétudes, ses angoisses et ses douleurs — il revenait chez lui haletant, essoufflé, hors d'haleine — il prenait le livre chéri, le couvait des yeux — et le regardait — et l'aimait comme un avare son trésor, un père sa fille, un roi sa couronne —

cet homme n'avait jamais parlé à personne si ce n'est aux bouquinistes et aux brocanteurs — il était taciturne et rêveur, sombre et triste — il n'avait qu'une idée, qu'un amour, qu'une passion: les livres — et cet amour, cette passion le brûlait intérieurement, usait ses jours, lui dévorait son existence —

souvent la nuit, les voisins voyaient à travers les vitres du libraire une lumière qui vacillait — puis elle s'avançait, s'éloignait, montait — puis quelquefois elle s'éteignait — alors ils entendaient frapper à leur porte et c'était Giacomo qui venait rallumer sa bougie qu'une rafale avait soufflée.

ces nuits fiévreuses et brûlantes, il les passait dans ses livres —

Plate 15 Gustave Flaubert: Zweig MS 146, f. 2r

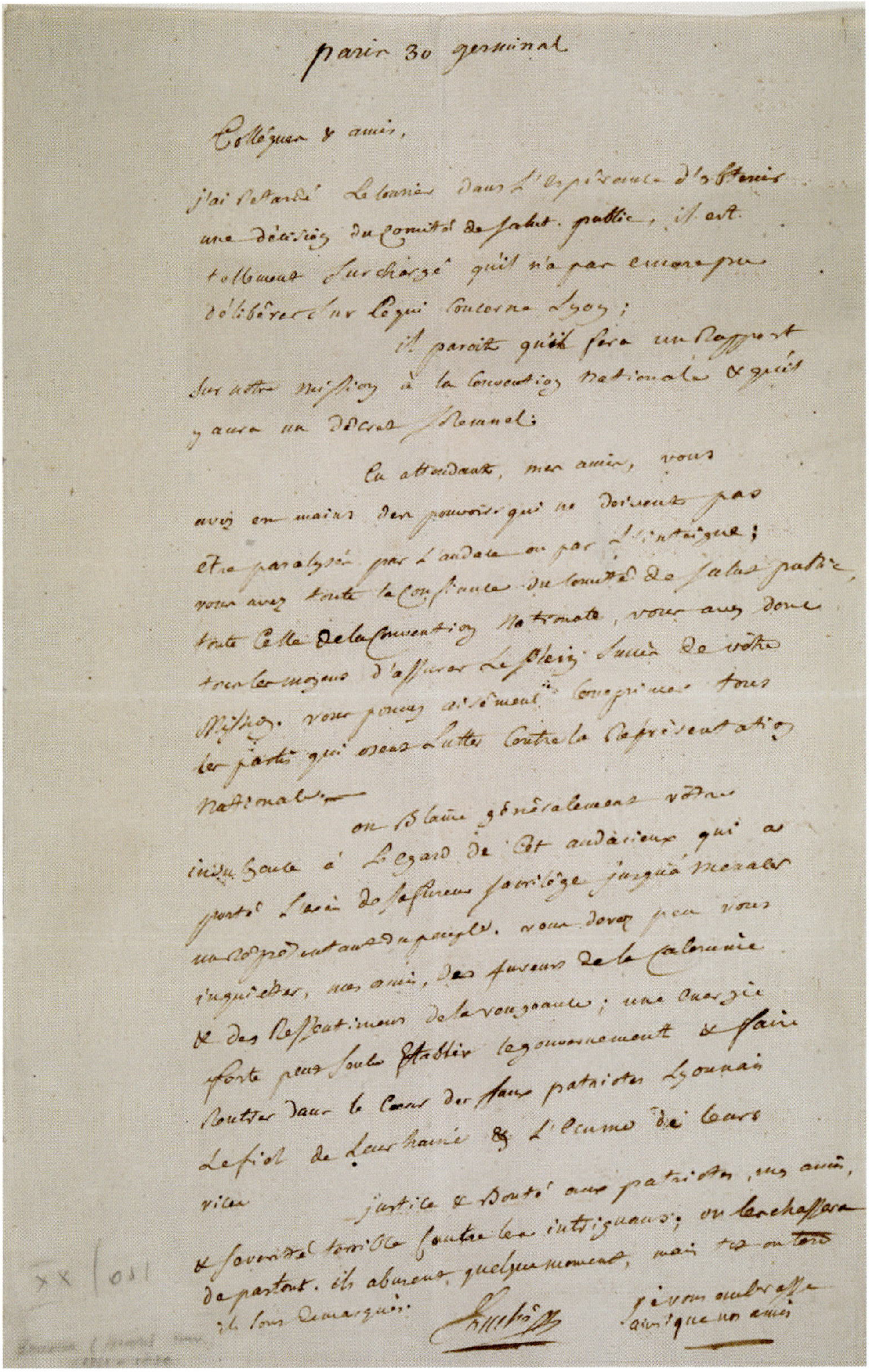
paris 30 germinal

Collègues & amis,

j'ai retardé le courrier dans l'espérance d'obtenir une décision du comité de salut public, il est tellement surchargé qu'il n'a pas encore pu délibérer sur ce qui concerne Lyon;

il paraît qu'il sera un rapport sur notre mission à la convention nationale & qu'il y aura un décret solennel;

en attendant, mes amis, vous avez en mains des pouvoirs qui ne doivent pas être paralysés par l'audace ou par l'intrigue; vous avez toute la confiance du comité de salut public, vous avez donc toute celle de la convention nationale, vous avez donc tous les moyens d'assurer le plein succès de votre mission. vous pouvez aisément comprimer tous les partis qui osent lutter contre la représentation nationale.—

on blâme généralement votre indulgence à l'égard de cet audacieux qui a porté l'excès de plusieurs sacrilège jusqu'à menacer les représentants du peuple. vous devez peu vous inquiéter, mes amis, des fureurs de la calomnie & des ressentiments de la vengeance; une énergie forte peut seule établir le gouvernement & faire rentrer dans le cœur des faux patriotes lyonnais le fiel de leur haine & l'écume de leurs vices

justice & bonté aux patriotes, mes amis, & sévérité terrible contre les intrigants; on les chassera de partout. ils abusent quelques moments, mais tôt ou tard ils sont démasqués.

Fouché

je vous embrasse ainsi que nos amis

XX | 051

Plate 16 Joseph Fouché: Zweig MS 147, f. 1r

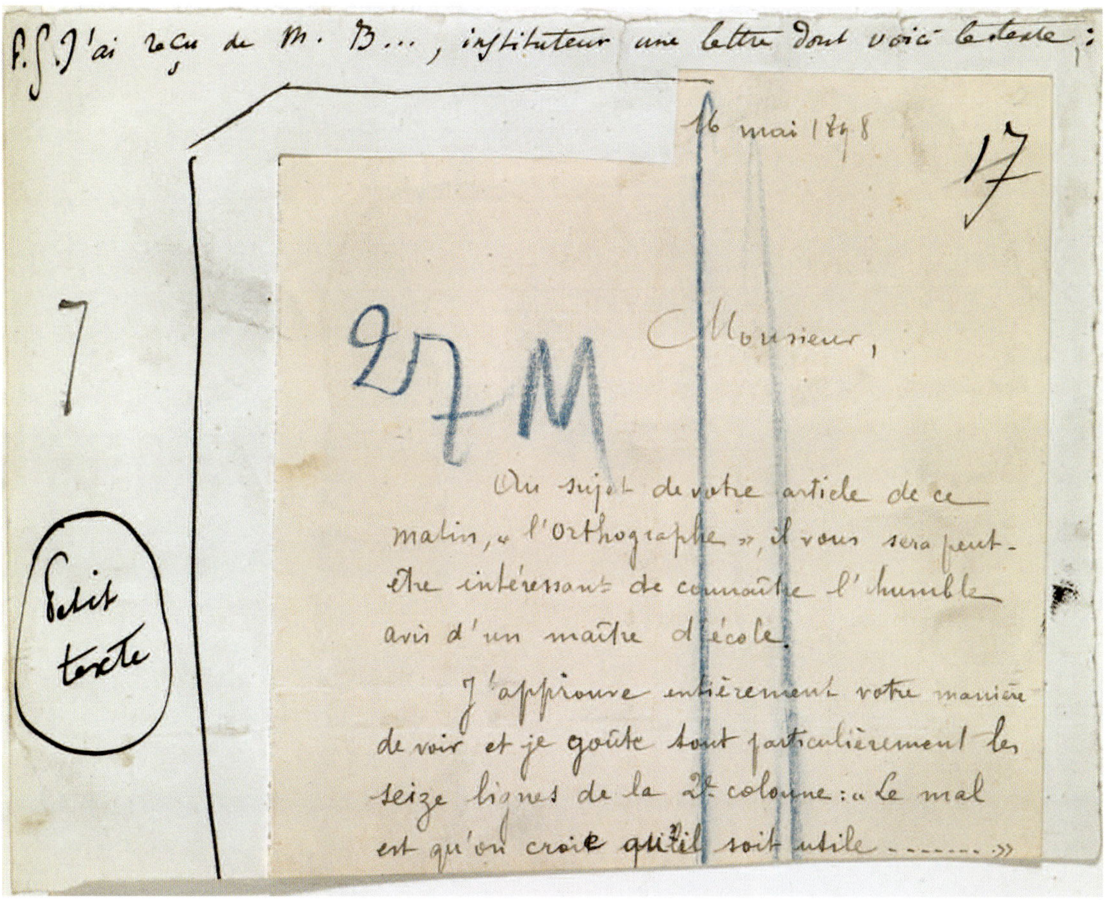

P.S. J'ai reçu de M. B..., instituteur une lettre dont voici le texte :

16 mai 1898

17

7

Petit texte

27 M

Monsieur,

Au sujet de votre article de ce matin, « l'Orthographe », il vous sera peut-être intéressant de connaître l'humble avis d'un maître d'école.

J'approuve entièrement votre manière de voir et je goûte tout particulièrement les seize lignes de la 2e colonne : « Le mal est qu'on croit qu'il soit utile ...... »

Plate 17 'Anatole France': Zweig MS 148, f. 1r

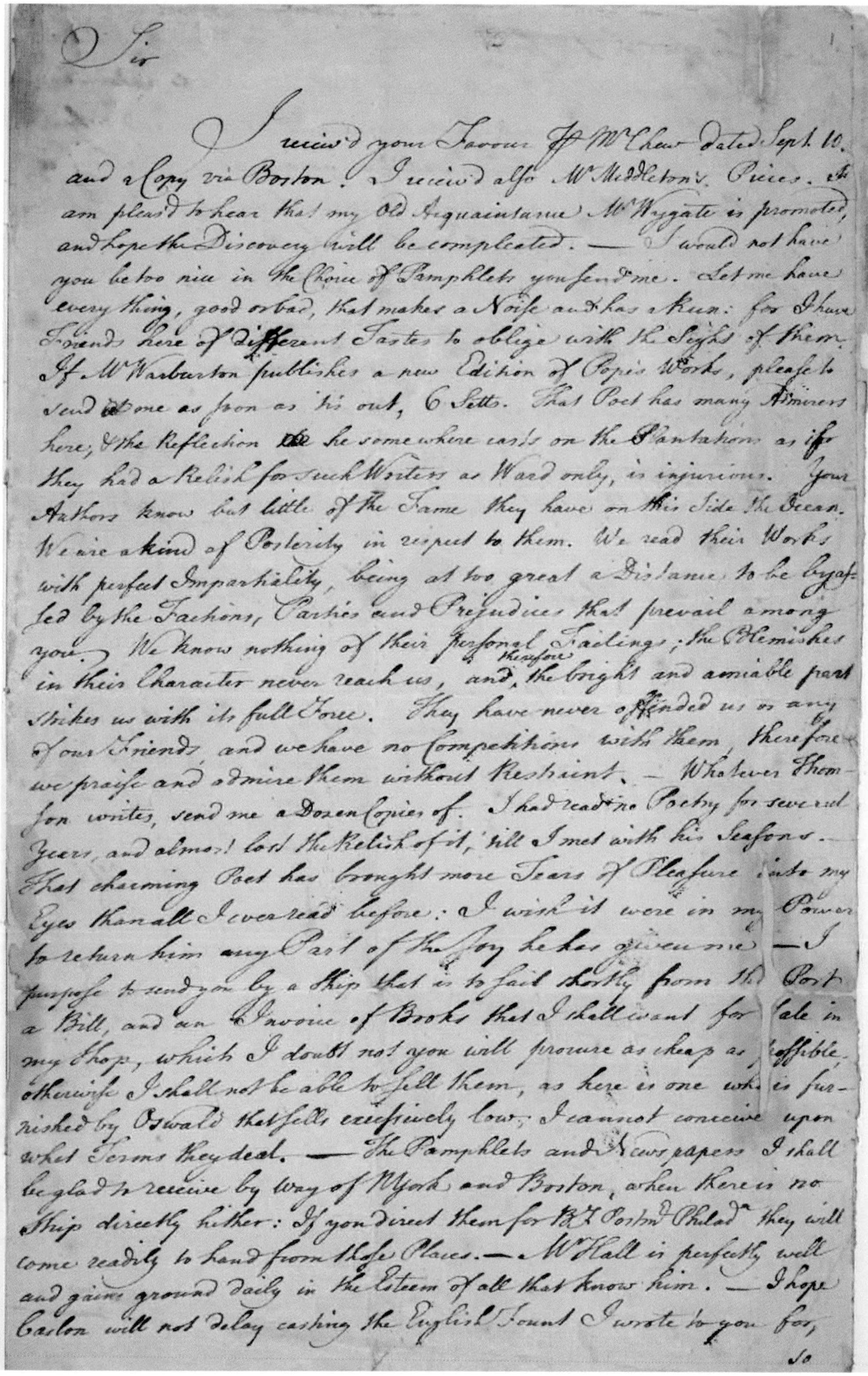

Sir

I receiv'd your Favour per Mr Chew dated Sept. 10. and a Copy via Boston. I receiv'd also Mr Middleton's Pieces. I am pleas'd to hear that my Old Acquaintance Mr Wygate is promoted, and hope the Discovery will be compleated. — I would not have you be too nice in the Choice of Pamphlets you send me. Let me have every thing, good or bad, that makes a Noise and has a Run: for I have Friends here of different Tastes to oblige with the Sight of them. If Mr Warburton publishes a new Edition of Pope's Works, please to send me as soon as 'tis out, 6 Setts. That Poet has many Admirers here, & the Reflection he somewhere casts on the Plantations as if they had a Relish for such Writers as Ward only, is injurious. Your Authors know but little of the Fame they have on this Side the Ocean. We are a kind of Posterity in respect to them. We read their Works with perfect Impartiality, being at too great a Distance to be byass'd by the Factions, Parties and Prejudices that prevail among you. We know nothing of their personal Failings; the Blemishes in their Character never reach us, and therefore the bright and amiable part strikes us with its full Force. They have never offended us or any of our Friends, and we have no Competitions with them, therefore we praise and admire them without Restraint. — Whatever Thomson writes, send me a Dozen Copies of. I had read no Poetry for several Years, and almost lost the Relish of it, till I met with his Seasons. — That charming Poet has brought more Tears of Pleasure into my Eyes than all I ever read before: I wish it were in my Power to return him any Part of the Joy he has given me. — I purpose to send you by a Ship that is to sail shortly from this Port a Bill, and an Invoice of Books that I shall want for Sale in my Shop, which I doubt not you will procure as cheap as possible, otherwise I shall not be able to sell them, as here is one who is furnished by Oswald that sells excessively low; I cannot conceive upon what Terms they deal. — The Pamphlets and News papers I shall be glad to receive by Way of N York and Boston, when there is no Ship directly hither: If you direct them for B.F. Postmr Philada they will come readily to hand from those Places. — Mr Hall is perfectly well and gains ground daily in the Esteem of all that know him. — I hope Caslon will not delay casting the English Fount I wrote to you for, so

Plate 18 Benjamin Franklin: Zweig MS 149, f. 1r

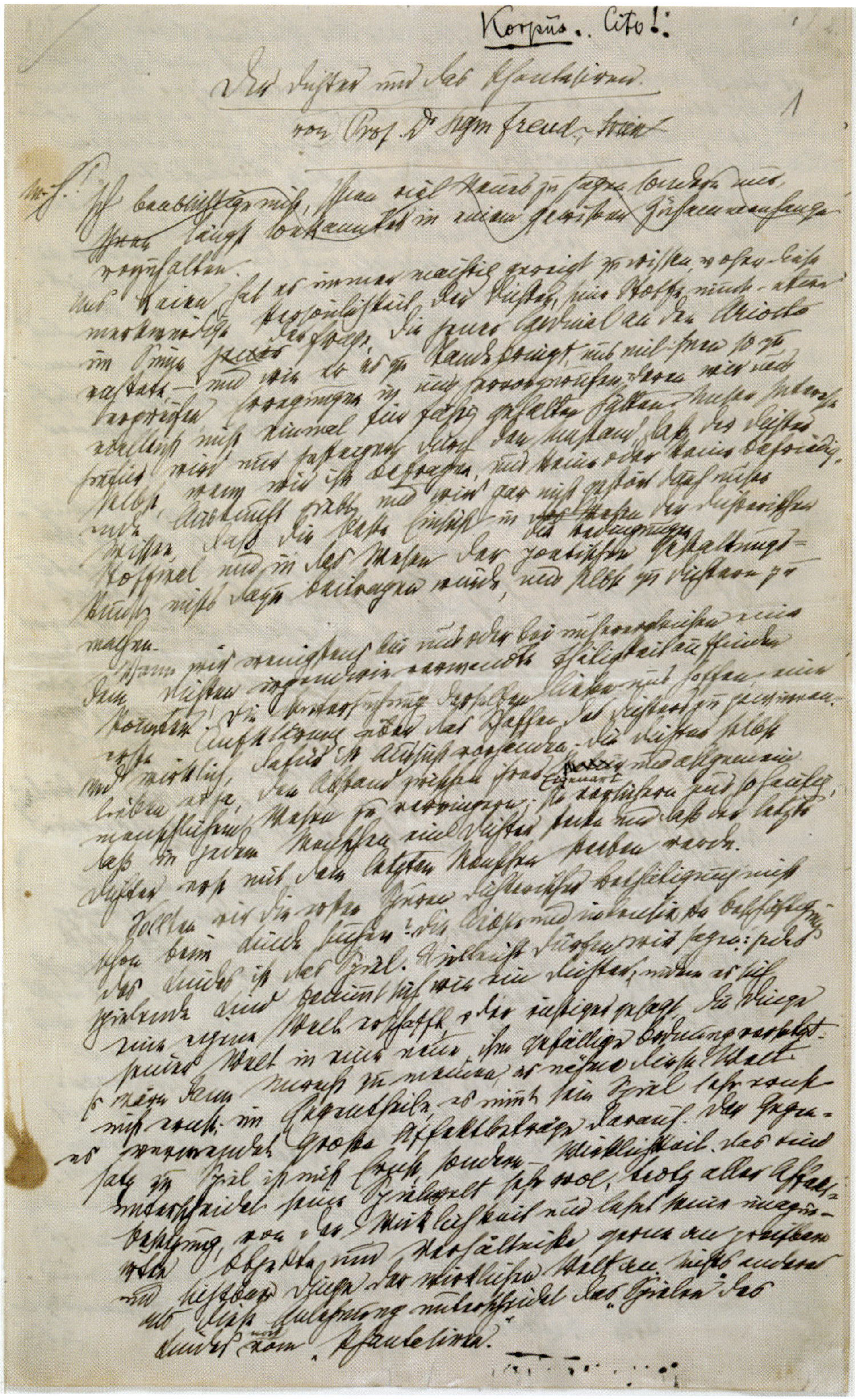
Korpus.. Cito!

Der Dichter und das Phantasieren.

von Prof. Dr Sigm Freud, Wien

1

Plate 19 Sigmund Freud: Zweig MS 150, f. 1r

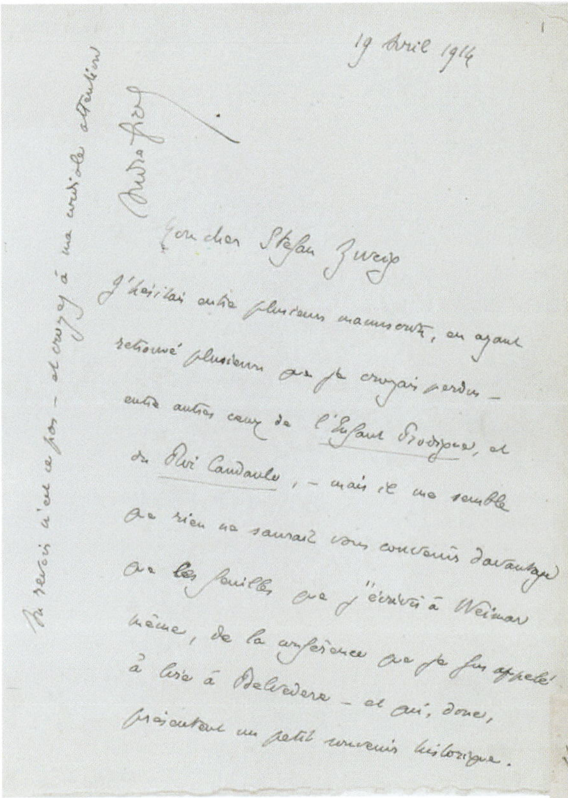

19 Avril 1914 1

Mon cher Stefan Zweig

J'hésitai entre plusieurs manuscrits, en ayant retrouvé plusieurs que je croyais perdus – entre autres ceux de l'Enfant Prodigue, et du Roi Candaule, – mais il me semble que rien ne saurait vous convenir davantage que les feuilles que j'écrivis à Weimar même, de la conférence que je fus appelé à lire à Belvedere – et qui, donc, présentent un petit souvenir historique.

Au revoir n'est ce pas – et croyez à ma cordiale attention

André Gide

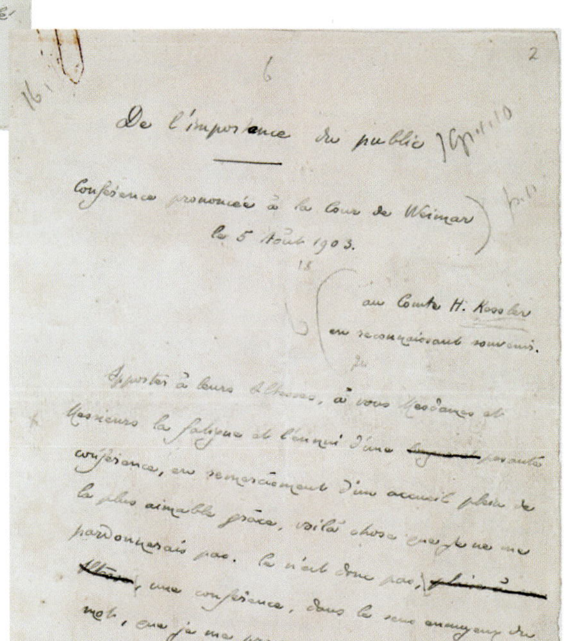

2

16 6

De l'importance du public

Conférence prononcée à la Cour de Weimar le 5 Août 1903.

au Comte H. Kessler en reconnaissant souvenir.

Apporter à leurs Altesses, à vous Mesdames et Messieurs la fatigue et l'ennui d'une ~~[illegible]~~ pesante conférence, en remerciement d'un accueil plein de la plus aimable grâce, voilà chose que je ne me pardonnerais pas. Ce n'est donc pas, ~~[illegible]~~, une conférence, dans le sens ennuyeux du mot, que je me propose de lire devant elles ce soir, – mais plutôt une causerie, et que je souhaite légère – où je m'efforcerai de dire en quelques mots ce que, devant un public moins cultivé je devrais ex–

Plate 20 (a) André Gide: Zweig MS 151, f. 1r (dedication to Zweig)

Plate 20 (b) André Gide: Zweig MS 151, f. 2r

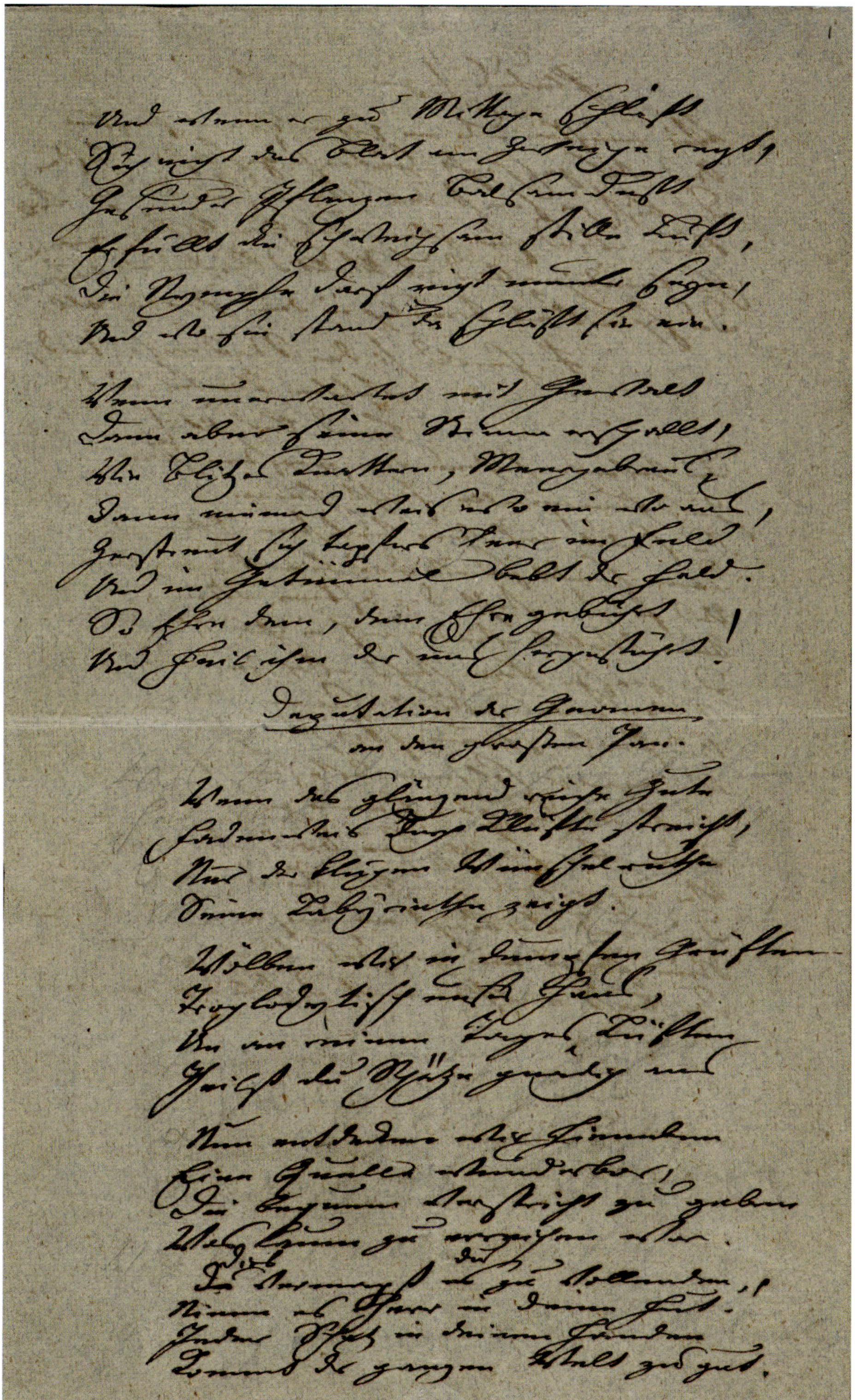

Plate 21 Johann Wolfgang von Goethe: Zweig MS 152, f. 1r

Plate 22 Johann Wolfgang von Goethe: Zweig MS 154, f. 1r

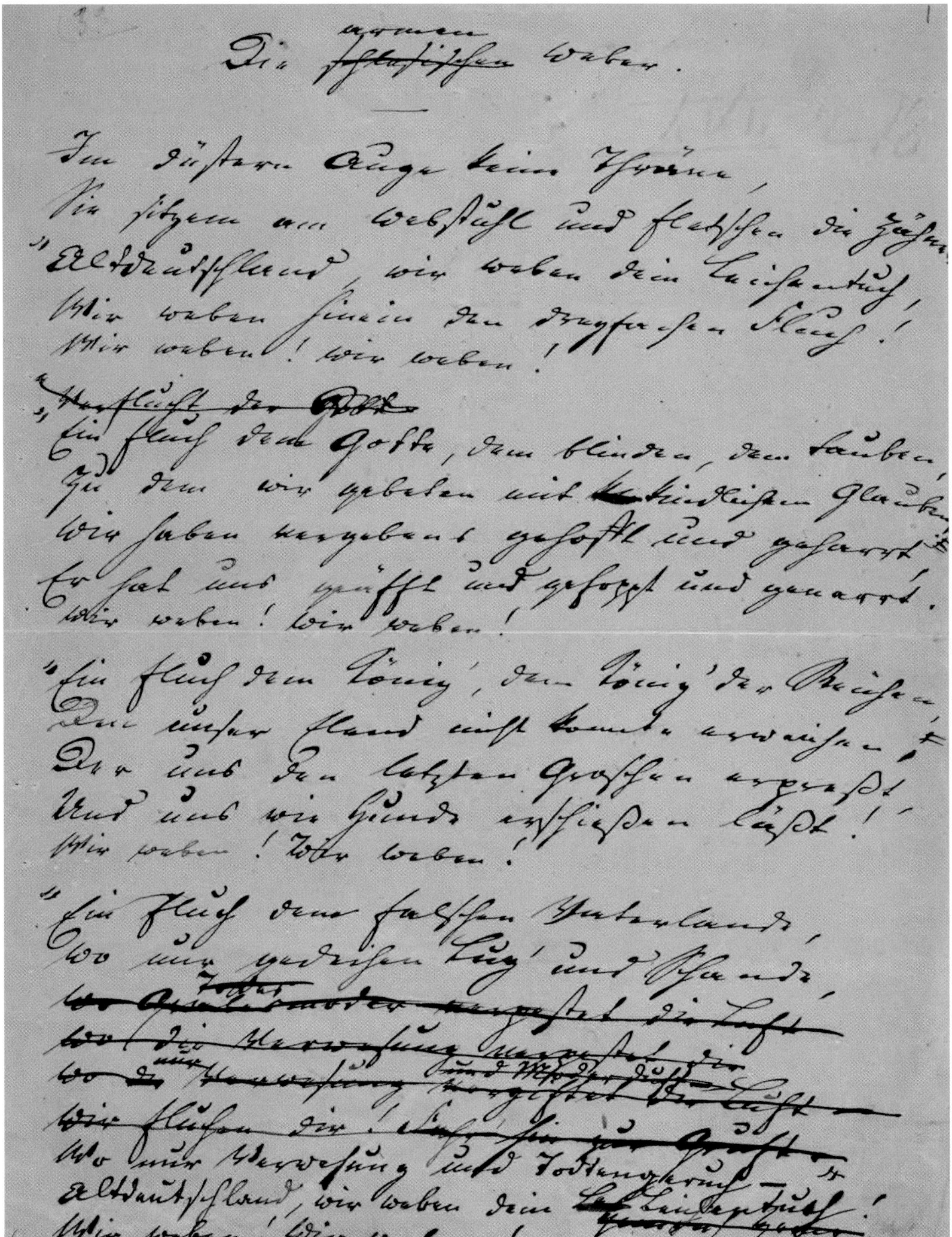

Die ~~schlesischen~~ armen Weber.

Im düstern Auge keine Thräne,
Sie sitzen am Webstuhl und fletschen die Zähne:
"Altdeutschland, wir weben dein Leichentuch,
Wir weben hinein den dreyfachen Fluch!
Wir weben! wir weben!

"Ein Fluch dem Gotte, dem blinden, dem tauben,
Zu dem wir gebeten mit kindlichem Glauben;
Wir haben vergebens gehofft und geharrt,
Er hat uns geäfft und gefoppt und genarrt.
Wir weben! wir weben!

"Ein Fluch dem König, dem König der Reichen,
Den unser Elend nicht konnte erweichen,
Der uns den letzten Groschen erpreßt
Und uns wie Hunde erschießen läßt!
Wir weben! wir weben!

"Ein Fluch dem falschen Vaterlande,
Wo nur gedeihen Lug und Schande,
Wo nur Verwesung und Todtengeruch –
Altdeutschland, wir weben dein Leichentuch!
Wir weben! wir weben!

Plate 23 Heinrich Heine: Zweig MS 156, f. 1r

Plate 24 Hermann Hesse: Zweig MS 157, f. 4r

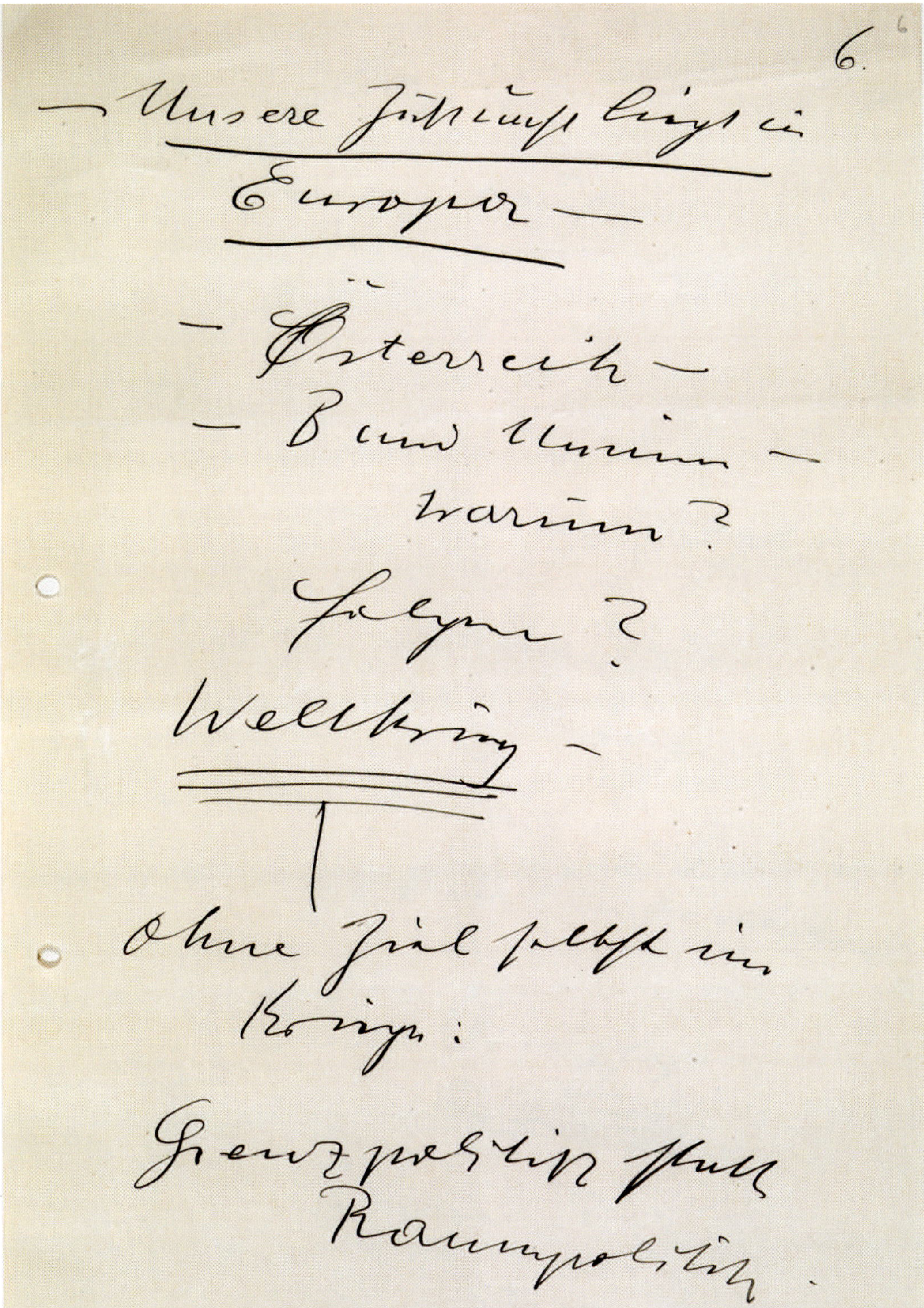

6.

– Unsere Zukunft liegt in Europa –

– Österreich –

– B und Ungarn –

warum?

Folgen?

Weltkrieg –

Ohne Ziel selbst im Kriege:

Grenzpolitik statt Raumpolitik.

Plate 25 Adolf Hitler: Zweig MS 158, f. 6r

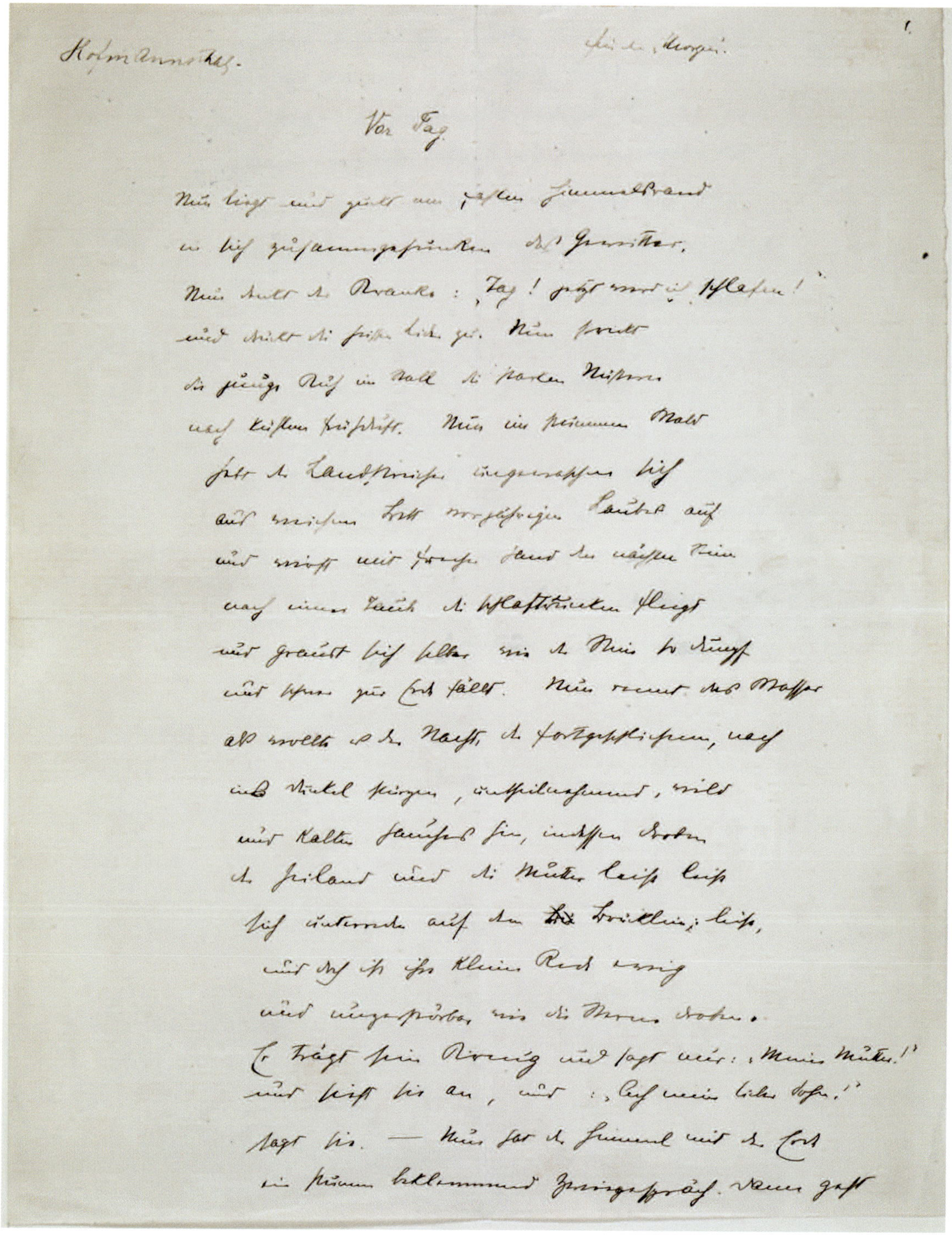
Hofmannsthal.

für den „Morgen".

1

Vor Tag

Nun liegt und zuckt am fahlen Himmelsrand
in sich zusammgesunken das Gewitter.
Nun denkt der Kranke: „Tag! jetzt werd ich schlafen!"
und drückt die heißen Lider zu. Nun streckt
die junge Kuh im Stall die starken Nüstern
nach kühlem Frühduft. Nun im stummen Wald
hebt der Landstreicher ungewaschen sich
aus weichem Bett vorjährigen Laubes auf
und wirft mit frecher Hand den nächsten Stein
nach einer Taube die schlaftrunken fliegt
und graust sich selber wie der Stein so dumpf
und schwer zur Erde fällt. Nun rennt das Wasser
als wollte es der Nacht, der fortgeschlichenen, nach
ins Dunkel stürzen, unbesänftigt, wild
und kalten Hauches hin, indessen droben
der Heiland und die Mutter leise leise
sich unterreden auf dem ~~Br~~ Brücklein: leise,
und doch ist ihre kleine Red ewig
und unzerstörbar wie die Sterne droben.
Er trägt sein Kreuz und sagt nur: „Meine Mutter!"
und sieht sie an, und: „Ach mein lieber Sohn!"
sagt sie. — Nun hat der Himmel mit der Erde
in stummem schlummernd Zwiegespräch. Dann geht

Plate 26 Hugo von Hofmannsthal: Zweig MS 159, f. 1r

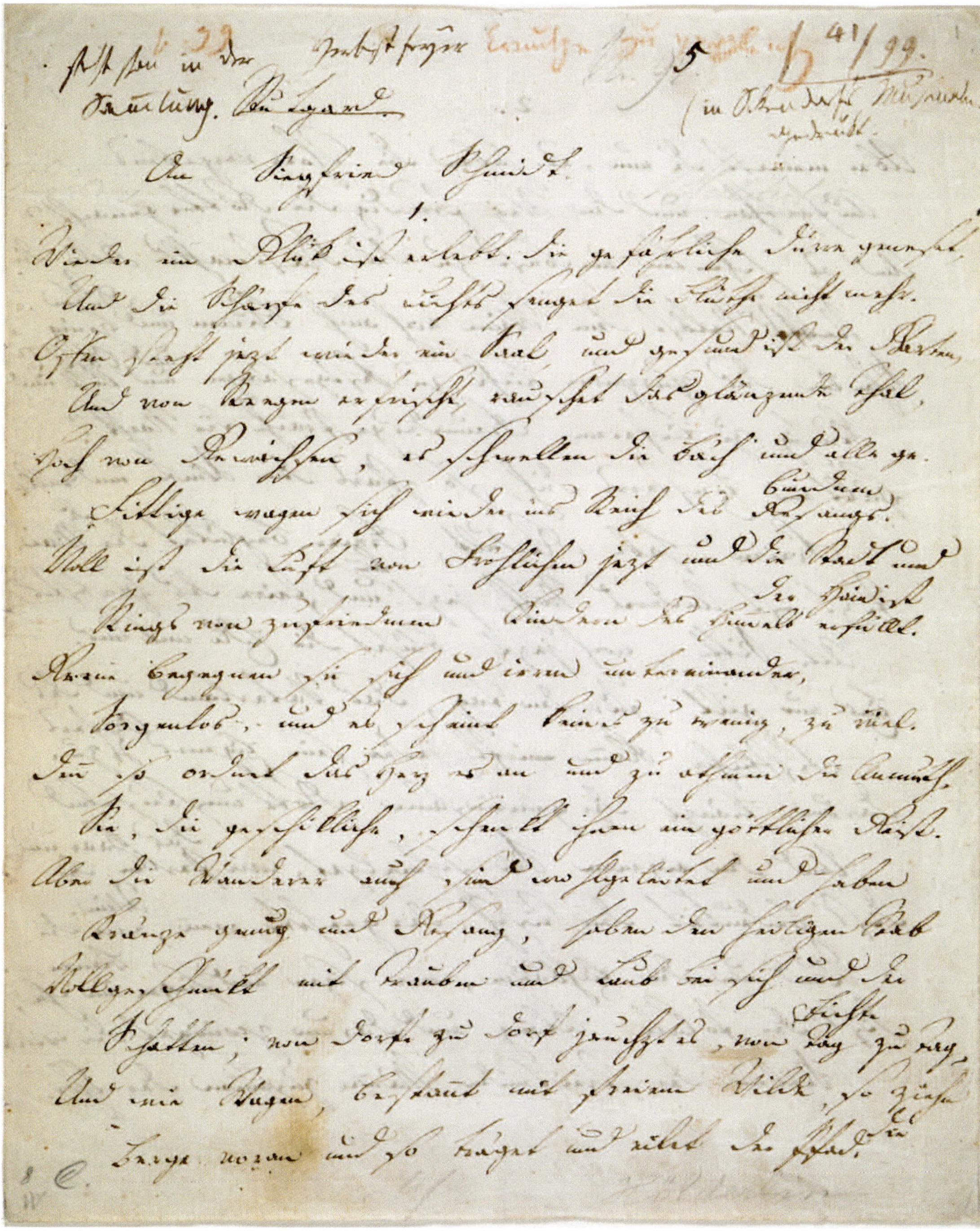

Plate 27 Friedrich Hölderlin: Zweig MS 160, f. 1r

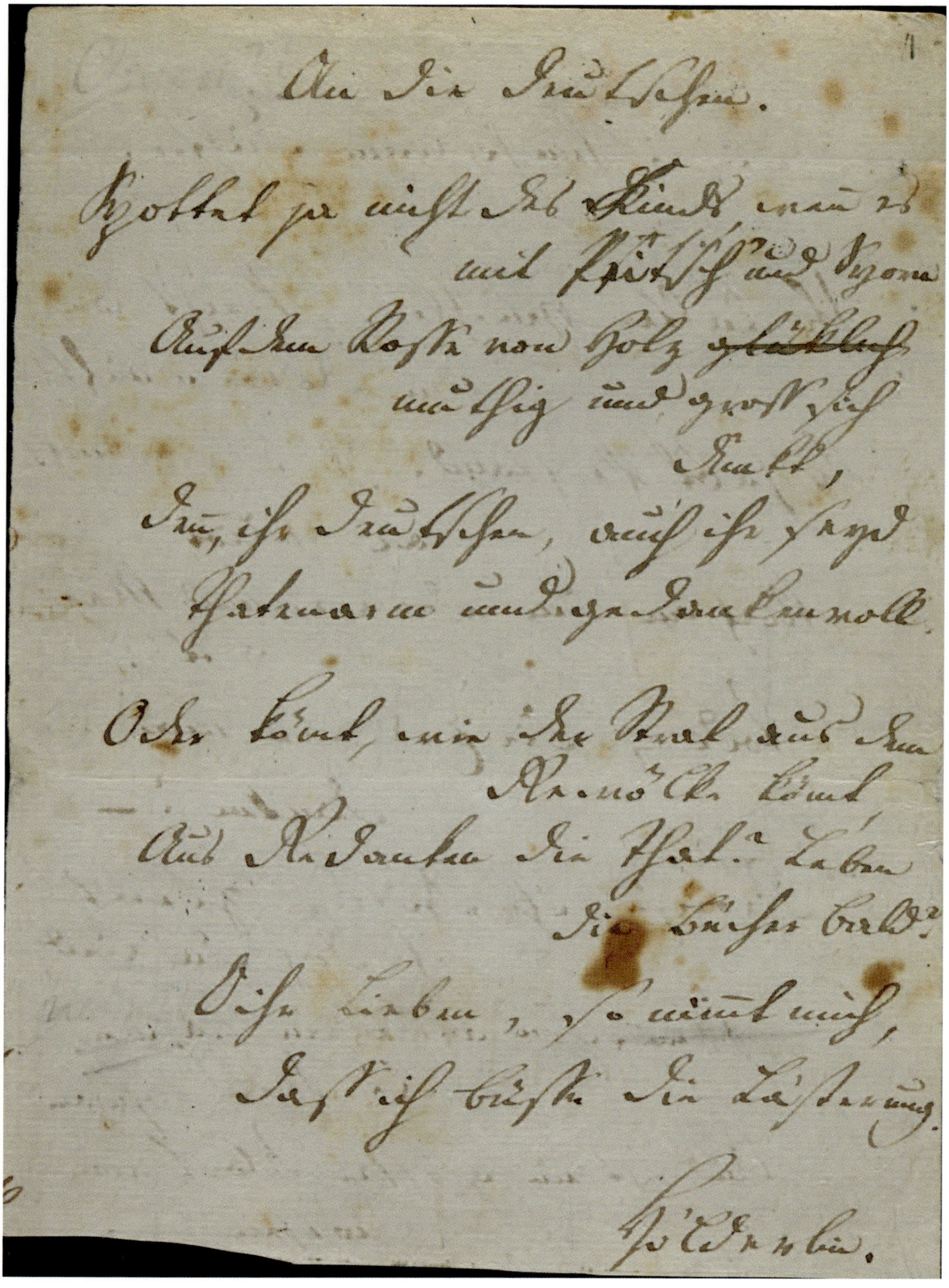

An die Deutschen.

Spottet ja nicht des Kinds, wenn es
mit Peitsch und Sporn
Auf dem Rosse von Holz ~~[illegible]~~
muthig und groß sich
dünkt,
Denn, ihr Deutschen, auch ihr seyd
Thatenarm und gedankenvoll.

Oder kommt, wie der Strahl aus dem
Gewölke kommt,
Aus Gedanken die That? Leben
die Bücher bald?
O ihr Lieben, so nimmt mich,
Daß ich büße die Lästerung.

Hölderlin.

Plate 28 Friedrich Hölderlin: Zweig MS 161, f. 1r

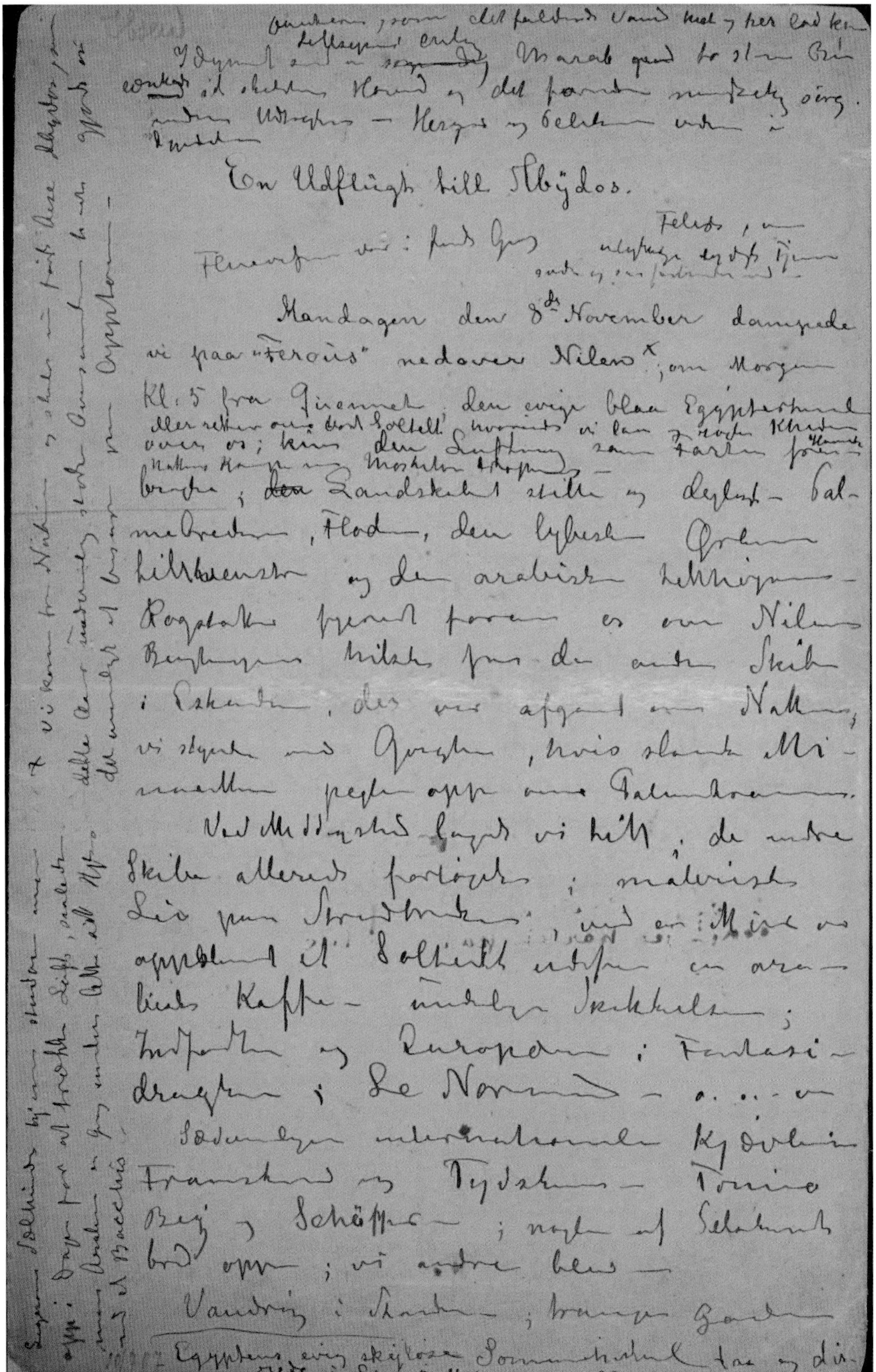
En Udflugt till Abydos.

Mandagen den 8de November dampede vi paa "Ferouz" nedover Nilen; om Morgen Kl. 5 fra Gizeh.

Plate 29 Henrik Ibsen: Zweig MS 162, f. 1r

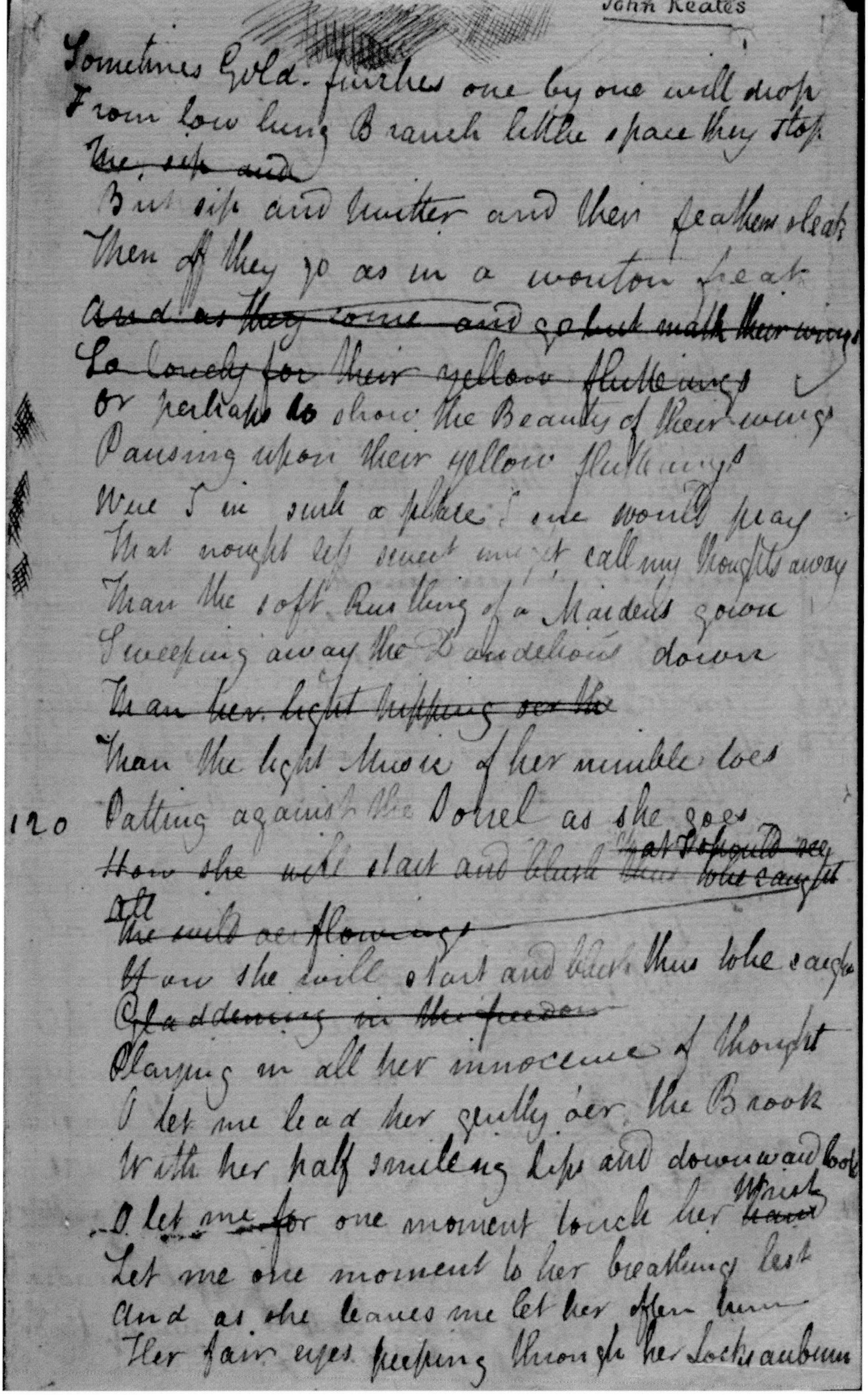

John Keats

Sometimes Gold-finches one by one will drop
From low hung Branch little space they stop
~~We sip and~~
But sip and twitter and their feathers sleak
Then off they go as in a wanton freak
~~And as they come and go but mark their ways~~
~~So lovely for their yellow flutterings~~
Or perhaps to show the Beauty of their wings
Pausing upon their yellow flutterings
Were I in such a place I sure would pray
That nought less sweet might call my thoughts away
Than the soft Rustling of a Maidens gown
Sweeping away the Dandelions down
~~Than her light tripping oer the~~
Than the light Music of her nimble toes
Patting against the Sorrel as she goes
~~How she will start and blush that I should see~~ ~~thus while caught~~
~~All the wild air flowings~~
How she will start and blush thus while caught
~~Gladdening in the freedom~~
Playing in all her innocence of thought
O let me lead her gently o'er the Brook
Watch her half smiling lips and downward look
O let me ~~for~~ one moment touch her Wrist ~~hand~~
Let me one moment to her breathing list
And as she leaves me let her often turn
Her fair eyes peeping through her Locks auburn

Plate 30 John Keats: Zweig MS 163, f. 1r

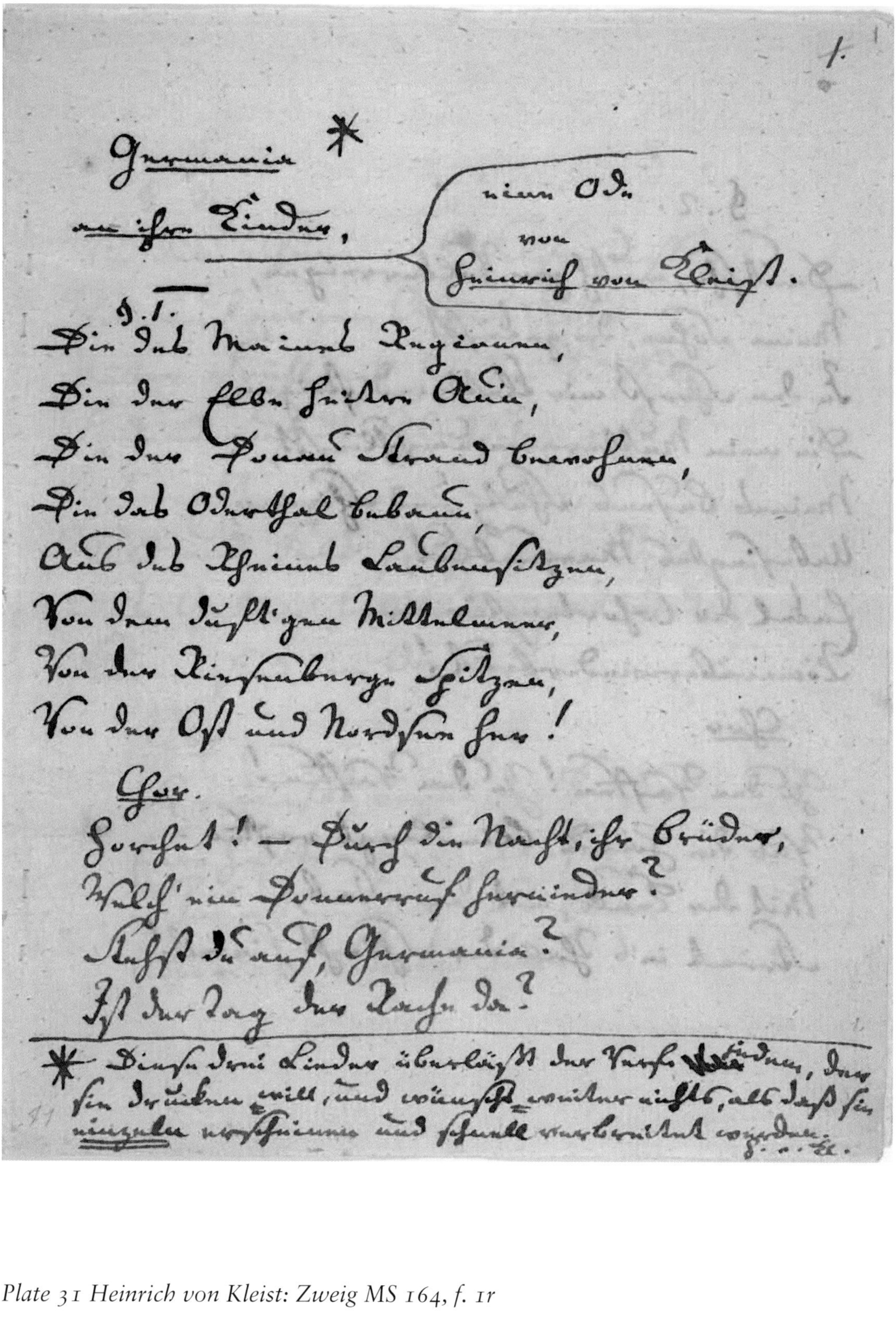

1.

Germania *
an ihre Kinder.

eine Ode
von
Heinrich von Kleist.

1.

Die des Maines Regionen,
Die der Elbe heitern Aun,
Die der Donau Strand bewohnen,
Die das Oderthal bebaun,
Aus des Rheines Laubensitzen,
Von dem duft'gen Mittelmeer,
Von der Riesenberge Spitzen,
Von der Ost und Nordsee her!

Chor.

Horchet! – Durch die Nacht, ihr Brüder,
Welch' ein Donnerruf hernieder?
Stehst du auf, Germania?
Ist der Tag der Rache da?

* Diese drei Lieder überläßt der Verfasser jedem, der sie drucken will, und wünscht weiter nichts, als daß sie einzeln erscheinen und schnell verbreitet werden. H. v. Kl.

Plate 31 Heinrich von Kleist: Zweig MS 164, f. 1r

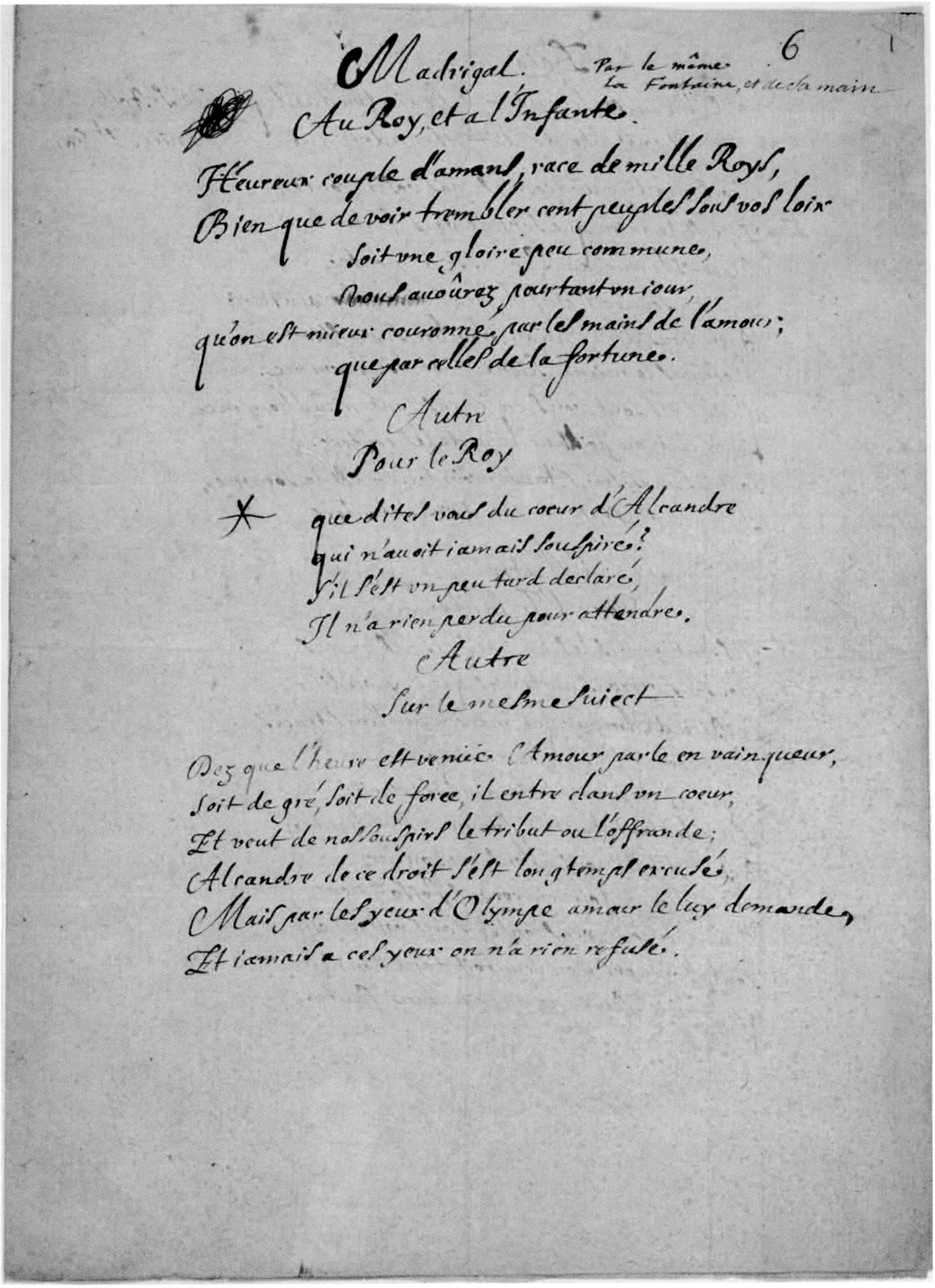

Madrigal. Par le même La Fontaine, et de sa main 6

Au Roy, et a l'Infante.

Heureux couple d'amans, race de mille Roys,
Bien que de voir trembler cent peuples sous vos loix
Soit vne gloire peu commune,
Vous auoûrez pourtant vn iour,
qu'on est mieux couronné par les mains de l'amour;
que par celles de la fortune.

Autre
Pour le Roy

* que dites vous du coeur d'Alcandre
qui n'auoit iamais souspiré?
S'il s'est vn peu tard declaré,
Il n'a rien perdu pour attendre.

Autre
Sur le mesme suiect

Dez que l'heure est venüe l'Amour parle en vainqueur,
Soit de gré, soit de force, il entre dans vn coeur,
Et veut de nos souspirs le tribut ou l'offrande;
Alcandre de ce droit s'est longtemps excusé,
Mais par les yeux d'Olympe amour le luy demande,
Et iamais a ces yeux on n'a rien refusé.

Plate 32 Jean de La Fontaine: Zweig MS 165, f. 1r

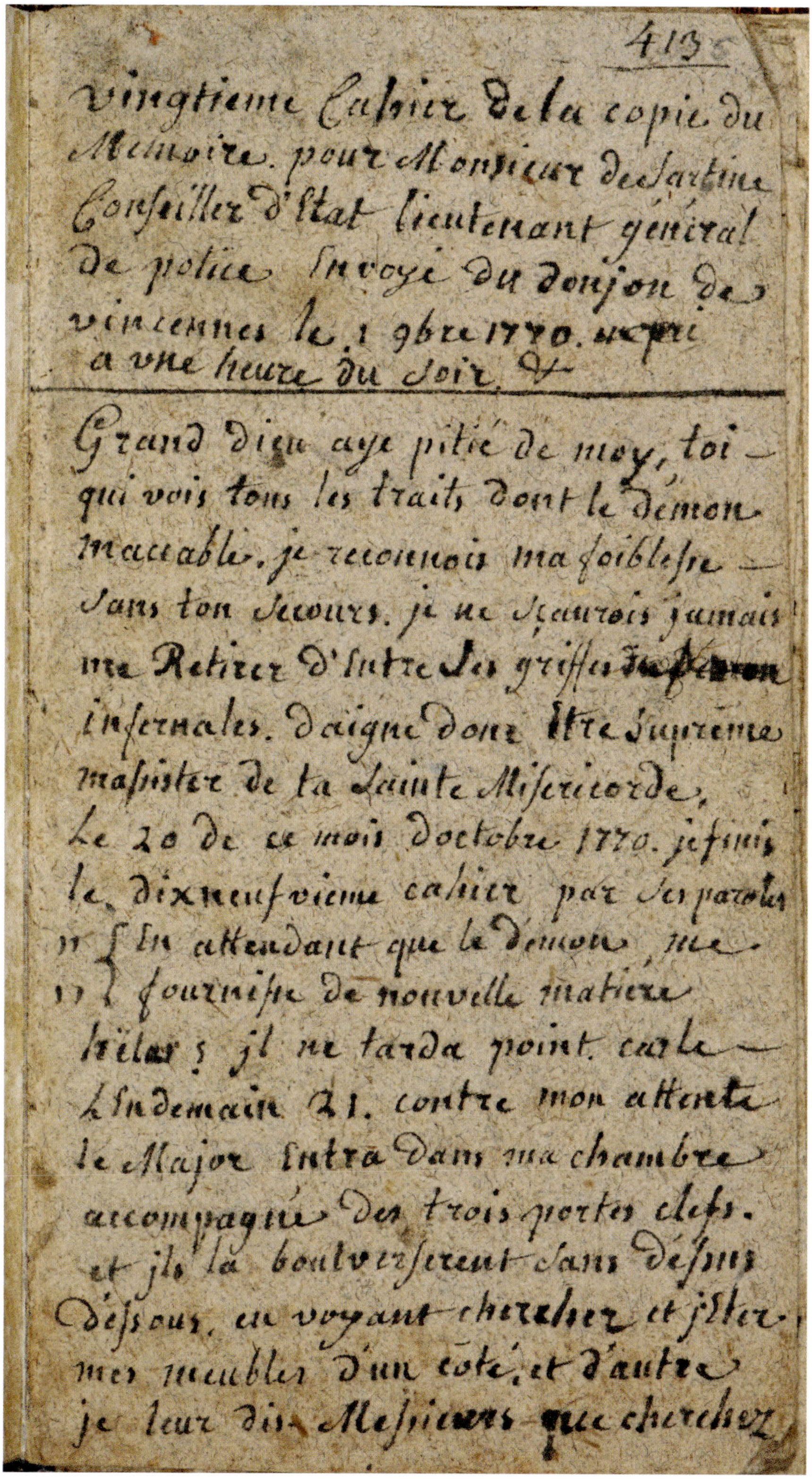

413

vingtieme Cahier de la copie du
Memoire. pour Monsieur de Sartine
Conseiller d'Etat lieutenant général
de police Envoyé du donjon de
vincennes le 1 9bre 1770. [illegible]
a une heure du soir.

Grand dieu aye pitié de moy, toi
qui vois tous les traits dont le démon
maccable. je reconnois ma foiblesse
sans ton secours. je ne sçaurois jamais
me Retirer d'entre ses griffes [illegible]
infernales. daigne donc Etre Supreme
m'assister de ta Sainte Misericorde.
Le 20 de ce mois doctobre 1770. je finis
le dixneufvieme cahier par ces paroles
" {En attendant que le démon me
" {fournisse de nouvelle matiere
écrire; jl ne tarda point. car le
lendemain 21. contre mon attente
le Major Entra dans ma chambre
accompagné des trois portes clefs.
et jls la bouleverserent sans dessus
dessous. en voyant chercher et jetter
mes meubles d'un coté, et d'autre
je leur dis Messieurs que cherchez

Plate 33 Jean Henri Latude: Zweig MS 166, f. 5r

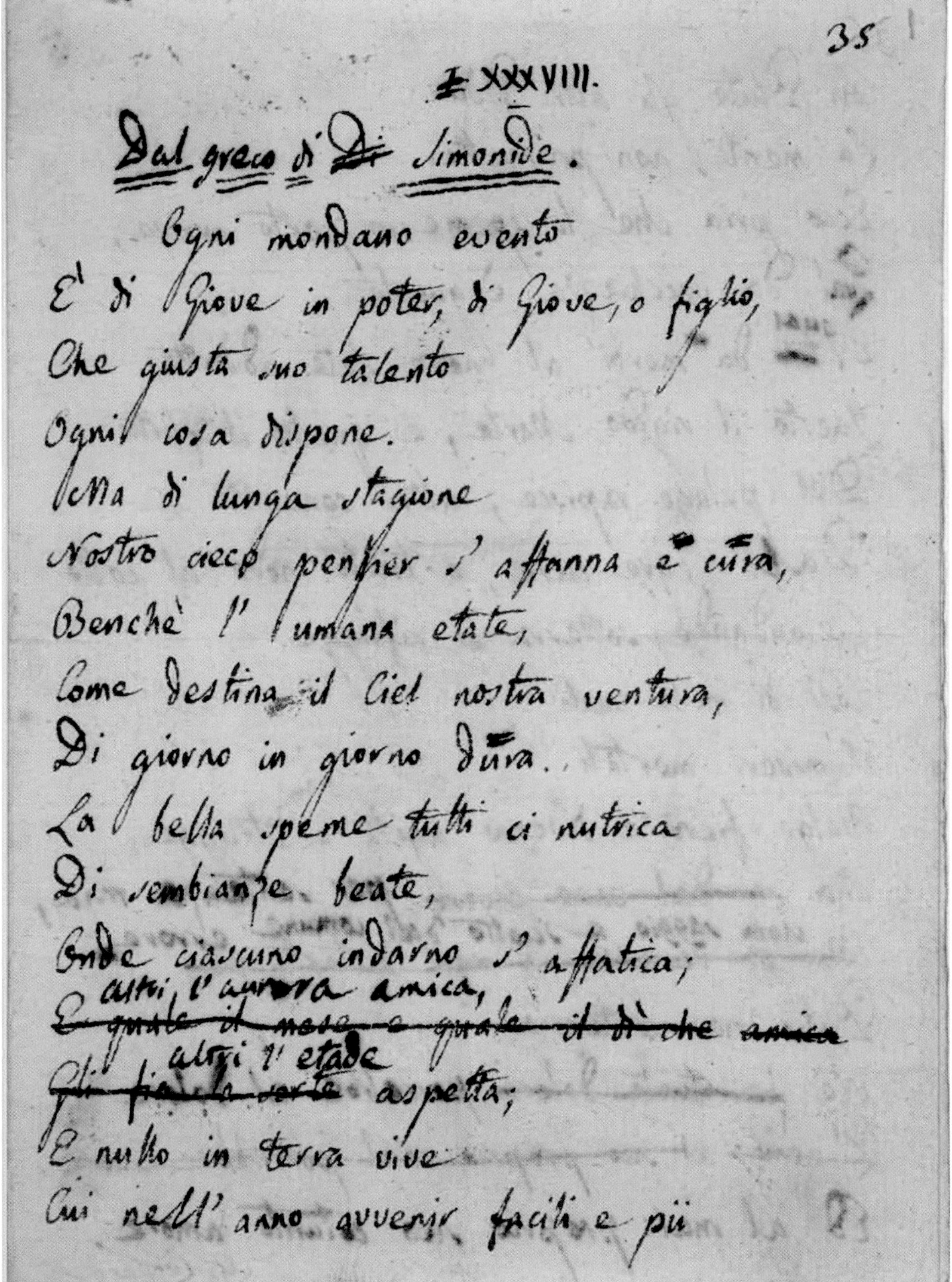
35

XXXVIII.

Dal greco di ~~Di~~ Simonide.

Ogni mondano evento
E' di Giove in poter, di Giove, o figlio,
Che giusta suo talento
Ogni cosa dispone.
Ma di lunga stagione
Nostro cieco pensier s'affanna e cura,
Benchè l'umana etate,
Come destina il Ciel nostra ventura,
Di giorno in giorno dura.
La bella speme tutti ci nutrica
Di sembianze beate,
Onde ciascuno indarno s'affatica;
altri l'aurora amica,
~~E quale il mese e quale il dì che amica~~
altri l'etade
~~Gli fia la sorte~~ aspetta;
E nullo in terra vive
Cui nell'anno avvenir facili e pii

Plate 34 Giacomo Leopardi: Zweig MS 167, f. 1r

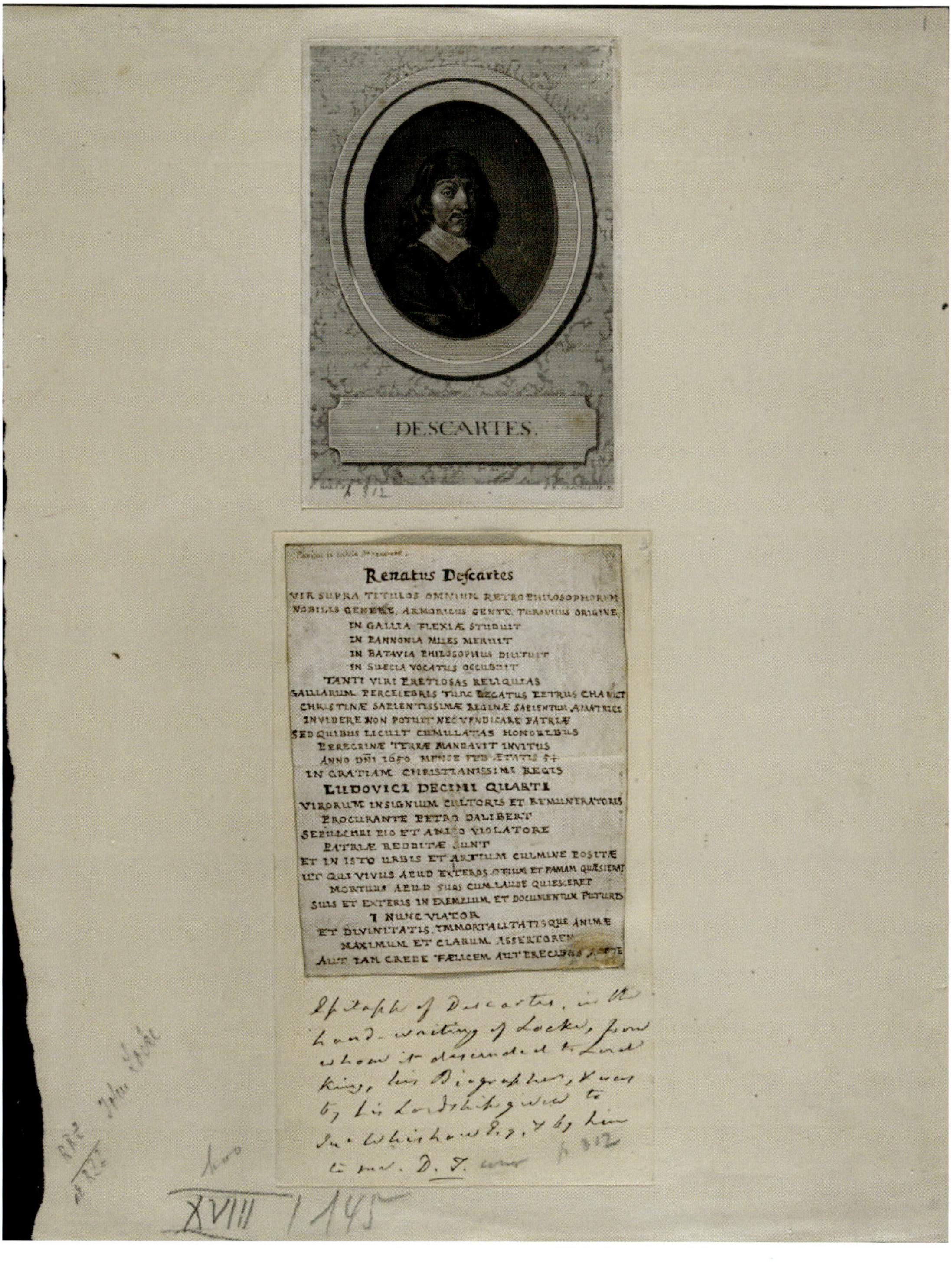
DESCARTES.

Renatus Descartes

VIR SUPRA TITULOS OMNIUM RETRO PHILOSOPHORUM
NOBILIS GENERE, ARMORICUS GENTE, TURONICUS ORIGINE
IN GALLIA FLEXIÆ STUDUIT
IN PANNONIA MILES MERUIT
IN BATAVIA PHILOSOPHUS DELITUIT
IN SUECIA VOCATUS OCCUBUIT
TANTI VIRI PRETIOSAS RELIQUIAS
GALLIARUM PERCELEBRIS TUNC LEGATUS PETRUS CHANUT
CHRISTINÆ SAPIENTISSIMÆ REGINÆ SAPIENTUM AMATRICI
INVIDERE NON POTUIT NEC VENDICARE PATRIÆ
SED QUIBUS LICUIT CUMULATAS HONORIBUS
PEREGRINÆ TERRÆ MANDAVIT INVITUS
ANNO DÑI 1650 MENSE FEB ÆTATIS 54
IN GRATIAM CHRISTIANISSIMI REGIS
LUDOVICI DECIMI QUARTI
VIRORUM INSIGNIUM CULTORIS ET REMUNERATORIS
PROCURANTE PETRO DALIBERT
SEPULCHRI PIO ET AMICO VIOLATORE
PATRIÆ REDDITÆ SUNT
ET IN ISTO URBIS ET ARTIUM CULMINE POSITÆ
UT QUI VIVUS APUD EXTEROS OTIUM ET FAMAM QUÆSIERAT
MORTUUS APUD SUOS CUM LAUDE QUIESCERET
SUIS ET EXTERIS IN EXEMPLUM ET DOCUMENTUM FUTURUS
I NUNC VIATOR
ET DIVINITATIS IMMORTALITATISQUE ANIMÆ
MAXIMUM ET CLARUM ASSERTOREM
AUT IAM CREDE FÆLICEM AUT PRECARE

Epitaph of Descartes, in the hand-writing of Locke, from whom it descended to Lord King, his Biographer, & was by his Lordship given to Mr Whishaw Esq., & by him to me. D. T.

XVIII / 145

Plate 35 John Locke: Zweig MS 168, ff. 1–4

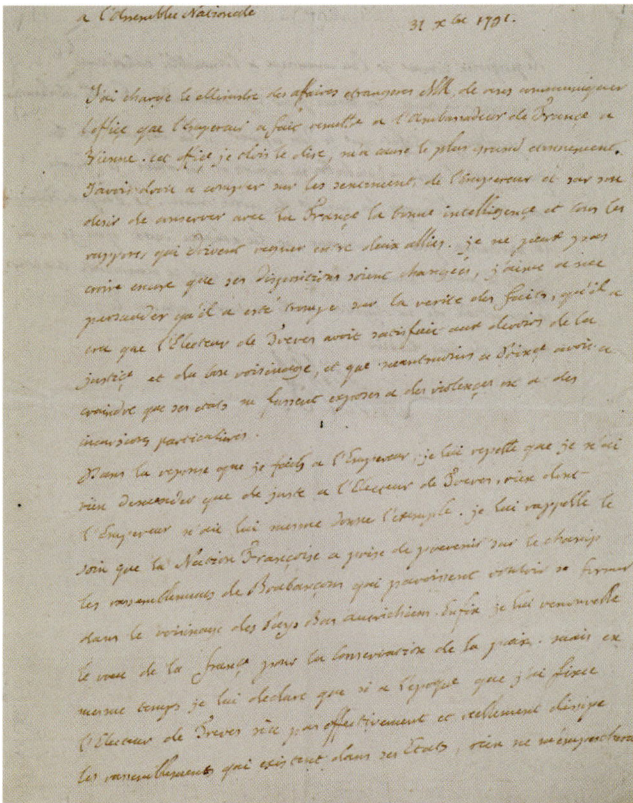
a l'Assemblée Nationale 31 Xbre 1791.

J'ai chargé le Ministre des affaires étrangeres Mr de vous communiquer l'office que l'Empereur a fait remettre a l'Ambassadeur de France a Vienne. cet office je dois le dire, m'a causé le plus grand étonnement. J'avois lieu a compter sur les sentiments de l'Empereur et sur son desir de conserver avec la France la bonne intelligence et tous les rapports qui doivent regner entre deux alliés. je ne peut pas croire encore que ses dispositions soient changées, j'aime a me persuader qu'il a été trompé sur la verité des faits, qu'il a cru que l'Electeur de Treves avoit satisfait aux devoirs de la justice et du bon voisinage, et que neantmoins la France avoit a craindre que ses etats ne fussent exposés a des violences ou a des incursions particulieres.

Dans la reponse que je fais a l'Empereur, je lui repette que je n'ai rien demandé que de juste a l'Electeur de Treves, rien dont l'Empereur n'ait lui meme donné l'exemple. je lui rappelle le soin que la Nation Françoise a prise de prevenir sur le champ les rassemblements de Brabançons qui paroissoient vouloir se former dans le voisinage des Pays Bas autrichiens. enfin je lui renouvelle le voeu de la France pour la conservation de la paix. mais en meme temps je lui declare que si a l'epoque que j'ai fixée l'Electeur de Treves n'a pas effectivement et reellement dissipé les rassemblements qui existent dans ses Etats, rien ne m'empechera

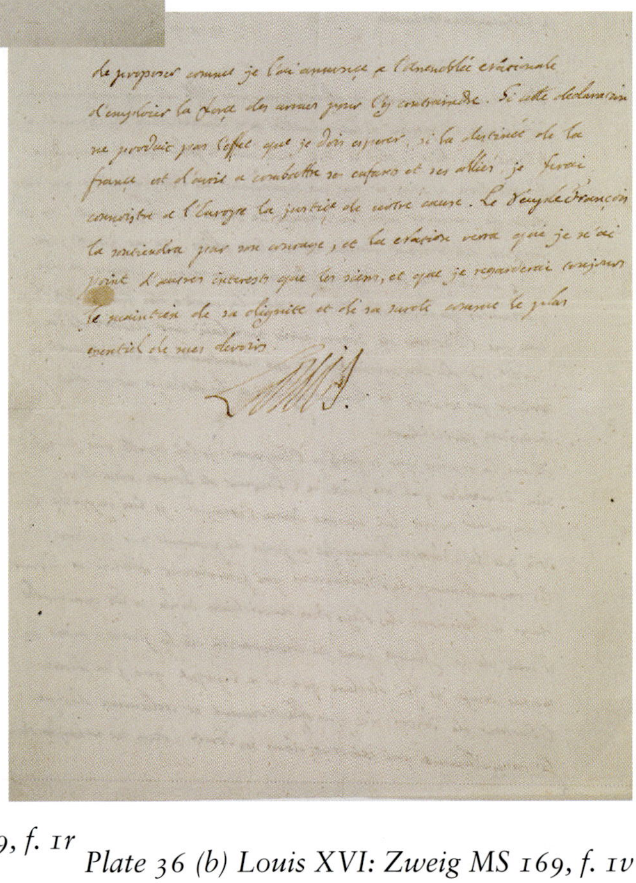
de proposer comme je l'ai annoncé a l'Assemblée Nationale d'employer la force des armes pour l'y contraindre. Si cette declaration ne produit pas l'effet que je dois esperer, si la destinée de la France est d'avoir a combattre ses enfants et ses alliés, je ferai connoitre a l'Europe la justice de notre cause. Le Peuple François la soutiendra par son courage, et la Nation verra que je n'ai point d'autres interests que les siens, et que je regarderai toujours le maintien de sa dignité et de sa sureté comme le plus essentiel de mes devoirs.

Louis

Plate 36 (a) Louis XVI: Zweig MS 169, f. 1r

Plate 36 (b) Louis XVI: Zweig MS 169, f. 1v

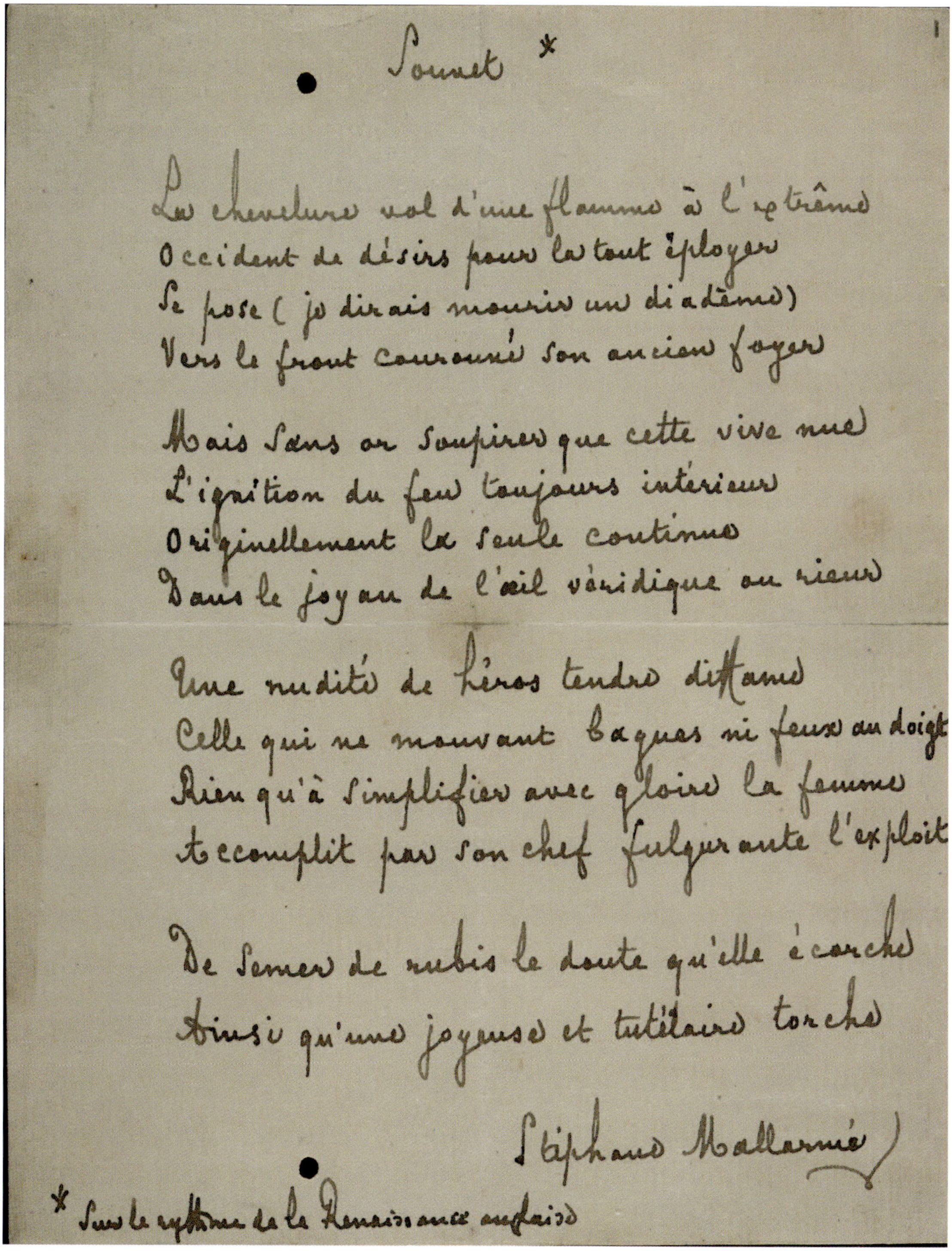

1

Sonnet *

La chevelure vol d'une flamme à l'extrême
Occident de désirs pour la tout éployer
Se pose (je dirais mourir un diadème)
Vers le front couronné son ancien foyer

Mais sans or soupirer que cette vive nue
L'ignition du feu toujours intérieur
Originellement la seule continue
Dans le joyau de l'œil véridique ou rieur

Une nudité de héros tendre diffame
Celle qui ne mouvant bagues ni feux au doigt
Rien qu'à simplifier avec gloire la femme
Accomplit par son chef fulgurante l'exploit

De semer de rubis le doute qu'elle écorche
Ainsi qu'une joyeuse et tutélaire torche

Stéphane Mallarmé

* Sur le rythme de la Renaissance anglaise

Plate 37 Stéphane Mallarmé: Zweig MS 170, f. 1r

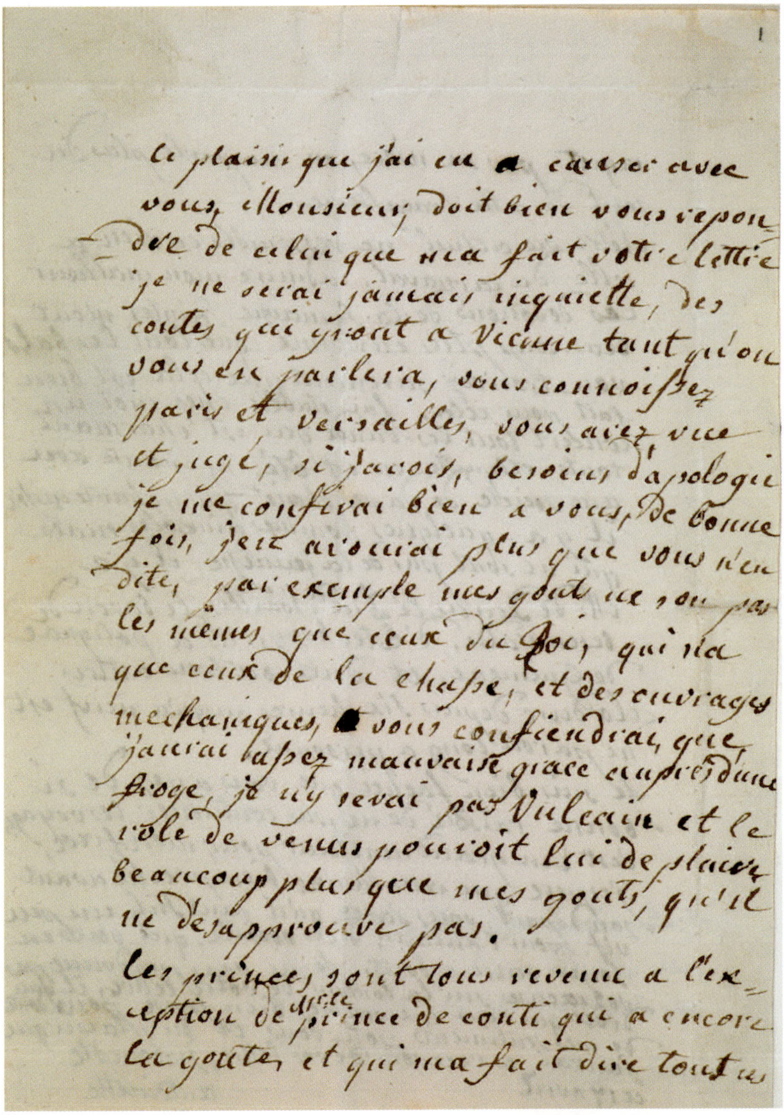

le plaisir que j'ai eu a causer avec
vous, Monsieur, doit bien vous repon-
dre de celui que m'a fait votre lettre
je ne serai jamais inquiette, des
contes qui iront a Vienne tant qu'on
vous en parlera, vous connoissez
paris et versailles, vous avez vue
et jugé, si j'avois besoin d'apologie
je me confirai bien a vous, de bonne
fois, j'en avouerai plus que vous n'en
dite, par exemple mes gout ne sont pas
les mêmes que ceux du Roi, qui n'a
que ceux de la chasse, et des ouvrages
mechaniques, vous conviendrai, que
j'aurai assez mauvaise grace auprès d'une
forge, je n'y serai pas Vulcain et le
role de venus pouroit lui deplaire
beaucoup plus que mes gouts, qu'il
ne desapprouve pas.
les princes sont tous revenu a l'exception de Mr le prince de conti qui a encore
la goutte, et qui m'a fait dire tout ce

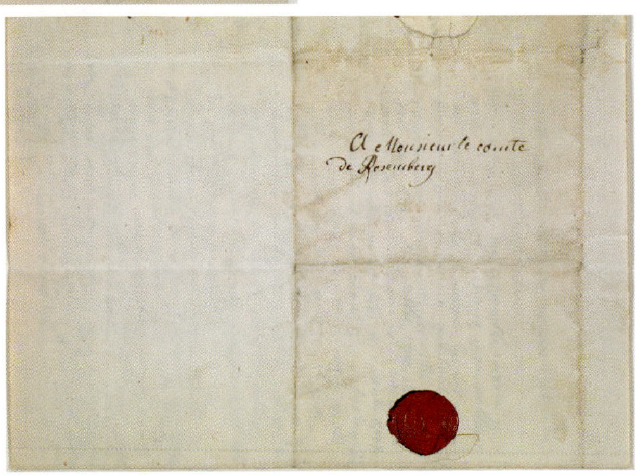

A Monsieur le comte
de Rosenberg

Plate 38 (a) Marie Antoinette: Zweig MS 171, f. 1r

Plate 38 (b) Marie Antoinette: Zweig MS 171, f. 2v (seal)

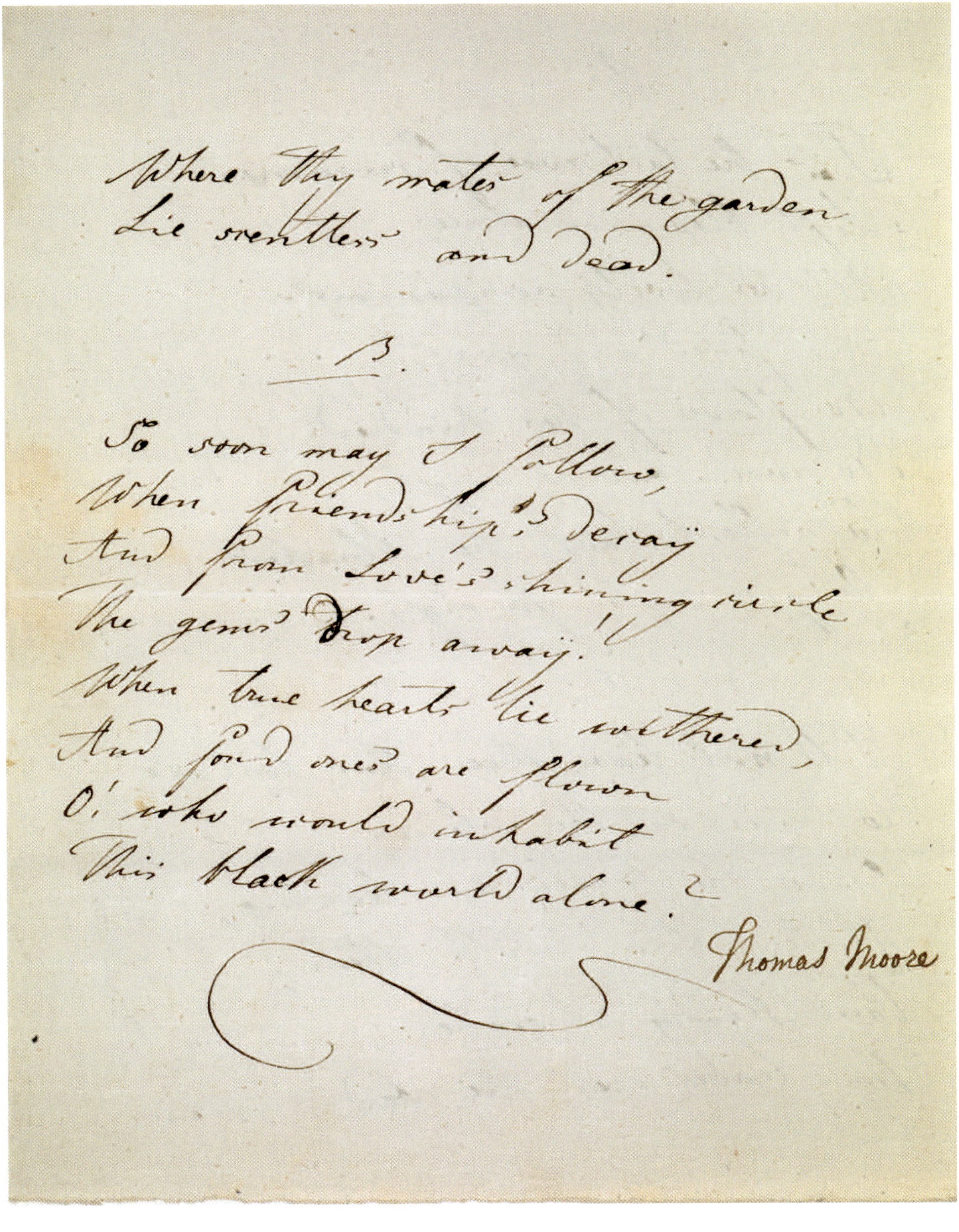
Where thy mates of the garden
Lie scentless and dead.

3.

So soon may I follow,
When friendships decay,
And from Love's shining circle
The gems drop away.
When true hearts lie withered,
And fond ones are flown,
O! who would inhabit
This bleak world alone?

Thomas Moore

Plate 39 Thomas Moore: Zweig MS 172, f. 1v

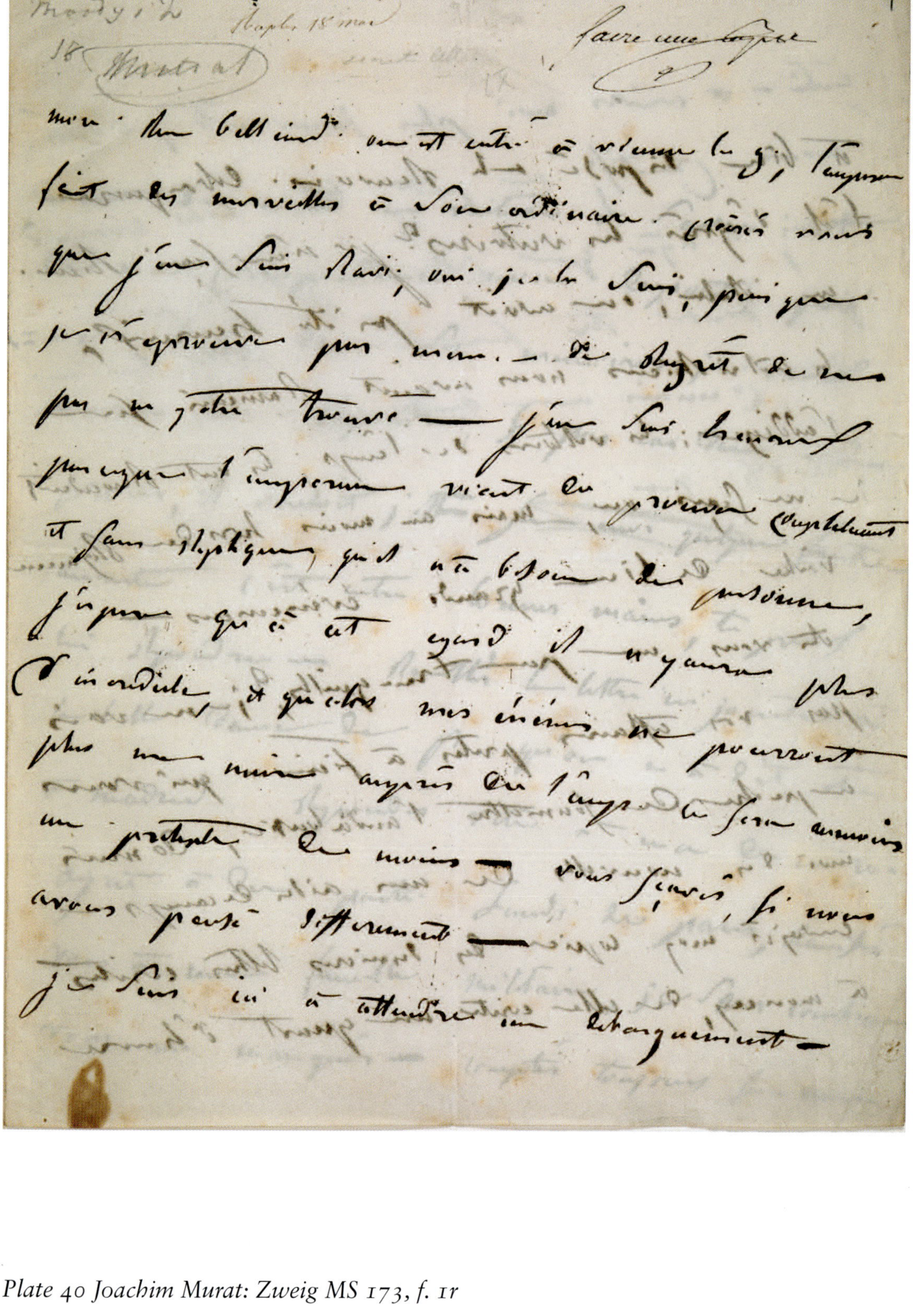

Plate 40 Joachim Murat: Zweig MS 173, f. 1r

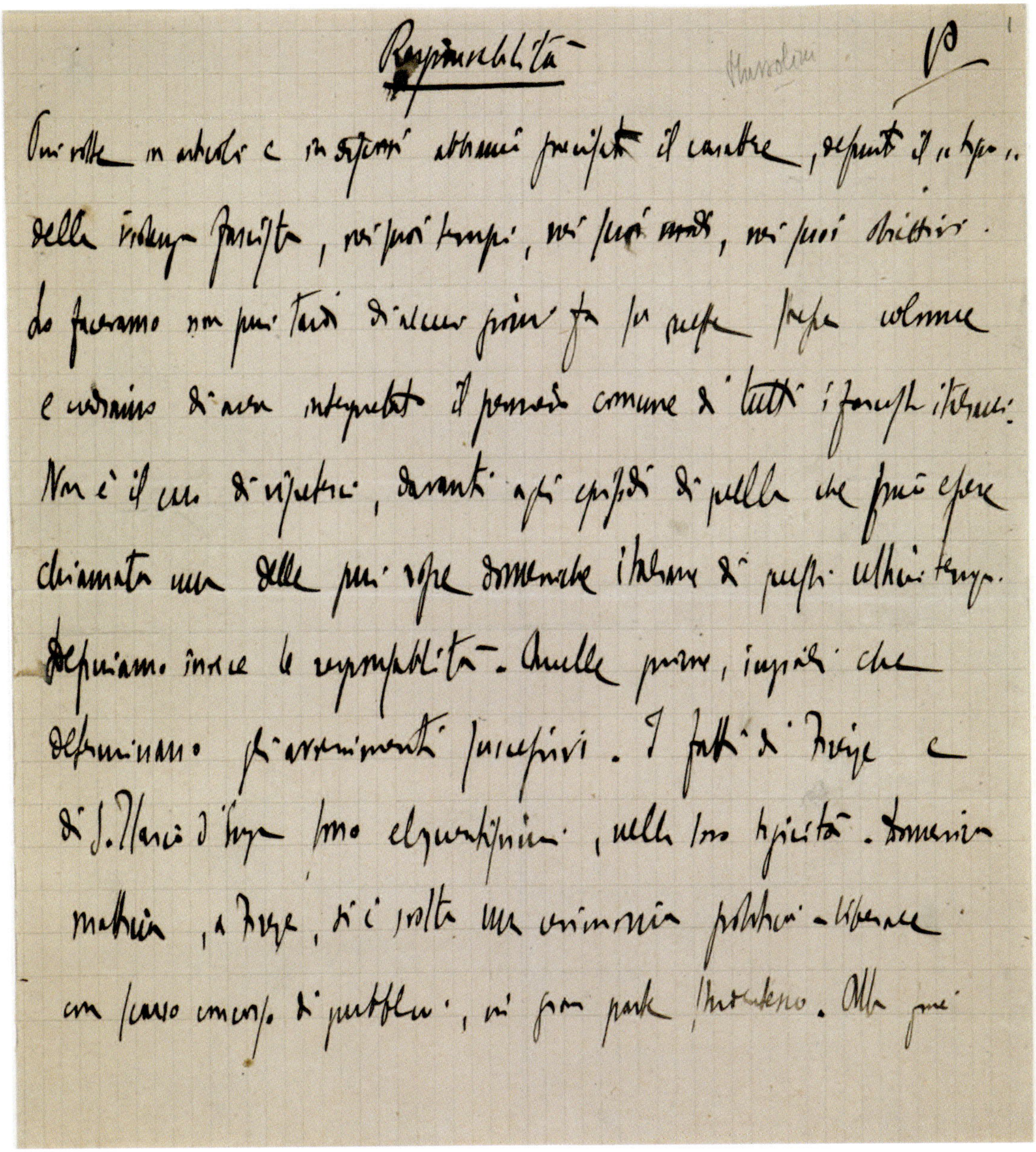
Responsabilità
Mussolini
13

Più volte in articoli e in discorsi abbiamo precisato il carattere, definito il "tipo" della violenza fascista, nei suoi tempi, nei suoi modi, nei suoi obbiettivi. Lo facevamo non più tardi di alcuni giorni fa su queste stesse colonne e crediamo di aver interpretato il pensiero comune di tutti i fascisti italiani. Non è il caso di ripetersi, davanti agli episodi di quella che può essere chiamata una delle più fosche domeniche italiane di questi ultimi tempi. Precisiamo invece le responsabilità. Quelle prime, iniziali che determinano gli avvenimenti successivi. I fatti di Treviso e di S. Marco d'Argo sono eloquentissimi, nella loro tragicità. Domenica mattina, a Treviso, si è svolta una cerimonia politico-liberale con scarso concorso di pubblico, in gran parte studenti. Alle prime

Plate 41 Benito Mussolini: Zweig MS 174, f. 1r

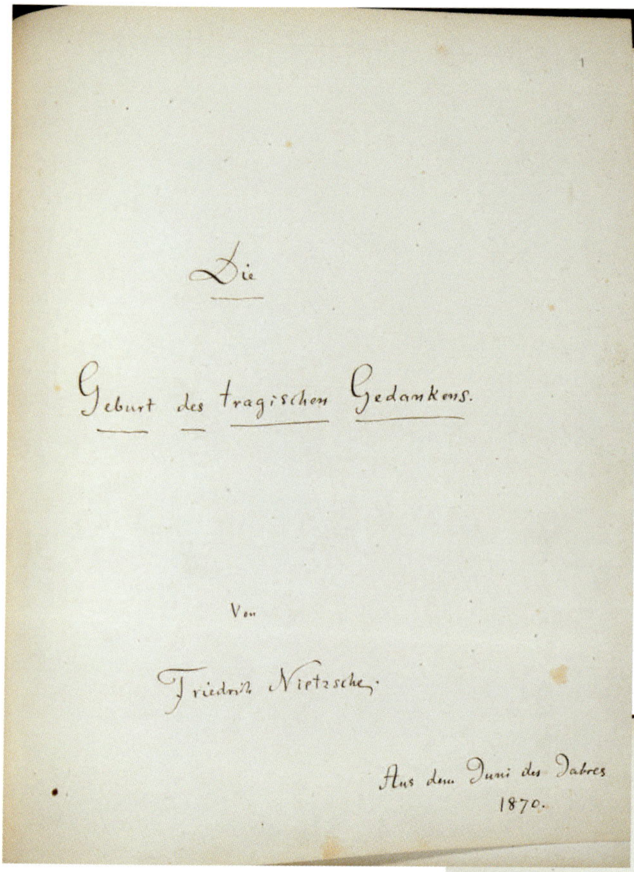
1

Die

Geburt des tragischen Gedankens.

Von

Friedrich Nietzsche.

Aus dem Juni des Jahres
1870.

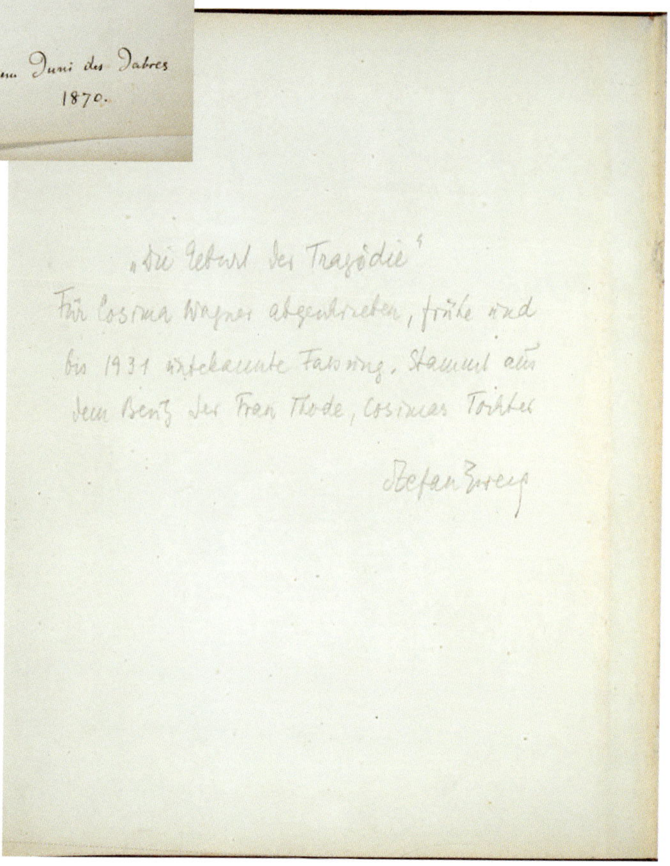
„Die Geburt der Tragödie"
Für Cosima Wagner abgeschrieben, frühe und
bis 1931 unbekannte Fassung. Stammt aus
dem Besitz der Frau Thode, Cosimas Tochter

Stefan Zweig

Plate 42 (a) Friedrich Nietzsche: Zweig MS 175, f. 1r

Plate 42 (b) Friedrich Nietzsche: Zweig MS 175, f. i v (note by Zweig)

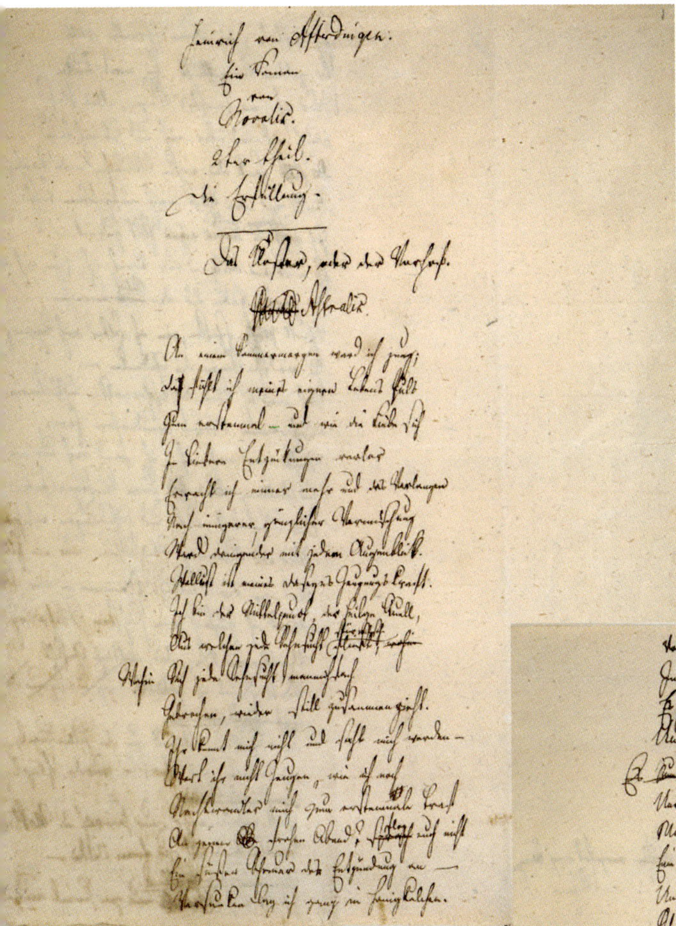

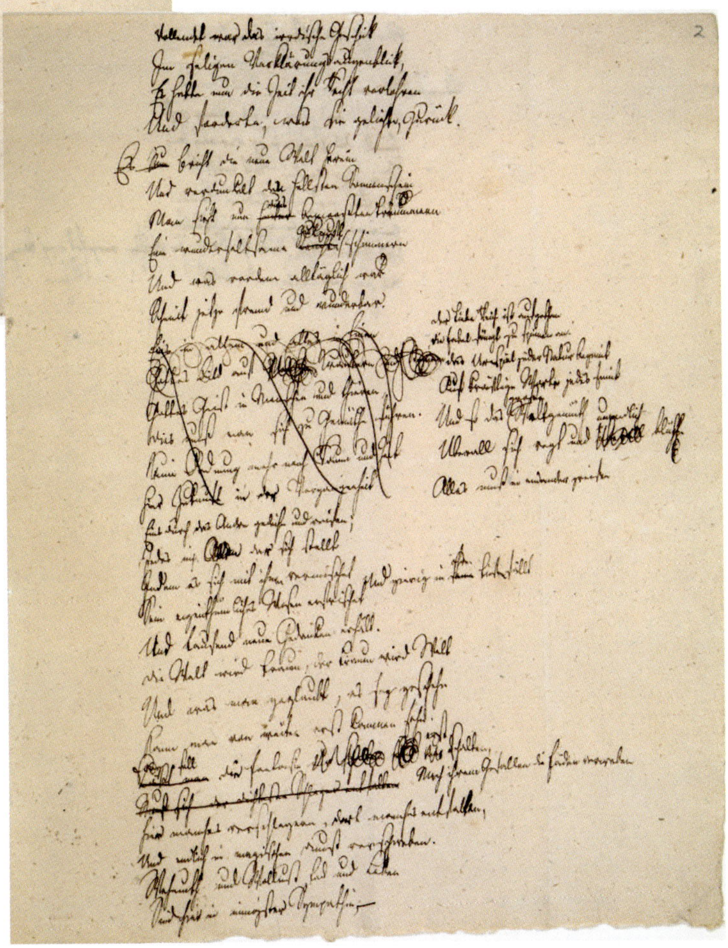

Plate 43 (a) 'Novalis': Zweig MS 176, f. 1r

Plate 43 (b) 'Novalis': Zweig MS 176, f. 2r

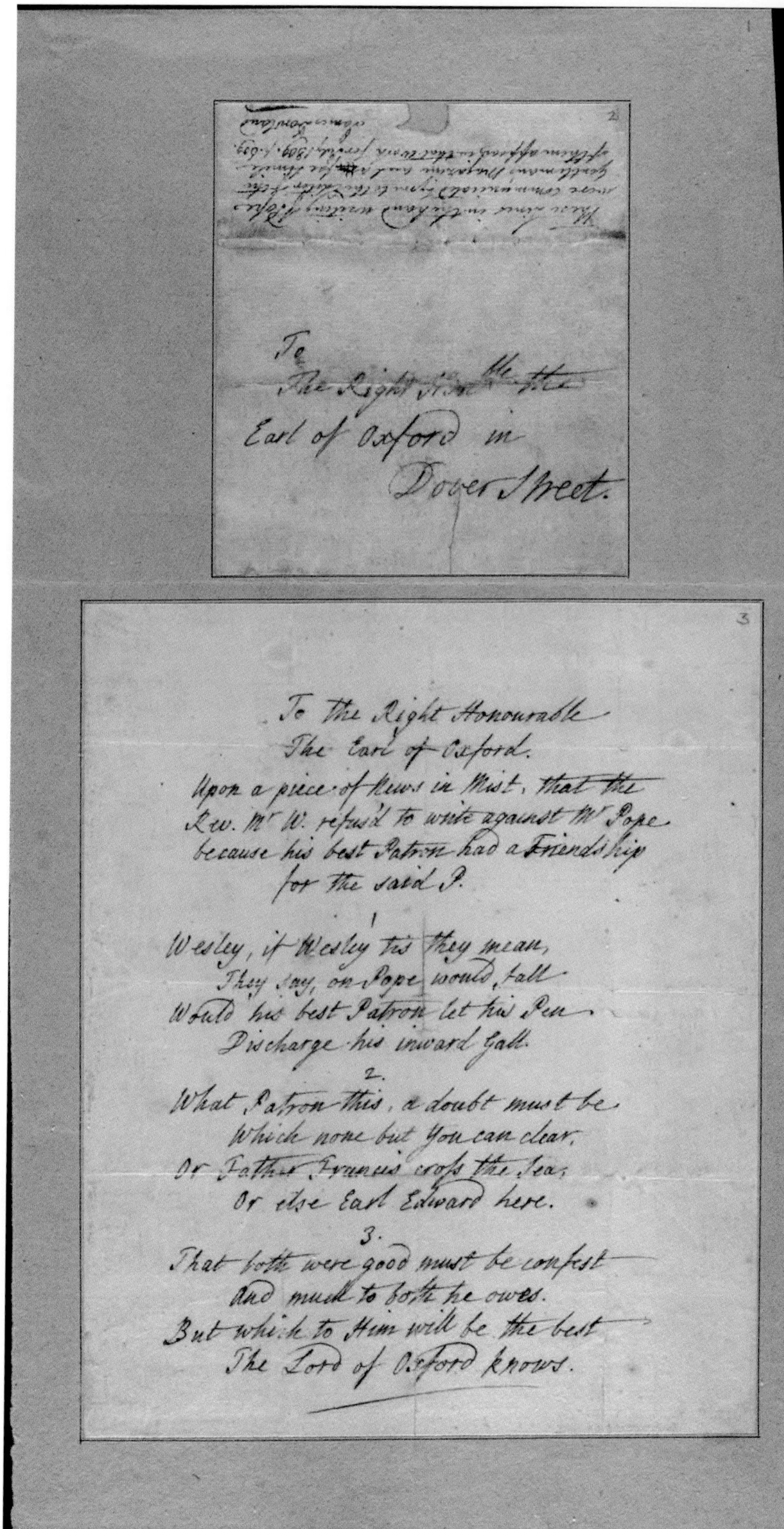

To
The Right Honble the
Earl of Oxford in
Dover Street.

To the Right Honourable
The Earl of Oxford.
Upon a piece of News in Mist, that the
Rev. Mr W. refus'd to write against Mr Pope
because his best Patron had a Friendship
for the said P.

1

Wesley, if Wesley 'tis they mean,
They say, on Pope would fall
Would his best Patron let his Pen
Discharge his inward Gall.

2.

What Patron this, a doubt must be
Which none but You can clear,
Or Father Francis cross the Sea,
Or else Earl Edward here.

3.

That both were good must be confest
And much to both he owes.
But which to Him will be the best
The Lord of Oxford knows.

Plate 44 Alexander Pope: Zweig MS 177, ff. 1–3

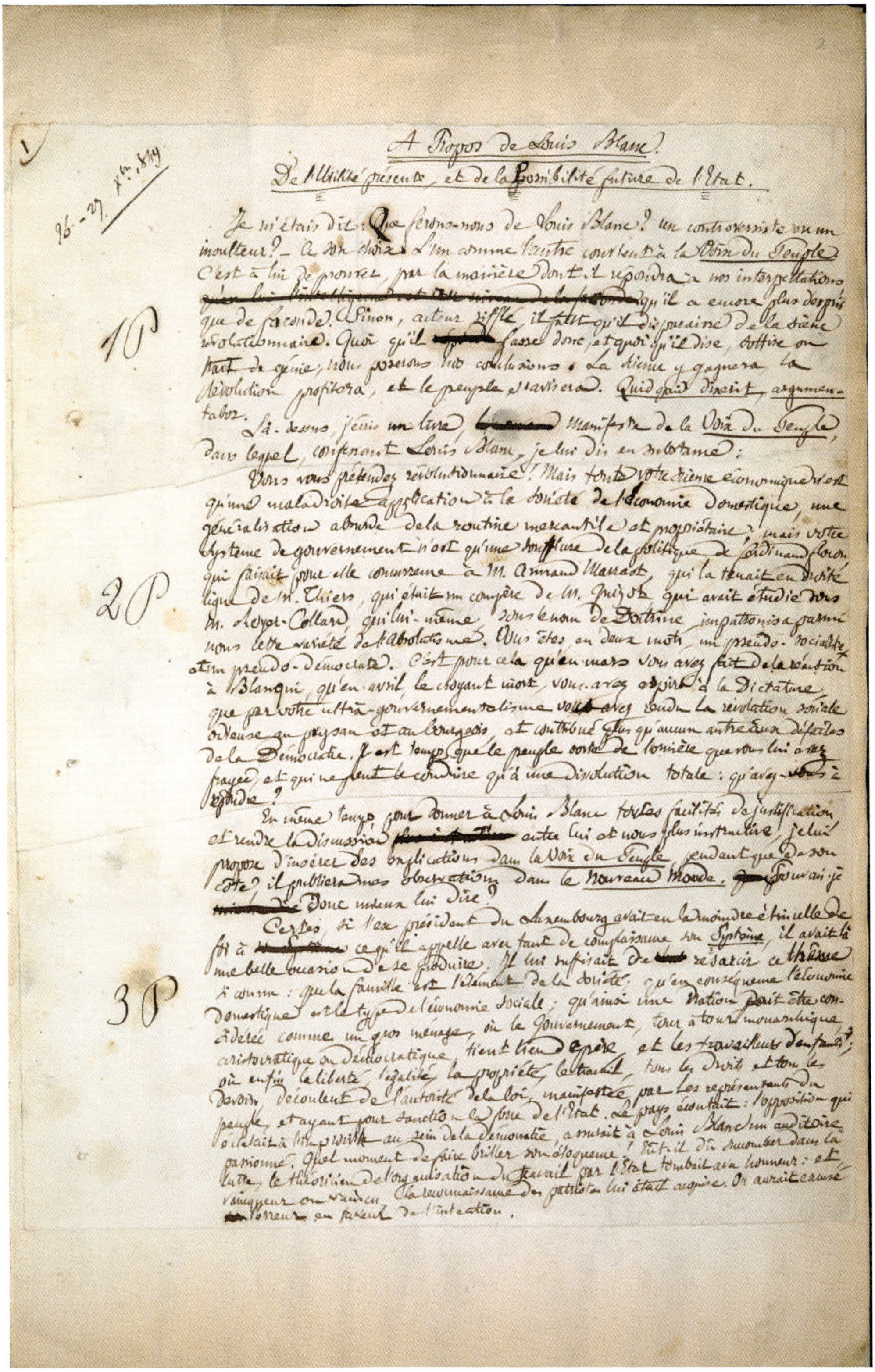

1 2

96–27 Xbre 1849

A Propos de Louis Blanc.

De l'Utilité présente, et de la Possibilité future de l'Etat.

Je m'étais dit : Que ferons-nous de Louis Blanc ? un controversiste ou un insulteur ? – Le choix de l'un comme l'autre convient à la Voix du Peuple. C'est à lui de prouver, par la manière dont il répondra à nos interpellations, qu'il a encore plus d'esprit que de faconde. Sinon, acteur sifflé, il faut qu'il disparaisse de la scène révolutionnaire. Quoi qu'il fasse donc, et quoi qu'il dise, sottise ou trait de génie, nous poserons nos conclusions. La science y gagnera, la Révolution profitera, et le peuple s'avisera. Quidquid dixerit, argumentabor.

1P

Là-dessus, j'écris une lettre, manifeste de la Voix du Peuple, dans lequel, apostrophant Louis Blanc, je lui dis en substance :

Vous vous prétendez révolutionnaire ! Mais toute votre science économique n'est qu'une maladroite application à la société de l'économie domestique, une généralisation absurde de la routine mercantile et propriétaire ; mais votre système de gouvernement n'est qu'une boursouflure de la politique de Ferdinand Flocon, qui faisait pour elle concurrence à M. Armand Marrast, qui la tenait en droite ligne de M. Thiers, qui était un compère de M. Guizot, qui avait étudié sous M. Royer-Collard, qui lui-même, sous le nom de Doctrine, impatronisa parmi nous cette variété de l'Absolutisme. Vous êtes en deux mots un pseudo-socialiste et un pseudo-démocrate. C'est pour cela qu'en mars vous avez fait de la réaction à Blanqui, qu'en avril, le croyant mort, vous avez aspiré à la Dictature, que par votre ultra-gouvernementalisme vous avez rendu la révolution sociale odieuse au paysan et au bourgeois, et contribué plus qu'aucun autre aux défaites de la Démocratie. Il est temps que le peuple sorte de l'ornière que vous lui avez frayée, et qui ne peut le conduire qu'à une dissolution totale : qu'avez-vous à répondre ?

2P

En même temps, pour donner à Louis Blanc toutes facilités de justification et rendre la discussion entre lui et nous plus instructive, je lui propose d'insérer ses explications dans la Voix du Peuple, pendant que de son côté il publiera nos observations dans le Nouveau Monde. Pouvais-je donc mieux lui dire ?

Certes, si l'ex-président du Luxembourg avait eu la moindre étincelle de foi à ce qu'il appelle avec tant de complaisance son Système, il avait là une belle occasion de se produire. Il lui suffisait de ressaisir ce thème si connu : que la famille est l'élément de la société ; qu'en conséquence l'économie domestique est le type de l'économie sociale ; qu'ainsi une nation doit être considérée comme un gros ménage, où le Gouvernement, tour à tour monarchique, aristocratique ou démocratique, tient lieu d'époux, et les travailleurs d'enfants ; où enfin la liberté, l'égalité, la propriété, le travail, tous les droits et tous les devoirs, découlent de l'autorité de la loi, manifestée par les représentants du peuple, et ayant pour sanction la force de l'Etat. Le pays écoutait : l'opposition qui s'élevait à l'improviste au sein de la démocratie, assurait à Louis Blanc un auditoire passionné. Quel moment de faire briller son éloquence ! Fût-il dû succomber dans la lutte, le théoricien de l'organisation du travail par l'Etat tombait avec honneur : et, vainqueur ou vaincu, la reconnaissance des patriotes lui était acquise. On aurait excusé l'erreur en faveur de l'intention.

3P

Plate 45 Pierre-Joseph Proudhon: Zweig MS 178, f. 2r

Plate 46 (a) Rainer Maria Rilke: Zweig MS 179, f. 1r

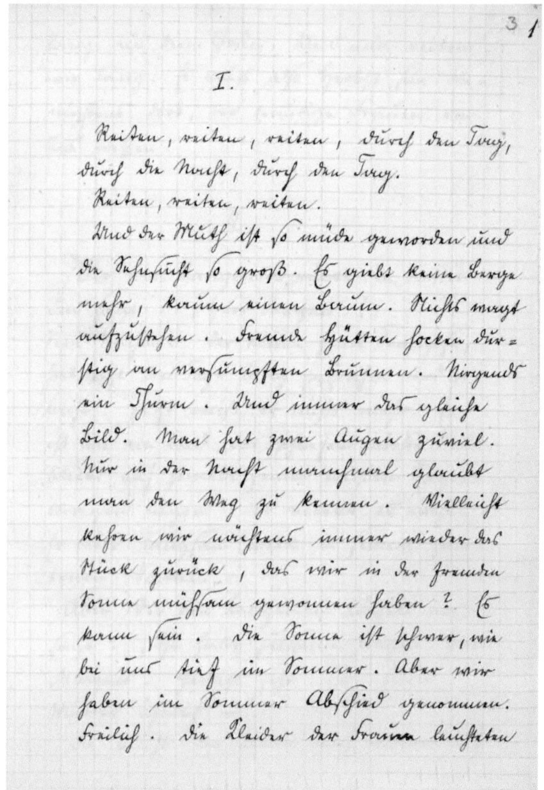

Plate 46 (b) Rainer Maria Rilke: Zweig MS 179, f. 3r

Plate 46 (c) Rainer Maria Rilke: Zweig MS 179, f. i r (note by Zweig)

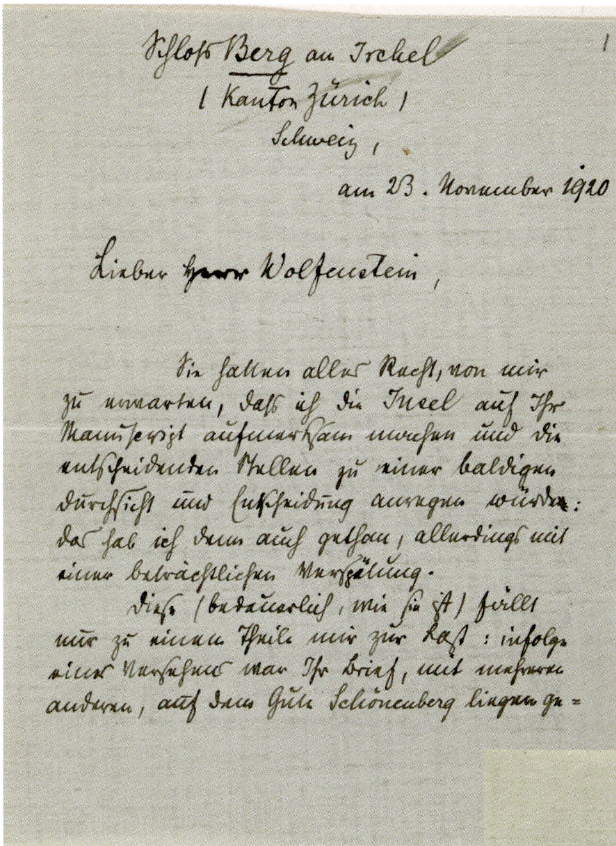

Schloß Berg am Irchel
(Kanton Zürich)
Schweiz,

am 23. November 1920

1

Lieber Herr Wolfenstein,

Sie hatten alles Recht, von mir zu erwarten, daß ich die Insel auf Ihr Manuscript aufmerksam machen und die entscheidenden Stellen zu einer baldigen Durchsicht und Entscheidung anregen würde: das hab ich denn auch gethan, allerdings mit einer beträchtlichen Verspätung.

Diese (bedauerlich, wie sie ist) fällt nur zu einem Theile mir zur Last: infolge einer Nachsehens war Ihr Brief, mit mehreren anderen, auf dem Gute Schönenberg liegen ge=

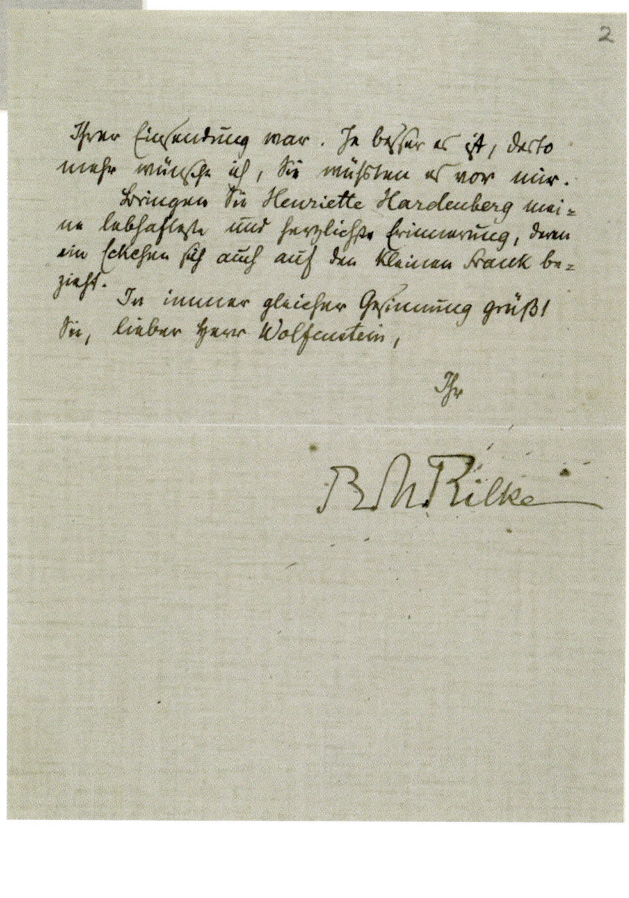

2

Ihrer Einsendung war. Je besser es ist, desto mehr wünsche ich, Sie wüßten es vor mir.

Bringen Sie Henriette Hardenberg meine lebhafteste und herzlichste Erinnerung, denn ein Lächeln sich auch auf den kleinen Brack bezieht.

In immer gleicher Gesinnung grüßt Sie, lieber Herr Wolfenstein,

Ihr

R. M. Rilke

Plate 47 (a) Rainer Maria Rilke: Zweig MS 180, f. 1r

Plate 47 (b) Rainer Maria Rilke: Zweig MS 180, f. 2r

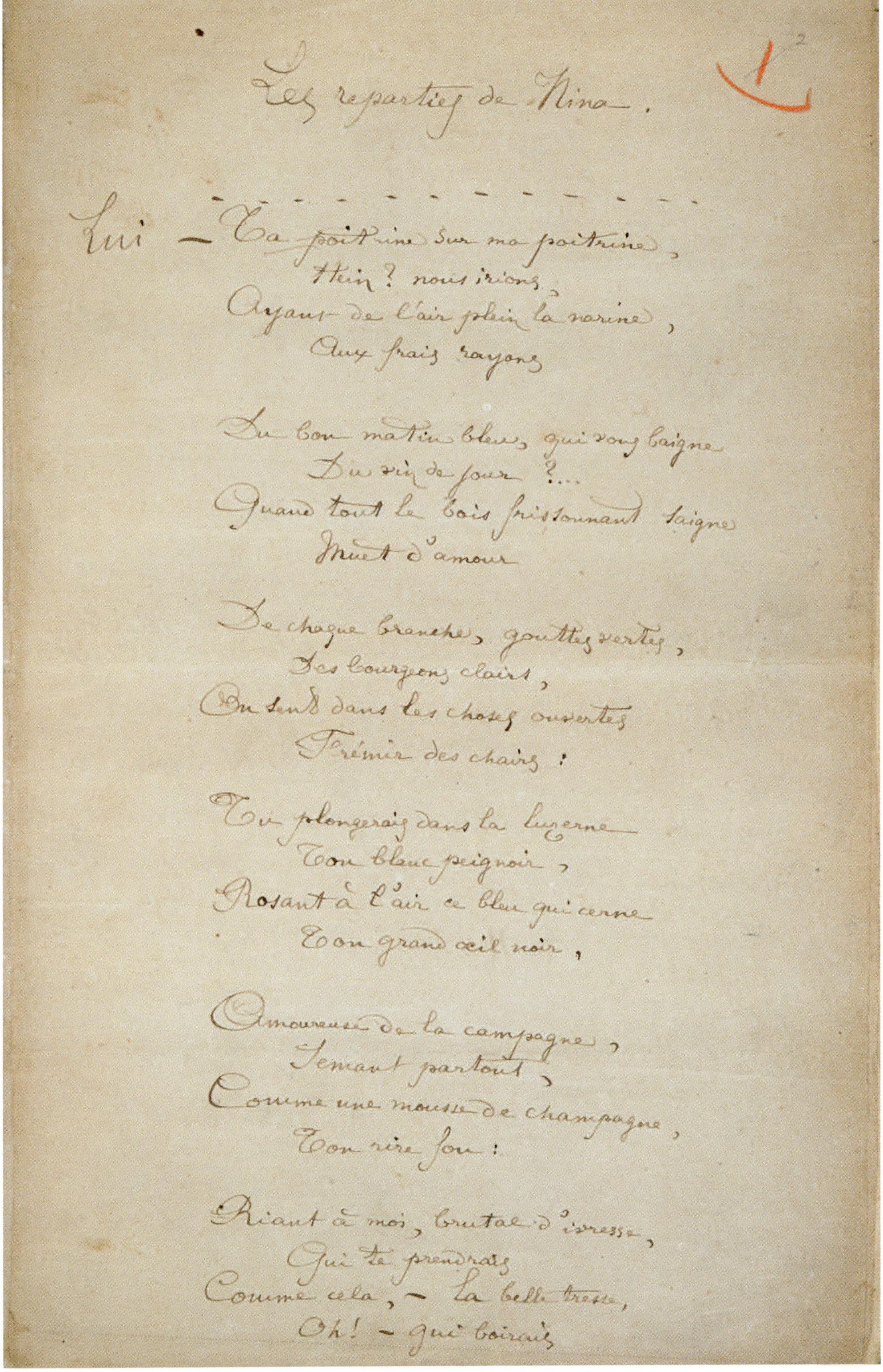

Les reparties de Nina.

Lui — Ta poitrine sur ma poitrine,
Hein? nous irions,
Ayant de l'air plein la narine,
Aux frais rayons

Du bon matin bleu, qui vous baigne
Du vin de jour ?...
Quand tout le bois frissonnant saigne
Muet d'amour

De chaque branche, gouttes vertes,
Des bourgeons clairs,
On sent dans les choses ouvertes
Frémir des chairs :

Tu plongerais dans la luzerne
Ton blanc peignoir,
Rosant à l'air ce bleu qui cerne
Ton grand œil noir,

Amoureuse de la campagne,
Semant partout,
Comme une mousse de champagne,
Ton rire fou :

Riant à moi, brutal d'ivresse,
Qui te prendrais
Comme cela, — la belle tresse,
Oh! — qui boirais

Plate 48 Arthur Rimbaud: Zweig MS 181, f. 2r

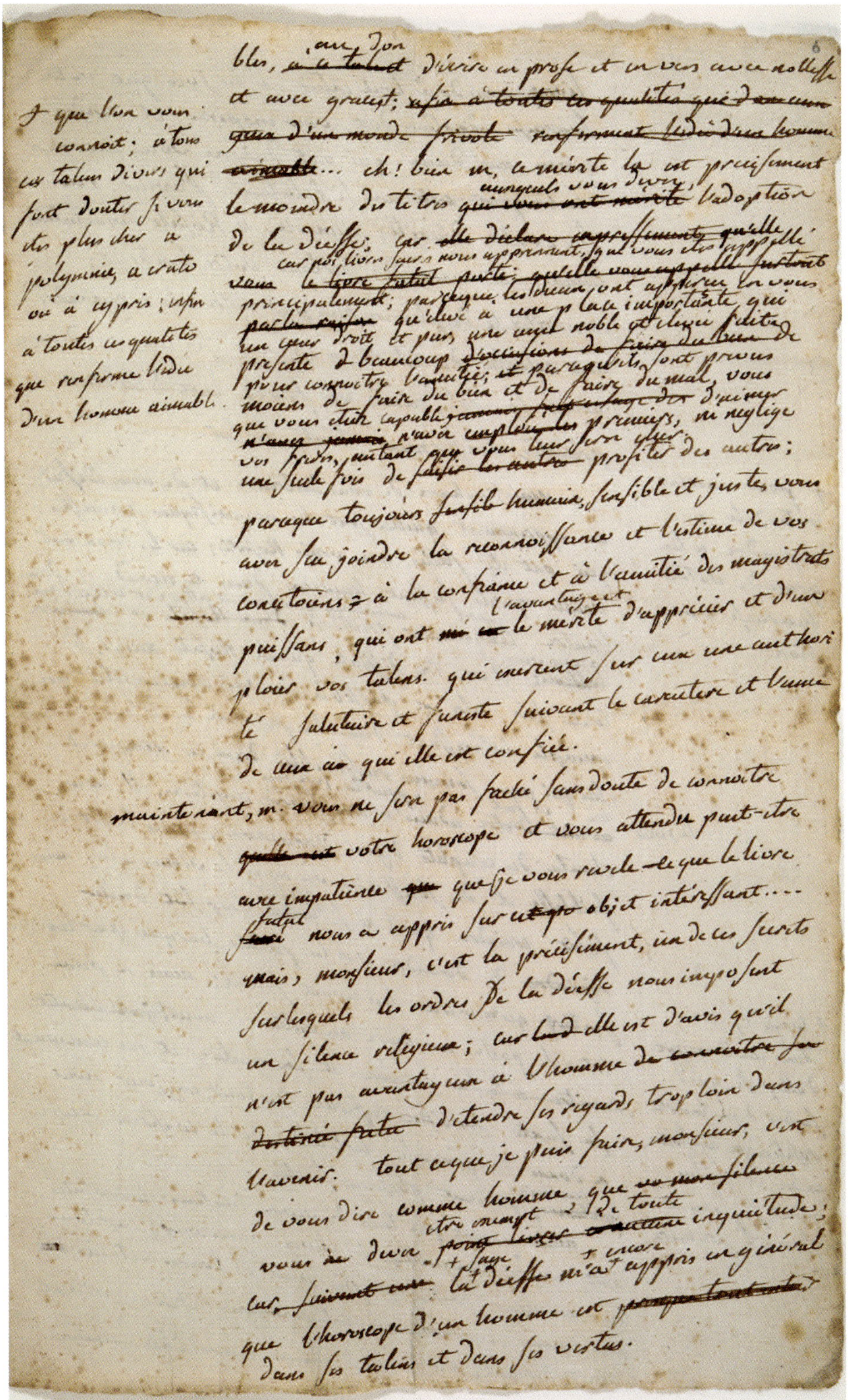

Plate 49 Maximilien de Robespierre: Zweig MS 182, f. 6r

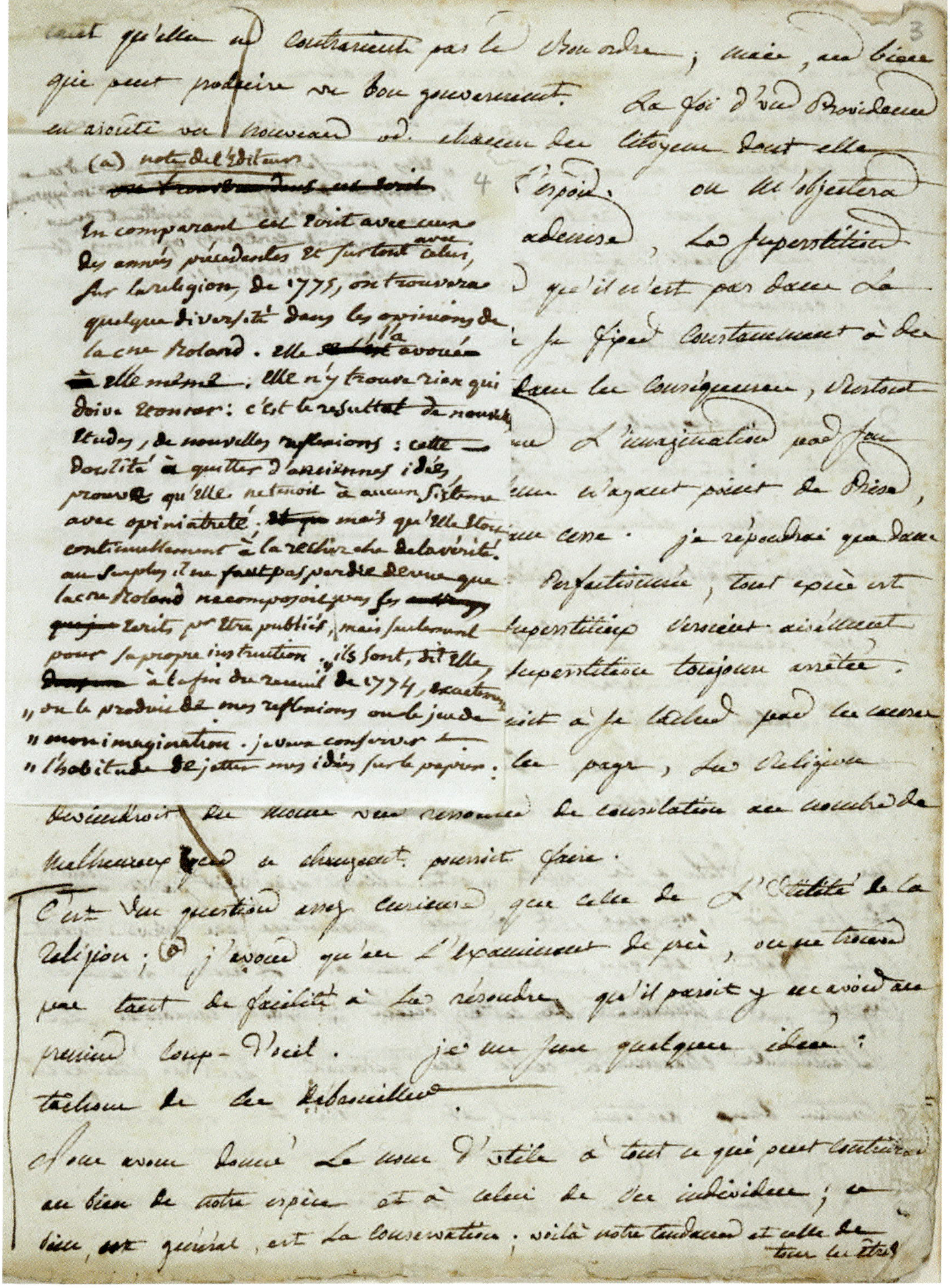

tant qu'elle ne contrarient pas le bon ordre ; mais, au bien qui peut produire un bon gouvernement. La foi d'une Providence en ajoute un nouveau où chacun des citoyens dont elle … l'espoir. … on m'objectera … adorer, la superstition … qu'il n'est pas dans la … se fixe constamment à des … dans les conséquences, surtout … l'imagination … n'ayant point de Dieu, … une … je répondrai que dans … perfectionnée, toute espèce est … superstitieuse … superstition toujours arrêtée … soit à se … les pays, les religieux deviendroit le moins une ressource de consolation au nombre de malheureux … à changement … faire.

(a) note de l'éditeur

~~…~~

En comparant cet écrit avec ceux des années précédentes et surtout avec celui sur la religion, de 1775, on trouvera quelque diversité dans les opinions de la cne Roland. elle ~~…~~ l'a avoué ~~à~~ elle même ; elle n'y trouve rien qui doive étonner : c'est le resultat de nouvelles études, de nouvelles reflexions : cette docilité à quitter d'anciennes idées prouve qu'elle ne tenoit à aucun sistême avec opiniatreté ; ~~et que~~ mais qu'elle étoit continuellement à la recherche de la vérité. au surplus il ne faut pas perdre de vue que la cne Roland ne composoit pas ses ~~…~~ écrits pr être publiés, mais seulement pour sa propre instruction. "ils sont, dit elle ~~…~~ à la fin du recueil de 1774, exactement
" ou le produit de mes reflexions ou le jeu de
" mon imagination. je veux conserver
" l'habitude de jetter mes idées sur le papier.

C'est une question assez curieuse que celle de l'utilité de la religion ; (a) j'avoue qu'en l'examinant de près, on ne trouve pas tant de facilité à la résoudre qu'il paroit y en avoir au premier coup-d'oeil. j'en ai jeté quelques idées : tâchons de les débrouiller.

Nous avons donné le nom d'utile à tout ce qui peut contribuer au bien de notre espèce et à celui de ses individus ; ce bien, en général, est la conservation ; voilà notre tendance et celle de tous les êtres

Plate 50 Jeanne-Marie Roland de la Platière: Zweig MS 183, f. 4 inserted on f.3

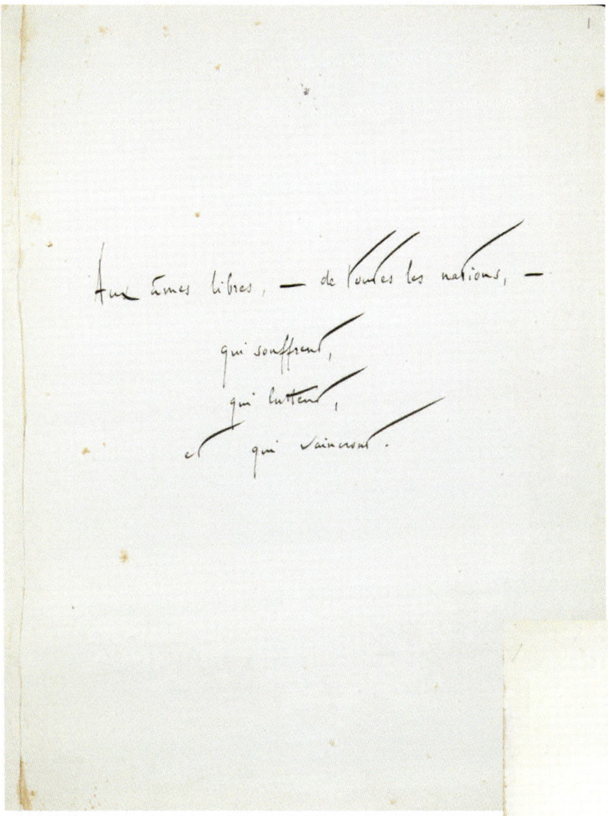

Aux âmes libres, — de toutes les nations, —
qui souffrent,
qui luttent,
et qui vaincront.

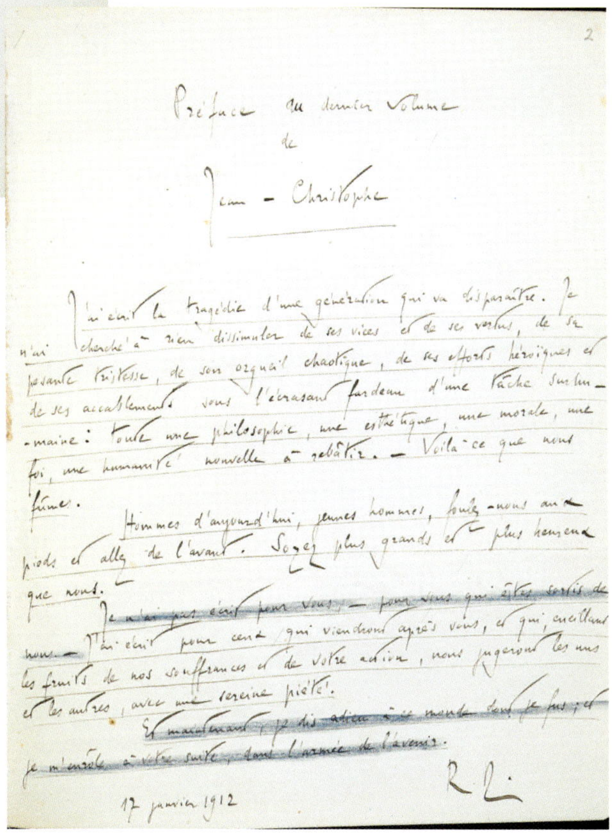

2

Préface au dernier volume
de
Jean-Christophe

J'ai écrit la tragédie d'une génération qui va disparaître. Je n'ai cherché à rien dissimuler de ses vices et de ses vertus, de sa pesante tristesse, de son orgueil chaotique, de ses efforts héroïques et de ses accablements sous l'écrasant fardeau d'une tâche surhumaine: toute une philosophie, une esthétique, une morale, une foi, une humanité nouvelle à rebâtir. — Voilà ce que nous fûmes.

Hommes d'aujourd'hui, jeunes hommes, foulez-nous aux pieds et allez de l'avant. Soyez plus grands et plus heureux que nous.

~~Je n'ai pas écrit pour vous, — pour vous qui êtes sortis de nous.~~ — J'ai écrit pour ceux qui viendront après vous, et qui, cueillant les fruits de nos souffrances et de votre action, nous jugeront les uns et les autres, avec une sereine piété.

~~Et maintenant, je dis adieu à ce monde dont je fus; et je m'enrôle à votre suite, dans l'armée de l'avenir.~~

R. R.

17 janvier 1912

Plate 51 (a) Romain Rolland: Zweig MS 184, f. 1r

Plate 51 (b) Romain Rolland: Zweig MS 184, f. 2r

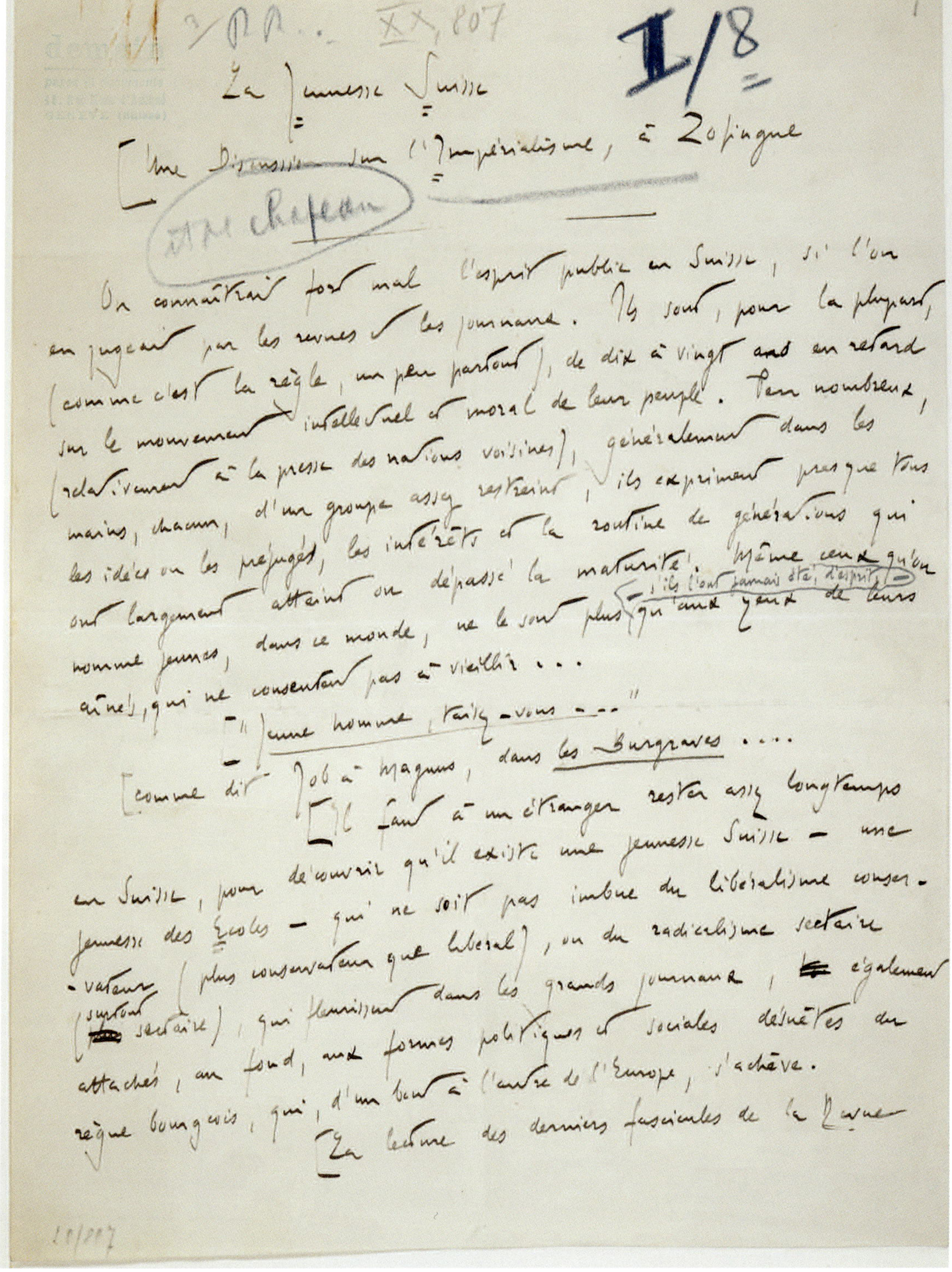

3/RR... XX, 807 — I/8 — 1

La Jeunesse Suisse

[Une Discussion sur l'Impérialisme, à Zofingue

Sans chapeau

On connaîtrait fort mal l'esprit public en Suisse, si l'on en jugeait par les revues et les journaux. Ils sont, pour la plupart, (comme c'est la règle, un peu partout), de dix à vingt ans en retard sur le mouvement intellectuel et moral de leur peuple. Peu nombreux, (relativement à la presse des nations voisines), généralement dans les mains, chacun, d'un groupe assez restreint, ils expriment presque tous les idées ou les préjugés, les intérêts et la routine de générations qui ont largement atteint ou dépassé la maturité. Même ceux qu'on nomme jeunes, dans ce monde, ne le sont plus — s'ils l'ont jamais été, d'esprit — qu'aux yeux de leurs aînés, qui ne consentent pas à vieillir...

— « Jeune homme, taisez-vous... »

[comme dit Job à Magnus, dans les Burgraves....

[Il faut à un étranger rester assez longtemps en Suisse, pour découvrir qu'il existe une jeunesse Suisse — une jeunesse des Écoles — qui ne soit pas imbue du libéralisme conservateur (plus conservateur que libéral), ou du radicalisme sectaire (surtout sectaire), qui fleurissent dans les grands journaux, également attachés, au fond, aux formes politiques et sociales désuètes du règne bourgeois, qui, d'un bout à l'autre de l'Europe, s'achève.

[La lecture des derniers fascicules de la Revue

XX/807

Plate 52 Romain Rolland: Zweig MS 186, f. 1r

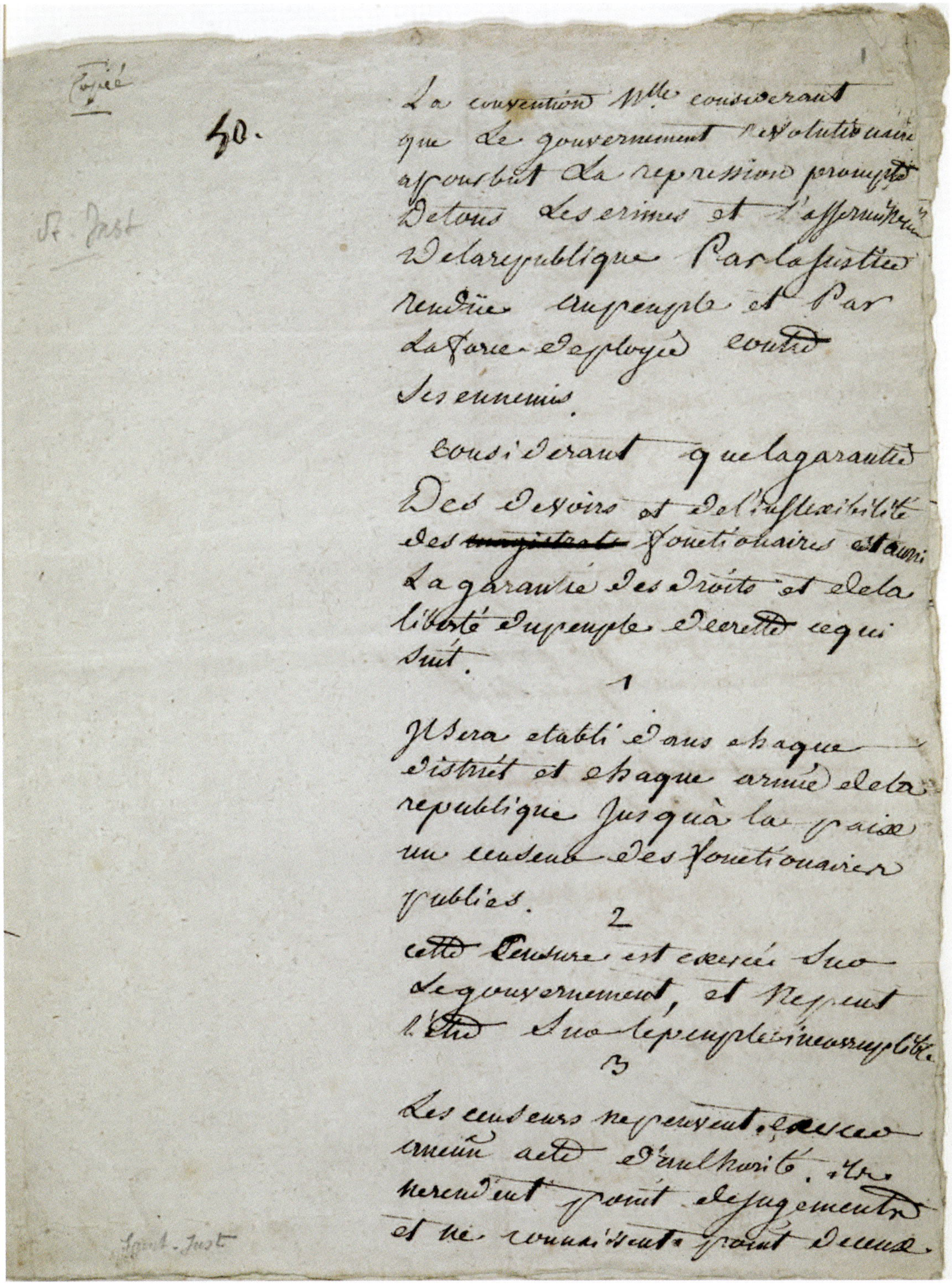
Copié

30.

St. Just

La convention Nle considerant
que le gouvernement revolutionnaire
a pour but la repression prompte
de tous les crimes et l'affermissement
de la republique par la justice
rendue au peuple et par
la force deployée contre
ses ennemis.

considerant que la garantie
des devoirs et de l'inflexibilité
des ~~magistrats~~ fonctionnaires est aussi
la garantie des droits et de la
liberté du peuple decrette ce qui
suit.

1

Il sera etabli dans chaque
district et chaque armée de la
republique jusqu'à la paix
un censeur des fonctionnaires
publics.

2

cette censure est exercée sur
le gouvernement, et ne peut
l'etre sur le peuple incorruptible.

3

Les censeurs ne peuvent exercer
aucun acte d'autorité. ils
ne rendent point de jugements
et ne connaissent point de ceux

Saint-Just

Plate 53 Louis-Antoine de Saint-Just: Zweig MS 187, f. 1r

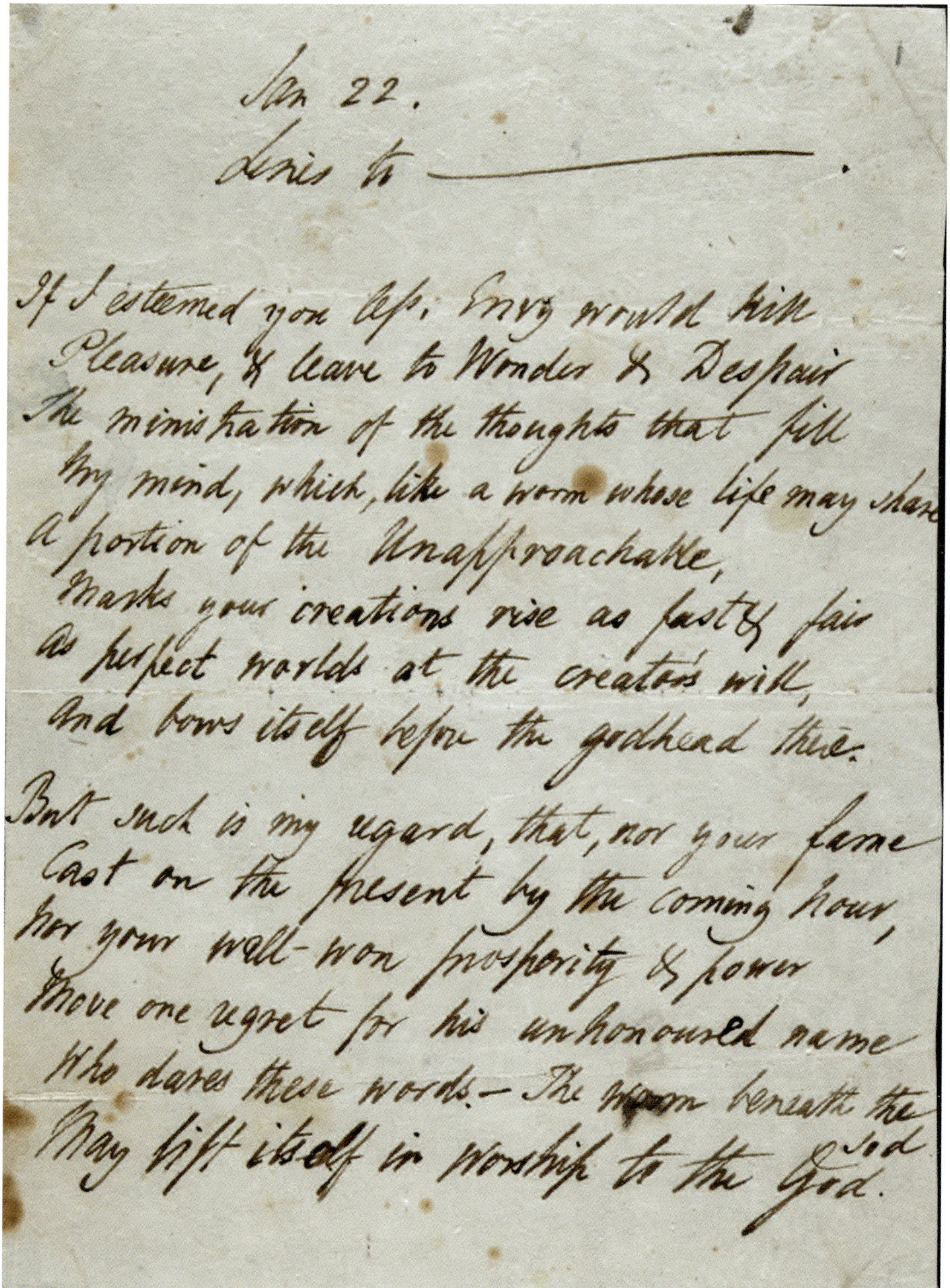

Jan 22.

Lines to ———

If I esteemed you less, Envy would kill
Pleasure, & leave to Wonder & Despair
The ministration of the thoughts that fill
My mind, which, like a worm whose life may share
A portion of the Unapproachable,
Marks your creations rise as fast & fair
As perfect worlds at the creator's will,
And bows itself before the godhead there.

But such is my regard, that, nor your fame
Cast on the present by the coming hour,
Nor your well-won prosperity & power
Move one regret for his unhonoured name
Who dares these words.— The worm beneath the sod
May lift itself in worship to the God.

Plate 54 Percy Bysshe Shelley: Zweig MS 188, f. 1r

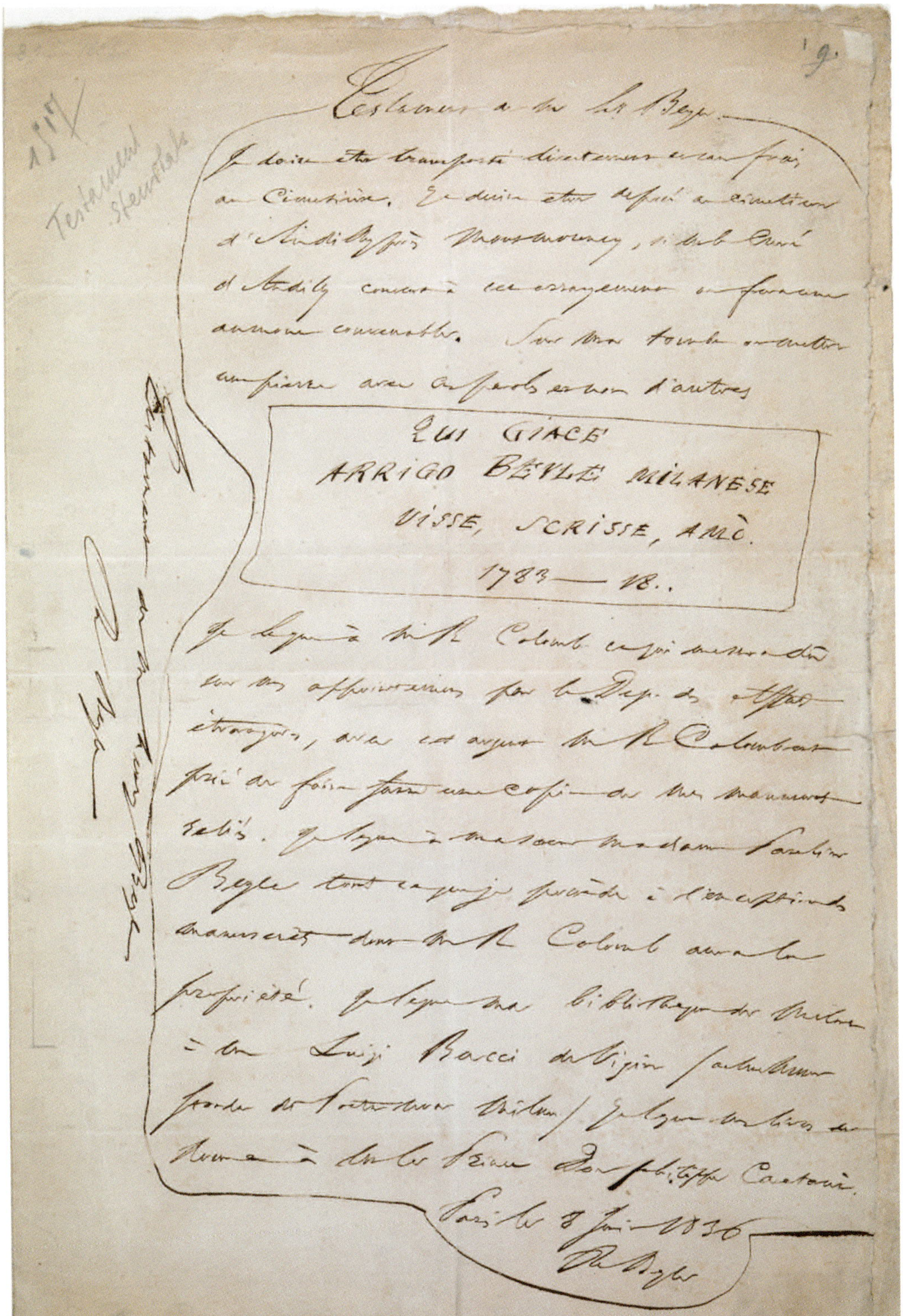
QUI GIACE
ARRIGO BEYLE MILANESE
VISSE, SCRISSE, AMÒ.
1783 — 18..

Plate 55 'Stendhal': Zweig MS 189, f. 1r

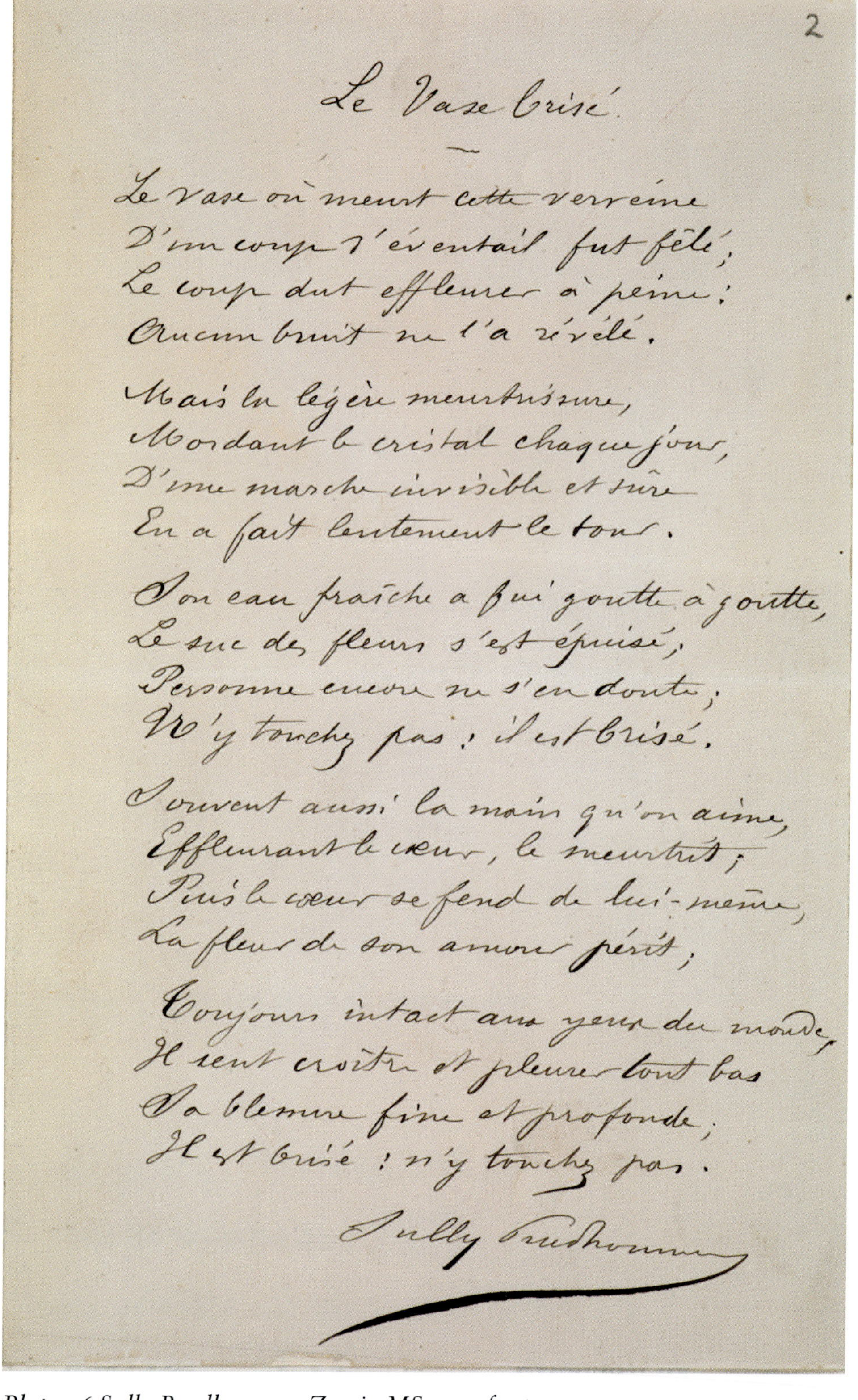

2

Le Vase brisé.

Le vase où meurt cette verveine
D'un coup d'éventail fut fêlé;
Le coup dut effleurer à peine:
Aucun bruit ne l'a révélé.

Mais la légère meurtrissure,
Mordant le cristal chaque jour,
D'une marche invisible et sûre
En a fait lentement le tour.

Son eau fraîche a fui goutte à goutte,
Le suc des fleurs s'est épuisé;
Personne encore ne s'en doute;
N'y touchez pas: il est brisé.

Souvent aussi la main qu'on aime,
Effleurant le cœur, le meurtrit;
Puis le cœur se fend de lui-même,
La fleur de son amour périt;

Toujours intact aux yeux du monde,
Il sent croître et pleurer tout bas
Sa blessure fine et profonde;
Il est brisé: n'y touchez pas.

Sully Prudhomme

Plate 56 Sully Prudhomme: Zweig MS 190, f. 2r

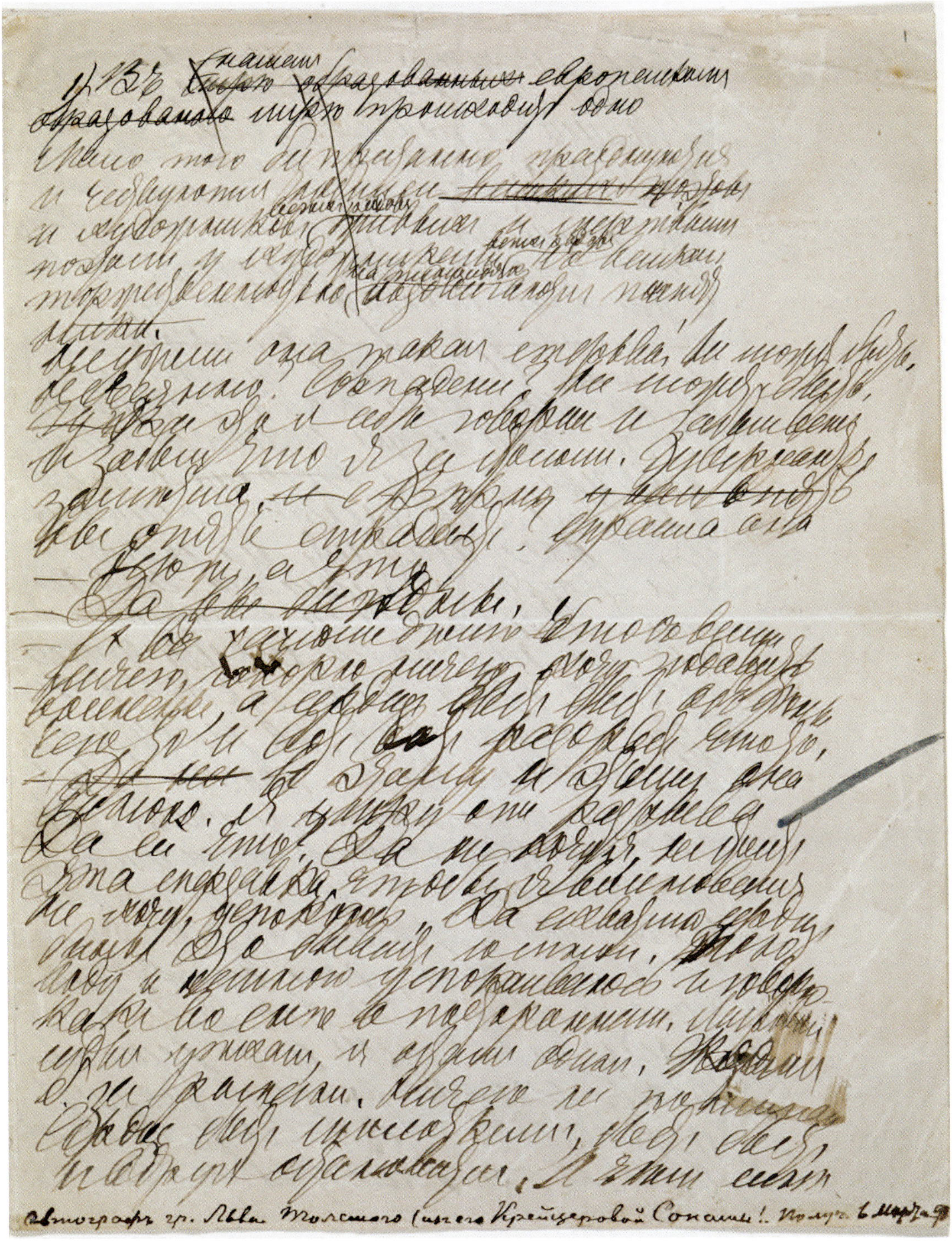

Plate 57 Leo Tolstoy: Zweig MS 191, f. 1r

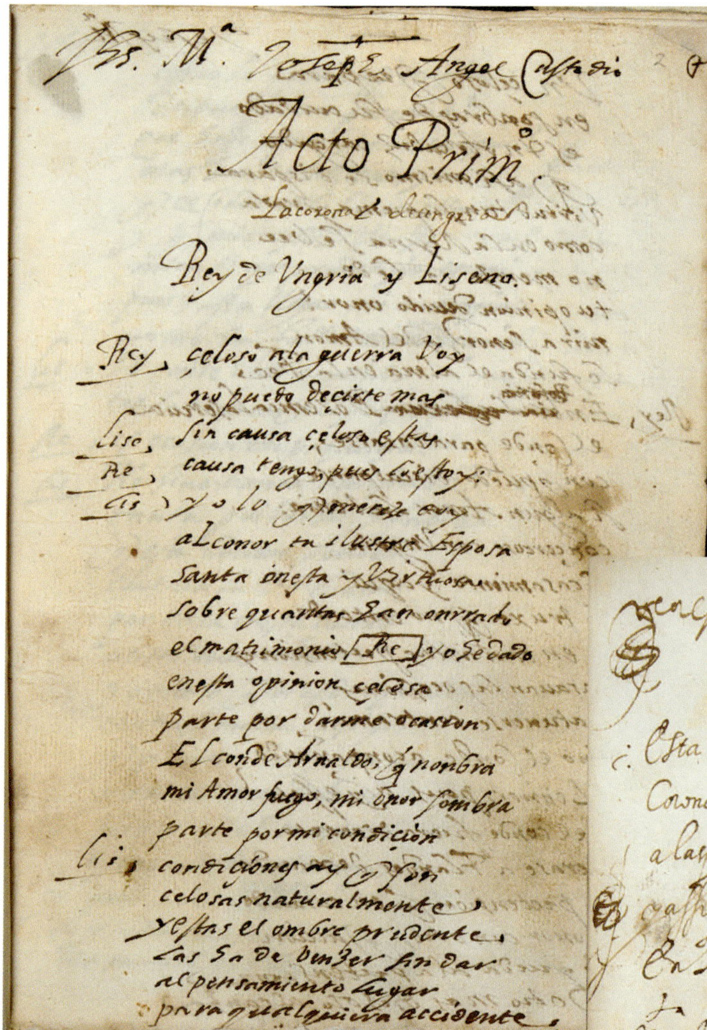

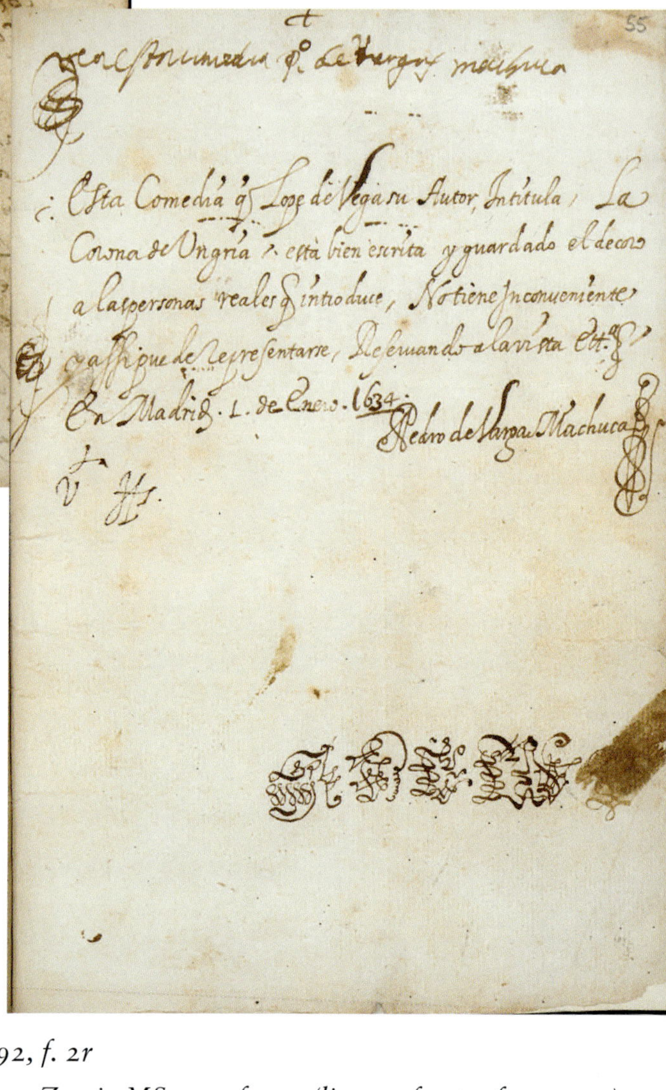

Plate 58 (a) Lope de Vega: Zweig MS 192, f. 2r

Plate 58 (b) Lope de Vega: Zweig MS 192, f. 55r (licence for performance)

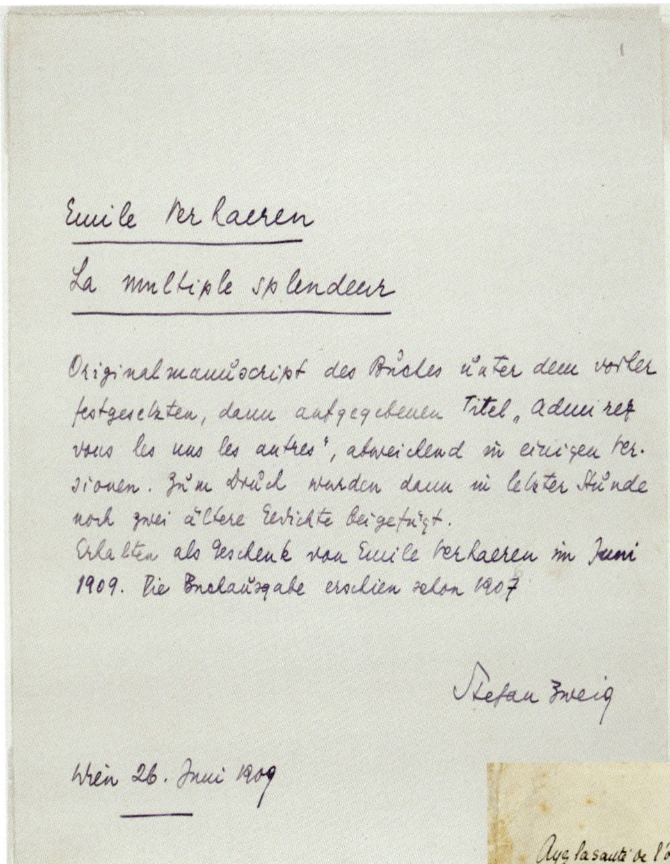

Emile Verhaeren

La multiple splendeur

Originalmanuscript des Buches unter dem vorher festgesetzten, dann aufgegebenen Titel „Admirez vous les uns les autres", abweichend in einigen Versionen. Zum Druck wurden dann in letzter Stunde noch zwei ältere Gedichte beigefügt.
Erhalten als Geschenk von Emile Verhaeren im Juni 1909. Die Buchausgabe erschien schon 1907

Stefan Zweig

Wien 26. Juni 1909

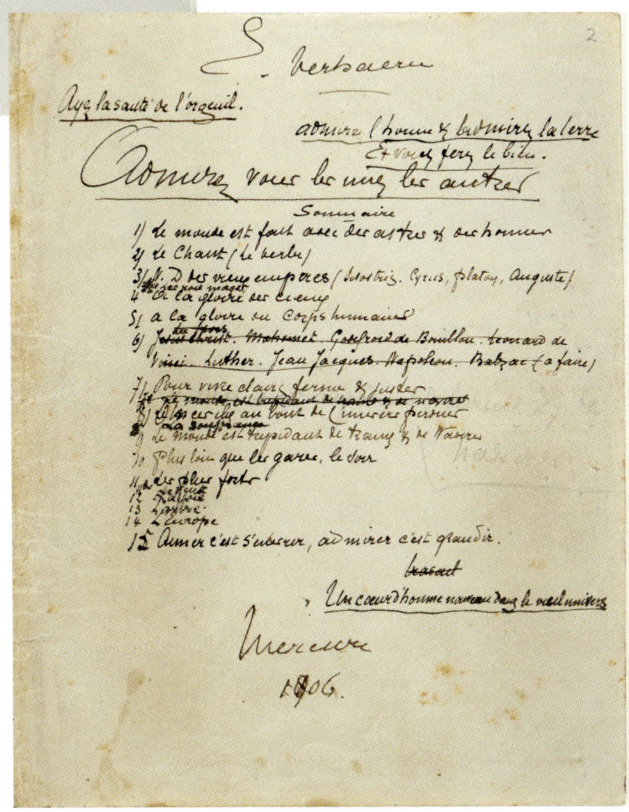

E. Verhaeren

Ayez la santé de l'orgueil.

Admirez l'homme et admirez la terre
Et vous serez le ...

Admirez vous les uns les autres

Sommaire

1/ Le monde est fait avec des astres et des hommes
2/ Le Chant (le verbe)
3/ ... des vieux empires (...)
4/ ... la gloire des cieux
5/ à la gloire du Corps humain
6/ ~~... Mahomet~~ Godefroid de Bouillon. Léonard de Vinci. Luther. Jean Jacques. ~~Napoléon.~~ Balzac (à faire)
7/ Pour vivre clair, ferme et juste
8/ ... au bout de l'univers ...
9/ Le monde est trépidant de trains et de navires
10/ Plus loin que les gares, le soir
11/ Les plus forts
12/ ...
13/ ...
14/ L'Europe
15/ Aimer c'est s'aimer, admirer c'est grandir.

Un cœur d'homme nouveau dans le vieil univers

Mercure

1906.

Plate 59 (a) Émile Verhaeren: Zweig MS 193, f. 1r (note by Zweig)

Plate 59 (b) Émile Verhaeren: Zweig MS 193, f. 2r

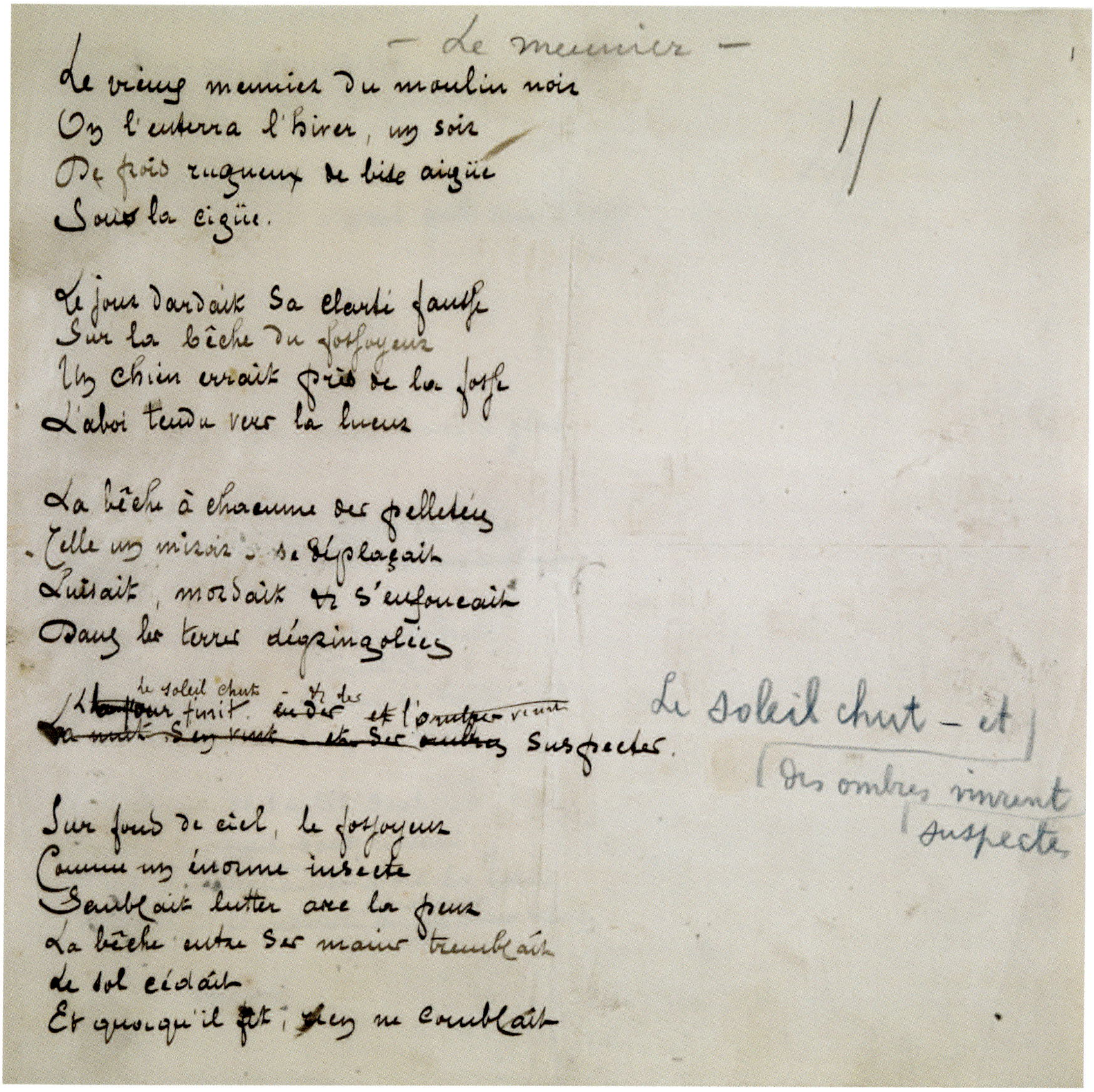

— Le meunier —

Le vieux meunier du moulin noir
On l'enterra l'hiver, un soir
De froids rugueux de bise aiguë
Sous la ciguë.

Le jour dardait sa clarté fausse
Sur la bêche du fossoyeur
Un chien errait près de la fosse
L'aboi tendu vers la lueur

La bêche à chacune des pelletées
Telle un miroir se déplaçait
Luisait, mordait et s'enfonçait
Dans les terres dégringolées

le soleil chut — et des
~~L'autour~~ finit ~~en des~~ et l'~~ombre~~ vinrent
~~La nuit s'en vint — et ses ombres~~ suspectes.

Le soleil chut — et
des ombres vinrent
suspectes

Sur fond de ciel, le fossoyeur
Comme un énorme insecte
Semblait lutter avec la peur
La bêche entre ses mains tremblait
Le sol cédait
Et quoiqu'il fît, rien ne comblait

Plate 60 Émile Verhaeren: Zweig MS 194, f. 1r

Table

~~410~~
412

Plate 61 (a) Paul Verlaine: Zweig MS 195, f. 2r

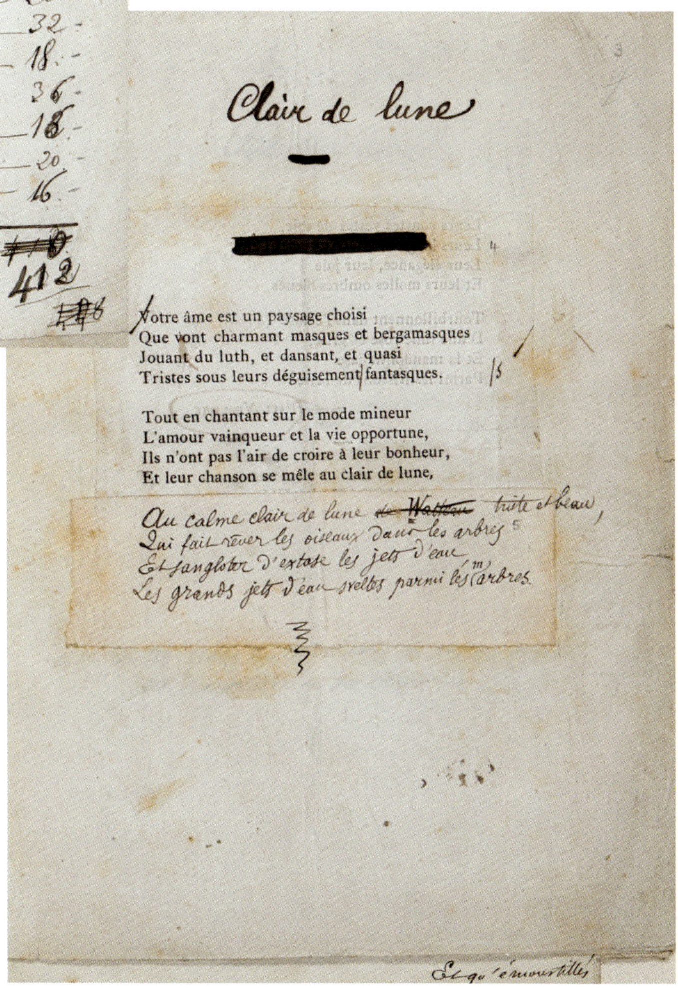

Clair de lune

[redacted]

Votre âme est un paysage choisi
Que vont charmant masques et bergamasques
Jouant du luth, et dansant, et quasi
Tristes sous leurs déguisements fantasques.

Tout en chantant sur le mode mineur
L'amour vainqueur et la vie opportune,
Ils n'ont pas l'air de croire à leur bonheur,
Et leur chanson se mêle au clair de lune,

Au calme clair de lune ~~de Watteau~~ triste et beau,
Qui fait rêver les oiseaux dans les arbres
Et sangloter d'extase les jets d'eau
Les grands jets d'eau sveltes parmi les marbres.

Et qu'émoustillés

Plate 61 (b) Paul Verlaine: Zweig MS 195, ff. 3–5

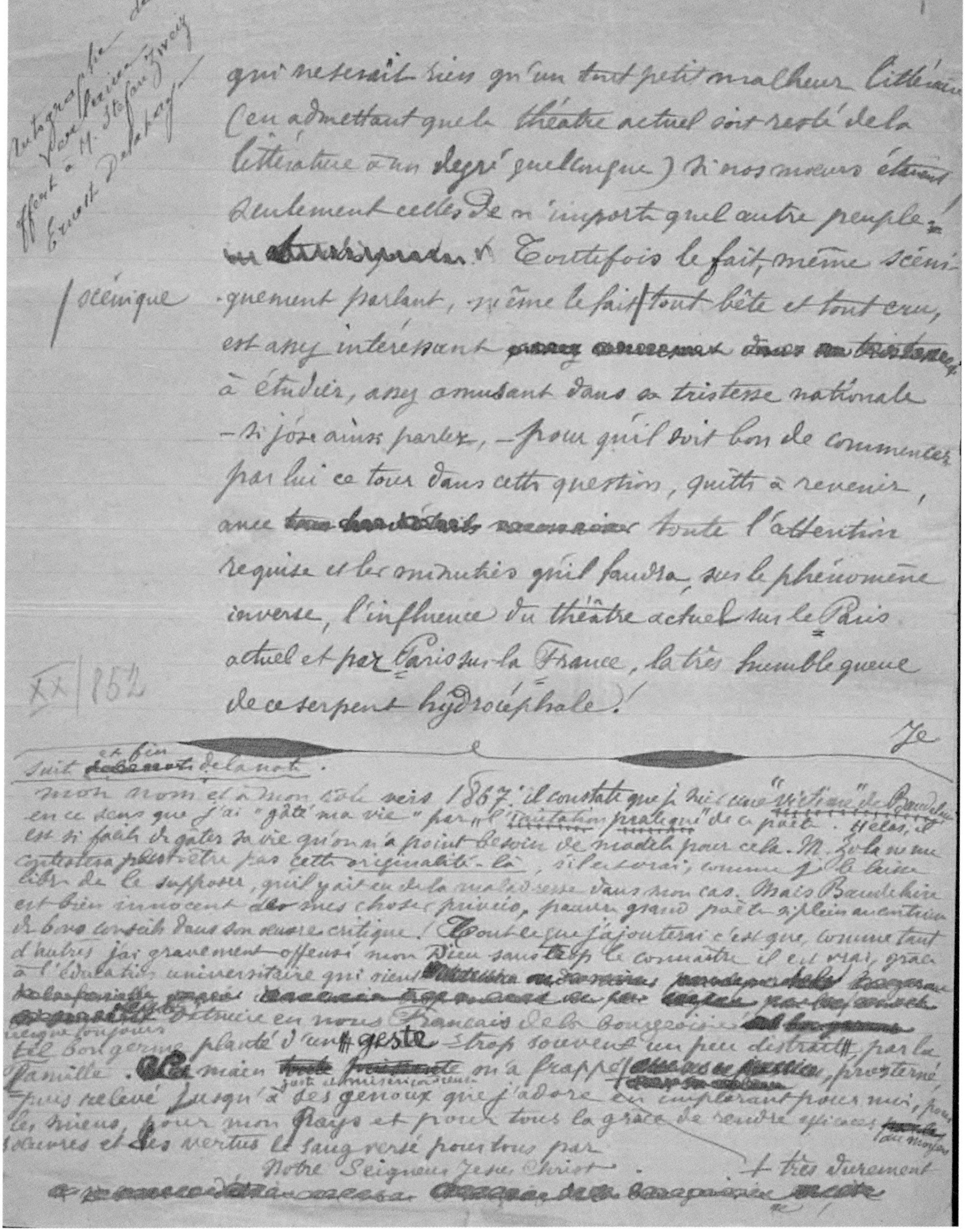

Autographe de Paul Verlaine offert à M. Stefan Zweig Ernest Delahaye

qui ne serait rien qu'un tout petit malheur littéraire (en admettant que le théâtre actuel soit relevé de la littérature à un degré quelconque) si nos mœurs étaient seulement celles de n'importe quel autre peuple! [illegible] Toutefois le fait, même scénique — scéniquement parlant, même le fait tout bête et tout cru, est assez intéressant [illegible] à étudier, assez amusant dans sa tristesse nationale — si j'ose ainsi parler, — pour qu'il soit bon de commencer par lui ce tour dans cette question, quitte à revenir, avec [illegible] toute l'attention requise et les minuties qu'il faudra, sur le phénomène inverse, l'influence du théâtre actuel sur le Paris actuel et par Paris sur la France, la très humble queue de ce serpent hydrocéphale!

XX | 852

Je

Suit et fin de la note.

mon nom et à mon tôle vers 1867, il constate que je suis une "victime" de Baudelaire en ce sens que j'ai "gâté ma vie" par "l'imitation pratique" de ce poète. Hélas, il est si facile de gâter sa vie qu'on n'a point besoin de modèle pour cela. M. Zola ne me contestera peut-être pas cette originalité-là, si je l'en crois, comme je le laisse libre de le supposer, qu'il y ait eu de la maladresse dans mon cas. Mais Baudelaire est bien innocent de mes choses privées, pauvre grand poète si plein au contraire de bons conseils dans son œuvre critique! Tout ce que j'ajouterai c'est que, comme tant d'autres j'ai gravement offensé mon Dieu sans trop le connaître il est vrai, grâce à l'éducation universitaire qui vient [illegible] détruire en nous Français de la bourgeoisie [illegible] règne toujours tel bon germe planté d'un geste trop souvent un peu distrait par la famille. La main [illegible] juste et miséricordieuse on a frappé [illegible], prosterné puis relevé jusqu'à des genoux que j'adore en implorant pour moi, pour les miens, pour mon pays et pour tous la grâce de rendre efficaces au moyen [illegible] œuvres et des vertus le sang versé pour tous par Notre Seigneur Jésus-Christ. + très durement [illegible]

Plate 62 Paul Verlaine: Zweig MS 196, f. 1r

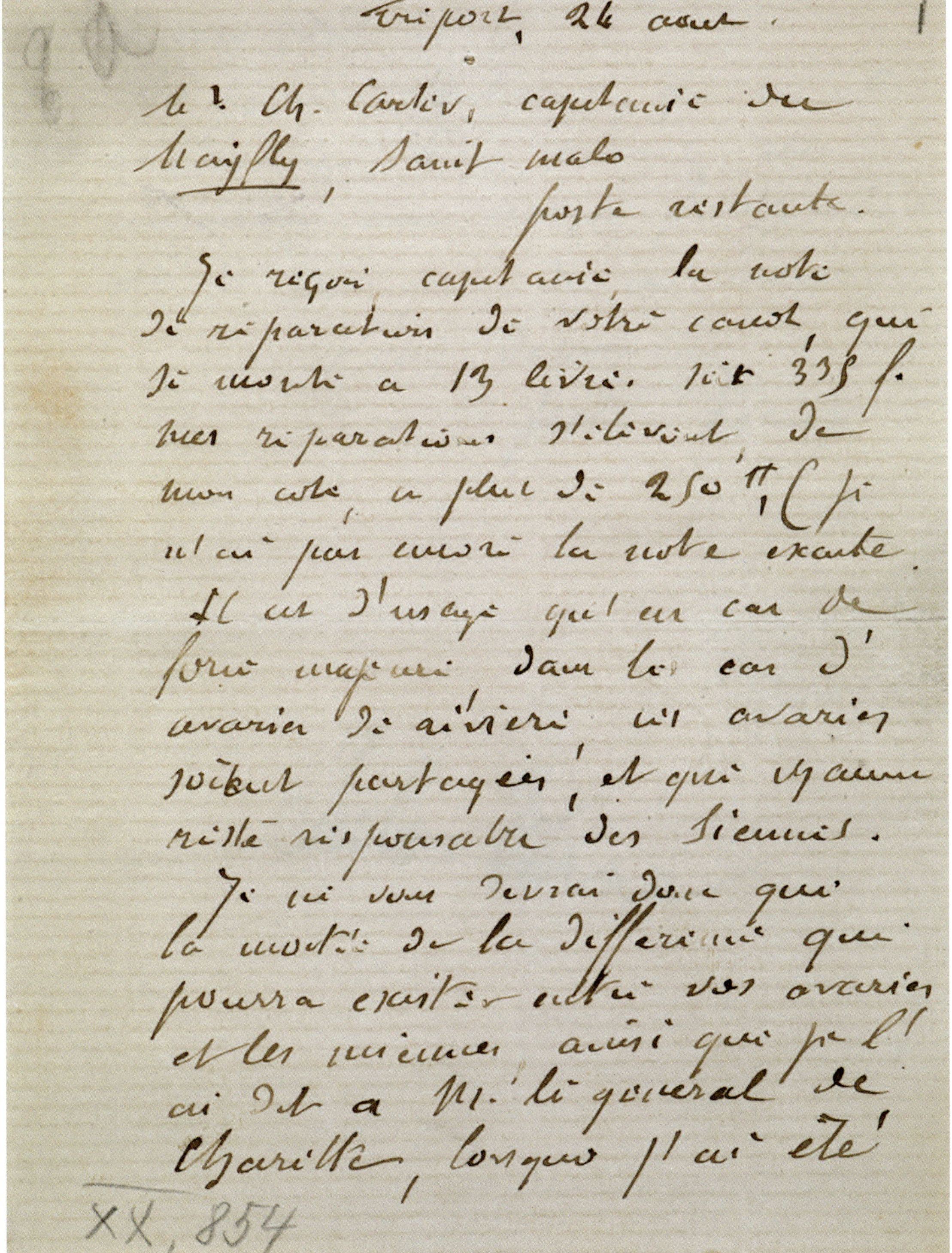

1

Tréport, 24 août.

Mr Ch. Cartier, capitaine du
Majesty, Saint Malo
poste restante.

Je reçois, capitaine, la note
de réparation de votre canot, qui
se monte à 13 livres, soit 335 f.
Mes réparations s'élèvent, de
mon côté, à plus de 250 ff, et je
n'ai pas encore la note exacte.
Il est d'usage que en cas de
force majeure dans les cas d'
avaries de rivière, les avaries
soient partagées, et que chacun
reste responsable des siennes.
Je ne vous devrai donc que
la moitié de la différence qui
pourra exister entre vos avaries
et les miennes, ainsi que je l'
ai dit à M. le général de
Charette, lorsque j'ai été

Plate 63 Jules Verne: Zweig MS 197, f. 1r

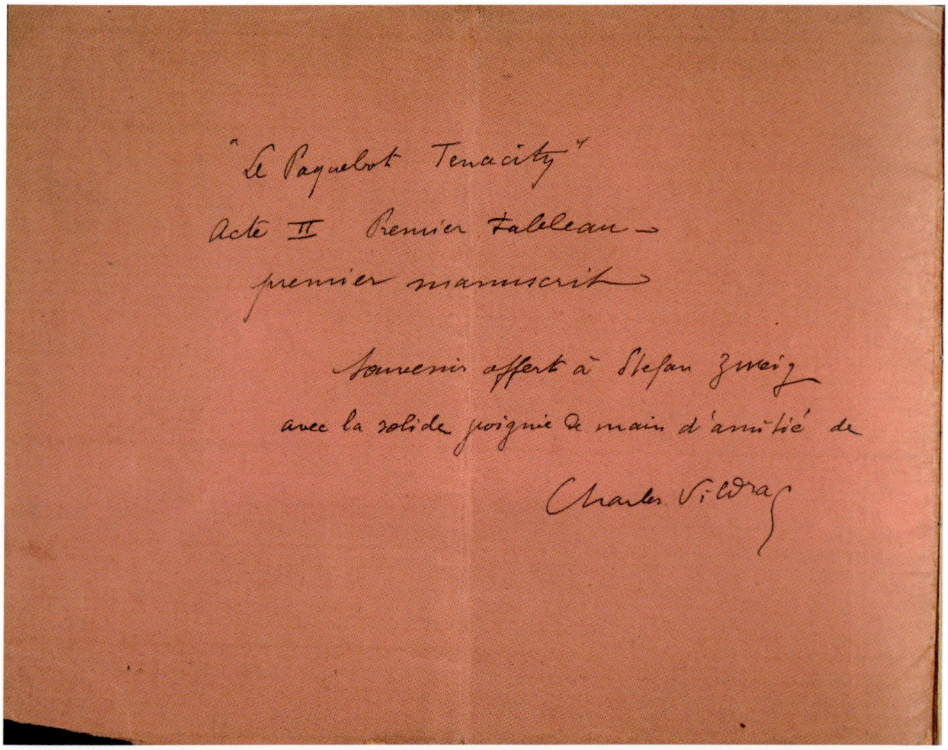

"Le Paquebot Tenacity"

Acte II Premier tableau —

premier manuscrit

Souvenir offert à Stefan Zweig

avec la solide poignée de main d'amitié de

Charles Vildrac

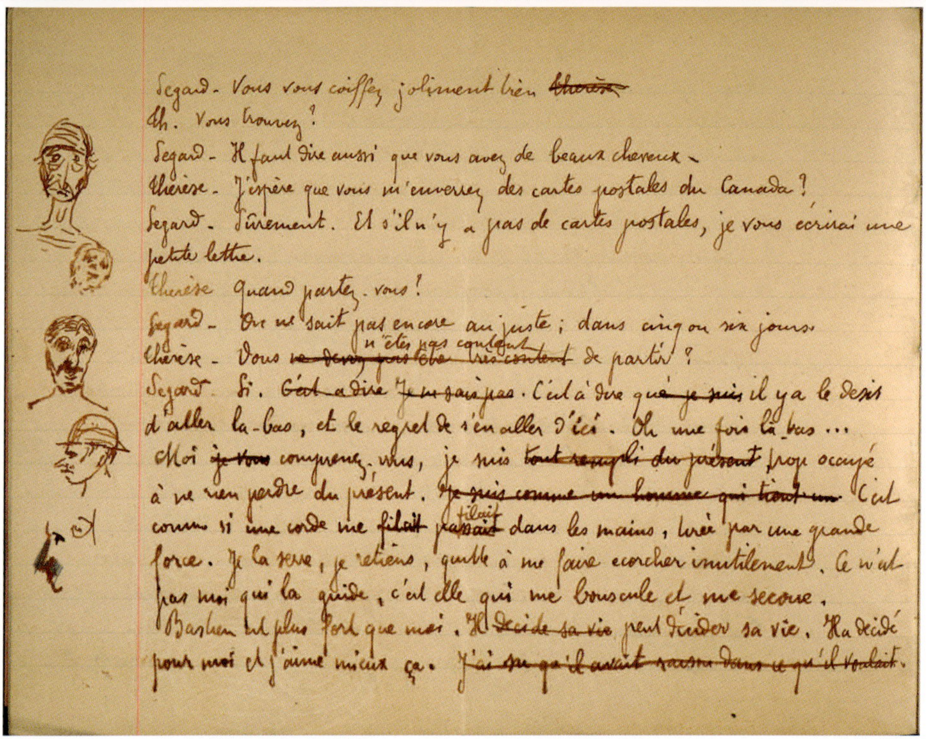

Ségard – Vous vous coiffez joliment bien ~~[illegible]~~

Th. Vous trouvez?

Ségard – Il faut dire aussi que vous avez de beaux cheveux –

Thérèse – J'espère que vous m'enverrez des cartes postales du Canada?

Ségard – Sûrement. Et s'il n'y a pas de cartes postales, je vous écrirai une petite lettre.

Thérèse Quand partez-vous?

Ségard – On ne sait pas encore au juste; dans cinq ou six jours.

Thérèse – Vous ~~ne devez pas être très content~~ n'êtes pas content de partir?

Ségard Si. ~~C'est à dire je ne sais pas~~. C'est à dire que ~~je suis~~ il y a le désir d'aller là-bas, et le regret de s'en aller d'ici. Oh une fois là-bas...
Moi ~~je vous~~ comprenez-vous, je suis ~~tout rempli du présent~~ trop occupé à ne rien perdre du présent. ~~Je suis comme un homme qui tient un~~ C'est comme si une corde me ~~filait~~ ~~passait~~ filait dans les mains, tirée par une grande force. Je la serre, je retiens, quitte à me faire écorcher inutilement. Ce n'est pas moi qui la guide, c'est elle qui me bouscule et me secoue.
Bastien est plus fort que moi. Il ~~décide sa vie~~ peut décider sa vie. Il a décidé pour moi et j'aime mieux ça. ~~J'ai su qu'il avait raison dans ce qu'il voulait.~~

Plate 64 (a) 'Charles Vildrac': Zweig MS 198, f. 1v (dedication to Zweig)

Plate 64 (b) 'Charles Vildrac': Zweig MS 198, f. 4v

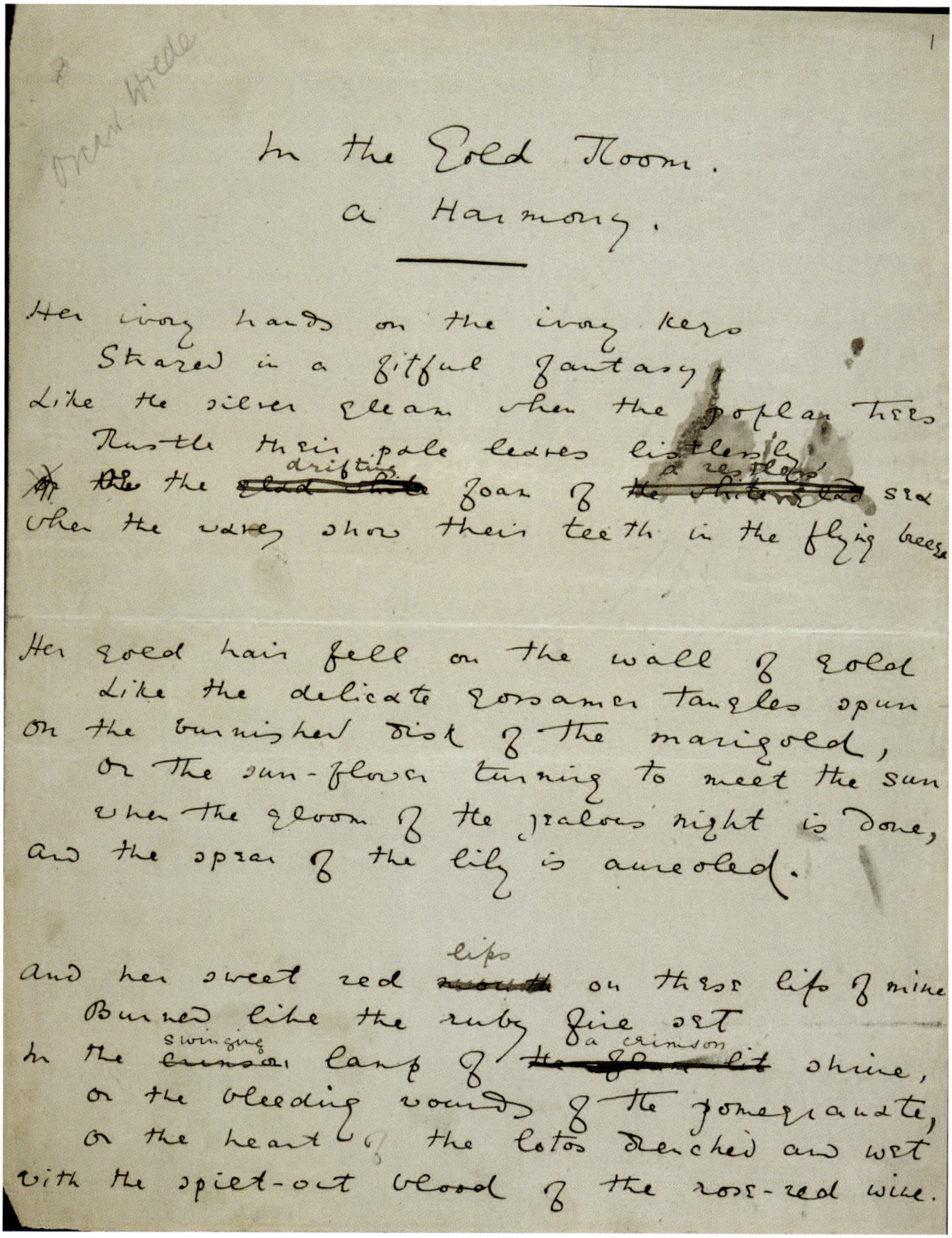

Oscar Wilde

1

In the Gold Room.
A Harmony.

Her ivory hands on the ivory keys
Strayed in a fitful fantasy,
Like the silver gleam when the poplar trees
Rustle their pale leaves listlessly,
~~Or~~ ~~the~~ the ~~gold white~~ drifting foam of ~~the white [illegible]~~ a restless sea
When the waves show their teeth in the flying breeze.

Her gold hair fell on the wall of gold
Like the delicate gossamer tangles spun
On the burnished disk of the marigold,
Or the sun-flower turning to meet the sun
When the gloom of the jealous night is done,
And the spear of the lily is aureoled.

And her sweet red ~~mouth~~ lips on these lips of mine
Burned like the ruby fire set
In the ~~crimson~~ swinging lamp of ~~the [illegible] lit~~ a crimson shrine,
Or the bleeding wounds of the pomegranate,
Or the heart of the lotos drenched and wet
With the spilt-out blood of the rose-red wine.

Plate 65 Oscar Wilde: Zweig MS 199, f. 1r

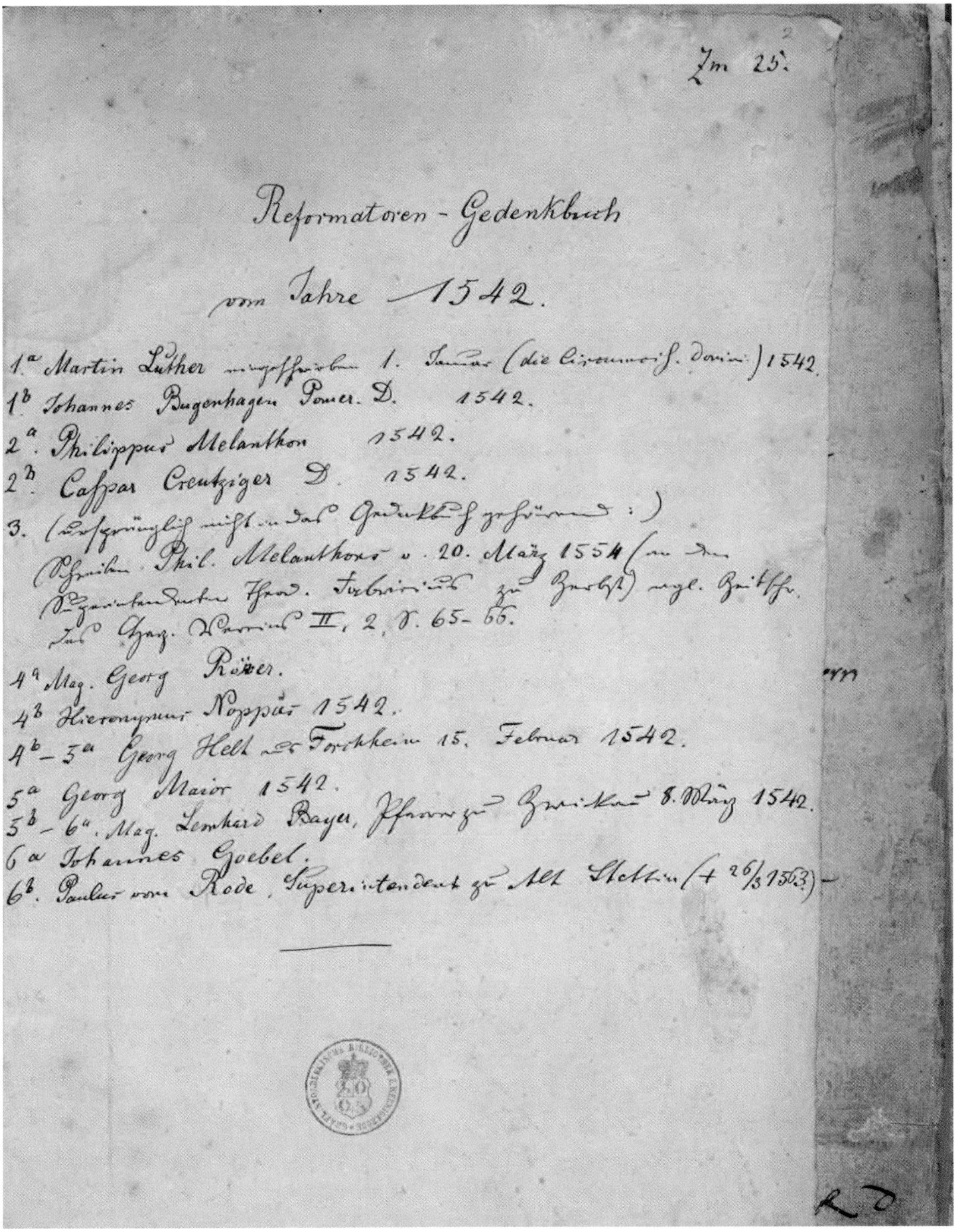
Zm 25.

Reformatoren-Gedenkbuch

vom Jahre 1542.

1a Martin Luther eingeschrieben 1. Januar (die Circumcis. domini) 1542.
1b Johannes Bugenhagen Pomer. D. 1542.
2a. Philippus Melanthon 1542.
2b. Caspar Creutziger D. 1542.
3. (ursprünglich nicht in das Gedenkbuch gehörend:)
Schreiben Phil. Melanthons v. 20. März 1554 (an den Superintendenten Theod. Fabricius zu Zerbst) vgl. Zeitschr. des Harz. Vereins II, 2, S. 65-66.
4a Mag. Georg Rörer.
4b Hieronymus Noppus 1542.
4b-5a Georg Helt aus Forchheim 15. Februar 1542.
5a Georg Maior 1542.
5b-6a. Mag. Lenhard Bayer, Pfarrer zu Zwickau 8. März 1542.
6a Johannes Goebel.
6b. Paulus vom Rode, Superintendent zu Alt Stettin (+ 26/3 1563)

Plate 66 'Reformatoren-Gedenkbuch': Zweig MS 200, f. 2r

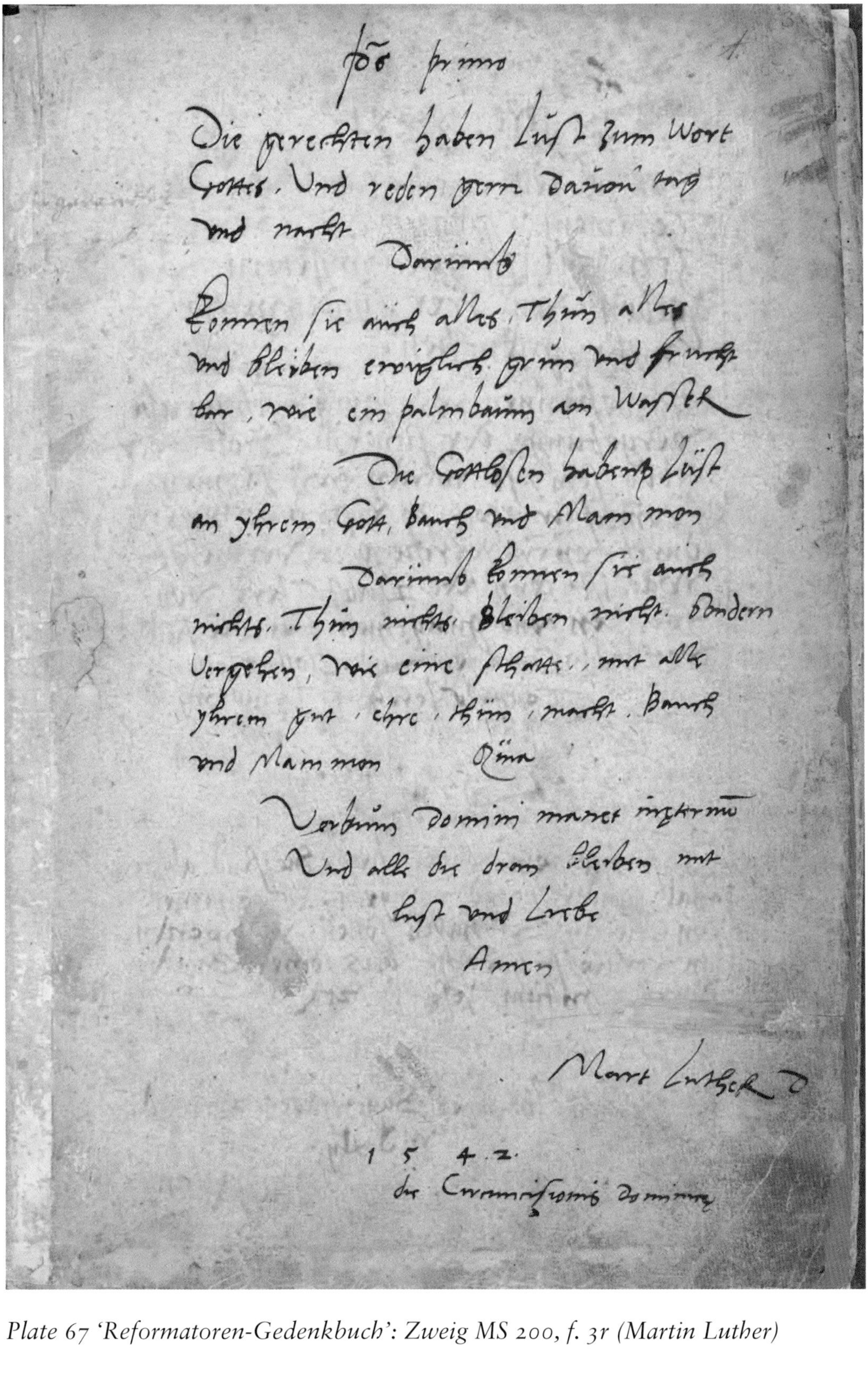
Pso primo

Die gerechten haben lust zum Wort
Gottes. Und reden gern davon tag
und nacht
Darumb
konnen sie auch alles thun alles
und bleiben ewiglich grun und frucht
bar, wie ein palmbaum am Wasser

Die Gottlosen habens lust
an yhrem Gott, Bauch und Mammon
Darumb konnen sie auch
nichts thun nichts bleiben nicht. sondern
Vergehen, wie eine spreue, mit aller
yhrem gut, ehre, thun, macht, Bauch
und Mammon Qua

Verbum domini manet in eternum
Und alle die dran bleiben mit
lust und Liebe
Amen

Mart Luther D

1 5 4 2.
die Circumcisionis domini

Plate 67 'Reformatoren-Gedenkbuch': Zweig MS 200, f. 3r (Martin Luther)

Fol. 1

PRIMERA PARTE
DEL INGENIOSO
Hidalgo don Quixote de
la Mancha.

Capitulo Primero. Que trata de la condicion, y exercicio del famoſo hidalgo don Quixote de la Mancha.

EN Vn lugar de la Mancha, de cuyo nombre no quiero acordarme, no ha mucho tiempo que viuia vn hidalgo de los de lança en aſtillero, adarga antigua, rozin flaco, y galgo corredor. Vna olla de algo mas vaca que carnero, ſalpicon las mas noches, duelos y quebrātos los Sabados, lantejas los Viernes, algun palomino de añadidura los Domingos, conſumian las tres partes de ſu hazienda. El reſto della concluìan, ſayo de velarte, calças de velludo para las fieſtas, con ſus pantuflos de

A lo

Plate 68 Miguel de Cervantes Saavedra: Zweig MS 201, f. 1

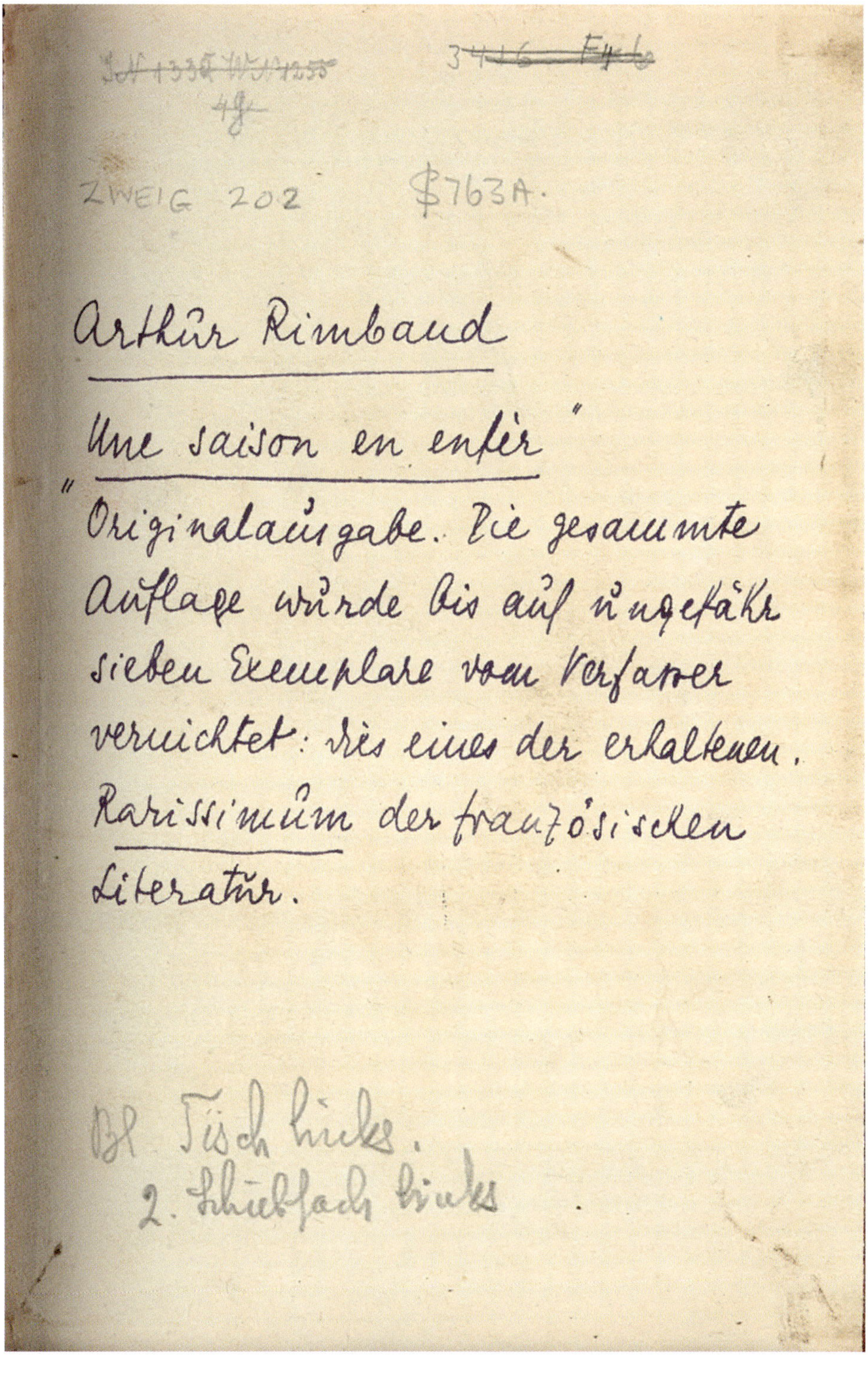
ZWEIG 202 $763A.

Arthur Rimbaud

Une saison en enfer

"Originalausgabe. Die gesammte Auflage wurde bis auf ungefähr sieben Exemplare vom Verfasser vernichtet: dies eines der erhaltenen. Rarissimum der französischen Literatur.

Bl. Tisch links.
2. Schubfach links

Plate 69 Arthur Rimbaud: Zweig MS 202, original box (note by Zweig)

Formauit DOMINVS DEVS hominem de limo terræ, ad imaginē ſuam creauit illum, maſculum & fœminam creauit eos.

GENESIS I. & II.

DIEV, Ciel, Mer, Terre, procrea
De rien demonſtrant ſa puiſſance
Et puis de la terre crea
L'homme, & la femme a ſa ſemblance.

Plate 70 Hans Holbein: Zweig MS 203, f. 9v

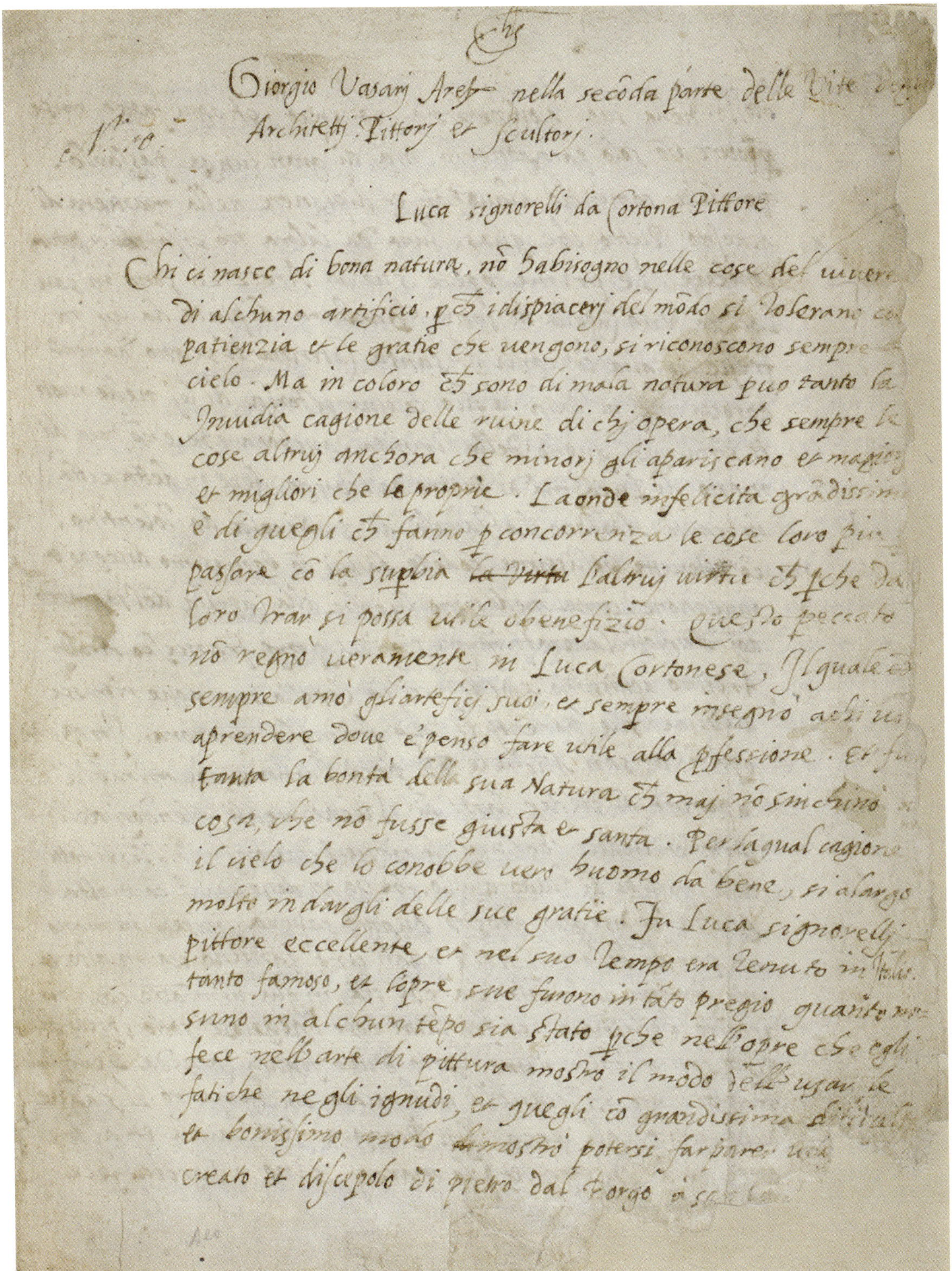
N.º 10

Giorgio Vasari Aret[ino] nella secōda parte delle Vite de gli
Architetti Pittori et Scultori.

Luca signorelli da Cortona Pittore

Chi ci nasce di bona natura, nō habisogno nelle cose del vivere
di alchuno artifitio, perche i dispiaceri del mōdo si tolerano co
patienzia et le gratie che vengono, si riconoscono sempre
cielo. Ma in coloro che sono di mala natura puo tanto la
Invidia cagione delle ruine di chi opera, che sempre le
cose altrui anchora che minori gli apariscano et maggiori
et migliori che le proprie. Laonde infelicita grādissima
è di quegli che fanno per concorrenza le cose loro piu
passare cō la superbia ~~la virtu~~ l'altrui virtu che perche da
loro trar si possa utile o benefizio. Questo peccato
nō regnò veramente in Luca Cortonese, Il quale che
sempre amò gli artefici suoi, et sempre insegnò a chi u
aprendere dove e' penso fare utile alla professione. Et fu
tanta la bontà della sua Natura che mai nō s'inchinò
cosa, che nō fusse giusta e santa. Per la qual cagione
il cielo che lo conobbe vero huomo da bene, si alargo
molto in dargli delle sue gratie. Fu Luca signorelli
pittore eccellente, et nel suo tempo era tenuto in Italia
tanto famoso, et l'opre sue furono in tāto pregio quanto ne-
ssuno in alchun tēpo sia stato perche nell'opre che egli
fece nell'arte di pittura mostrò il modo dello usar le
fatiche negli ignudi, et quegli cō grandissima difficulta
et bonissimo modo ~~dimostrò~~ mostrò potersi far parer vivi
creato et discepolo di piero dal borgo a san se

Plate 71 Giorgio Vasari: Zweig MS 206, f. 1r

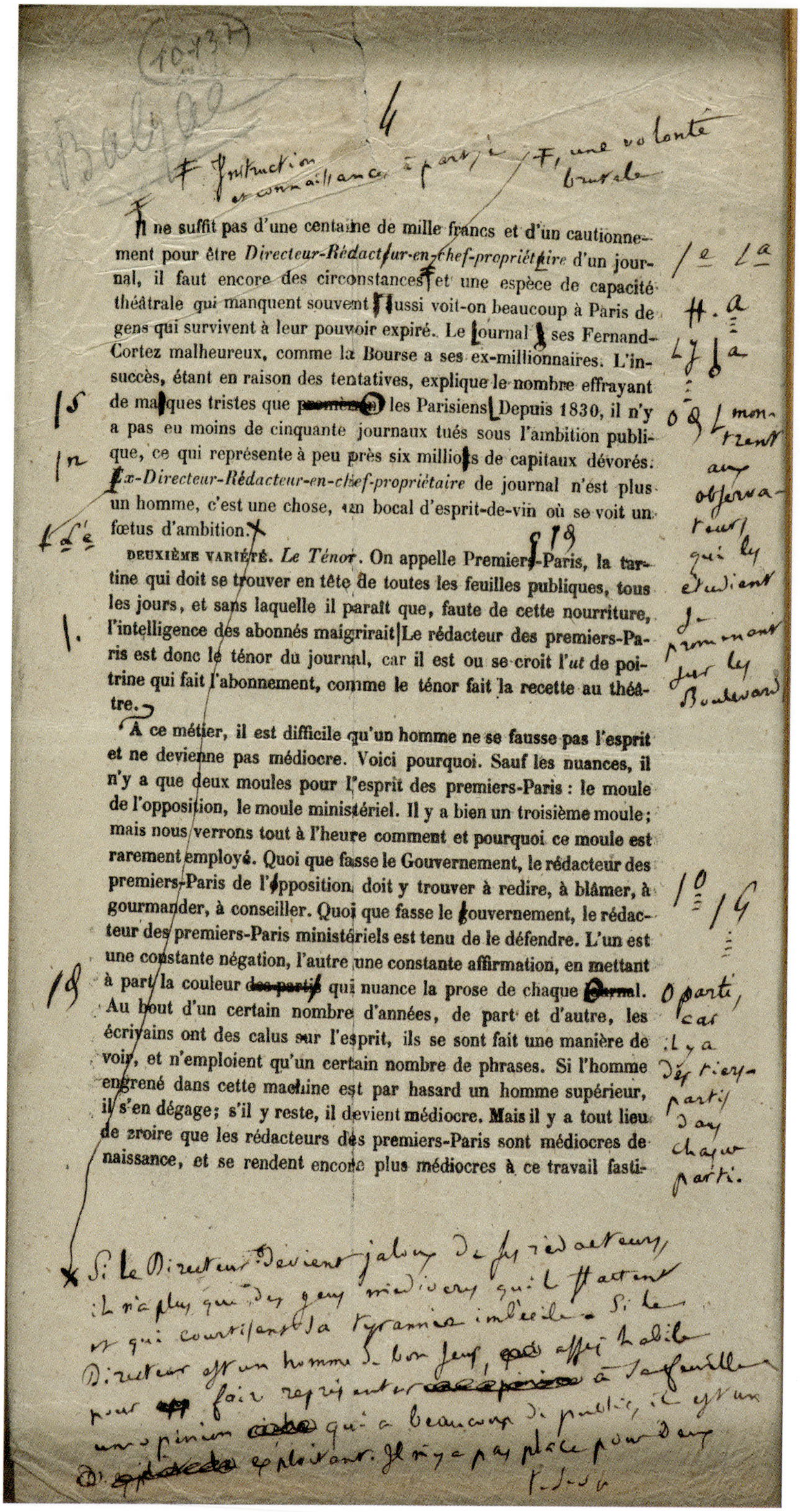

Il ne suffit pas d'une centaine de mille francs et d'un cautionnement pour être *Directeur-Rédacteur-en-chef-propriétaire* d'un journal, il faut encore des circonstances et une espèce de capacité théâtrale qui manquent souvent. Aussi voit-on beaucoup à Paris de gens qui survivent à leur pouvoir expiré. Le Journal a ses Fernand-Cortez malheureux, comme la Bourse a ses ex-millionnaires. L'insuccès, étant en raison des tentatives, explique le nombre effrayant de masques tristes que promènent les Parisiens. Depuis 1830, il n'y a pas eu moins de cinquante journaux tués sous l'ambition publique, ce qui représente à peu près six millions de capitaux dévorés. *Ex-Directeur-Rédacteur-en-chef-propriétaire* de journal n'est plus un homme, c'est une chose, un bocal d'esprit-de-vin où se voit un fœtus d'ambition.

DEUXIÈME VARIÉTÉ. *Le Ténor*. On appelle Premiers-Paris, la tartine qui doit se trouver en tête de toutes les feuilles publiques, tous les jours, et sans laquelle il paraît que, faute de cette nourriture, l'intelligence des abonnés maigrirait. Le rédacteur des premiers-Paris est donc le ténor du journal, car il est ou se croit l'*ut* de poitrine qui fait l'abonnement, comme le ténor fait la recette au théâtre.

A ce métier, il est difficile qu'un homme ne se fausse pas l'esprit et ne devienne pas médiocre. Voici pourquoi. Sauf les nuances, il n'y a que deux moules pour l'esprit des premiers-Paris : le moule de l'opposition, le moule ministériel. Il y a bien un troisième moule; mais nous verrons tout à l'heure comment et pourquoi ce moule est rarement employé. Quoi que fasse le Gouvernement, le rédacteur des premiers-Paris de l'Opposition doit y trouver à redire, à blâmer, à gourmander, à conseiller. Quoi que fasse le Gouvernement, le rédacteur des premiers-Paris ministériels est tenu de le défendre. L'un est une constante négation, l'autre une constante affirmation, en mettant à part la couleur des partis qui nuance la prose de chaque journal. Au bout d'un certain nombre d'années, de part et d'autre, les écrivains ont des calus sur l'esprit, ils se sont fait une manière de voir, et n'emploient qu'un certain nombre de phrases. Si l'homme engrené dans cette machine est par hasard un homme supérieur, il s'en dégage; s'il y reste, il devient médiocre. Mais il y a tout lieu de croire que les rédacteurs des premiers-Paris sont médiocres de naissance, et se rendent encore plus médiocres à ce travail fasti-

Plate 72 Honoré de Balzac: Zweig MS 216, f. 1r

Plate 73(a) Johann Wolfgang von Goethe: Zweig MS 217, f. 1r
Plate 73(b) Johann Wolfgang von Goethe: Zweig MS 217, f. 1v

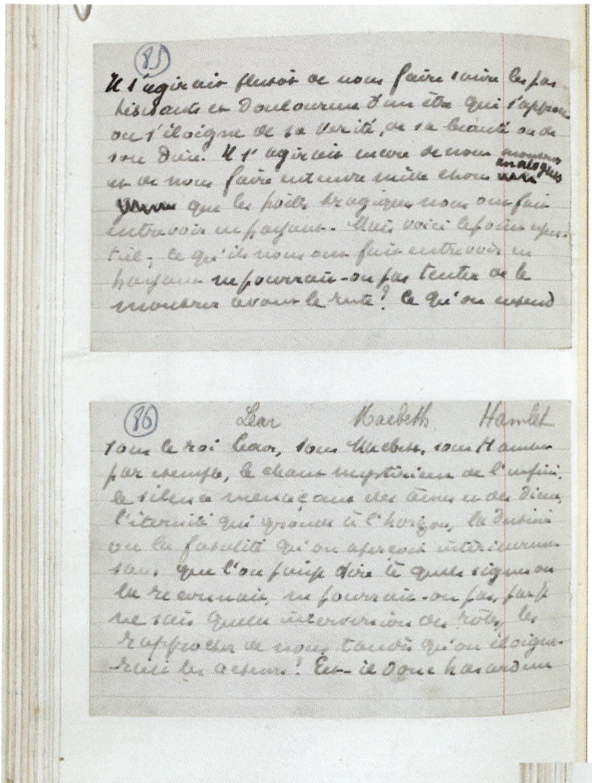

(85)

Il s'agirait plutôt de nous faire suivre les pas hésitants et douloureux d'un être qui s'approche ou s'éloigne de sa vérité, de sa beauté ou de son Dieu. Il s'agirait encore de nous montrer et de nous faire entendre mille choses analogues que les poètes tragiques nous ont fait entrevoir en passant. Mais voici le point essentiel; ce qu'ils nous ont fait entrevoir en passant ne pourrait-on pas tenter de le montrer avant le reste? Ce qu'on entend

(86) Lear Macbeth Hamlet

sous le roi Lear, sous Macbeth, sous Hamlet par exemple, le chant mystérieux de l'infini, le silence menaçant des âmes et des Dieux, l'éternité qui gronde à l'horizon, la destinée ou la fatalité qu'on aperçoit intérieurement sans que l'on puisse dire à quels signes on la reconnait, ne pourrait-on pas, par je ne sais quelle interversion des rôles, les rapprocher de nous tandis qu'on éloignerait les acteurs! Est-il donc hasardeux

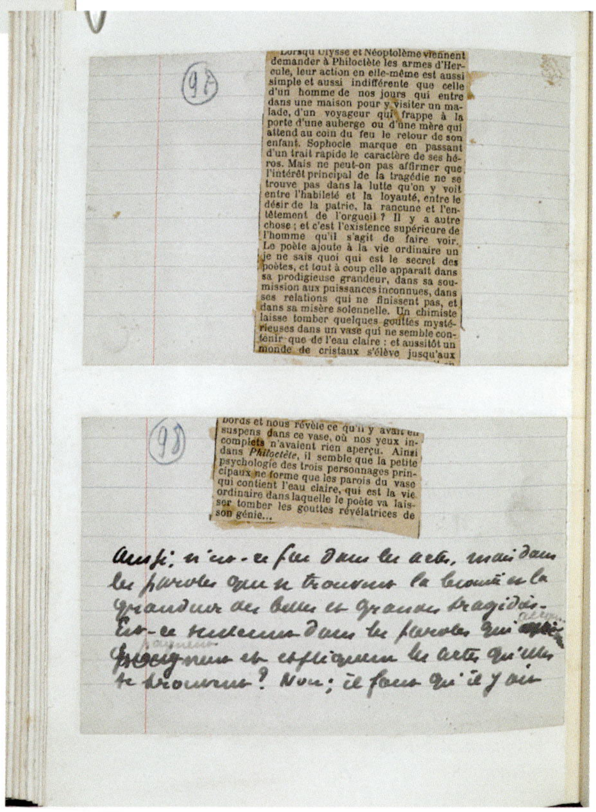

(97)

Lorsqu Ulysse et Néoptolème viennent demander à Philoctète les armes d'Hercule, leur action en elle-même est aussi simple et aussi indifférente que celle d'un homme de nos jours qui entre dans une maison pour y visiter un malade, d'un voyageur qui frappe à la porte d'une auberge ou d'une mère qui attend au coin du feu le retour de son enfant. Sophocle marque en passant d'un trait rapide le caractère de ses héros. Mais ne peut-on pas affirmer que l'intérêt principal de la tragédie ne se trouve pas dans la lutte qu'on y voit entre l'habileté et la loyauté, entre le désir de la patrie, la rancune et l'entêtement de l'orgueil ? Il y a autre chose ; et c'est l'existence supérieure de l'homme qu'il s'agit de faire voir. Le poète ajoute à la vie ordinaire un je ne sais quoi qui est le secret des poètes, et tout à coup elle apparait dans sa prodigieuse grandeur, dans sa soumission aux puissances inconnues, dans ses relations qui ne finissent pas, et dans sa misère solennelle. Un chimiste laisse tomber quelques gouttes mystérieuses dans un vase qui ne semble contenir que de l'eau claire : et aussitôt un monde de cristaux s'élève jusqu'aux

(98)

bords et nous révèle ce qu'il y avait en suspens dans ce vase, où nos yeux incomplets n'avaient rien aperçu. Ainsi dans *Philoctète*, il semble que la petite psychologie des trois personnages principaux ne forme que les parois du vase qui contient l'eau claire, qui est la vie ordinaire dans laquelle le poète va laisser tomber les gouttes révélatrices de son génie...

Ainsi; n'est-ce pas dans les actes, mais dans les paroles que se trouvent la beauté et la grandeur des belles et grandes tragédies. Est-ce seulement dans les paroles qui accompagnent et expliquent les actes qu'elles se trouvent? Non; il faut qu'il y ait

Plate 74 (a) Maurice Maeterlinck: Zweig MS 218, f. 44v

Plate 74 (b) Maurice Maeterlinck: Zweig MS 218, f. 47v

Index

References to catalogue entries are in **bold.** References to plates are preceded by 'pl.' or 'pls'.